Cherokee Outlet Cowboy

Cherokee Outlet Cowboy

Recollections of
Laban S. Records

By Laban Samuel Records
Edited by Ellen Jayne Maris Wheeler

University of Oklahoma Press : Norman and London

This book is published with the generous assistance of the Kerr Foundation, Inc.

Library of Congress Cataloging-in-Publication Data

Records, Laban Samuel, 1856–1941.
　　Cherokee outlet cowboy : recollections of Laban S. Records / by Laban Samuel Records ; edited by Ellen Jayne Maris Wheeler.
　　　p.　cm.
　　Includes bibliographical references and index.
　　ISBN 0–8061–2694–9
　　1. Records, Laban Samuel, 1856–1941. 2. Cowboys—Cherokee Strip (Okla. and Kan.)—Biography. 3. Ranch life—Cherokee Strip (Okla. and Kan.)—History.—19th century. 4. Cherokee Strip (Okla. and Kan.)—History. 5. Kansas—History, Local. 6. Ranch life—Kansas—History—19th century. I. Wheeler, Ellen Jayne Maris, 1936– . II. Title.
　　F702.C42R43　1995
　　978.1—dc20　　　　　　　　　　　　　　　　　　　　　　　94–37534
　　　　　　　　　　　　　　　　　　　　　　　　　　　　　　　　CIP

_F 702 C42 R43_

_9591_

The paper in this book meets the guidelines for permanence and durability of the Committee on Production Guidelines for Book Longevity of the Council on Library Resources, Inc. ∞

2　3　4　5　6　7　8　9　10

To all the cowboys who rode the ranges of the thundering prairies and especially those who rode on the great Cherokee Strip—a country larger than all New England—we owe the heritage of pioneering spirit. Their lives, filled with deprivation, hazards, and loneliness, and the often exciting, extraordinary events of this forty-year era have captured the imagination of the world as has no other period in the history of the American people.

Contents

CONTENTS

Illustrations

Preface

Laban Samuel Records was a wiry, leathery-skinned, wind-blown, toughened cowboy with steely-blue, piercing eyes under his beloved high-crowned Stetson hat. He was a range rider from 1873 to 1887, when cowboy life was its wildest and wooliest. He was only five feet four inches tall, and never weighed more than 135 pounds, but he could ride and compete with the best of them. He was the son of a Methodist minister who established several churches in the pioneer country of Chautauqua County, Kansas. Laban read newspapers to the illiterate cowboys around the campfires. Likewise he read the classics by kerosene lamp to his own children when the family gathered in the parlor after supper in their Oklahoma Territory homestead.

Laban Records was my grandfather. This book contains the story of his cowboy days, extracted from his own handwritten, penciled manuscript of over one thousand pages, written on ruled notebook paper about 1937. This manuscript passed on to his eldest son, Dr. Ralph Records, then a history professor at the University of Oklahoma. Uncle Ralph extracted several stories from the manuscript and published them in the *Chronicles of Oklahoma* and other southwestern journals and magazines. It was his intent to publish the entire manuscript in book form. He interviewed his father and included other stories and explanatory material. When his untimely death left the project unfinished, I solicited the advice of the late Dr. Arrell Gibson, also a history professor at the university. After reading Uncle Ralph's manuscript, he agreed that it was publishable, made minor revisions, and presented it to the Oklahoma Historical Society for publication. I presented the Oklahoma State Library with the original manuscript, which had been passed down through my mother, Edith Lucinda Records Maris.

This edition uses Laban's own colorful cowboy language, rather than the academic version used by Uncle Ralph. Some stories from Uncle Ralph's manuscript—Shep and the coyotes, the buffalo hunters, and brief descriptions of some of the people—are included, with a historical chronology of events. Some name spellings were changed when they were found in contemporary newspaper accounts. Laban's spellings are in parentheses in the index.

It has been a great joy to relive some of the stories that I heard as a little girl, both from my grandfather and my mother, about early Oklahoma. It is an added pleasure to make these reminiscences available for a firsthand account of this colorful era of American history.

ELLEN JAYNE MARIS WHEELER

Oklahoma City, Oklahoma

Acknowledgments

Especial gratitude is given to Dr. Alvin Turner, Dean of the School of Social Science, Northwestern Oklahoma State University, Alva, for his advice and encouragement. Many thanks to the library staff members of the Western History Collection of the University of Oklahoma, the Oklahoma Historical Society Library, Oklahoma City University, and the Oklahoma City Public Library. Also to former librarians Betty Jean Mathis of the Oklahoma State Library and Mary Rausch of the Western History Collection for their untiring efforts in going the extra mile to solve a tedious research problem.

I am also indebted to my husband, the Rev. Dr. J. Clyde Wheeler, himself an author, who lent his support and help in the organization of this manuscript, and to his co-worker Dr. Newton Flora.

This project was also helped by other interested friends and colleagues. Elmer Allen and Reid Daffer of Reidprographics printed the various revisions at their expense. Clay Maxwell redrew the cattle brands on his scanner. Madge McGrew, Herman and LaDonna Meinders, and Robert Yount have also given monetary donations to help with publication costs.

E.J.M.W.

Chronology

1849	Andrew Drumm and Henry Goddard go to the California gold rush and become small-time cattlemen.
1856–1870	The Records family resides in Indiana.
1859	Tip McCracken moves with his family from North Carolina to Texas; the boys carry guns for protection from Indians.
1860	Fayette Thomas moves with his family from Alabama to Texas.
1869	Charlie Curry comes up the Texas Trail to southeastern Kansas.
1870	The Records family moves to Peru, Kans.; Father Samuel establishes Methodist congregations; Charles and Laban become freighters. Ike Pryor comes up the trail. Drumm drives cattle across Indian Territory; the Wilson brothers join him.
1871	The Records family builds a house and a school; Samuel performs horseback marriages and foils the saloonkeeper. Isaac Gibson and other Quaker agents live among the Osages. Cal Watkins lives in Osage country.
1872	The Osages are moved to Indian Territory. Billy Conner hunts near Bird Creek.
1873	Charles and Laban buy cattle in the Cherokee and Chickasaw nations and meet Chief Nopawalla. Samuel produces a thirty-acre wheat crop. Elias Booth disappears. *Fall:* Vigilantes hang a victim.
1874	Drumm is the first cattleman in the Cherokee Outlet (U Ranch). George Mefford and "Darb" Horsley go on an unsuccessful buffalo hunt. Oliver Ewell and Justis drive cattle on the old trail to Chanute, Kans. The area is hit by a grasshopper plague. *July 4:* Pat Hennessey is killed

by Indians; Billy Malaley finds the body. *Nov.:* Alfred Sams, Barney Mann, and Laban and Frank Records work for the Osage agency. Bob Marshall digs a well. Burk Burnett sells beef to Osages. J. C. Records takes charge of Hickory Station. Freighter Rube Marshall in snow storm near Lake City, Kans.

1872–92 Frank works among the Pawnees as ferry builder across Arkansas River, government farmer, and chief of police. Adolphus Carian studies for the ministry and converts many Pawnees.

1875–78 Laban works for his father, Samuel, and buys yearlings at Webbers Falls.

1875 *Jan.:* Laban's work ends at agency. *Summer:* Osages scalp Otoe boy. Oliver Ewell and his brothers and "Crate" Justis buy cattle in Texas.

1876 "Ez" Iliff and Mike Meagher arrest a Withers brother at A. W. Rumsey's store.

1878–86 Laban observes stagecoaches.

1878 "Gus" Johnson buys 4,000 Texas cattle and divides them into four herds; Bill Dunlap, Ike Berry, L. C. Farris, and Bill Hudson are in charge of each herd. Frank Bates meets "Shanghai" Pierce on Texas cattle-buying trip and brings McCracken, Sam Fling, Thomas, and Jerry Frey up the trail. John Dugan (West) and "Red Neck" Brown come up the trail. Laban stays at the Wendel Hotel in Caldwell. *Spring:* Heavy rainfall, then drought, lasts until June 1880. *Aug.:* Laban punches cows in Dodge City and meets "Wild-Horse" Johnson, a Mexican sheep herder, and "Gus" Johnson. Buffalo bone industry grows. Jesse Evans brings 20,000 cattle to Dodge City. Laban sees Milt Bennett, Tony Day, and Pierce in Dodge City. *Sept.:* Ewell and Justis establish ranch above ⅍ ranch and hire Laban to herd steers. Cheyennes attack whites in the Dull Knife Raid, Tom Murray is killed, and Wiley Payne's brother is wounded. Laban discovers Evans's body at Sheete's camp. Ewell and John Gobie join forces. *Nov.:* Laban meets Tom Morris, works for Comanche County Pool, and returns to Peru via Kiowa, the Ewell-Justis and L. C. Bidwell camps,

Grouse Creek, and Elgin. Stanley Parsons invites his neighbors to Thanksgiving dinner. *Dec.*: Charlie Siringo works on Ƨ ranch.

1879   Thomas returns to Texas. The Streeter family moves to a Kiowa ranch from Ohio. *Jan.*: Frank rides to Medicine Lodge and visits Fred Bunker, Henry Goddard, and Jim Springer. *Apr.*: Frank, Laban, and Turner drive cattle to "Barbeque" Campbell's range. New northwest trail is established. Laban attends first Outlet roundup (pack horse). Watkins moves to Supply, Indian Territory. *July*: Jim Henderson and Troy Stockstill are killed by the Barker gang. Laban works on Ƨ ranch with Sam Prudent, George McDonald, Frank Tracy, Thomas, George Cunningham, and Barrett and Jim Buzard; he meets Dugan. *Fall*: C. M. Scott and Mike Meagher spend a night at Ƨ camp. Tracy and McDonald go to Wolf Creek for 2,500 cattle. Laban bluffs five Cheyenne hunters and kills a panther. Mexicans steal Ƨ mare herd.

1879–80 *Dec.-Feb.*: Tracy and Laban hunt and trap on Ƨ.

1880s   *Early*: Wes Fay escapes from a stagecoach.

1880   Tracy goes to Wichita. Laban works for Curry in Medicine Lodge. Ike Pryor and Thomas come up the Texas Trail. A water well is dug at Medicine Lodge. *March*: Laban stays at Ben Miller's ranch headquarters. Bill Dunlap works for Bill Quinlan in Cheyenne Motle. Day Fling, Wheeler Timberlake, Watkins attend Roundup close to Fort Supply. Day and Watkins claim same cut. John Payne and John Langford roast turtles along the trail. *Apr.*: Laban works at ⌃ ranch. Timberlake has a tenderfoot line rider. *June*: Southern cattle arrive. Bates buys 1,400 yearlings from Kingsbury and Dunson. *Summer*: Young Short brings a small herd to winter at ⌃. Day takes charge of a range in west Outlet with 4,000 head on 200,000 acres. Frank buys yearlings in the Cherokee Nation. *Nov.*: Laban freezes his feet on return trip from Caldwell. Frank gets Laban to return to Medicine Lodge to work in their winter camp. Frank becomes ill. P. H. Chapin family ranches in Barber County.

xvii

1881   Tom McNeal writes "War between China and Scots."
S. W. Lard drives 800 cows from Arkansas for Chapin.
Scout Amos Chapman escorts U.S. soldiers to Indian war
council. Abner Wilson manages the general roundup and
Laban rides for Frank. They cross swollen Driftwood
Creek. Pat Gallagher is gored. Richard King and Mifflin
Kenedy send horses through the Outlet to southern
Kansas. *Spring*: Bates buys saddle horse herd from
Kingsbury & Dunson. Mitchell boy is killed by lightning.
May: Charles and Laban drive cattle to Pratt County.
Summer: Bob Bigtree, Bob Munson, Jim Martin, Doug
Hill, and Jim Talbot come up the Texas Trail. *June*: A
tornado strikes. Laban meets a man looking for cow-
chips. Pierce is in Caldwell. Laban drives Charles Col-
cord's cattle for Bates. Theodore "Boff" Baughman tells
tall tales. *Fall*: Laban returns to ⊹ ranch. A rattlesnake
kills Laban's horse. McCracken tries to rope an antelope. Bill McMillan's steers get into ⊹ range. Shep helps
with the cattle. Laban finds "Dutch George's" horse.
Dec. 17: The Talbot gang raids Caldwell.

1881–82   *Winter*: Laban is away from ⊹ ranch. Young and George
Short hold cattle at U ranch.

1882   McCracken is Campbell's foreman. Barber and Comanche counties are settled. George Leonard dies.
Early spring: Frank chairs an immigration debate.
McNeal gives lectures and writes newspaper columns.
Bates and Payne reorganize ⊹ ranch; Laban returns and
rides "old Morg." He and Hank Smith get hurt in the
general roundup and a hailstorm hits. Laban meets
young Colcord and visits the Medicine Lodge shooting
gallery. Nate Priest's gun club battles the cowboys. *July*:
"Gus" Johnson is killed by lightning. Pierce detains the
stagecoach at Caldwell. *Fall*: When the fencing of great
cattle ranges begins, Laban is working for Payne on Skeleton ranch. He delivers a herd to ⊹ ranch.

1883   *Mar.*: Dodd is killed at Hunnewell. Pat Carnegie dies of
pneumonia. George Gorelon swallows his teeth. A panther runs into Hank Meredith's dugout. The last big
Strip roundup goes across both Canadian rivers and

among cattle rustlers, then into Caddo country. Laban meets White Bead and passes the Mennonite mission on the Arbuckle Trail. Cragin Co. buys out Timberlake, and Thomas becomes manager. *Sept.*: Tim Birmingham gets married.

1884   Calvin Hood, Preston Plumb, and Billy Malaley dissolve their Texas Panhandle ranch. Hood is injured in a cattle-train wreck. Laban sees "Terrapin Jim" Wilson and "Cap" Johns in a Medicine Lodge saloon. *Mar.*: Bates swims the Salt Fork. John Potts is killed at ƀ ranch. Charles buys 300 cattle in White County, Ark. Neighborhood roundup is held at the ranches of W. E. Campbell and Drumm and Crooked Creek Pool. Laban and Bill Wilson entertain girls at hotel in Kiowa. *Apr.*: CSLSA sends money to Cherokees. The trail changes to follow Eagle Chief Creek. *Apr. 30*: Several men attempt to rob the Medicine Lodge bank. Running Buffalo is killed at Cantonment. *Summer*: A black cloud forms for a day. *July*: Laban makes two cattle drives to Caldwell. A tornado hits near Pond Creek Flat. Berry loses his money in a card game. "Missouri Dave" Thomas tries out his program. Laban crosses the swollen Salt Fork, and his cattle stampede. Oscar Thomas is killed in Caldwell. *Oct.*: C. M. Hollister is killed by Bob Cross. Laban has a serious injury and leaves ↑ ranch.

1880s   *Early*: Caldwell has a bear, Ben Wheeler teases Louis Segerman, and Johnny Blair pulls a prank. *Middle*: Last general roundup is held in Barber County. Jim Elston serves as captain of the BCSGA. Troubles arise with settlers. Cowboys hold a dance in Kiowa's new town hall.

1885   The Medicine River floods near Kiowa. First Bud Moore, then McCracken become foreman of ↑ ranch. *Summer*: Laban ships cattle to Kansas City. *Fall*: Charlie and Laban place steers on Pole Cat Ranch.

1886   *Jan.*: Laban travels to Pole Cat Ranch. Heavy snow kills Tom Morris's cattle. "Gus" Hegwer dies in a snow storm. *Spring*: Laban and Malaley conduct a roundup. Laban holds his cattle in Lane near Cadwell; he meets John Eaton at the Leland Hotel, sells steers to Payne, ships cattle to Kansas City, sees Day for the last time, and sees a "Boomer" camp. *Winter*: Laban is foreman of **JD P** ranch. "Erv" Timberlake and Rumsey relive Civil War days.

1887   *Mar.*: A range fire breaks out. Van Leven comes to spay heifers. Laban has hard fall. *Aug.*: Laban quits the range, meets Scott Cummings at Kiowa, goes into the shipping and meat market business in Peru, and uses a cowboy snake-bite remedy on father. William Shanklin holds a meeting at Peru Methodist Church. *Dec. 28*: Laban marries Dora Belle Barker.

1889   Frank meets Gordon Lillie. K. P. Lawrence shows Laban his eagle house on the Arkansas River. Little Soldier dies mysteriously at Hominy Creek. William McKinney ("Ranicky Bill") stakes a claim on Turkey Creek. Bill Quinlan builds a home on his ranch for his family. Chris Madsen is in charge of government issues at Fort Reno. *Apr.*: Mother Lucinda dies at Peru.

1892   *Apr. 19*: Laban stakes a claim in Cheyenne-Arapaho Run but runs into difficulty at Kingfisher Land Office. *Aug.*: Meteorite hits near Laban's claim. Laban meets Tom Ferguson, "Ranicky Bill," and Deck Spurlock in Kingfisher. *Oct. 6*: Laban files his claim. *Nov.*: Laban moves his family to the homestead.

1893   *Sept.*: Laban rides Flax in the Strip Run.

1894   Laban meets Morris along a road near Hennessey.

1904   *Feb.*: Father Samuel dies at Peru.

1918   Laban meets George Short in Lawton.

1932   Ike Pryor is president of American National Live Stock Association. Outlet cowmen dedicate Drumm monument at U ranch.

Cherokee Outlet Cowboy

ONE

Westward to Kansas

I was born at Milton, Switzerland County, Indiana, 8 July 1856, the youngest of eleven children. My father, Samuel Records, born in Ross County, Ohio, 30 March 1812, married Lucinda M. Cadwell, formerly of Jamesville, New York, at Neville, Ohio, 28 January 1836. I was given my grandfather's name; he was the son of a Revolutionary soldier, Captain Josiah Records, whose father, John, of English heritage, was from Delaware. Each successive generation, like innumerable other families, moved farther west, from Delaware into Virginia, thence to Ohio, later to Indiana, then Kansas. When the last frontier passed, I was ready to seek a homestead in Oklahoma.

My father, Samuel Records, taught school in his early manhood. He was licensed to preach 24 August 1844 at Patriot, Indiana; ordained deacon 12 November 1848 at Rising Sun, Indiana, in the Ohio River Valley; and ordained elder 10 October 1852 at Rushville, Indiana. We moved to Tippecanoe County, fifteen miles northwest of Lafayette in 1858. Father bought forty acres of timber land, six miles to the south near Montmorency where we traded. We got mail at Octagon, four miles east. Later I attended Fairview, a country district school.

Father purchased a small hickory rocking chair when I was four years old and gave it to my mother. Daily at ten o'clock Mother went to her room, placed the open Bible in this chair, knelt, and prayed for the salvation of her children. When she passed to her reward 9 April 1889 in her seventy-second year, all of her eleven children had accepted the faith. Father died in Peru, Kansas, February 1904.[1]

Winter weather was too severe in northern Indiana. Usually I suffered from malarial fever each summer. In 1870 Father concluded he should leave and take up government land in Howard County, Kansas, as my older brothers, Elisha and John, had done. Perhaps climate and living conditions would be better there. We stayed in Indiana for one last wheat harvest. Father sowed 100 acres which made thirty bushels

3

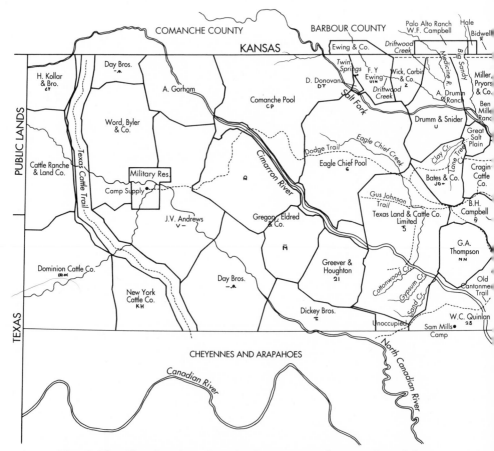

Map 1. The Cherokee Strip Live Stock Association leases. Adapted from a map in the Western History Collections, University of Oklahoma Library.

to the acre and sold for a dollar a bushel. He sold all his cattle and put up Timothy hay in the large meadow which sold by the rick.

My oldest brother, Henry, was married and remained in Indiana at Rising Sun. Eight of us children and my parents made the trip. Father brought six head of horses to Kansas, two wagons, and a spring wagon or surrey. My mother and four sisters rode in the light wagon which had a good cover of top and side curtains. The wagons had bows and

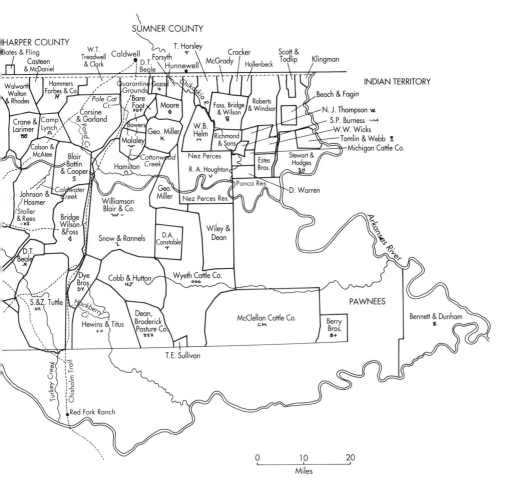

heavy canvas sheets drawn tightly over them for easier transportation across the Missouri or Mississippi Rivers if there were any bridges.

As we passed through Springfield, Illinois, I saw the Lincoln monument, a tall white shaft. We crossed the Mississippi on a steam ferry large enough to carry all our wagons at one trip. We crossed the Missouri at Hannibal on a small treadwheel ferry operated by a small, fat, blind sorrel mule. Father asked the operator if that little mule

5

Laban Samuel Records (1856–1940), as a young man when he was visiting his parents in Peru, Kansas, while working as a Cherokee Strip cowboy. Courtesy of Western History Collections, University of Oklahoma Library.

Samuel Records (1812–1904), born in Ross County, Ohio, the youngest of twelve children, was orphaned at age ten. He was ordained a Methodist minister in 1852 in Rushville, Indiana. His border Kansas circuit extended from Havana to Cedar Vale. He started churches at Elgin, Jonesburg, Peru, and Sedan. Courtesy of Western History Collections, University of Oklahoma Library.

Lucinda Cadwell Records (1817–89), the fifth of nine children, migrated west to Ohio with her parents from New York in 1834. There she met Samuel and encouraged him to enter the ministry, since her younger brother was also a minister. Her family descended from John Cotton, the Puritan minister from Boston. Courtesy of Western History Collections, University of Oklahoma Library.

could furnish power enough to run the boat. He replied that he could turn the wheel and carry all that could be piled onto it. We had to make two trips before we could resume our journey.

Until that trip I had never seen but one Negro in my life. When we got into Missouri, they were everywhere. I recall seeing about thirty young Negroes having a jolly time. They appeared striking with white teeth shining through such black faces.

We stopped at Rantone, Missouri, and rested the teams over Sunday. I thought the Missouri country was the most attractive I had seen. The majority of the houses were brick and many of them were two stories high. Lawns, orchards, yard fences, ornamental trees, and many other features made me feel that we had reached the place where we ought to stop. Father replied that we would have to go where land was free in southeastern Kansas; it was called Howard County then.

We passed through Humboldt, Kansas, and turned south to camp on the Verdigris River for a few days. One day brother Turner and I were under a high bank near the water, fishing in the river. Mother was the only member of the family at the wagon. Directly I heard the sound of horses' hoofs and peculiar-sounding human voices.

I asked my brother what that was. He hadn't noticed anything. The noise was so close I jumped to my feet and ran to the top of the high bank. About ten feet from me was an old blanket Indian mounted on his horse; others were behind him in single file as far as I could see around the bend in the river, riding in a little trot. It so astonished me that I stood and looked for awhile; I had never seen anything like that before.

Mother was alone and I thought she must be terribly frightened. I broke for the wagon as fast as I could run and there she was on the outside, walking around, arranging some clothes, not even looking at the Indians.

"Just look at them Indians!" I remarked. "Aren't you afraid?"

She replied, "Why no, I was born and raised right between the Oneida and Onondaga Indians in New York; they were always visiting back and forth. They looked so much like these Indians, it seemed very homelike to me."

They turned to a crossing on the river and let their horses drink as they crossed the stream. They rode into a timbered horseshoe bend on the south side where excellent grass abounded and made camp. As soon as night came, the squaws gathered dry wood, built large fires,

9

and when I went to sleep that night, the Indians were pounding away on their tom-toms.

We finally arrived in Howard County. The land was poor near Peru. Father traded four horses and a wagon for twenty-five head of long-horned Texas cattle to break out sod. All horses were traded off save two. The steers were easily broken.

We built a 16 x 18 feet, 1½ story house of logs, carefully scraped and hewn. A fireplace was built in the lower front room, enclosed with carefully-hewn rocks from the base up, including the mantle. Rafters, sheeting, and hand-hewn shingles were fashioned from native walnut. In nearby Peru was a shingle mill. Large walnut logs were cut, squared in blocks, and boiled in a vat until soft. They were sliced with a knife, operated by hand power. The high-grade shingles lasted many years.

The house which was 3½ miles southwest of Peru was soon finished. That year the county was cut in two. The north half became Elk County; the south, Chautauqua County with Peru as the county seat. The first postmaster, named Clark,[2] was a peg-legged lawyer. Brother Charles was kicked out of the post office and Father came down and secured an apology.

A trial was held in county court. The peg-legged lawyer-postmaster was interested in the first case of Judge Hinkle's court. When Clark became too overbearing, Judge Hinkle grabbed up a rock and carried it back and laid it down on the desk and said, "If you interrupt this court again, I'll knock you down and fine you $10."

We had no schooling in 1870. Father was contracted to haul lumber for the first school house, 2½ miles south of Peru, in October 1871. Reuben Crone built the house; Elisha Records layed the foundation; and Jim Caldwell, a plasterer and bricklayer, built the flue. Crone purchased the lumber at Coffeyville, Kansas, thirty miles away. The school, named Oakland, still stands today.

Brother Charles and I hauled the lumber for this house with ox teams. Crone went with us to see that we cared properly for the lumber. At age fifteen this was one of the hardest jobs I had confronted in my life. We used two wagonloads with four yokes of big, full-grown, long-horned Texas steers.

There was no east-west road leading into Coffeyville. When we arrived at the west bank of the Little Caney River, we followed a road south to a point near the Kansas boundary, then turned into the well-traveled road to Coffeyville, a developing cow town. We found two

10

factions, north and south, nearly in a state of war over which name to use for the new town. It was there I first saw cowboys in full regalia. All the buildings were frame houses. Two new railroads were engaged in a construction race to determine which one should obtain the government's consent to enter Indian Territory. The M. K. T. [Missouri, Kansas, and Texas, or "Katy"] won the race and the rich profits of the Texas cattle drives. We arrived in time to load our wagons for the return trip. We left after dark and selected a camp site in a bluestem grass meadow near running water so our oxen could graze and have plenty of water. Crone camped with us but returned the next morning to the lumber company to settle the payment.

I drove the lead wagon and got into two bad scrapes because of my inexperience in driving bull teams. First I permitted the leaders to travel too rapidly downhill. The wheelers could not hold the heavy load alone. When the wheels struck the bottom of the gully and started up another hill, the unusual strain broke the log chain. We stopped. Charles unhooked the chain from his wagon, hitched all eight steers to my wagon, and cracked his whip. The load went uphill in a hurry.

When we arrived at the west bank of the Little Caney, we doubled the four yokes for each wagon. When we started up the river bottom, a cold October rain began. Crone overtook us. Since he had been an infantryman in the Civil War, he knew how to march. He preferred to walk on alone to Peru. In time, after we had crossed the river, we came to Davis Creek which was banked full of water.

Had I asked for Charles to double team, I could have avoided my second accident. The hind wheels of my wagon sank into the mud as I crossed to the other side of the creek. I unhitched my team and hooked them on front of Charles' team. He stood on top of his lumber and made the wheelers pull while I waded and urged the leaders. We were successful so we tried the eight on my load. The chains broke and it was dark so we dropped the chains and turned the oxen loose. We ate the little food in our grub box, made a lean-to out of the lumber and slept on it during the night. We slept in wet clothes but they were dry when we awoke at daybreak.

The next day the sun was shining as we crossed the prairie with only one wagon. I was too stiff to walk. Charles told me to ride on the load while he walked and belabored the oxen. About half way home Father met us; he suspected something had happened. He sent me home on his horse while he and Charles rode the wagon home, unloaded it,

11

returned to pull my stalled wagon out of Davis Creek, and deliver the load to Peru.

Since my father was a Methodist preacher, he sent out word that he would have preaching every other Sunday in his house. He organized societies from Elgin to Cedar Vale on the west side, from Sedan to Elk City on the north side, and from Havana to Caney on the east side in Montgomery County.[3] He built churches in Jonesburg, Sedan, and rode horseback all of the time, mostly without roads.

Bent Darnell, a young man who had a claim in West Hickory Valley 1½ miles south of our house, had a married neighbor named Harris, whose wife's sister lived with them. It was an unusually cold winter and a heavy snow lay on the ground when these four persons came driving into Father's place, wanting him to marry Darnell and Mrs. Harris' sister. Father asked them if they had a license; they had never heard of such a thing, for the Harrises didn't have a license when they were married in Missouri. They asked where to get one and what it would cost. Father told them Peru was the county seat and they could easily secure one for a $1.50. So the two men unhooked their team from the wagon, mounted bare-back, rode to the county clerk's office, procured the license, and got back in forty-five minutes. That was doing things in double-quick order, riding seven miles through deep snow and getting the license issued, besides.

One summer Father was plowing corn with a two-horse cultivator. When he came to the end of the row, there sat a man and a woman on horses; they wanted him to marry them. Father told them all right; he had better unhitch his team, go to the house to clean up for the wedding. They objected, saying they lived about ten miles south in Indian Territory. They had left home early that morning, had ridden to Sedan where they got their license and dinner, and decided on Father to perform the marriage ceremony. Since that was the case, he would marry them as they sat on their horses. The young fellow handed Father the license; Father said it should have a witness or two but since they were so sorely pressed for time, he would have it recorded without witnesses. As soon as the ceremony was said, they started off in a high lope and kept it up as far as he could see them.

In 1871 Father was preaching in Peru in the front part of a store building as there was no church building. The usual quota of saloons was in Peru. Some fellows thought it would be smart to get a half-witted fellow in liquor, have him mount his horse, and ride into the door of the building where the services were being held. Father was standing by the door, talking to the people. As the horse started into the door, Father took the horse by the bit, turned him around and out, closed the door, and continued his discourse without interruption.

The Kansas law governing saloons required a prospective saloonist to circulate a petition and secure a majority of the voters in that precinct as signers. A saloon keeper named Roper was running a saloon in Peru and his license was ready to expire in 1872. The law required a renewal every six months.

We had bought the fodder of a cornfield in West Hickory Valley south of us. I had to herd our cattle away from the corn shocks that stood in part of the field. Snow lay on the ground and it was pretty cold; I would go up to the renter's house to warm my feet once in awhile.

The renter's name was Cole. While I was down in the field, I saw Roper drive up to Cole's house; I knew what he was after. When I went up to warm my feet, after awhile I said, "I reckon you signed Roper's petition, didn't you?"

He said, "No, I didn't."

I replied, "I thought you were in the habit of sampling it once in awhile."

He said he would have to plead guilty to the charge but he didn't sign the petition for two reasons: "The first reason, I knew Dad Records would be along in a little while with a remonstrance and I would be ashamed to turn him down. The second reason, my wife sends me to town to get coffee or sugar and if there is a saloon there, I spend my money in the saloon. But if there isn't any saloon, she gets just what she sent me after." He turned to his wife and asked, "Isn't that so?"

She answered, "That's the way it has been working so far."

Roper was circulating his petition by riding in a two-horse buggy. Because the snow had covered certain rocky places in the road, he couldn't drive as fast as he would ordinarily. When I was down in the field, again looking after the stock, I saw Father ride in to Cole's place on horseback. He was always a hard rider and was taking the same route which Roper had taken.

Finally he overtook Roper, rode up beside him and said, "Mr. Roper, I've got a remonstrance here which I'm circulating against a saloon in Peru and I don't aim to miss any legal voter in the precinct." Father asked Roper if he would sign it.

13

Roper replied, "No, I won't sign your remonstrance, for it isn't necessary; I know when I'm licked. I'll tell you what I'm going to do. I'm going right straight to Peru, put up all of my saloon fixtures, sell 'em to the highest bidder, and leave the country. It won't be necessary for you to go any farther with your remonstrance." And Roper did what he said.

Father raised some wheat but not as much as he had produced in Indiana. In 1873 he raised thirty acres of wheat which he bound and shocked. He asked Jim Preston, who owned a horse-powered grain separator with "Darb" Horsley and George Mefford, if they would thresh his grain. He stacked it on a hill near his granary a mile west of the field.

"That hill is so sidling I am afraid the separator will upset and I might get killed," Preston replied.

"Jim, if you do get killed, I will take charge of your funeral and preach you a better funeral sermon than you ever heard in your life!" Father admonished.

Jim laughed heartily and added, "Just for that we will pull up that hill and do your threshing." The job was finished and no one was killed.

Wheat was selling at $2.50 a bushel at threshing time but the great panic soon hit. A neighbor, Bill Alford, had a large wheat crop but was in no hurry to sell. Independence, the nearest railroad point, was thirty miles distant. The roads were in poor condition which required a full day's hauling time. When Alford and a neighbor began their journey, it took them until the next noon to arrive because of the neighbor's balky team; they had to double team at every hill. By this time the market had dropped off $1.50 a bushel.

The next summer was the year of grasshoppers and drought in the Southwest, Kansas in particular.[4] The hoppers came in mass formation. My brother-in-law, Supply D. Shattuck, had died and was to be buried and my family had gone to the funeral. I was sick and couldn't attend. As I lay on the couch in the front room of our home, which was built in a post oak grove, I could see the trees. Of a sudden, a heavy shade like a cloud obscured the sunlight; it was accompanied by a heavy roar like the wind. No leaves on the trees were stirring. This excited my curiosity. I stepped to the east door, looked out, and saw what seemed to be a sea of brass coming down to earth. For a moment I was so amazed and at a loss to understand. Suddenly I saw the

14

grasshoppers. They had flown as far as they could; now they were falling perfectly exhausted to the ground.

The chickens were around the house and seemed to be greatly pleased to meet such a feast. They ate until they were filled then began to act frightened and ran to the hen house to get away from the great feast which they had enjoyed a few moments before. This gave me an idea; I walked over to the hog pasture to see how they were making out. The hogs were wading among the piles of hoppers and eating them by the mouthfuls. The grasshoppers stripped all the vegetation; our corn stood in the shock. We had planted about 200 acres, but when we noticed the tassels were dying, we began to cut the stocks for feed. We knew we would have no corn but we must have fodder. The hoppers merely trimmed the outsides of the corn shocks.

George Mefford, John Goraby, Nathan Bessey, and "Darb" Horsley decided to go west and kill some buffalo for their winter's supply of meat. The buffalo were not numerous in the vicinity of their camp for the main herds had passed to other grazing grounds.

One morning these men saw a buffalo grazing not far from camp. Goraby and Horsley took their guns and started toward the buffalo from different angles to intercept it in either direction. Horsley got close enough to shoot; not being an experienced buffalo hunter, he aimed to break the buffalo's neck. When he fired, the buffalo dropped as if dead. He went up to cut its throat to bleed it, but the shock of the knife brought the buffalo out of its stupor; it leaped to its feet and charged. Horsley eluded its charge by dropping low and grabbed its long hair by one hand while the other hand held the knife. He cut and slashed at the animal's belly until he was entangled in its entrails and covered with blood. Goraby came up but was afraid to shoot for fear of hitting Horsley. The buffalo tore off most of Horsley's clothing, bruised his body, and peeled patches from his skin but was unable to gore him. The buffalo soon collapsed and Goraby helped Horsley out of his predicament.

Horsley's associates said he had been bragging how he killed buffalo. After this experience they said if that was the way he killed buffalo, they should just as well return to the settlements. Since buffalo were so scarce there, Horsley and his companions gave up the hunt and returned to Chautauqua County.

In early Kansas there were some mysterious happenings. Often people thought they had to take the law into their own hands. Young Elias

15

Booth lived in Chautauqua County and his nearest relative whom we knew, Mrs. Sam Hoadley, was an aunt with whom he stopped when he came. One day in 1873 he told his aunt he was going to meet a man in Indian Territory not far from here. He left and no one ever saw him again. His aunt's little son complained that Booth had taken his knife when he left.

A few years afterwards some boys were hunting rabbits and their dogs chased a rabbit into some shelving rocks in a rocky cliff. When they climbed up, they found the skeleton of a man. They reported to officers, the skeleton was taken out, but there was no object to identify it except a little knife. When Mrs. Hoadley heard about the knife, she brought her little son who looked and said it was his.

It was assumed that the skeleton was that of Elias Booth. A monument was set up and marked: "Elias Booth died in 1873." The manner in which he met his death has always remained a mystery. He had no enemies, no visible wealth.

In the fall of 1873 when the grass began to become a little dry, the cattle began to be unruly and break into cornfields. We thought it best to put them under herd in the afternoon after they had watered and we corraled them at night.

One evening as I was working the cattle towards the corral, I saw twelve or fourteen men riding west, carrying guns. Not following any road, they were keeping under cover of hills and timber. I wondered who the men were and what they had in view.

The next day as I was bringing up the cattle just about sundown, I saw three men riding from the west along the public road. I rode to the road when the men passed close by. I recognized and spoke to Mason. He was riding and leading the horse of a man who had his hands tied behind. His roan horse had a bald face and white feet. Another man rode behind him, carrying a gun.

People in Peru said about 9 P.M. Mason came, trying to get help to rescue a man from a vigilante committee. As he went along a brushy road, a bunch of men stopped him and took the man from him. Mason couldn't get anybody to go with him, so he went to his home near Caney. Mason had been taking the fellow to Caney to stand trial for some minor offense.

The next day people who lived in Hickory Valley south of us saw a horse grazing around with a saddle on it. When it remained in the vicinity after noon, some of the neighbors went to investigate. The horse had come down a little road which extended back among the hills and trees. They followed the trail back and found a man hanging in a small tree about six or eight inches in diameter.

The word was spread; I went over to look. The horse and man were the same ones I had seen in Mason's charge. The limb to which the fellow was hanged was so weak it had to be propped up at the end by a dead limb to prevent the fellow's feet from touching the ground. I thought this was the most brutal disposing of man I had ever seen. The authorities took the horse and saddle to pay for the fellow's burial expenses.

TWO

Bullwhackers, Mule Skinners, and Cattle Buyers

Brother Charles and I were freighting from different points in southeastern Kansas in the early 1870's—Humboldt; Cherryvale, about 40 miles away; Elk City; and Thayer.

On one trip from Thayer we had two yokes of cattle, pulling a load of freight and facing a south wind. When night overtook us, we were on an open prairie country. We saw a small house; there were a man, wife, and several children; we asked if we could camp for the night. Since his family occupied the whole house, we would have to find a place to sleep. The wind was still blowing terribly hard. He had a granary which was built tight and would turn the wind but it was almost full of shucks. When we got ready to go to bed, we went inside the bin and laid on those shucks that were naturally warm. I never put in a more comfortable night in my life.

The man gave us everything he could afford: a fine bed, plenty of forage, water for the oxen, and a good fire to do our cooking on the stove in his house.

On another trip from Cherryvale we had a load of flour. Night overtook us on the road and a storm came up; we couldn't sleep on the ground. We had a good wagon sheet stretched over good wagon bows, so we slept on the sacks which we stood on end to make room for other types of freight. The hard-packed flour sacks were like sleeping on a pile of rocks.

In going from Peru to Cherryvale we would intercept and follow the Santa Fe Trail half way between Peru and Independence, which was the nearest railroad point for Peru. The trail turned northwest to cross the Elk River where there was a ripple and the same type of low-lying bank as that of the Verdigris at Independence. The trail, after crossing a few miles south of Elk City, veered a little to the south as it went west up the Salt Creek Valley. I have followed this trail from Cherryvale all the way to Dodge City. While on herd along the Santa Fe Trail in the early 1870's along this portion of the trail, I observed the mode of traveling by ox trains.

Some of the terms which were used in freighting across the plains help in understanding the manner in which this business was conducted. For example, a yoke of cattle was two steers; a team of oxen might comprise three or four yokes of steers. A team of oxen, as to numbers, depended upon the load to be pulled. The mode of travel was simple, just three or four teams pulling alongside each other so the drivers could be close to their meals. The travel order was: two men rode in front of the ox or mule train on horseback; one on each side of the trail to cover as much of the country as possible to avert a surprise attack. They must not ride too far ahead lest they be cut off from the train. Also one man rode in the trail behind the train to guard against attack from behind. If the drivers got the signal to corral, the lead team was turned either to the right or left, according to the lay of the ground, and driven in a circle to turn inside the last team in the train. That put all the teams behind wagons and made a breastwork behind which to fight. This was also the regular order in camping for the night. There was an opening in the circle to let the teams in or out. Oxen were left out under guard at night. Horses and mules were placed inside the wagon barricade for they could be stampeded more easily than oxen.

When the wagon train was moving, one bullwhacker walked along the left side of the team with a plaited, ten-foot leather lash fastened to a smooth, four-foot hickory stick. There was a soft leather popper on the end of the lash. An expert bullwhacker could make it sound like a gun report.

The yoke was made of hickory or ash; the bows were taken from hickory saplings and bent to fit the steer's neck and were long enough to pass through the yoke far enough to permit a hole to be bored through the bow in which to place a key to hold the bow in place. The hole through the center of the yoke, which contained a bolt of that size, and the lower end of the bolt had a loop in which a rim was fastened. If there were more yokes of oxen ahead of the wheel yoke, the pulling chain was passed through this ring; if one or more yokes of oxen pulled a wagon, the end of the tongue was carried in that ring.

If a span of mules or a team was used, according to the load, the mule skinner rode the mule on the right side of the wagon tongue and controled the mules in the lead with a jerk line. He had a rope extending from his saddle to a long pole fitted into a socket in the wheel-brake; it gave the driver power to control the load going downhill. He carried a short stock whip with a lash long enough to reach all of the mules.

The oxen or mules were hooked to the wagons but once a day. After the stock grazed in the morning, they were driven until late afternoon, then given time to fill on grass and water before they were corraled or tied for the night. If the stock were all broke to handle and they were in a civilized country, it wouldn't take much time to start or stop. If wild, the steers were not unyoked until well-broken. Their tails were tied together so they could get their yokes turned upside down while out grazing.

To loosen the oxen, the chains were unhooked, dropped to the ground, the key taken out of the bow, the bow pulled out of the yoke, the oxen walked out, the bow replaced, and the key stuck through the hole. Then it was ready to pick up the next morning. This procedure was repeated for each ox. To hook up the team, the right-hand bow was taken, the yoke was picked up, the right-hand end of the yoke put on the right-hand ox's neck, then the key put in its place. Next, the bow of the near, or left-hand end of the yoke was taken out, the yoke held up, the near ox told to go under, which well-trained oxen readily did.

The mule had a bridle, collar, harness, and tugs of light chains or leather fastened to the harness, buckled around the collar to pull as the brake was supposed to hold back the wagon going downhill.

On another trip to Cherryvale we crossed the Verdigris River at Independence where the Santa Fe Trail crossed it. The main hotel there was in a hay shed; public houses were scarce. People usually traveled in covered wagons and camped where night overtook them; they had no need for hotels other than to occasionally eat out.

When we got to Independence, it was our good or bad fortune to meet an ox train crossing the river. Cattle or mule trains always had the right of way; the general public had to stand aside until the whole train had succeeded in crossing. We were held up an entire day. This gave us a good chance to observe all of the details of crossing a flooded stream with an ox train and the feats of swimming oxen across the river. When a train began to cross a stream near a hamlet or town, it was quite an event for the residents to see.

There was no bridge. They used a ferry for their wagons. In loading, one yoke of oxen would pull the wagon which was a large government wagon with a common farm wagon trailed at its rear, having a short tongue. The yoke of cattle which pulled the wagon and trailer remained hitched to the wagon. When the ferry landed across the river, another team would be hitched in front of the two oxen on the ferryboat; then they could pull the load to high ground.

If the stream was banked full of water, the team would have a straight pull and require fewer oxen. The other oxen and mules, if any, swam across the river as the owner of the train would rather not pay ferry charges.

The drivers or bullwhackers were usually a rough, rolicky bunch of men who were fond of showing what they could do while they swam the livestock across the streams. To get such a job, a man had to be a good swimmer because he was liable to be put to the test, crossing these streams without bridges. Only one yoke of oxen at a time was permitted to swim the stream. They could put as many in the stream at one time as they wished but they must not chain two yokes together; each yoke must be independent. The drivers had their fun by standing on the steers' backs, whooping and yelling, jumping up and down, and swimming around among the steers as they swam across.

On this trip there was one large young man named Tom who seemed to be overcharged with energy and fun. He enjoyed displaying his swimming feats to attract attention. He had a large, expensive black hat which made him most noticeable. He tried different stunts, finally one that attracted everyone within hearing distance. He had a loud voice which he liked to exercise. He suddenly began to shout for help that he was drowning. Everybody came to see what they could do to save him, so realistic was his mimicry. Part of his yells were gurgling up through the water. Suddenly in the midst of the excitement, he went swimming off, laughing. Some were really sorry that he didn't drown because he had been so foolish.

The next time he tried, he did not attract any attention. The third time Tom began to yell, no one paid any mind until his fine black hat was seen floating down the river. Then they knew that he did need help but it was too late.

One of the other drivers who was an excellent swimmer said, "Well, Tom won't need that hat anymore and I can't stand here and see that fine hat float down the river." So he showed his powerful swimming by plunging into the river and soon had possession of the hat. The hat started on toward Santa Fe, New Mexico, but Tom stayed in the Verdigris riverbed.

On the road from Independence to Cherryvale we camped on Drum Creek where the notorious Bender family lived and saw what was called the Bender Hotel. They did not pretend to keep people overnight but served meals. There is no telling how long they could have kept killing and robbing people who stopped with them had they not killed Dr. York and his young daughter. He was too prominent and was missed quickly; searching parties soon learned where he had been seen last.[1]

I never ate at the so-called Bender Hotel but my wife's father and another man ate dinner there one time. My father-in-law recalled the curtain which hung closely behind them when they ate. Those who were marked for plunder were struck on the head with an axe or a hammer from behind the curtain. A trap door in the floor let the body fall to a cellar below. All of this was discovered when the Benders were charged with numerous mysterious homicides.

The Benders disappeared mysteriously. They must have met death by violence for neighbors noticed that the horses and cattle were left without any care or protection. This was another example of the old neck-cracking vigilante committees which often operated independently of the law of the land. They were more of a curse than a benefit to the community.

We also traveled into Indian Territory to buy cattle. We heard of a stockman who might repay us. When we inquired where he resided, a man directed us to ride by a schoolhouse. He gave additional directions to lead us to the stockman's ranch.

As we were riding along the road, a gray squirrel ran across the road and up a tree a short distance ahead of us. When we came opposite the tree, I saw it lying flat on a limb. I told the boys I would get it for our next meal. I drew my cap-and-ball six-shooter and shot it through the head. I dismounted, picked it up, and tied it to my saddle. We soon came to the schoolhouse; the teacher had dismissed the pupils for recess. It was a Cherokee Indian school, the first and only one I ever saw in Indian Territory.

When we saw that all were Indians, we decided to learn more. We told one of the pupils to tell the teacher that we wanted to see him. When the teacher came to the door, it was a woman! Her hair was caught up; she was dressed as white women did in those days. Her clothes were neat and becoming. She spoke good English. She said she was a full blood Indian but her figure did not resemble that of the

22

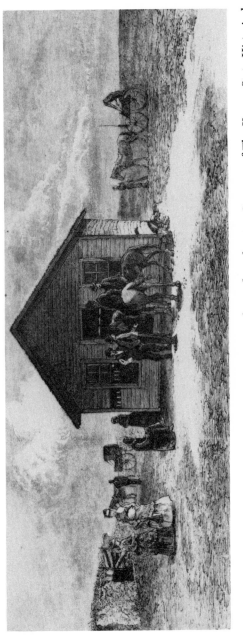

The Benders' shanty, near Cherryvale, Kansas. A museum is located on the site. Courtesy of The Kansas State Historical Society, Topeka, Kansas.

average blanket squaw. I have forgotten where she said she was educated; she said she lived in that community. When she finished her education, she got the Cherokees there to send their children to the subscription school.

She gave us directions to reach the ranch, then asked me what I was going to do with that gray squirrel.

I replied, "I'm going to give it to you."

She said, "I would like that."

I began to untie it. She told one of the boys to get the squirrel and thanked me.

This school occupied a substantial 1½ story log building. It was enclosed with the front rail fence style that both Cherokees and white people used in that country. This style could be built out of heavy flat rocks which could be used as a step to walk over the fence, or of heavy rough lumber with a platform usually six feet square on top. A woman could lead a horse alongside this fence and easily mount it. Courting couples frequently occupied these places.

In August 1873 brothers Frank, Charles, and I accompanied neighbor John Vanarsdall, a widower, to the Chickasaw nation to buy steers. We camped on Big Caney. He brought his personal effects and his little boy and girl. Old Chief Nopawalla of the Little Osages and five or six others came to our camp to claim one of our horses.[2] We talked it over and thought we convinced them the horse did not belong to them. When we left the camp and started on our way, the little girl was driving the team. Charles and I remained behind to put out the campfire. Frank and Vanarsdall were on horses ahead of the wagon. Our path wound around through a heavy thicket of haw bushes.

As the wagon was going out of sight, I heard the little girl scream. I rode to the wagon as quickly as I could and had my six-shooter drawn. There stood old Chief Nopawalla holding one horse by the bit. Another Indian was on our horse, going through the woods as fast as he could.

I thought the war was on. As I brought the gun down to shoot him, Chief Nopawalla threw up his hand toward me and said, "Please don't shoot, you'll scare the young lady."

I had known the chief several years and did not know that he knew a word of English. It so astonished me that I didn't shoot.

We substituted another horse, Vanarsdall's own mount. He drove the wagon down to Frank Labadi, a Frenchman. Frank rode to Hick-

Charles Marion Records (1852–1901) attended Kansas State College, Manhattan, to study veterinary medicine. Charley settled in Kingfisher County and is buried in Emmons Cemetery near the old Craige Chapel, which the Records brothers helped establish. Courtesy of Western History Collections, University of Oklahoma Library.

ory Station to see sub-agent Jake Coffman who went with Frank to Chief Nopawalla to tell him if he did not have the horse at Labadi's by 10 A.M. the next day, Coffman would take the whole bunch of Indians down to Fort Smith. That meant a mighty hard trip for the Indians; the marshals usually took them in irons. By 10 A.M. the horse was restored.

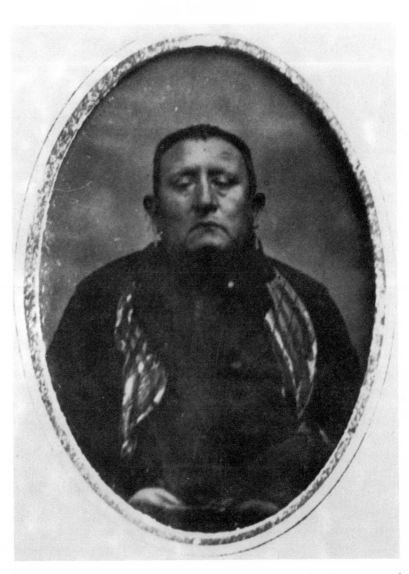

Osage Chief Nopawalla was a leader of the Little Osage band. Courtesy of Archives and Manuscripts Division of the Oklahoma Historical Society.

Two residents of Lake City, Kansas, were freighting for the government from Wichita to Fort Cobb, Fort Arbuckle, and other points in the Southwest. The day before a storm struck, they started from Lake City to Wichita to get supply loads for the government garrisons. About half way they camped for the night. They had anticipated a pleasant trip, but they awoke before daybreak in the midst of the worst storm they had ever encountered. They saw they and their teams would all freeze if they stayed there so they turned their teams loose. Since they were rugged and stout men, they thought they could drift with the storm and find some place to stop. They had not gone far when they discovered their legs were frozen from their knees down. They decided they would not survive and talked over what to do. Since they were going to freeze to death anyhow, they would do their friends a favor by going to the top of a hill so their bodies could be found readily. After they sat awhile one fellow began to cry and Rube Marshall asked, "What's the matter?"

"It's too damn cold to freeze to death here. Let's go down in a hollow and die where it ain't so cold," was the reply.

They had not traveled far down the small canyon when they found a good dugout which had served a settler or as a line camp for a cow camp. If they had found it first, they would not have suffered much inconvenience. When their teams arrived home, neighbors formed a searching party and finally found them two or three days later. Their legs had been frozen so long that surgeons amputated them above the knees. Since they were employees of the government, friends secured congressional support for pensions for them.[3]

I have often seen Marshall, who settled on a claim ten miles north of Kingfisher, Oklahoma, on his small sorrel mule. He had a platform at home on which he climbed onto the mule when the animal walked alongside of it, then he rode to Kingfisher.

Brother Charles and I accompanied Elmore Connor and Nathan Lonsdale of Sedan in 1875 to buy yearlings at Webbers Falls. We crossed the Arkansas River near Cane Creek to buy corn for our horses. Up that creek was a Negro settlement among the Creek Indians. We saw a continuous string of one-room log cabins and log corn cribs filled with snapped corn. We found shucked out corn for fifty cents a bushel which was the equivalent of half bushel of shelled corn.

We passed into Choctaw country and stopped at a small town to inquire about livestock and travel conditions. We saw a large Negro woman approaching, carrying a bucket of water on her head and two buckets in her hands.

"Watch me make the woman spill some of that water," Connor said. As she walked past us, Connor bowed, scraped, and said, "How do you do, Madam?"

She bowed slightly and returned the salutation without spilling a drop of water.

Further east, two days later we found a white man who would sell horses for $15-$17. Charles brought one for $12. When we entered Arkansas, we found nothing to our liking and returned west, passed through Fort Smith, crossed the Arkansas River bridge, and traveled along the north bank to Webbers Falls. We were there about ten days and rain fell nearly every day or night. We met Bill Bradley, a well-to-do planter, who raised hogs, corn, and potatoes. Since we could not trade with the Indians without a permit, we employed him to do our trading. As we left with our herd of newly bought steers, our host accompanied us with his span of well-matched chestnut-sorrel horses until we crossed the bridge.

We had the cattle swim across the swollen Grand River where we lost two yearling steers. When the steers came out into the open prairie, the sun came out for the first time in ten days. The old bell was pealing in the Fort Gibson tower; it seemed that we had suddenly arrived at a different country.

THREE

Life in the Osage Nation

In 1871 the Osage Indians were drifting aimlessly about in southern Kansas, annoying the settlers, scaring women and children, and picking up things which did not belong to them. This caused much complaint. Finally a small band of them camped on a hill a short distance west of Peru. They set up their long, canvas-wrapped tepee poles, which made an imposing sight. This action caused increased complaints and some of the settlers began to talk of quitting their claims and leaving the country.

Brother Elisha had a Civil War Spencer seven-shooter carbine; in his four years of army-life practice he could "make it talk fast." As there seemed to be no other way to cause the Indians to move just after darkness, he took this gun filled to capacity and rode close to the Indian camp until he could see the tall tepees and not mistake a man for one of them. He pointed his carbine at the tops of the tall tepees and began shooting at top speed until the seven-shooter was empty. He walked back to his horse, mounted, and rode home. He said nothing about it to anyone for years. This put a stop to Osage camping in that part of Kansas.

At daybreak the next morning, neighboring settlers saw the Indians on the move; they never stopped until they reached Big Caney River in Indian Territory.

In 1872 the national government had just moved the Osages to Indian Territory. They continued to take things and some of the whites decided to retaliate. Eight or ten armed whites went down into the Territory looking for horses and met the Little Osages led by Nopawalla.

All got away save the chief who was captured. The whites were the rough element. The Indians came with their guns and began to shoot. They killed a white man named John Selters, then freed the chief.

Osages continued to trade in the border Kansas towns. A merchant named Knapp in Peru traded goods to Chief Nopawalla for two Indian ponies. A short time later Nopawalla and six to five other Indians rode past Father's residence to Peru where they remained until after darkness.

Next morning Knapp's two Osage ponies were missing, along with one of Father's two-year-old mares. I was sick at the time and had been in bed more than ten days.

As soon as I could get up, I saddled a horse and without telling anyone where I was going, rode down into Indian Territory to see if I could find the horses. I saw no one until I crossed the Big Caney a few miles downstream from Hickory Station. I started over the wide bottom land south of the river when I saw a mounted Indian. When he saw me, he came riding swiftly. He asked me in Osage what I was after. I replied in Osage that I was hunting horses. He rode a short distance with me then without saying another word put his horse at top speed in the direction I was going. He soon came to a bunch of horses which he drove into the hills as fast as they could run. I saw he had beaten me and I had no business being on such a mission in my condition. So I turned back.

I crossed the Caney River at the same ford and rode up the east side of Hickory Creek where I came upon a herd of Texas cattle which was being driven toward Missouri. They had followed the old cattle trail[1] to Coffeyville until the Big Caney. As they crossed the water, the lead steers up on the north bank, an Osage Indian shot and killed a large beef. This stampeded the herd and caused the drivers to lose the trail.

They asked me where it was. I thought that I had crossed it before overtaking them. While I was talking to them, I saw an old blanket Indian riding past. I hailed him in Osage and asked him where the trail was. He said it was north of us. I told him he was lying but he stuck to his story and rode away.

Since the Texas cow outfit had camped for the night and were eating their supper, they asked me to eat with them. I told them my story, got off my horse, and drank a cup of coffee, saying I was afraid to eat anything. They seemed to fall for me when they saw me carrying on a conversation in Osage. They wanted me to stay all night. I couldn't do that for I hadn't told any of my relatives where I was going.

I mounted my horse and told the boss he should go a short distance with me to see if the Indian knew where the trail was. We hadn't ridden far when we found it. Since there had not been any driving along the trail during the summer of 1871, the trail was very dim.

I arrived home at sunset. When my folks heard where I had been,

30

they were astonished beyond measure and wondered how I could stand it. They wanted me to go to bed for a few days at least. But when I told them what I had learned, all agreed that it would take some scheming to get the horses.

Brother Charlie saw Knapp and they went to see Nopawalla. Knapp told the chief that he would give the Indians a certain quantity of goods if they would deliver the horses to Peru on a certain day. The Indians agreed and returned the horses. Knapp said he would assure all of the expenses as we had a difficult time locating the horses. His goods were not fit for a white person to use, anyway.

Knapp sold his horses as soon as they were returned to avoid having to redeem them again. It seems that when an Indian gets a horse and because of its freedom of action in the Indian's wild life, the horse seldom forgets it. The next chance a horse like this gets, it will follow them off again. Our horse was not long in the hands of the Indians. We kept it well away from the road and had no more trouble with it.

Cal Watkins, a Kentuckian, had "went" to Texas and brought a 1000 head of cattle up the eastern trail that led to Baxter Springs, Kansas, in 1870.[2] He turned northwest from the trail after he had passed through the Five Civilized tribes and intended to settle in southern Kansas near Elgin on the Big Caney River. When the line was established in 1871, Watkins found that he had stopped too soon and was in the Indian Territory. So he stayed among the Osages, leased land, and did extensive farming and stock raising until 1879. He always took his family along.

Watkins was a big, powerful man, but the bone between his elbow and shoulder was missing in the left arm. He had been shot and the bone was shattered. Watkins lived up to and observed his religious views of right and wrong. If there were any poor people in the country, and there were always some of them present at Christmastime, he would bestow gifts on the poor freely; whatever he gave was the best. If it was pork, he gave hams; if beef, the hindquarters. Of course he raised an abundance of corn and other grain but no wheat. He gave sacks of corn meal; he thought it should be good enough for the poor as it was what he lived on.

Hard Rope's band of the Big Osages[3] rounded up all of the horses that were running loose and drove them off. No one "seen" the Indians doing it but after two days their trails were discovered.

Watkins organized a bunch of armed men and followed their trail to

31

Osage Chief Hard Rope was a leader of the Big Osage band. Courtesy of Western History Collections, University of Oklahoma Library.

the Verdigris River. When the pursuing party got to a hill where they could see the Osage camp, they thought it was too big to attack successfully. The whites held a war council. There was one vote for going into the camp; all the others voted for "Home Sweet Home."

Cal Watkins said, "Well, you fellows can all go back." They turned back, and Watkins mounted his horse and rode down to the Osage camp; he knew the chief would be in the center of the camp. It was the custom among all Indians that the chief must have the largest lodging place, for all the other Indians would come to him for the councils and other deliberations. He rode up, dismounted, and an Indian stepped to the door. Watkins handed him his bridle rein.

The Indian motioned him inside; Watkins walked in and sat down beside the fire. Soon the old chief's dinner was brought in. Watkins and Hard Rope ate together. Afterwards they lit their pipes. An interpreter came in and said Hard Rope wanted to know what he wanted. Watkins, with a little diplomacy, told the interpreter that a few days ago some of the chief's young men had "drove" off some of his horses. The chief wanted to know where they got the horses, how many, and the description of each one. Watkins described them with their brands.

The old chief said, "Tomorrow morning your horses will all be brought into camp." He invited Watkins to stay all night. After breakfast the Indians came leading all of his horses and helped him get started on the road back to his home. That was the last time the Indians stole any horses from Watkins.

Quakers from Iowa held the important government posts at various Indian agencies during the seventies. Isaac Gibson[4] was the agent at the Osage Agency that later became the present-day Pawhuska. His sub-agent was Timothy Wittiby. Varney was in charge of the Hominy Station. Samuel Comer was in charge of Hickory Station, a trading post and sub-agency, two miles south of Jonesburg on the freight line from Coffeyville to Pawhuska. In 1873 Comer was transferred to the Osage Agency. Since he and Wittiby were equal in rank, their orders often conflicted and resulted in some pretty sharp controversies.

Samuel Comer had a large carbuncle on the back of his neck at one time which made him cross and irritable. When their orders clashed one day, they got into a heated argument and Timothy Wittiby lost his temper, "Samuel if it wasn't for my religion I would whip thee."

Samuel replied, "If it wasn't for this boil on my neck, I would whip thee." Quakers always used their Christian names and referred to each

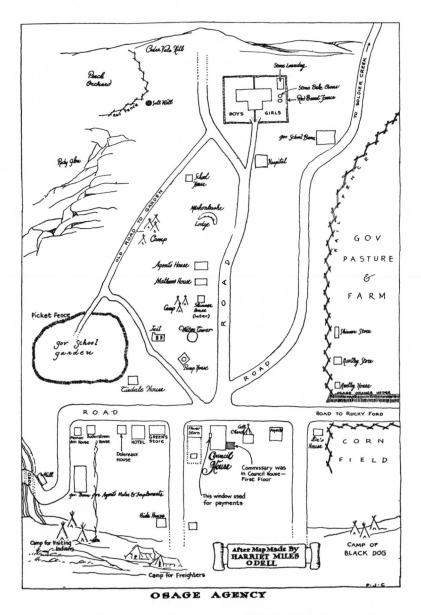

OSAGE AGENCY

Map 2. Map of the Osage Agency. From *Wah'Kon'Tah*, by John Joseph Mathews. Copyright © 1932 by the University of Oklahoma Press.

other as "thee." In their worship they opened their services about like other sects, then they would be seated to wait until the spirit moved them.

A young Quaker named Andrew Hisey, a roustabout, lived with Timothy Wittiby. He seemed to be very zealous in the worship of the Quaker faith. One night while they were assembled and all seated waiting for the "Spirit to move them," Andrew arose suddenly, as if the Spirit had moved him, and said, "In the language of the poet," stopped and said, "I've forgotten the poet's name," then paused again. He continued, "Well, I'll declare I've forgotten what the poet said," and sat down.

Wittiby's house was a frame or box-house with only one room. There was a loft over the room on which loose boards had been laid on the joists. A ladder leaned against the joists and Andrew used this upper space for his bedroom. One night he shifted too far out on the ends of the boards and fell to the floor below, causing marks on his face. When he came around some of the employees the next day, some of them asked what had happened to his face. Wittiby was present and didn't like the manner in which Andrew answered. Wittiby added, "Yes, he fell down flutterty-floppity."

When Samuel Comer left Hickory Station in 1873 and took charge of the beef issues at the Osage Agency, he came to Father's neighborhood and bought a bunch of beeves. He hired Charley Beers and me to drive the cattle to the agency where they were butchered and issued to the Indians.

Comer and his assistants were having difficulty trying to teach the Osages how to dress the beeves in the white man's fashion. Once I saw him ask an Indian to shoot a beef and his government expert butcher took charge of dressing it. The Indians were wanting the beef badly but when they saw the butcher cutting the meat, they put up a great protest. They did not know how to handle or prepare such pieces of meat. Some left in disgust without any meat and Comer had a hard time disposing of it. The government butcher told Comer it might take a generation to teach the Indians how to prepare and cook a beef according to the white man's formula. They let the Indians shoot another beef and dress it their way while the butcher observed.

The Indians swarmed about the second beef, and the government butcher became so disgusted with their performances that he left before the Indians got the carcass torn to pieces. Some were getting

35

meat; others, bones; still others got the entrails; all seemed to be well pleased with their cuts. They loaded up and started for their respective wigwams to prepare their usual feast.

In 1874 my older brother, John Cotton Records, got a commission to take charge of Hickory Station succeeding Samuel Comer. My brother did not have to move to the station, as he could quit Saturday noon, drive only eight or ten miles up to his home in Kansas, and report back sometime Monday forenoon.

There was a sawmill at Hickory Station. John Varnarsdall, who lived on an adjoining farm with John Cotton, had the contract to furnish cordwood for the furnace to run the steam engine which operated the saws. They rode back and forth together.

One Monday morning as they were riding to the station, they stopped at a little branch to let their horses drink. They saw a man's face sticking up out of the water. There was a house not far distant where they found two boys and sent them in different directions to the neighbors for help. Soon several men assembled and the body was dragged from the water. No one knew the fellow nor why he had both hands cut off at the wrists.

The following spring a farmer was plowing in his field near where the body was found and turned up two hands, each with a star tatooed on its back. It was concluded that the murderer had done this to prevent identification which might furnish a clue as to the perpetrator of the crime. Neighborhood meetings were held, inquiries made, committees appointed to investigate, but no evidence was uncovered.

In November 1874 after we had taken care of what little we had raised on our farm, Alfred Sams, a neighbor boy, and I got jobs cooking for government employees at the Osage Agency. Alf cooked for the sawmill; I cooked for the teamsters, carpenters, and stone masons. Some were our neighbors in Chautauqua County—Rufe Mason, "Gent" Stearns, Charlie Thompson, Jim Wilson, and brother Frank. Our bunkhouses were close together; we called them just across the street from each other. We had two rooms for sleeping. Sams, a rather reckless housekeeper and cook, didn't put in much time around his bunkhouse. He would come over and visit with me quite a bit.

There was also an old man named Holmes who came to the agency. He cut up the tree tops from which the saw logs had been taken by the log crews and sold the wood to people about the town, as everyone burned wood. The wood didn't cost Holmes anything. He camped outdoors and slept in the government barn. When the weather turned cold, I saw him out, trying to cook in the cold wind and told him to bring his frying pan and coffee pot to cook on our stove when we were not using it. He could set his flour and other things in our bunkroom on a bench which stood next to the door.

One day Alf came over to visit awhile. I told him to watch something which I was cooking; I must go uptown to get something essential for the meal and wouldn't be gone long.

When I returned, I didn't go into the kitchen but went into the bunk-part of the house. I saw a pile of beef entrails lying on Holmes' flour sack, soaking into his flour. I set down the groceries, picked up the entrails, and heaved them out to a bunch of hogs which were running at large. They had a feast on some Indian's beef. I thought this was one of Alf's smart tricks, as he was very fond of doing funny things.

I went into the kitchen and asked, "Al, why did you put them beef guts on the old man's flour?"

He replied that he hadn't been in the bunkroom during my absence and didn't know what was there. I told him what I had found and done with it. He recalled an Indian came and stuck his head in the door to ask if he could lay a piece of beef in there. Al told him he could but never looked at it. Al returned to his own bunkhouse.

About nightfall an Indian pushed the door open, "Whare my beef?"

I grabbed a stick of stove wood, "You dirty gut eater, get out of here or I'll break your head!" He dodged out mighty quick; that was the last I saw of him.

In those days prairie chickens were numerous in the Southwest. Barney Mann, a half-breed Sioux, was working for the government in 1874. Everyone was killing and eating the chickens.

One winter night a group was sitting around a fire when Mann grabbed a chicken, hanging at a convenient place, took out the entrails, forced the contents from through the anal orifice, wrapped the entrails around a stick, dissolved some salt in a cup of water, dipped the entrails into the cup, then held them over the coals in the fireplace. When they became crisp, he bit off those portions, then dipped the other end into the cup of salt water, and repeated the roasting until he had eaten all of it.

A young Englishman who had recently come to this country saw what Mann was doing, "Ah, just look what the nawsty hawg is doing."

37

The boys began to laugh. Mann said, "I wish I could take him out on a buffalo hunt sometime."

While I was cooking at the agency, an Osage named Joe, whom I liked very much, would come to visit. He had a bad scar on his head which was caused by a wild mustang pony which he had roped. It struck him with its front foot. Such animals kick, strike, and bite. They are as vicious as a wolf. We have caught them and tied them to logs; they would never eat or drink water in the daytime, only at night.

Joe brought two young bucks, dressed in Indian costume. When he came in, I spoke to him and he said, "How."

I could not carry on a conversation although I knew a large number of Osage words. When I found he wouldn't talk, I told him if he did not take these two Indians out of my cook shack, I would put a few more scars on his head. Since he had been so friendly before, it made me mad when he refused to talk to me in the presence of the other two.

Soon after he poked his head into the door and said, "If you'll let me come in, I will talk to you."

I said, "Come on in and I'll hear what you have to say."

He said when he left the Osage mission school, the Quaker teachers gave him citizens' clothes and instructed him to teach the others the white man's language. When pupils dressed in white men's clothes, that created much opposition among the older members of the tribe. They beat him, tore his clothes off, and made him wear his old garments. If they ever caught him talking to a white man, they beat and kicked him, accusing him of making light of them to the white men.

That fall a well was dug a little southwest of the government barn at the Osage Agency for the purpose of furnishing water for the work stock which were kept in stalls underneath the barn. Bob Marshall, a professional well-digger, had gotten the government contract to dig a big open well which was walled up with stone.

While he was digging, the government agent was issuing beef which were purchased from Burk Burnett.[5] The agent's employees were trying to pen some of the beeves which were to be butchered. One large steer with long horns broke from the pen and came running past the well from the north.

John Soderstrom, a Swede, was windlassing the dirt out of the well for Marshall. As this steer approached, Soderstrom picked up a hand spike—a hickory stick about five feet long, green and heavy—stepped

38

up on top of the bench bank on which the barn stood, directly in the path of the wild steer. The steer saw him and turned a horn to hit him about the pit of his stomach. Soderstrom swung that big, heavy club with all his power on top of the steer's head. The shock caused the steer to lose aim and raise its head so that its forehead hit Soderstrom in the breast. He sailed off downhill with arms and legs extended, then fell on his back. The steer ran right over him, pinching one side of his hand slightly, never hurting him a particle.

There were twenty-five or thirty Osages standing in the front end of the barn to keep out of the way of the wild steers. They haw-hawed and laughed for several minutes.

Soderstrom said, "I thought I didn't stood against him."

That remark tickled those of us white fellows watching. That started the Indians on another round of laughter.

All this time Bob Marshall was in the bottom of the well, raving and snorting, wanting to get out. Then Soderstrom windlassed him out to stay until all of the beeves were disposed.

After the well was finished, there was plenty of water. Many Indians had never seen a well before. They seemed amazed that the temperature of the water was so much cooler than creek water. The well was curbed with good lumber, but the Indians could stand and look down into the water as they pulled up the bucket. They liked to drop small objects down into the well to see the effect of the little waves. I have seen squaws gathered around to look down, pick a fat louse off themselves, drop it into the well, and watch it swim around.

After Bob Marshall finished his well contract at the Osage Agency, he returned to Kansas where he resided and continued his well-digging. He was working on a job and had the well sunk to a depth of twenty feet when he put in a blast of black powder with a fuse attached to loosen the rocks in the bottom of the well. He lighted the fuse and was hoisted out. For some unexplained reason the fuse was slow to ignite. He waited for some time, then walked up to the mouth of the well, lay on a support at the edge of the well, and was looking down, when suddenly the blast went off and threw stones far out of the well. One stone weighing several pounds hit him in the head and killed him instantly.

John Soderstrom stayed in Pawhuska and built an ice house at the agency. If the winter was sufficiently cold to make handling ice profitable, he would fill the house which was cold enough to freeze ice for commercial purposes. He took a board and marked the ice in squares so he could cut them in cubes.

One day he marked and sawed a great number of the blocks. He used a common one-man, wood saw about five feet long. He engaged men and teams to haul sawdust from the government sawmill in which to pack the ice. That night it turned cold and froze again. Soderstrom believed the freezing would cause him to saw out these blocks of ice a second time. He got out early in the morning to investigate. If the ice blocks needed re-sawing, he was to notify his haulers to come late. Hearing no countermanding orders, all turned out to work.

They saw the ice had been disturbed considerably but Soderstrom wasn't in sight. They became suspicious that something was wrong. The indications showed he had ventured out too far; the blocks had broken loose; he had fallen into the water and drowned.[6]

Thus the first government well-diggers at the Osage Agency fell victims to their own professions.

On every beef issue day the town and woods about would be filled with Indians who had come to get their beef allowance. The cowpunchers were having their usual trouble penning the beeves to be slaughtered. Generally one or two would break away, followed by a chase.

On this particular day a wild steer came from the east, directly toward our cook shack. The road was filled with Indians who were walking toward the shack. They saw the steer at about the same time as I. Throwing open the door of the bunkhouse, I stepped out in front where they could see me plainly. I began to holler, "Kulolo wa sha-sha." (Come here, my friends).

A number of them started directly toward me. I stepped back inside, shut the door, and fastened it. Some were so close they jumped on top of the bunkhouse; others took to the pile of cordwood; some dodged behind trees; the steer missed them all. I stepped outside and began to laugh loudly. They all seemed to enjoy the joke for they were accustomed to such rough stuff.

As other Indians came up from behind, I saw the fellows nearest me pointing at me and telling the new arrivals something. Then they broke into a laugh, so I thought they had done better than John Soderstrom who "didn't stood against him."

When Burk Burnett of Texas brought up his two thousand head of cattle and sold them to the government, he camped on Bird Creek just

40

above Osage Agency. He kept his work horses and mules in the government barn. The morning before he started back to Texas, he walked from his camp to Isaac Gibson's office.

Among Burnett's hands was one large, powerful Negro, called Tom, who tended the work horses and performed heavy work around camp and the ranch. The Burnett family had raised him and he remained after the abolition of slavery. Tom attended to the horses and mules. One of the fine black mules had a mean disposition and would kick once in awhile.

Just as Burnett approached the barn, the mule kicked Tom who grabbed a board and began to beat the mule. Burnett stopped at the door and hollered, "Hey, there, what's a goin' on?"

Tom threw down his stick and replied, "That damn black mule kicked me!"

"A damn black mule kicked a damn black nigger," Burnett said, walking toward the agency as though nothing had happened.

I was coming out of the barn and had heard it all. As I stepped in front of the door, Tom was standing just inside. I asked, "You allow that feller to talk that way to you?"

The Negro's face showed a grayish cast as if he was scared nearly to death. His eyes widened, his mouth opened, he looked at me a little bit and replied, "Why, dat's Massa Bunett!"

Amused, I walked away rapidly to the cook shack, laughing. I didn't want him to know I was just tormenting him.

When the Indians came to share the beef issue, they would spread their buffalo and cowhide blankets on the bare ground; their wigwams were built over the bedding. In the center of the ground area was a barren spot for their fires to cook and warm themselves. The hides or skins were spread in such a way to leave the hole in the roof for a little of the smoke to go out. The Indians lay on the thin bedding next to the cold, damp ground and it would become mighty cold before morning by the first of December. Toward morning I could hear some Indians coughing and they made the woods ring.[7]

One night, perhaps 1 or 2 A.M., I heard one Osage who seemed to be carrying on a conversation in a very loud tone. The next time I saw Bill Conner,[8] an educated half-breed Osage, and told him about what I had heard in the Osage camp so late one night. He said the Indian was praying to the "Great Spirit" for the prosperity of his people and for its continuance.

41

I asked, "Do they do such things as pray to a Supreme Being?"

He replied, "Yes, they're very religious in their way." But their religion didn't seem to be of much value to a white man.

The Osage Indian School was in a large stone building. We employees were permitted to attend the night sessions which were usually singing and were conducted in one large room which might seat five hundred people. Some Indians sang well; pitch, time, and rhythm were good whether they could speak a word of English or not. It was amusing and instructive to us who were listeners. All of the Indians appeared to be full bloods from six to eighteen years old. It was not difficult to induce the young to attend because the government fed them.

Billy Conner told me his experiences before the Osage Agency was started. He and a bunch of young Indians went on a hunt down in the country. They camped at night on the south bank of Bird Creek, lay down in the tall grass, and went to sleep. They hobbled their horses to graze in the grass. When they woke up, a prairie fire was upon them. They had to leap like frogs over the bank into the water. Everything they had—saddles, bridles, guns—was burned up, but their horses had time to get out of the way. It was in early winter and they nearly froze.

They peeled bark, put it on their horses' lower jaws, and rode back to Hickory Station, twenty-five or thirty miles northeast. They had told the squaws of a great abundance of meat they were going to bring back. They knew what their fate was and true to custom, the squaws met them, armed with clubs and sticks to give them a sound beating. Then the squaws built up the fires and put on big kettles to make a good feast.

The government built houses for the Osages but they did not know how to use them. At first they put their harness, dogs, and worthless plunder inside, then built their teepees in front of the houses.

One day in 1874 at Pawhuska I was talking with Conner and he pointed to a rocky point, "My, how things have changed here. Two years ago me and some other Indians came down here on a hunt; I came out on that rocky point and sat down to rest. I looked down in the valley where this town is built, and I thought it would be a long time before the white men would occupy this land here. Now look at these big buildings and the business that's being done here."

I told some of the boys what he had said. Captain Ogese whirled around and remarked, "Bill Conner, who is he? Nothing but a renegade white man." Ogese had married a full-blood Osage woman. They had only one child, a daughter.[9]

A man named Tom Adams came up with Burk Burnett's herd and later married Captain Ogese's daughter. They had one daughter and the wife died shortly afterwards. When I last saw Adams, he had a case pending in court in which he was attempting to establish a claim to a head right of allotted land. I never learned how his suit terminated.[10]

Horse racing was a great sport among the Osages as with other tribes I have observed. They would first excite the horses by riding them in a large group of running horses, the riders shouting and singing. As they raced, the riders lay forward, dug their heels in the horses' flanks. Excited Indians who watched were apt to bet their blankets, buffalo robes, and ponies on their favorite horse. Sometimes the loser was left naked, afoot, without anything to eat.

Government employees were forbidden to attend these races under penalty of losing their jobs. Sometimes on beef-issue days a race would take place in sight of the agency. Then employees could see the race without losing any time. One clerk was caught by Agent Gibson. He gave the excuse that he was studying the behavior and character of Indians. He kept his job.

By January 1875 my work as a cook ended. Brother Frank remained and was appointed to run the sawmill during that winter. It was not uncommon for strangers to come into the Osage Country searching for work. If they didn't find it, they would leave; no questions were asked. One day two men came to Frank and wanted to know if they could find work in the Osage Agency. Of course he couldn't give them any definite information. They asked permission to camp nearby. He told them they could camp wherever they pleased, there was plenty of work, and the government well was near. The two men camped under some big trees between the sawmill and the barn. They tied their horses at the back end of their wagon by their feed box.

The men went to bed in their covered wagon. A storm struck and broke off a previously storm-damaged tree about twenty feet above the ground at least two feet in diameter. The top struck the ground first and the recoil pitched the heavy tree with such force that it fell across the middle of the wagon, smashed the box in two, and killed both men instantly. They had no identification marks to tell who they were or where they originated.

In the summer of 1875 a very prominent Big Osage Indian of Chief

Hard Rope's band died near the Arkansas River. Since they were usually at war with some other tribe, it was an Osage custom, and I think among all tribes, when a prominent Indian died, to bury a fresh scalp with the deceased. In a council the Osages decided to honor this ancient custom.

Since they had no enemies in reaching distance, about twelve Osages took the ancient vow, put on their war paint, and started west to kill the first Indian they met. Some distance away on the Otoe reservation, they met a boy whom they killed and scalped. Before they could get clear away, the Otoes discovered what happened. They started in pursuit and sent runners after Generals Caddison and Gatchell[11] who had supervision over all the Indians in Indian Territory west of the Cherokees. The Otoes appeared in Osage country in war paint.

A detachment of soldiers had just escorted the Pawnee Indians into the territory and was camped on the Arkansas near the Pawnee Agency. The army officials sent them to see that the Pawnees and Osages were disarmed sufficiently to prevent them from making a general assault against each other. The officers called a council of the Otoe and the Big Osage chiefs. They were told they must have a peaceful settlement without bloodshed.

Since the Otoes seemed to be the aggressors, they were asked their reasons for entering the Osage reservation. They stated eloquently the great things they had done. Under this aggravating condition, they plead for the privilege of taking vengeance on the Osages. After the Otoe orator finished, the officers called on Hard Rope to represent the Osages. He arose and began to belittle the Otoes; they were nothing in his sight. Although the Otoe chief had made great threats and boasts that they were men with pricks; the Osage, Hard Rope, said they had pricks too.

Generals Caddison and Gatchell, the representatives of the great White Father in Washington, were held responsible for the amicable settlement of all disagreements among the Indians under their jurisdiction. They told the council that although the Osages had committed a grievous offense, they were indebted to the Otoes and must immediately go into negotiations for a peace treaty. If they didn't, the officials would have to take the whole tribe to Fort Smith before the Federal Court to locate the guilty Osages who would be executed for murder. The Osages did not wait long to make up their minds; several had been to Fort Smith in irons. They decided to pay the Otoes

44

liberally for the transgression with ponies, blankets, and supplies. The Otoes went back heavily laden, declaring they could live peaceably and happy the rest of their days.

The only eagle nest I ever saw was on Little Caney River in Indian Territory near Eagle Ford. In this western country eagles and large hawks did not hesitate to roost on the ground, but they usually selected a spot on a high point. The nest was about as large as a common wagon box, about 10 × 4 feet. It was not more than twenty feet from the ground up to the nest. The nest was built of sticks and limbs, placed in the forks of the tree limbs. It was difficult for wild animals to climb to it. The eagles had nested there for several years but it was not bullet-proof. The hunters soon killed them.

The eagles had such terrible claws that they were never in fear of being attacked by any animal. Predatory animals knew it didn't pay to attack these birds; the loss of flesh and blood could not equal the flesh of a hawk or an eagle, should they succeed in killing one. Coyotes learned it did not pay to eat the craw or the gizzard of a hen.

K. P. Lawrence, who lived on the Arkansas River, did most of his trading at Arkansas City, Kansas. A breeder of fine trotting horses and drivers, he found some excellent trotters in Arkansas City to which he bred his mares. He showed me his stock horses which he had raised; there were at least twenty-five which he got by trading eagle feathers to the Osages.

I do not know how he got his start in eagles, but he had a 28 × 18 foot house with a good two-story roof, containing cross beams on which eagles roosted. The whole building was well-braced and enclosed with woven wire instead of lumber. There were no sidings but the corners of the structure were boxed in. His eagles were loose in the building when I was there in 1889. I saw the carcass of a deer inside. Lawrence hired an Indian to bring him a deer once in a while. He also got other kinds of meat and kept the eagles well-supplied. They would gorge, then sit around a few days without eating. I asked how he got the feathers out.

He said, "Oh, that is easy." He took a blanket, folded it several times, wrapped it on his arm, then stepped into the house, and closed the door behind him. When one made a dash to kill him, he held up the bandaged arm. The old eagle would bury his talons into it and hang on while Lawrence pulled out its feathers. The more he pulled, the tighter the eagle would grip. Lawrence handed the feathers to his attendant who took care of them. Lawrence would back out of the door and slip his arm out of the blanket as he stepped out. The eagle would let go and Lawrence could recover it.

He had a good market for feathers. The Indians would trade deer for them. It never cost Lawrence anything to keep the feather trade going.

Lawrence told me that Billy Conner, his wife's cousin, found an eagle frozen in the ice on the Arkansas River. Conner had been hunting along the river and saw an eagle sitting on the ice. He watched awhile and observed that the eagle did not move. He went up to see what was the matter and found the eagle was frozen dead.

The eagle apparently had been flying over the water, looking for fish. There was an old water-soaked chunk about two feet long and four inches in diameter which must have been floating downstream in the open water. When the eagle saw it moving, he swooped down and thrust his powerful claws into the soft chunk with such force that he couldn't withdraw them. It was too heavy for the eagle to lift clear of the water. A cold wave came and froze the eagle tightly in the ice.

All Indians have their legends which they regarded sacred. Old Indians are guarded in telling them to one another and never to strangers. The Indians are loath to discuss with white people the doings of the Great Spirit. As they sit around their ceremonial fire of their tribal councils, there is no more awe-inspiring story told than that of Little Soldier, a full-blood Osage Indian, whom later Osages called the man who would never die as other men die.

The explanation about this legend can be given by the white men and Indians who were present as members of the searching party. It is not an ancient legend nor pipe dream, but a mystery of the present time. Residents of Hominy and Pawhuska who were at the inception of this legend admitted it had them buffaloed. It was told to me by the only survivor of Hominy Station, Chal Byers, a reliable eyewitness, a man whom I knew in Chautauqua County when he was a small boy.

At the birth of an Osage child it was the custom of the father or mother to name it. One or the other would walk about with eyes closed for a few moments, then open them. The first thing they saw would be the baby's name. Also, if they saw the setting sun, it would be Sundown, which was the name of a member of the Little Osage band. They may have their names changed or something added later. An

Indian named Good Man at birth had on his first hunt killed a bear and it made him Good Man Bear Meat.

To become a member of the full-blood braves, the aspirant had to isolate himself from all of the members of the tribe and hold communion with the Great Spirit for about ten days until he had an inspiration. Then he would return with the story of his vision. Some would come with the good qualities of the elk, others, of the bear, etc.

When Little Soldier returned from his period of communion, he told how it had been revealed that he should never die as other men do. The old braves accepted it and said nothing. Little Soldier later became very prosperous, owning several hundred horses when Byers knew him.

One morning in 1889 Little Soldier and his nephew, Kemohah, went deer hunting along a branch of Hominy Creek about eight miles east of Hominy Post. They separated with the understanding that Little Soldier was to start at the mouth of the creek and come upstream. Kemohah was to go to the headwaters and start downstream. Whoever came to a deer herd first was to shoot the deer and chase the rest in the opposite direction so that the other hunter could have a chance at the kill. Kemohah was the first to meet and kill a deer. The others ran downstream as planned. Kemohah waited to hear the report of Little Soldier's gun but he heard nothing. He drew the deer and hung it to the limb of a tree, then started in search of his uncle. He found Little Soldier's horse about a mile downstream, fifty yards from the creek bank. His saddle gun was still in its scabbard; his blanket was thrown across the saddle; but Little Soldier had disappeared. Kemohah made a hurried search for his uncle; he rode rapidly to camp to tell the startling news.

The young men scoffed, "Kemohah don't know where Little Soldier went. Kemohah never murdered Little Soldier for his horses."

But the older men were not so skeptical. Kemohah's story was only the inevitable fulfillment of prophecy and they accepted it seriously. Kemohah took little comfort from the faith of the older men, and he was so worried because of the skepticism of the young Osage men that he rode twenty miles to Pawhuska and surrendered to the officials.

On his way he stopped at Hominy Station and told Byers about the strange disappearance. Byers, two other white men, and several young Indians who were sure that they would find Little Soldier's body near where Kemohah had murdered him went to the scene and found the

47

deer just as Kemohah had left it. There was the horse with gun, scabbard, and blanket lying back on the horse's rump as if he had thrown it from his shoulders when he dismounted.

Kemohah returned next morning with the Indian police and joined Byers and the search party for a second search up and down the creek all day. They thought that a party of Creek Indians had captured him by roping him as no blood stains could be found. They soon gave up that theory as the most expert trailers in the searching party could find no traces or any other evidence where they found Little Soldier's horse. This also eliminated the idea that he had gotten thirsty and had gone to a deep hole and drowned. They followed the sand bars along the side of the creek for several miles and saw nothing but deer tracks where they had gone into and out of the creek.

The searching party gave up the quest and no one to this day knows what became of Little Soldier. Kemohah was cleared blame by the officers, but he was strangely moved by the mysterious disappearance of his uncle. Kemohah lived forty-three years and never mentioned his strange experience.

According to Indian belief the Great Spirit lifted Little Soldier to the Happy Hunting Ground. The prophecy which Little Soldier made came true—"He had not died as other men had died."

FOUR

Cowpunching in Dodge City

After I left the Osage Agency, I worked at Father's in between cattle-buying trips until August 1878. Sam Taylor, one of our neighbors who had worked at Dodge City the previous summer, suggested I accompany him back there to seek work among the numerous cattlemen who congregated there. We reluctantly took along "Hi" Moore, another neighbor, because he had no money. Taylor and I bought two horses and a wagon in which we carried our saddles. Shortly after we left Grenola, Moore took sick, then again when we arrived in Dodge.

I helped him along the street, watching for signs of a cheap lodging house. Presently we met a rough-looking old fellow and asked him where we could find one.

"You don't want to take him to any such place! They'll do nothing but rob you!" He turned and pointed to a sign and said, "There's an old lady in charge who will treat him right. It won't cost you anything."

When I entered, out came a husky old lady. I asked her for a room for this young fellow. "All right," she said. "Some of you girls, come here; you're needed!" she called.

Three or four painted, rouged girls came; I realized this was no lodging house. They promptly removed his clothing and placed him in his assigned room with expressions of sympathy. I told the madam I would call to see Moore each evening to see how he was getting along.

Meanwhile, Sam Taylor met his former employer at the stockyards, and they went to that cattleman's range several miles up the Arkansas River. At the stockyards I met Bill Lindsay, a ranch foreman, who hired me to work in the branding pens. Later I worked for various cowmen from Colorado, Texas, and Kansas who were changing the road brands on the herds of through cattle which had come up the Texas Trail[1] that season to their own ranch brands.

The stockyards belonged to the Santa Fe Railroad which furnished all the tools and repairing materials. I found the spades exceedingly sharp when I carelessly set one on the toe of my boot. It cut a hole

49

Front Street, Dodge City, 1878. Courtesy of The Kansas State Historical Society, Topeka, Kansas.

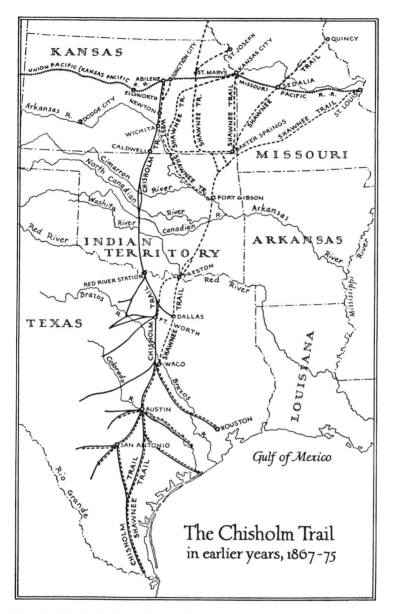

Map 3. The Chisholm Trail in early years, 1867–75. From *The Chisholm Trail*, by Wayne Gard. Copyright © 1954 by the University of Oklahoma Press.

through the leather and made a gash in my big toe. When I quickly dropped it to the ground, it cut off the point of my boot sole.

After one day's work in the chutes, I was sent out on herd in the daytime, then to pen cows at night. I sold the wagon and my horse to Cox and Boyd's livery barn as I was furnished a mount at work. When a chuteful was branded, the cattle were turned out to the herd which I held as close as possible to the branding pen. I usually rode to a small knoll-like formation where I could watch the herd.

I saw a fellow circling a bunch of wild horses toward the branding pen with a peculiar outfit. He had a span of fine horses, hooked to a low, four-wheeled vehicle which had long axles, a slat-bottom arrangement without any bed, and he had an original way of sitting in it. He could lie and sleep in the vehicle. The harness was not hooked to a double-tree but was fastened to each end of the axle-trees just inside the wheels. There were no collars for pulling, but their heads were thrust through leather contrivances, and breast straps served as collars, no checks inside for lines. They were on the outside and the horses were held by a single check line, extending from one's head to another.

He motioned to me, wanting to know how long that pen would be in use. I told him it would be used all afternoon.

He said, "My name is Johnson, 'Wild-Horse' Johnson.[2] This outfit was made to chase wild horses." This was his profession. If anyone inquired, he would try to pen the horses at Kinsley, Kansas. He had followed them four or five days, two days before he could get close enough to turn them. He believed that he could have driven them into the pen if it hadn't been in use. "Some of these horses are branded and I always advertise them when I get them into the pen. If the owner appears and establishes his claim, usually he pays me a good fee to bring the horse to him. I claim all the horses without brands and offer them for sale."

His driving horses, used to round up the wild horses, were high-headed, long-necked, long-legged, and excellent travelers. I never saw anyone inquiring about him and I do not know what became of him. He certainly had that bunch of wild horses under good control, for when he was talking with me, they stopped as if waiting for him.

After work I looked after "Hi" Moore. Four days later he decided he wanted to go back to Chautauqua County. When I told Lindsay about Moore's predicament, he told me about the cowboy's half-fare ticket on the Santa Fe, if I approached "Gus" Johnson,[3] the general manager of freight and passenger traffic, the right way. Lindsay could not appear with me because of suspicion of collusion between foremen and cowhands. I was to tell Johnson that Moore was from Dickey's cow outfit at Buttermilk Lakes.[4]

I found "Gus" Johnson, told him a young cowboy across the street, ill and broke, wanted to return to eastern Kansas by rail. Since I would have to buy his ticket, I wanted to make it as light as possible.

"Bring him over, let me look at him," Johnson said.

I went over and told "Hi" to get himself ready to be put on exhibition.

Johnson took one look at him and said to the agent, "Issue one half-fare to Atchison."

I paid the fare, then paid Moore's lodging which was little, and helped him to his car. He was the happiest fellow I had seen in a long while. I felt more like kicking than kissing him goodbye; he never did repay me.

While on herd north on the sand hills, I saw for the first and only time, a mirage, directly above Fort Dodge. An exact duplicate of the fort appeared several hundred feet in the air with teams and soldiers, afloat and horseback, as if on the ground.

Fort Dodge was near the Arkansas River, and as I looked up that winding stream, I could see no timber. Near sundown, I could look upriver and see how rapidly it seemed to fall as it formed one bend after another toward me. Each bend, as it faced me directly, seemed to contain a little lake, and there seemed to be a number of them like layers, laid on one another.

There seemed to be lots of fish in the river. Settlers found fish could not be caught by hooks, but groups banded together, formed a line, and waded across the water to drive the fish toward a sand bar. When they made a good drive, the schools of fish become frightened and swam into the shallows and got stranded on a sand bar. It was great sport for the cowpunchers who noted similar tactics that they used in rounding up fish. If a fish tried to break back, the cowpunchers would yell, "Head him off," along with other similar roundup terms.

I saw prairie dog towns for the first time. The farther west I traveled, the larger and more numerous they were. The large dog towns lay beyond the settlements. Invariably they were in buffalo grass areas. If bunch and bluestem grass began to crowd into their towns, the prairie dogs fought against the grass as long as they could; if they lost, they moved. When the tall grass surrounded the dog burrows, it was

53

easier for predatory animals to catch them. The dogs worked toward high divides where grass was short and dangerous enemies could be sighted readily.

There were vast areas white with buffalo bones where they had been slaughtered for their hides. This was the main cause why the Indians went on the warpath. They depended on the buffalo for meat and their skins for tents, clothing, and bedding. Since they had lived in this manner for so many generations, the Indians considered that the buffalo belonged to them and the whites were robbing them of their rightful possession. When they saw this ruthless slaughter which wasted everything except the hides, they felt justified in killing every white man.

Thus the bone industry was created.[5] I saw many trainloads of bones leaving Dodge City. It was lucrative for the white man, especially freighters. Dodge was the end of the railroad; often these freighters, who worked from there to Santa Fe and other points, had to lay over while waiting for sufficient supplies to come by train. It was expensive, so they hit upon a plan of gathering the dry buffalo bones with their teams and wagons to haul to Dodge. They received $8 a ton for the bones and made considerable money.

The freighters had one government wagon with a bed, five or six feet deep; trailing behind was a common farm wagon with a stub tongue. They had a system of piling bones so that every available bit of space was occupied. The two wagons must have carried several tons in one trip. The loaders arranged the pelvic bones, half inside and half out, along the edges to enable the haulers to carry tremendous loads. Because of the immense quantity of bones, the railroad company built a separate track for them to drive alongside and unload. The railroad officials prepared special cars for the bones which could be loaded from the top and the side.

Later that summer I met a Mexican sheep herder with a large flock of sheep. He was afoot and carrying an old cap-and-ball dragoon pistol, used to scare away coyotes and wolves. He could talk good English but was slow about speaking for fear somebody might take advantage of him. When he found I was not trying to take advantage, he became very sociable.

He told me how he maneuvered. The owner of the sheep told him when and where to meet him. The herder carried a little memorandum book in which he made a mark for each day. He never stayed in the same camp more than one night but kept moving to make the meeting places. He made water holes, springs or streams of water, and carried a water canteen to drink. His boss told him to come to the stockyards in Dodge City on this particular August day, so he could look over the sheep to pick out some fat ones to ship to market.

I asked if he would like to buy a horse. He replied yes. He had often been in places where it was dangerous to be afoot. I sold him an old, gentle horse. I didn't think he would want a saddle but I sold him one anyway. He was greatly pleased with his new outfit.

I met a government scout in Dodge City, who was staggering from one saloon to another, drunk and boasting about what a famous scout he was. A day or so later I met a couple of cowhands, Bill Neeley and Boone, who were working for Oliver Ewell, who owned a ranch with C. M. "Crate" Justis on the Eagle Chief Creek in the Cherokee Strip southwest of Kiowa, Kansas.[6] They had purchased 1000 head of cows at Smoky River, Kansas, and were ready to take the herd south, where they had another 1000 head of Texas steers. They needed another man and I told them I would go.

We left with the herd about 12 September and headed across Comanche County on the Texas Trail. Ewell took charge of the grub wagon until Selmo, his Mexican cook, overtook us the following day. I was put on point to keep the cattle moving and because I could count them. No one else would attempt it; Ewell said he was a poor counter, himself. Every counter of 500 or more had a string with leather buttons. For every 100 he slipped a button to the other side of the saddle horn. When Ewell tried me out, I counted only 998. That pleased him wonderfully; he told me to keep that string on my saddle horn. Every two or three days he would tell me to take count. It could not be done going down or uphill to any certainty but on level ground where the herd was walking at a regular gait.

The first day out, the same scout I had seen in the saloon saw our herd. I rode back and told Oliver Ewell where I had seen him. Ewell replied, "I think that is about the caliber of all of these scouts. They are out looking among cow herds to see if they can find any Indians." For several mornings after that we could hear the cannon boom the sunrise salute at Fort Dodge.

The second morning out when I was turning the cattle back toward the trail, I found a freshly-killed, four-year-old buffalo bull lying in the sand hills. The shot pierced the body close to and behind the shoulder blade, the mark of a professional hunter. The flesh of one whole hind

55

Oliver P. T. Ewell (1849–1931) was born in Virginia and went west with his brother. The partnership he formed with J. M. "Crate" Justis in 1874 lasted until 1909. Courtesy of Western History Collections, University of Oklahoma Library.

M. Socrates "Crate" Justis (1857–1938), partner with Oliver Ewell, retired from their Cherokee Outlet ranch on the Eagle Chief Creek to Kiowa, Kansas, where this picture was taken in 1937. From the author's collection.

quarter was missing. I told Mr. Ewell about it and suggested we might get some fresh meat since we had rather meager fare. But he was afraid and would not touch it.

When Boone called me to go on guard the third morning, he said our saddle horses were all gone. I made a swing completely around the

57

herd but found no trace of them. At the first streak of day, I awoke Ewell and told him Boone had let the horses get away. He awoke the cook and told him to get me something to eat before I went after them. I asked for instructions. When he inquired if the wind had been out of the north all night, I told him it had as far as I knew. Ewell thought riding north was most logical. The horses doubtless were thirsty and would travel in the direction from which we had come. I found them about five miles out from camp, grazing and walking north.

When I returned, the herd and cowhands had gone on down the trail, for Ewell wanted to reach a watering place sufficient for a herd of 1000 by noon. Ewell, alone, remained and was the worst worried man I ever saw. I had ridden away in such haste that I had forgotten my gun. Soon we overtook the herd and I returned to the point.

Our grub wagon was about to run out; the cattle were trail weary and slow. That day I saw an antelope herd on the west side of the trail; a large antelope buck to the east was trying to get to the band. He tried to go behind but the wagon scared him. He came back and stopped on a hill to look. I jerked out my six-shooter and dismounted, for a heavy wind was blowing, rested my arm across the saddle seat, and fired at the antelope.

I thought at first I had missed, by the way he ran. I stood and watched since I had seen no evidence of the bullet skipping beyond. He made a false step; I jumped on the horse and went after him. As I came up, he fell flat on the ground. I jumped off and ran up, but his horns looked so desperate, I thought I would not take any chances afoot. As he reared, I shot and creased the back of his neck and he died. I bled the antelope. Ewell came rushing up and told me to get back on the point; he would dress it. The chuck wagon driver drove up and the two loaded the antelope into the wagon. There was rejoicing in the cow outfit now that we had fresh meat.

The next morning Ewell told me we were out of flour. I rolled up a half hind quarter of the antelope in my slicker, tied it behind my saddle, and went to the tent of a cow camp which we could see about a mile away. I told the cook I had brought him some fresh meat; we were about out of flour.

He said, "There's a sack of flour; I've used very little of it; just take that." I started back.

When I arrived, Oliver Ewell said, "That was a pretty good shot you made to bring in meat and flour."

FIVE

The Dull Knife Raid

That summer the northern Cheyennes broke away from the Fort Reno reservation in an attempt to get to the Bad Lands of the Dakotas.[1] About 10 September I was told that government officials at Fort Reno had telegraphed Fort Dodge. The following day I was on herd just east of Dodge City when I saw a detachment of fifty infantrymen, marching double-quick, four abreast, up the Arkansas River, presumably to intercept the Cheyennes. The commanding officer was mounted on a fine horse, riding a few rods ahead. A few rods behind, an ambulance followed, pulled by four mules—two wheelers and two leaders. I was astonished that the government would send soldiers afoot to look for wild, mounted Indians.

If the Indians had been fed and had proper medical care, they probably would have been content. There was so much government red tape that they were not given the beef and medical attention as they should have. Lots of Indians died of malaria and this started trouble.

Under the direction of their two shrewd chiefs, Big Horn and Dull Knife, they smuggled rifles, ammunition, and all needed supplies they could transport on pack horses. They seemed to be so docile to the soldiers on guard that the officers became negligent of duty. Of nights the Indians would build big fires and dance around them until after midnight and seemed to be contented. When daylight came, the camp showed no Indians until near noon. Many came to trade; it seemed they had no intention of leaving.

In the meantime the Indians sent out runners to pick out a route they could travel after night. After the Indians had allayed all suspicion, one night they built up their fires as usual and had them tended by men and women who were too old or sick to go on the warpath. Under cover of darkness the two chiefs took ninety warriors and some of the healthiest squaws and started up the North Canadian River. They traveled Indian style which left a plain trail. About daylight they

Cheyenne Chiefs Little Wolf and Dull Knife were the two leaders of the Northern Cheyennes' move back to their homelands in what was called the "Dull Knife Raid." After considerable hardship and loss of life, their people were finally settled on a reservation in southwestern Montana. Courtesy of National Anthropological Archives, Smithsonian Institution.

began to scatter, turned north, left the river, and met at a certain point which the runners had previously picked out.

As the old Indians moved about their campfires and kept adding fuel to the fires, the soldiers saw nothing unusual. This strategy gave the fleeing warriors virtually twenty-four hours of flight before the soldiers missed them.

It was afternoon before the soldiers suspected anything. They took the trail until they came to the point where the Indians had scattered. They finally found the trail again and followed until they overtook the Indians' rear guard. These Indians came back to hold a parley.

The commanding officer had told the soldiers not to kill any Indians but to bring them in alive. The soldiers sent word back that they had overtaken the Indian rear guard and they were unarmed. They sent these Indians forward to Dull Knife to tell him and his band to come back or the soldiers would take them by force. They thought all the Indians were unarmed, but they had repeating Winchester rifles and the latest-modeled, single-shot, breech-loading buffalo guns which were effective in firing at objects a mile away.

The Indians sent runners ahead to pick out a favorable battle-ground. It lay in broken hollows and gullies which led into the Cimarron River. The soldiers brought reinforcements and two wagons of supplies, each drawn by a four-mule team. Dull Knife sent back a runner to tell the soldiers not to follow any farther; they would not come back but would fight. The soldiers had orders to go take the Indians.

The Indians were not in sight. They lay hidden behind banks and opened fire on the unsuspecting soldiers who barricaded themselves behind their two wagons. They stood off the Indians and escaped complete massacre with few killed and wounded. They sent word back to Fort Reno that the Indians were well-armed and would fight and die rather than be brought back.

After the fight the Indians' main column moved northwest but sent out scouts on either side to gather in all horses and supplies and kill all white men.

Meanwhile on the trail, we approached a stream to water the herd and let them graze the next day near noon. We saw a man riding rapidly toward us. Mr. Ewell rode out to meet him; the two talked a moment. Then Ewell rode rapidly to Bill Neeley and me. He told us that Indians had killed Evans, the man's cook. They stole all their horses, save the one he was riding and one other with a rider who had not returned to camp.

The rider, Dave McAnally, was from Scheete's cow outfit, the 7U, a member of the Comanche County Pool.[2] Since he had only three cartridges left, he asked us how we were supplied with forty-five ammunition. We had none to spare. Ewell told Neeley and me to return with McAnally to see what we could do. Ewell, Boone, Justis, and Selmo stayed with the herd.

As we rode up to the camp, McAnally stopped his horse suddenly and said, "Get your guns and watch them banks."

We sat a moment. I asked, "What's the matter with you?"

McAnally replied, "Right there is where I set part of a sack of flour. There was a gun stick laying there and they're both gone now!"

We could see Evans' body lying on the white sand of the creek bed. Neeley and I rode to the bank. Dave walked and led his horse. I noticed a shoe laying on the ground near the bank. Dave said it was the foot of a boot which the cook had cut down to make into shoes. Dave also told us that the twenty-five-year-old Evans was a native Kentuckian.

It was easy to reconstruct the events which led to the cook's death. He had a fly tent to make shade by tying four corners of a wagon sheet to four posts set well in the ground. The sudden appearance of the Indians caused him to attempt to escape by taking cover in near-by Soldier's Creek. As he neared the bank, he was shot through the body under the left shoulder blade. He must have been alive when he struck the sand, for his hands had been thrust out to break the fall. He turned his face so it would not strike the sand. The evidence indicated that an Indian jumped down and shot him through the jugular vein at the angle of the jawbone. The close-ranged shot singed his beard on the side of the face.

As we looked under the fly tent, we observed that the Indians had carried away everything, excepting a New Testament which the cook had been reading. McAnally picked it up and put it in his pocket. While we were viewing Evans' remains, John Doyle and a man named McCarty rode up. Both had cattle in the Comanche County Pool and were well-armed. McCarty was an old plainsman, hard of hearing, and had long whiskers of the wild and wooly type. I met him often later while working for the Pool and found out that he had killed the buffalo. They accompanied us back to Ewell's herd.

Over dinner we talked about how to dispose of the body. We had no spade or shovel to dig a regulation grave. Finally McCarty said, "I suggest we leave him lay where he is. We can dig a trench in the sandy creek bed with our bare hands, deep enough to lay him in." He added, "I have an extra saddle blanket and we can roll him in that, let him down in the trench, and heap sand over him." McCarty's suggestion was carried out from beginning to end.

McAnally had borrowed the flour at Nelson's camp and had set it down on the ground by a gun stick when he discovered what had happened to his cook. An Indian returned to get the hickory gun stick, because it would be useful in cleaning his gun and he got some flour for good measure. Only a few minutes had elapsed from the time he left his camp until our arrival. It was only a half mile from our herd which had just taken to the stream, and we could see McAnally's camp as we sat on our horses.

Gus Birdsall, Scheete's foreman, had taken the wagon and team to Kinsley after supplies. He missed the Indians for some unaccountable reason.

It is especially so, when considering the fate of Tom Murray who insisted it was not necessary to carry a gun. He had taken a discharged cowpuncher to Kinsley and on his return, he was leading the other fellow's saddled horse. He met a bunch of Indians who killed his horse. He mounted the other horse, but it was also shot and killed. When Murray did not get back to his destination on time, members of his cow outfit went in search of him. Knowing that Indians were in the country and had killed several people and Murray never went armed, they naturally feared for his safety.

They found the first horse. By following the direction it was going when it was killed, they discovered the second dead horse, then found Murray's body in a washout.

Murray was engaged to Miss Swank, who published a poem in his memory. Later she married Bill Lindsay, who took charge of the ranch after Murray was killed.[3]

About an hour after Evans' body was found, Wylie Payne's brother met up with these Indians while in a line camp on his brother's extensive ranch.[4] He had a new six-shooter but it cost too much to shoot. He bought a cap-and-ball six-shooter just for practice. He threw his white-handled six-shooter into his bunk and stuck the cap-and-ball six-shooter in his new scabbard on the new belt, full of cartridges.

While out riding his line, he saw about six Indians coming from his dugout. As they neared him, he saw that they had carried off everything of value that he possessed. Being the tenderest kind of a tenderfoot, he did not know what to do. A more experienced man would have fired his pistol as he ran, and the few Indians would not have cared to follow him.

He just ran down, one of the six rode alongside young Payne, touched his six-shooter and said, "Swap, John?"

Payne said, "No."

The Indian pulled up the cap-and-ball pistol a little farther, repeated the question, and again, Payne refused. The Indian jerked Payne's six-shooter from the holster and fired at his neck. The bullet creased the back of his neck; he fell to the ground, seemingly dead. The Indian sat on his horse, emptied, and threw the gun at him, then rode off with Payne's horse. A ball penetrated the arm that lay across Payne's face.

They had been gone only a minute or two when Payne regained consciousness. When he raised up and peered out of the grass, he saw one of the Indians rein up and turn around. He heard him coming and knew he had something that the Indian wanted. Payne thought of his new belt, full of cartridges, for the six-shooter which the Indians had taken from the dugout. He shifted his position so that the belt buckle would come up and the Indian could remove it easily.

The Indian dismounted, unbuckled Payne's belt, pulled it off, remounted his horse, and rode after the others. Payne raised up, watched the Indian ride over a small knoll out of sight, then got up and started toward the pool headquarters.

Ben Lampton,[5] an old buffalo hunter, was there alone. He had first eaten his dinner and did not know anyone was in miles of him. Payne ran through the doorway, caught his foot on the sill, fell into the room at Ben's feet, and yelled, "Indians."

Ben grabbed his old buffalo gun and jumped out. He couldn't see an Indian anywhere. He asked Payne what had happened.

In Comanche County, Kansas, a man, his wife, and her sister heard about the raid. They lived in a dugout on their claim. The man had hired out to do general ranch work; the women were employed as cooks.

One forenoon they saw a column of Indians headed straight for them. The man was so badly scared that he ran into his dugout, picked up a shotgun and fired into the air once. The Indians were perhaps a half mile away. When they saw the smoke and heard the report of the gun, the whole column turned to avoid the range of what they supposed was a buffalo gun, and perhaps a buffalo hunter's camp.

Going on down the trail, we overtook a mixed herd of 700 cows and steers owned by John Gobie, a New Yorker, who had been engaged in women's lingerie. He came to western Kansas for rest and recreation. Pleased with his physical recuperation, he bought a herd at Dodge and was headed for southwestern Barber County when his outfit heard about Dull Knife's raid. Three cowhands quit, the herd stopped near the trail, but the fellows wouldn't leave for fear of meeting the Indians.

Gobie was as pleased to see us as we, him. We threw our combined herds together, making 1700 head of cattle, two wagons, thirty saddle horses, and twelve men. The increased number of men with their guns would be effective at close range. Gobie had a fine heavy-duty shotgun. His foreman, John Sullivan,[6] carried a Smith and Wesson forty-five six-shooter, and Charlie Gobie, his brother, a Colt's forty-five; the rest of us had six-shooters.

Sullivan, an old seasoned cowpuncher, had a head as slick as a billiard ball. His nose was long and hooked and he always had a great quid of tobacco in his mouth. When he told stories, he was a sight to behold. As he came to the climax, he was trying to chew, spit, and finish the story at the same time.

John Gobie appointed himself chief cook and was a good one. We liked his bread, but he looked funny, dressed in his fine clothes—a derby hat, an expensive necktie, and shoes instead of boots. We respected him though, because he threw in with us.

That night Ewell put two men on guard every two hours instead of the regular lone man. One was to sit on his horse at camp while the other rode around the herd to the wagon. Then they changed places. Ewell's men, Neeley and his cousin, Boone, took the first shift. They argued who was to ride first while Ewell removed his trunk and other effects from the wagon to make a breastwork. When he finished, they were still arguing.

"Boys, you had better be going out," Ewell said. They did not move.

"Mr. Ewell," Sullivan said, "that is unusual to crawl under a wagon to fight Indians. If they do shoot, the splinters will do you more damage than the bullets."

Just then, like a flash, the great herd of cattle stampeded and came straight at us. The two wagons beside a rocky gulch scattered the herd and saved us.

At the first hoof beat, Neeley and Boone leapt from their horses, yelling. Neeley boomed like a foghorn, "They're after us, boys. They're after us!" They dived headfirst under the wagon, beating the rest by at least a neck.

"A hell of a place to fight Indians, under a wagon!" said Sullivan as he and I jumped down the four-foot rock ledge. We stood there a minute or two. All was quiet. We decided to round up the cattle and see what started the stampede. When we found two old horses near the spot where it originated, we agreed some Indians found the horses unfit and resorted to the old custom of flopping their blankets to stampede cattle. We soon got the trail-weary cattle settled down for the night.

Shortly after this, John Sullivan killed a rabbit and Selmo cooked it. I was late getting to supper after dark. Selmo had saved the rabbit saddle for me. He seemed to like me, despite the joking I had given him when his horse fell and skinned his face so much. He had been after an antelope when his horse stepped in a hole and dropped, as if dead. The jolt discharged his gun which creased his horse.

The same afternoon the rabbit was killed, we lost the house cat which had been with the grub wagon. At noon we had stopped at a place where sand rats were numerous. The cat got out of the wagon, as usual, and began to catch them. When we called to her, she would not come. Sullivan had a heavy, coarse voice, and when he called, "Kitty!" she became frightened and refused to heed anyone.

When night came, Boone missed the cat and wanted to know what had become of her. I told Boone in front of Sullivan that we had eaten the cat and Sullivan had lied about having killed a rabbit. Sullivan enjoyed being a part of the conspiracy. Boone believed it and tried to heave up his supper.

We had fun at Boone's expense the mornings thereafter because he was lazy and difficult to get out. If I woke up first, I made a noise like a cat fight. If Ewell woke up first, he came over, shook me, and told me to squall like a cat. Boone would come out of his bed, swearing.

One day we saw a red range of hills in the distance; the nearer we came, the redder they looked. When we got to them, we found ripe plums. It was the only time I had seen so many, especially that time of year. I had seen ripe plums from the latter part of June to September, but this was October. They grew on small bushes. We slipped our bushel dish pan under a plum bush and gave the bush a quick jerk; in a few moments it was piled full. We filled our saddle pockets and everything we could find, for fresh plums were quite a treat.

When the Indians entered Comanche County south of Dodge City, about twenty cowboys went with the soldiers to intercept them. The Indians had already passed Dodge; cowboys and soldiers followed about two days but never overtook them. When the cowboys returned, they found themselves without jobs. When "Happy Jack" Shepherd was asked to accompany them, he replied that he had not lost any Indians and refused to go.

I knew only one of the cowboys who lost a job following the Indians. Bell was born and reared along the Rio Grande and "come" up the Texas Trail during the summer of 1878. In the chase he found a discarded Indian mare, a buckskin. The usual Indian method was to cut the throats of the horses they discarded on their flight, so followers couldn't use them. The mare was a good animal, but her feet had become so tender that she was left behind. She wore a small Indian brand on a shoulder so he named her Madam Dull Knife.

Bell was an awfully careless fellow. He was riding a horse for the Comanche County Pool where he found work later. He was acting the fool with his six-shooter when he accidentally creased his horse with a shot from his gun. The horse was knocked to the ground. When the shock wore off, the horse got to its feet again.

Bell boasted he could stand the cold winters of western Kansas because he had seen frost several times in the Rio Grande Valley. Also he had been up in the mountains once or twice and had seen snow falling. He was humorless, the type of fellow who could not be joked. He told about many leopards of the Rio Grande mountain country, and a fellow who caught some of them was offered $300 dollars for a pair.

I said, "He must have been wanting leopards mighty bad to offer $300 for them." He took great offense and thought I was accusing him of lying.

After he finished work with the pool, branding and marking calves and through cattle that were driven up the Texas Trail that year, he decided to return to the Rio Grande Valley. Since his Indian mare had recovered, he decided to ride her. He and Bill Beauchamp fitted some horseshoes to the mare's feet so she could stand the trip. Madam Dull Knife had not been handled much, and the two fellows had to throw her before they could shoe her. It seemed like a long, dreary route for a man to go alone from Dodge City to the Rio Grande Valley in 1878; no one heard how he made out.

SIX

The Comanche County Pool

In November 1878 Ewell went to winter quarters; I went back to Comanche County by way of Kiowa and Medicine Lodge, Kansas, and went to work for the Comanche County Pool, southeast of Dodge City, as a cattle brander. The pool was a group of ranchers with large and small holdings. To cut down costs they formed an association and selected a president and a board of directors to handle complaints. Jesse Evans was general manager. He and his outfit brought 20,000 cattle from New Mexico to Dodge City that year. His foreman, Charley Nelson,[1] could not give me over a month's work, for they would soon have all of their cattle branded and line camps established. Besides the line riders, they needed one other man to stay at headquarters camp to attend to the work teams and similar jobs.

A cowpuncher furnished his own saddle, bridle, saddle blankets, and clothing; but he was furnished with horses and rope. I used rope usually about thirty feet long; others used fifty feet. I wore out several saddles and still have the remains of my L. C. Gallup saddle made in Pueblo, Colorado, which I purchased in 1880 from the Yorke, Parker, and Draper dry goods company in Caldwell.[2]

In winter I wore high-heeled, airtight boots with arctics over them. From feet up to knees my legs were covered with heavy cowhide leggings. I wore thin cotton socks called nickel socks; my feet never did sweat. I wore heavy, full-length, fleece-lined underwear; my pants were all wool. Overalls were worn over the pants in cold weather. I wore a knit, woolen blouse next to my woolen shirt. I wound a red 4' × 6" woolen, knit comforter around the blouse and stuffed the ends down under my belt. Most fellows preferred this type of garment around their necks in cold weather. The overcoat was heavy but not exceedingly long. Dressed in this fashion, I did not care if I got caught out in the open at night; I had a good comfortable bed in which to sleep anywhere.

Cowboy belts were usually about 2½ inches wide with a buckle at one end and several holes at the other to adjust to the size of the fellow. It was made of good soft leather, well-sewn. The prevailing color was drab yellow; some were black. Down the center was a full-length extra piece which had a loop on top in which cartridges were tightly fitted.

My first hats on the range were rather low-crowned but a little wider-brimmed than I later wore. I purchased a dark gray Stetson hat at Medicine Lodge for $9. I wore it several years. Later my Spade ranch foreman, Sam Fling, found that my hat exactly fitted his head. When his father died in Iowa, he borrowed this hat when he went up to settle his father's estate. He was called back later to Iowa and he told me that he did not want to appear without that hat. So I traded for his and wore it until he returned.

One winter I had a pair of soft, neat, fine-fitting gloves with a pair of wool-lined mittens over them. When I wanted to adjust anything about the saddle, I merely removed the mittens. I could handle anything because of the pliability of the airtight gloves.

The headquarters camp was placed near the geographical center of the ranges, determined by available water supply, wood, grass, and level ground. Convenient spots were chosen for corrals, branding chutes, catch pens for the calves, horse stables, and a wagon shed.

The headquarters ranch house was constructed of cedar logs. There were two rooms. One was a regular house built of logs which were notched and saddled at the ends. It was built independently of the other room which was a stockade. The log part was erected first; the stockade on the east came later as an afterthought or as their need for more room increased. The logs stood on end in a trench, squared smooth to stand close together. There were separate outside doors for each part, both on the south. The west-room door was made of flooring boards but neither room had a floor. The first log, full-length, split out half way through, where the door was to be placed. A 2 × 6 scantling was nailed to the log ends at the sides of the door. The door was hung by hinges to the 2 × 6 jamb.

The furniture was selected according to need. If permanent, the cowmen usually installed bunks. First a pole was set in the ground with the upper end spiked to the girder or ridgepole in the roof. A pole was nailed to the upright in a horizontal plane with the other end nailed to another upright pole at the end of the room. Slats of small poles were laid across the horizontal pole, and at short spaces under the slats were

69

placed short chunks or stobs to support it. Small saplings were split and laid over the slots to be supported by another horizontal pole at the end of the room in the corner. Usually one could find some kind of lumber to put on the slats on which to lay the bedding. If no lumber, a flint cowhide would serve as a good foundation for a bed. Grass, hay, or burlap sacks might be laid on top. The burlap sacks were filled with dry grass or hay for the tick. We called them "stuffed with prairie feathers."

Each fellow furnished his own bedding. He usually bought two good blankets at a store; mine came from Medicine Lodge or Caldwell. When two men bunked together, they could have four good blankets. Good dugouts were usually warmer than log houses.

The contents of the kitchen consisted of tin utensils for knives, forks, spoons, plates, and cups. The bucket was made of cedar, bound together with brass hoops. The bucket bail was attached with a wooden grip. The cook was furnished long-handle spoons and forks for handling boiled meat or vegetables. There was a "cook" stove but we prefered the "bake" ovens found in the line camps. They were also carried in wagons to roundups.

We had various kinds of meat. If there were not any good stray beeves with the herd, we might have deer or turkey. The company always furnished bacon, never ham; navy beans in bulk; canned corn and tomatoes; dried apples, peaches, prunes; coffee; sugar; salt; pepper; syrup; pickles; and pepper sauce. We were not furnished butter, but the company allowed us to milk cows if we treated them decently. There was usually a caddy of tobacco on hand for the boys. It was charged out to their account by the foreman. I was never burdened with this.

When we baked sourdough bread, flour and water with salt thrown in was set close to the fire where it could be warm all of the time. That's what made it sour. Sometimes it became too sour; the cook had to stir it and add more flour and water until it was ready to bake. Baking soda was added. The dough was put in a well-greased skillet which was set on a bed of coals in the fireplace. We preferred to cook in the fireplace in the winter rather than fool with the stove. The bake oven was a round iron kettle, six or eight inches deep, standing on three legs, covered with a heavy iron lid. The lid had a half-round cast-iron handle on the top side through which a poker or a stick could be inserted to lift the heated lid. We usually set the oven on a bed of coals, as well as the lid. When they were hot enough, we placed the dough in biscuit or loaf form in the hot oven, covered it, and piled more coals on top. When we smelled the baking bread, we took a poker and lifted the lid. If the bread seemed to be burning, we knocked off some of the coals.

Line camps, invariably dugouts, were not intended to be permanent. It would not reveal good business judgment to have expensive buildings, as the location might be changed any season for many reasons. The dugout was dug well back from the face of the bank so it could be enclosed without expense. When the dirt was removed to make at least a six-foot-deep room, it was thrown back from all sides and ends. A suitably sized ridgelog was placed through the center, lengthwise, to permit the log ends to rest firmly on the bank at each end of the dugout. There would be no side logs, but rafters for the roof were the same length, edged close together. The outer ends rested on the ground; the inner ends, on the ridgelog. There was a downward pitch from the ridgelog which caused rain or snow to drain off the roof. After the roof was covered with small side poles, thick mud was spread overall into cracks and crannies and allowed to dry. Over this was spread about six inches of dirt. More mud was spaded on the roof to stop leaks. Only prolonged rainfall could penetrate the roof.

Instead of cutting the doorway directly in the center of the dugout's front, the trench might start directly in front of the entrance. Usually it was turned in a circle to enter the dugout at its corner. This would give a solid rest for the front end of the ridgelog and stop the wind from taking in direct current. A door was not required.

A shed and a small pen or corral could be built out of native timber to protect the four horses for the line riders. They were combined with the dugout to form a windbreak during storms, and the roof of the shed was additional protection.

Two line riders usually occupied one camp. They rode in opposite directions and covered a large area. Supplies of canned fruit, tomatoes, and corn; dried apples and currants; bacon; flour; and grain for the horses, usually shelled corn, were brought from the headquarters ranch by a teamster and kept inside the dugout.

When the fencing of the great ranges began in 1882, fewer riders were needed. Line camps were discarded and all riders bunked at the headquarters ranch houses. Neighboring ranches arranged to cooperate in building common fences which were patrolled by the ranch which had built that portion of fence.

71

A crew of Comanche Pool cowboys in camp, 1884. Courtesy of The Kansas State Historical Society, Topeka, Kansas.

Cattle drifted against these fences during storms, but they were protected from lightning as the ground wire was placed on every third or fourth post. Whenever a line of cattle happened to crowd along a fence which lightning struck, not many were killed. I believe this occurred only when the barb on the wire happened to be pointed directly at a cow.

Nearly all cowboys, whether they could or not, attempted to sing. When cattle were uneasy, it was important for one who was on guard as he rode around the bed ground to whistle or sing. Whenever weather was bad, cattle were uneasy, nervous, and high-strung. If a guard rode along in the dark perfectly quietly and his horse should accidentally step into a hole, he would throw his other foot to the ground with such force to catch his weight that it would cause a loud popping noise. The cows would jump up and be off in a thundering stampede. When a horse stepped into a hole while the cowhand was whistling or singing, the cows paid no attention. When the cattle were well-filled with grass and water in pleasant weather, one could almost run over them without causing a stampede.

I met young Payne at the Comanche Pool. He related his experiences with the Indians and showed me his wounds which had nearly healed. I also met Ben Lampton who told me about the buffalo pool formed by some men at Wichita. They paid him board and thirty cents for each buffalo hide. It was the happiest moment in his life. He started walking southwest from Wichita with a forty-five Sharpe's square-barrel gun and 200 rounds of cartridges in his belt. His knapsack was filled with a small frying pan, ground coffee, bacon, flour, salt, and matches.

The company sent teams and wagons two days later to haul supplies and hides. The drivers listened for the gun report to find him, located their camp near fuel and water, and began skinning buffaloes. A skinner was supposed to skin at least ten buffaloes daily at fifty cents a head. The hides were stretched taut, flesh side up, with cedar pegs the size of a man's finger. When the hides were dried, they could be loaded easily. I have seen abandoned camp grounds with as many as a half bushel of these sharpened pegs.

It was the custom for buffalo shooters to go afoot into the buffalo county. They were men of cool courage. Many times their lives hung by a thread, because the Indians were after them when they saw the source of their meat and clothing disappearing. The shooters were

73

safer than the skinners and drivers of teams. A lone hunter would not let a man come directly to him. He could tell the difference between a cowpuncher's equipment and Indian apparel. The Indian rode differently and carried his gun on the opposite side to that of a white man. When he saw Indians approaching, he walked to the highest knoll, laid down his gun, loosened his pack, set it down, then waved his hand to indicate which way he wanted them to go. If they did not observe his signals, he opened fire. These long-ranged, accurately-sighted guns caused sore damage.

Steady firing caused the gun barrel to heat up. If the hunter was good with a six-shooter, he could use it while his gun cooled. The hunter stopped before night, built a fire, and cooked his supper. Instead of sleeping near the campfire, he picked up his gun and knapsack, followed a route which he had picked out during the day, and bedded down in the splendid buffalo grass. This was done to forestall surprise Indian attacks. When he lay down, he laid his gun with the butt end at his shoulder and the muzzle pointing down at his feet. If anything approached toward his feet, he could shoot without rising. If a hostile person came near his head, he could roll over into shooting position.

The buffaloes traveled in herds, usually from north to south or vice versa. If a shooter happened to be at a point where a great herd passed, he could kill many buffalo in a short time. It was safer to occupy a point on a bluff which would divide the herd. It was dangerous to be in front of a migrating herd. After several days traveling they would be well strung out and moving in a narrow column. The fastest travelers were in front. If a good shooter secured a good position, he could make a heavy kill as the column passed. It was best to shoot the left side of the animals and aim to penetrate the body close behind the left shoulder blade.

Buffalo hunters liked what they called a "stand" on the buffalo. They watched to see where a herd was apt to water. They usually grazed to water after they had almost finished grazing. Then they would go to a high divide where the wind blew to free the insects, lie down, and rest. Hunters would hide near such places to shoot as they came out. They would wait until many had laid down before they began to shoot.

After the slaughter of the buffaloes was past, Lampton built a dugout in the hilly country where he cut and sold cedar timber. When that business played out, he stayed until Jesse Evans came looking for a suitable dugout for a line camp.

When I went to work for the Comanche County Pool, Nelson told me to turn my horse loose with a gray mare and a colt. The mare wore a bell on her neck so Nelson could easily find her in the sand hills. My four-year-old horse was scarcely half broke. When I was dismissed in December, Nelson said he would catch my horse. It had become wild that month, running loose. The morning I was to leave, Charley told me to get on his horse, go hunt the three horses, and drive them into the corral.

The corrals were round, so any kind of stock could stampede and not put too much pressure on a given point. When I drove them to the corral, my horse seemed more mustang than domesticated. Nelson caught the mare and led her out with the colt. Since the corral fence was round, Nelson could not corner my wild horse.

I stood in the gate and kept the horse from escaping while Nelson, who was as fine a roper as I ever "seen," was trying to rope him. A good, sound snubbing post was standing close to the gate. Nelson didn't have his gloves on and decided there was only one way to get a good shot at the horse with his rope. He told me to step back from the gate into the corral and let the horse think the coast was clear. Nelson took his stand near the snubbing post; the horse "seen" his chance and made a dash for the open gate. Like a flash the rope noose went around his neck. With equal swiftness, Nelson threw three turns of rope around the post and set back on it; the blue smoke rolled off as the rope burnt it. It also burnt Nelson's hand terribly. He took my rope, made a hacimo on the horse's head, and turned him over to me to see if I could hold him. I did. Nelson wanted to know if I could ride the horse. I nodded, so he turned the horse over, for he was late getting off to do his work.

I told Bill Dunlap about Nelson in later years and Dunlap said, "Do you know what he would have done if you had said you couldn't have ridden the horse?"

I answered, "No."

"He would have jumped on the horse and rode him, himself, just for fun. I have seen him do it many times," replied Dunlap.

He told of a young fellow who worked for Nelson and was given a string of horses. One was terribly bad to pitch. One day the young fellow got hold of this lead horse and wasn't getting onto it as he

75

should. Nelson was lying around in camp not feeling well. When he "seen" the young fellow wasn't moving off as he should, Nelson came out and asked him if he was afraid the horse would throw him. When he answered yes, Nelson walked up to the horse and lit into the saddle before it had time to see what he was going to do. The horse "throwed" his head down and went at it. Dunlap said it surely was a sight to see Nelson riding that bucking bronco. When the horse discovered he had no show in that game, he just quit. Nelson rode him back, dismounted, and told the young fellow to mount the bronco, for he believed the horse had had enough.

Dunlap said Nelson was a kind-hearted fellow. He "seen" Nelson at a roundup, so busy he hadn't noticed much what was going on. As he came riding around the herd, he "seen" a boy setting on a big work horse, crying.

Nelson stopped and asked, "What's the matter?"

The boy told Nelson his folks lived not far away. He had come down to this roundup to look for their only cow which had strayed. He "seen" the cow in the herd and went to get her. The fellow who owned the outfit told the boy to let that cow alone; he wouldn't allow anybody to cut that cow out of the herd.

Nelson asked, "Where is your cow? Show her to me."

The boy began to inquire what he was going to do. Nelson told the boy, "I'll get her for you."

The boy began to beg Nelson not to get the cow. He might get into trouble with the owner of the herd who had made such big threats.

Nelson said, "Show me the cow. I'll tend to the trouble." He told the boy to get back a little way; he would drive the cow out by him. The owner seen Nelson cutting the cow out and came dashing up, swearing at him to let that cow alone; he would attend to her. Nelson swung his old gun up and told the fellow not to turn that cow back. If he did, it would be the last one he ever turned back. He might run over little boys, but he couldn't run over him. The boy tried to thank Nelson. Nelson told him not to do so but drive the cow on home; if the fellow bothered him anymore, he should tell Nelson.

As I left the Comanche County Pool, I started for Kiowa. When I arrived at Big Mule Creek, a settler was just building a good-sized log house; about six men were helping with the house raising. At least four women were cooking dinner. When I decided to ride up, one man jumped down from the building. They all ran inside and looked out

76

through the cracks. I thought if I looked that tough, I'd better go around them. I shifted my course to not ride nearby. When I got about opposite the house, one fellow came out, carrying a Winchester and a big hogleg hanging to his hip. He motioned to me and I discovered it was "Ez" Iliff, a deputy officer.[3]

A year or so before, two brothers named Withers[4] were with a bunch of cattle rustlers. One brother went to New Mexico; the other appeared in Barber County. Iliff secured U.S. Deputy Marshal Mike Meagher's help.[5] The two went to A. W. Rumsey's store.[6] Meagher hid in the cellar while Iliff remained in the store above. Finally Withers came into the store and walked close to a trap door which could be opened into the cellar. Iliff suddenly threw his arms around Withers and pinned his arms to his sides so Withers could not reach his guns— he was a two-gun man.

Iliff yelled, "Mike!" and the door flew open from the floor. Mike came out and put handcuffs on Withers.

This made Iliff and Withers deadly enemies. Withers swore he would kill "Ez" Iliff if it was the last thing he ever did. Withers got away some time later and went to New Mexico. He sent word back to Barber County that he still was hoping to see the day when he could kill "Ez" Iliff. That explained why Iliff came out to get a good look at me.

One or two years later A. W. Rumsey received a letter from one of his own friends in New Mexico which said, "Tell 'Ez' Iliff that he can lay his six-shooter aside. Withers was killed just a short time before."

I stopped at Kiowa to get my mail and look for work. I got a letter from the folks at home. I found no work in Kiowa but met some old acquaintances, Tom Greer and Jim Preston, who had just arrived from the Choctaw Indian Country with 1000 head of steers. A severe snow-storm struck. First came rain, then sleet, and finally, snow. Greer had been a partner in a general store in Peru, Kansas; Preston, a former Texan, had also resided in Peru in the early seventies. I stopped with them in their tent.

The storm came near morning, and they had trouble trying to keep their cattle from drifting with it. The cattle scattered among the breaks south of Kiowa. Preston was absent from camp and was across the Cimarron to the southwest, looking for a range for their herd. After the storm passed, they moved their herd to Yellowstone and established camp there. I rode toward Chautauqua County.

I learned in Kiowa that Ewell and Justis had moved over the Salt

Fork divide and built a large dugout and bank stable on the Eagle Chief bank. I called on them and stayed all night.

After breakfast Ewell told me about his old Black Mammy and to hear him talking without seeing him, you would think he was a Darky. He opened his old family album. The first picture in it was his Old Black Mammy. I laughed for I thought he was showing me a joke book. He was as astonished at me as I was at the picture. He told me how delighted she was to see him when he visited his old home. She shouted, slapped his back, hugged him, and cried.

I planned to stop next at Bidwell's camp[7] on the southern line of Kansas, but they had moved into winter quarters. It was getting dark; I saw a light, rode to it, and found a settler, his wife, son, and daughter who had taken a claim a year or so before. He gave me a hearty welcome and told me that cowboys had always treated him well and helped him. He told me to dismount, come in out of the snow, and stay all night. They had two dugouts. One had two rooms occupied by the family. The boy took me to the other dugout, a bank stable, to put up my horse. There was lots of corn and plenty of hay.

I ate supper and slept comfortably in the annex with the son, among the chickens. This is how the family protected them from the numerous coyotes.

When the mother announced breakfast the next morning, I heard her call the daughter. A volley of vicious invectives followed. The mother talked so rapidly I only heard something about a cowboy.

"Why in hell didn't you wake me up and tell me last night?" the daughter interrupted.

The mother returned and announced, "Pet has lost so much sleep lately that she is very irritable."

Before we finished, Pet came in, all smiles. While she was eating, the deputy sheriff from Anthony, Kansas, came with a summons for her to appear as a witness in a serious criminal case. She swore she knew nothing about it.

"Now, Pet, go with him," her father said. "You will be paid for your time and get your board while they hold you."

"I will not go a step until I find out what this cowboy is going to do!" Pet replied.

"This cowboy will be going on," I replied.

Pet put on her galoshes, a fine fur coat, took me by the hand and said, "I like the looks of you. If you will stay, I will stay!"

"I must go," I answered and prepared to resume my journey.

She stepped out, saw the two-wheeled cart with room for only one person, pulled by one horse, then told the deputy, "I'll make you sit in my lap to keep the cold north wind off! If we get stuck in a snow drift, I'll kick you off and make you push the cart with me in it!" As I rode off, they were still wrangling.

The next night I stayed at a cow camp on Grouse Creek. I arrived at Elgin, Kansas, the next night within ten miles of my home. The farther east I rode, the less snow there was. I visited my folks in Peru until April 1879.

Because the hilly ranges of Chautauqua County were overcrowded and cropped short, we had begun to consider plans where our own herd of about 150 yearling steers and cows could be moved to the excellent ranges in western Kansas. When Frank went to Comanche County in the fall of 1878, he had planned to go in with Jim Henderson whose small ranch was on the Medicine River.

The following January Frank rode to Medicine Lodge and visited some old Chautauqua County people—Fred Bunker, Henry Goddard, and Jim Springer had taken claims west of Medicine Lodge and established quite a cattle ranch there.[8]

Bunker spent most of his life as a sailor. On the old sailing vessels he learned to climb and rig sails. One old rough sea captain called out, "Say port, you haymaking son of a bitch!" after Bunker had mistakenly said starboard. He ultimately made several trips around the world. Once he deserted ship in a Chinese port and hid in a stack of pumpkins for three days, eating nothing but raw pumpkin, until the vessel sailed away. He made connection with another vessel.

Goddard was an old plainsman who had gone to California during the gold rush. He made a little stake then wanted to return east. He finally found another young man, and they set out with a saddle horse and pack horse apiece. Emigrants annoyed them by asking about wood, water, grass, and danger from wild Indians, causing them to lose several hours' traveling time. They finally thought of a way to save time. When they met a wagon train, the two would yell as they rode past, "Plenty of wood, grass, water, and Indians ahead."

Springer was a Civil War veteran and well-schooled in camp life. He received a bullet wound through his left hand which cut the tendon that controlled the middle finger, making it useless. It closed rigidly toward the palm. It was difficult for the average stake rope to pass

79

under this finger. One morning he roped his saddle horse which ran, dragging several feet of rope through the crook of his finger. The knot on the end broke the finger and the rope badly burned it, giving such a painful injury that he went to Medicine Lodge for medical treatment.

Brother Frank fell in with a fellow who was going to Comanche County. The fellow lost his direction and they had to sleep out that night. While they were wandering around, they found a long trench with rifle pits, each about 4 × 6 feet apart. Near each pit were five or six empty cartridges. In the trenches lay skeletons of two soldiers. The uniforms were torn nearly to pieces and the buttons were marked United States Government. Since this trench lay near the point where some regular soldiers had intercepted Dull Knife's warrior band, we assumed that these men were killed in the skirmish.

Frank went to Henderson's log house, found it vacant, and stayed there until he could find another cowman to take over our cattle. Henderson had sold his cattle and was planning to accompany Troy Stockstill to the Choctaw country to buy another herd.

I had met Henderson and Stockstill near Medicine Lodge. Henderson was quiet and unassuming. Stockstill had extensive property holdings in Medicine Lodge and resided in a two-story brick house. He wanted to set out a fruit orchard but knew nothing about it. I advised him to order trees from Stark Brothers in Missouri. In the summer of 1895 when I was at the Lacy, Oklahoma grocery, I met Scott Davis, a former Barber County and Cherokee Strip cowpuncher who took a claim in 1889 near Lacy. He had a load of peaches to sell from Stockstill's widow and commented that it was the best orchard in the Southwest. I bought some, planted the stones on my homestead, and had splendid luck.

In July 1879 Henderson and Stockstill left Medicine Lodge with a regular cow outfit to purchase a herd. A cowhand, named Candee; a cook; and a ten-year-old boy accompanied them. They bought 800 head of cattle and were returning when the notorious Barker outlaw band intercepted them.[9] They saw all but Candee who had eaten his dinner first and had returned to the herd to relieve the two owners. The outlaws killed the owners as they rode to camp. Candee heard the shooting, returned, saw the outlaws, and rode away, waving his hat, serving notice that he was going for help. They decided to kill the cook and take the boy, but the boy pleaded so pitifully for the cook's life that they rode off and left them both. They took horses, cattle, saddles, and other equipment. I heard the details of this unfortunate affair from Candee ten years later in Sedan, Kansas.[10]

On his trip brother Frank met "Barbecue" Campbell[11] who consented to let him occupy part of his range. In April brothers Frank, Turner, and I drove our cattle from Chautauqua County. On the way we found that one of our horses wouldn't pull uphill but ran away, regardless of the load, if we fired a gun near him. Often we had to start this horse in that manner. The mare, when teamed with this horse, was true to pull, quick to learn at the crack of a gun, and was soon ready for it.

There were great flocks of prairie chickens and it was mating time when we went out to Barber County. These birds always gathered on the highest ground on the prairie and the males made a "booing" noise to attract attention. They paid little attention to a wagon and team or a man on horseback. This enabled a person to ride or drive close and shoot some birds for they were as good to eat as domesticated chickens.

One day we had quite a bit of fun when brother Frank was driving the wagon after we had gotten the team well trained. We came into sight of a flock of prairie chickens. Frank drove along close to them, fastened up the lines on the front end of the wagon, took aim at one of the birds, and fired. The team broke into a keen run, took Frank unawares, and threw him on his back in the wagon. The team had run so far when he finally got hold of the lines, that he never went back to see whether he had killed any of the prairie chickens. I hollered and asked what he was running from; the birds were not after him.

When we arrived in Barber County, brother Turner got a short job with a cow outfit close to the Kansas state line. When he finished, he rode down the Texas Trail as the drive was heavy that spring. When he got just past the 5 ranch, he met a herd waiting because there were not enough men to handle it properly on the trail. Two men had gotten into a shooting scrape the day before. One killed the other. The fellow was buried on a large sand hill in the edge of the blackjacks.

Later that summer I was following a trail which led me out to a large sand hill and I rode up to look around. There I found a fresh grave. When I returned to camp, I inquired if they knew anything about it. None had. Several years elapsed before I met brother Turner again. He told me about his getting the job because of the killing, and that he had gone with the herd up the Texas Trail to Ogallala, Nebraska.

81

Moses Turner Records (1855–87) entered Baker University at Baldwin, Kansas, in 1877. His wages from cowpunching helped pay for his A.B. degree, which he received in 1886. He was supply preacher at Sedan and the Chanute Circuit of the Methodist church. At his untimely death, he was working for the Reverend John Dennison, the presiding elder of the Kansas Conference. Courtesy of Western History Collections, University of Oklahoma Library.

There he sold his cow pony and went down to Baldwin, Kansas, to enter Baker University, where he had previously attended school, to study for the Methodist ministry.

When we got to Barber County, I attended the '79 roundup which was conducted with pack horses instead of a wagon. There was no cook in such an outfit. The pack horses merely carried the bedding. The men were expected to eat at the nearest ranch house or wherever a roundup was being held. This method was discontinued because cattlemen found it was too cumbersome; ranches could not feed all the men and they never knew when we would arrive.

SEVEN

Roundup Time in the Spring

Cattlemen of the Strip did not have any general roundups until spring 1879. They were well-pleased with roundups and looked forward to them. Cowpunchers did not anticipate much pleasure. We did not have time to renew old acquaintances or to cultivate new friendships. Work was hard and exacting, a steady grind with no relief, and the dangers increased four-fold. Cowpunchers lost much sleep and rest because of night watches, cyclonic storms, swollen streams, hailstorms with dangerous lightning, and coping with "burnt cattle."[1] We were often cut off from our outfits, and even when we were with our grub wagons, there were no fires with nothing but raw grub to eat. To keep the saddle horses of one outfit from mixing with those of another, one or two cowpunchers had to ride in front of the horses to hold them back from others at the rear of another outfit.

A general roundup was to collect all of the stray cattle which had drifted from their respective ranges to other herds on other ranges. A few times on these roundups, if we found a calf that was too young or too weak to travel and its mother belonged to a ranch that was some distance away, it was placed on a horse, carried to the grub wagon, and hauled for a day or so until it could travel. We had to watch the cow, for she would turn back to the place where the calf was born.

An unfortunate incident happened on a general roundup to cowpuncher, Tom Snow,[2] who was cutting out cattle. He rode a good saddle horse which was trained to do all kinds of work in the cattle business, but the horse's wild nature was not much under control. It moved at a rapid gait and stepped into a hole. Tom turned loose to be thrown out of the way, but one of his feet was forced through a stirrup. He lay on his back as the horse leaped up. As the horse began to back away, Tom jerked out his six-shooter, cocked it, pointed it at the horse's vital parts, and began to talk to keep him quiet, if possible. All who saw it rode rapidly to Tom and his horse, formed a ring around them, and the first fellow who got into reach of the horse's head, grabbed the bridle reins. He held the horse; two others dismounted and picked up Tom. A fourth fellow came and pulled off his boot so his foot could be pulled out of the stirrup. How it got there in the first place seemed very peculiar.

The only time I ever saw a horse drop dead was at another general roundup. It had been raining and the whole country was muddy. Consequently it was hard on horses to work in the mud. We were south of the Cimarron near the Glass Mountains where we had worked all day without changing horses. Abe Manee,[3] a good hard-working cowman, was riding a good dark bay cutting horse that was willing to work without urging. It was just sundown as we finished and started to leave the herd with the cut.

One cow wheeled to go back. Abe's horse "seen" it, made a dash, and headed it back into the cut. At that instant the horse dropped dead. We dismounted and helped Manee get his saddle and bridle. We set the saddle on end behind another one of the boys, took the ladigo strap, put it over one shoulder and under his arm, and tightened it enough to hold the saddle without bothering him. Manee got on behind Tom Wilson and we started on with the cut to our camp.

I discovered a locoed horse is dangerous to ride and particularly hazardous as a cutting horse. Such animals have eaten a poisonous loco weed. When horses and cattle are subject to eating this weed, they do not shed their winter coat of hair in the springtime as animals should. One can't lead a badly locoed animal; it will pull back until it drops dead. But my locoed horse did shed and would lead pretty well. He was very foolish at times when I was cutting cattle. Instead of following an animal, he would lose sight of it and follow another one. A good cutting horse will keep his eyes on the cow first started.

If a horse stepped in a hole and fell, the rider sometimes lost his life. I was slightly acquainted with young Charley Hill who was with a wagon and a bunch of saddle horses, headed for Caldwell to receive a cattle herd. They camped near the state line southwest of Caldwell. The following morning Hill's horse stepped in a hole and threw him to the ground. The horse's hoof struck Hill in the temple, killing him.

Occasionally when we were near the settlements, someone came and challenged the boys to a foot race. Such fellows wanted to win some money. The cowboys had rather do this than anything else, for these visitors usually were smart alecks and could get into some pretty bad scrapes.

85

Both sides put up all kinds of bets or pretended ones. We lay out a track as long as the fellow wanted. The cowboys took positions along both sides so the runners would have to run in a straight line. The cowpunchers stood, making posts of themselves, with ropes in their hands. The two runners started off great to win. If the newcomer looked like he was going to beat the cowpuncher, some of the fellows with ropes would heel him and he would take a hard fall, knocking the wind out.

Most of us bet on the newcomer and he usually bounced to his feet, wanting to whip everybody in sight. The madder he became, the more he wanted to fight. The rest of us paired off, pulled off our coats, and got ready to fight. At that point some jerked their six-shooters and threatened to have justice or kill somebody. The fellow begged for the men not to kill each other. Usually about that time all of us had to saddle up and start to work.

One fellow named Thompson from Barber County, fifty-two years old, got out and ran foot races with young and old alike. One spring we had a good runner, Fred Dudley, who could defeat any cowpuncher around. Thompson came to our wagon and wanted to know if anybody there could run. We told him we'd put up Fred Dudley against him. Fred said he hadn't run for so long that he preferred a trial run before the match. Thompson agreed. They ran the preliminary, but Dudley did not run as fast as he could and it was a tie.

When Dudley came back, he told me he didn't learn anything about how fast the fellow was since they had tied. "If I can talk him into running again, I'll test him with every pound I've got." He did but the race resulted in another tie. Then Dudley told me, "Don't bet anything on me against that old man. He can run right off and leave me any time he wants to."

Some cowboys couldn't resist the lure of easy money in racing horses. John Langford had a cream-colored, fine-looking horse which he used but lost more money than he won.

One day Fred Beebe and another boy came out to our general roundup, riding two of the smallest ponies I ever "seen." Fred's family lived in the east edge of Medicine Lodge; I knew them well. Bill Parker happened to be there, and he wanted to get a race between "them" two ponies. He bet a quarter that Fred Beebe's pony could outrun the other one.

Old Bill rode a big, long-legged horse. The two ponies did not stand higher than mid-sides to his horse. He carried a great cow whip, something a cowpuncher had no use for. It had a short handle and a long plaited lash with a good popper on the end. He always played some joke by swinging it. Somebody bet a quarter on the other pony. Bill went to do the starting, but no one knew what else he would do.

Just as they got ready to run, Bill hit Beebe's pony on the hip and it sounded like a pistol. He yelled and kept pouring it on the pony. Soon the other pony became frightened, quit the track, and Beebe won the race.

I said, "Bill, it was a shame the way you whipped that little pony. What did you do it for?"

"Oh, I had to; I couldn't afford to lose that quarter."

Dave Greever[4] had a large bay cow horse named Hoover. He was known all over the range for winning so many races. The only race I ever "seen" John Payne's horse run was against old Hoover when he had been cutting all day in the mud. Payne's handsome yellow horse had rested all day and was given twenty feet advantage, but old Hoover came out almost a length ahead.

Cowboys frequently played pranks on one another, especially tenderfeet who were not cowpunchers, but hanging around cow camps near the settlements. When they tried out their stunts on young fellows, I enjoyed that as much as any. Sometimes they found someone asleep under a wagon and tied a rope to his foot with the other end tied to a wheel. They shook the wheel and yelled, "Whoa!" As the fellow jumped to his feet, he struck his head against the wagon box or running gears, and this scared him worse than ever. He might conclude that he had been kicked for he was just coming out of a sleep.

One fellow got such a fright that he ran the length of the rope and fell. He then jumped up and ran the length of the rope again in another direction. He fell again before he realized that he was a victim of a prank.

Some pranks I didn't approve. One man named Bort, a rather well-to-do small cowman in Barber County, had heard I was going to take a wagon on the general spring roundup in the Southwest. He had a farm with work stock but only one cow horse and a small bunch of good cattle. A few had gotten away during the previous winter. He wanted to go with me for a few days and was willing to pay his part. I told him to come along; it wouldn't cost much, if anything.

He was getting old and slightly nervous. After he finished dinner, he

87

lay down under the wagon to take a nap before time to start again. Someone discovered him, grabbed hold of the wagon wheels, shook them, yelling, "Whoa!" The old man awoke and attempted to jump to his feet, but he struck his head against the running gears of the wagon, then fell out from under the wagon. He "seen" that it was a joke and decided not to get under the wagon anymore.

The next day after dinner, he took his nap away from the wagon. The boys "seen" him asleep. A couple got their saddles, ran over him, shook their saddles, yelling, "Whoa!" Bort jumped on all fours, and one of the boys dropped his saddle on top of him as if he were a horse. He looked like a little pony trying to buck off the saddle. The dazed, bewildered old fellow with his long hair and full beard looked so comical.

He came to me, "I 'shust' can't stand this any longer. Them boys, they 'shust' run me crazy." He wanted to know if I would gather his cattle for him. I told him it would be no trouble. We would round up all Barber County cattle and we knew his brand. So he saddled up and started back; he had had enough.

Sam Fling and Wheeler Timberlake followed the Spring 1880 roundup out close to Fort Supply. When they returned to the ⚕ and TL Bar ranches, they told about meeting up with Cal Watkins and his outfit of rollicking boys who were tough as young mules. One of them could run on all fours like a dog and outrun every man who bantered him for a race. Another could outrun a horse by running twenty-five yards to a post around which he turned with great speed by throwing out his arm, then keep ahead on the return lap.

In this roundup four small or two large outfits would throw together and have a grub wagon which carried all supplies, bedding, food, and cooking utensils. There was one horse wrangler with each wagon. Cowmen in the Strip referred to a general roundup with a wagon as a Colorado roundup, so I assumed that Colorado cattlemen had used a grub wagon prior to us. A beef was killed nearly every day. Each wagon took turns butchering for the whole outfit. They had to be careful about the killing, for there were men looking out for their own ranch's interests.

Anthony was the nearest railroad point to the cattle ranges of Barber and Comanche Counties when the country was settled circa 1882. The farmers were unable to fence their fields, and the cattlemen did not want to destroy their crops as they drove their herds to Anthony to be shipped. When large beef herds passed between two unfenced farms, they stopped on an uncultivated place and were taken through between farms in small bunches. Then they were close-herded on another uncultivated area while the herd was being driven through the narrow land to the open ground beyond the two farms. The riders were divided so that some watched each portion of the herd as it was being transferred. It took more time and a great deal more work; but, by cooperation with the farmers, very little destruction was done.

The small farm was the most important factor for the termination of the range cattle industry. Barber and Comanche Counties have some good farming land but should remain largely cattle ranch country. Much of western and northwestern Oklahoma is more suitable for cattle grazing rather than farming.

I heard considerable comment concerning the Texas fever and the "Dead Line"[5] on the roundup of 1879. In 1878 the fever had become so bad along the southern border of Kansas that domestic cattlemen in Barber County formed an organization and elected officers to look after its interests. Bill Springer was president. I had known him since 1870 in Chautauqua County. He was instructed to proceed to Kiowa near the state line and post notices forbidding Texas cattle from crossing into Kansas. When these notices appeared, it created consternation among the owners of longhorn cattle. Some asserted if they had seen Springer posting these signs, they would have hanged him. There were heated comments on both sides. Oliver Ewell angrily asked me who Springer was and whether he was a large cattleman.

Farmers of Barber County were also at odds with the cattlemen. They wanted herd laws; the cattlemen, free range. Herd law meant that cattlemen must keep their cattle under close herd or in fenced pastures.[6] This became a political issue because the law must be enacted by the state legislature. In the fall campaign, the free range cattlemen's candidate, Perry Ewing, was elected to the Kansas legislature.

When we arrived at "Fine" and Perry Ewings' ranch on Driftwood Creek,[7] I saw Oliver Ewell and "Crate" Justis. They met Bill Hudson, "Gus" Johnson's manager of all his herds, and recommended me. He hired and sent me to the ⅋ ranch on the Eagle Chief Creek in Indian Territory.

EIGHT

Line Riding on the 5̄ Ranch

In April 1879 I reported to Jim Buzard, foreman of the outfit on the Eagle Chief Creek. The big 5̄ range, held by A. H. "Gus" Johnson, extended to the Glass Mountains, south of the Cimarron River, as far east as the present site of Fairview, Oklahoma.[1] Johnson dealt in cattle by the thousands. In the summer of 1878 he bought 4000 head of Texas cattle, some at Dodge City, others as they came up the Texas Trail. There were 1000 head of Mexican steers, called "grub ears," with ears cut off so no one could change the ear marks. He wintered them on the ranch along the Eagle Chief.

The next spring Johnson divided them into four herds. He sent the "grub ears" to the Ninnescah River valley in Pratt County, Kansas, west of Wichita to fatten on bluestem grass. This section of Kansas was too open for winter range and there was no buffalo grass. Moreover, settlers had not appeared. Buzard, the foreman, had the cow herd of 1800. Bill Dunlap, Ike Berry, L. C. Farris, and general manager, Bill Hudson, had herds of 1000, each.[2] Calves were not counted until they were branded and marked. Each herd had four riders, a cook, and a boss. There was no horse wrangler. When the herd was on the move, the cook drove the wagon; one of the riders served as horse wrangler. He unhitched and unharnessed the team, turned it loose with the horse herd, remuda, and helped the cook gather cow chips for fuel. When the herds moved toward the settlements, farmers came to these cow outfits and offered to buy the cow chips because of the scarcity of fuel. By the end of October 1879, all the beeves were driven to Wichita and marketed.

Although we seldom used the word "remuda" when we spoke of saddle horses, we did call the mares and colts collectively, the "cavva-yard." Tip McCracken told me about a tenderfoot horse wrangler formerly in his outfit. When the boy drove the saddle horses into the corral near the ranch house, the boss noticed that one of the horses was lame. He asked the boy what caused it. The boy replied that the horse ran against the corner of the "cavva-yard!"

When I started to work on the 〒 range, all the bosses advised the cowpunchers to ride lines in pairs because of the Dull Knife Raid. Barrett[3] and Jim Buzard, George McDonald, Frank Tracy, Fayette Thomas, George Cunningham, Sam Prudent, and I were the riders.

Bill Dunlap camped in a dugout along the south side of the Cimarron opposite the mouth of the Eagle Chief the previous winter. He had deposited several hundred dollars in a bank in Wichita. One day while riding his line, his dugout caught fire and burned his camp equipment, supplies, and personal effects, including his bank deposit receipts. He felt a little uneasy, so he decided to go to Wichita to look after his deposit. He hired Sam Prudent to ride in his place. When he returned, there was need for more men and Sam stayed.

I rode a line from headquarters to meet Sam in a line camp along the north side of the Cimarron. A big, husky fellow, he couldn't learn to mount a horse. He took hold of the saddle horn with his left hand, then the cantle with his right hand, put his foot in the stirrup, and lifted himself up into the saddle. He let go of the cantle which was not so bad with a perfectly gentle horse, but these frisky horses left him open for trouble. One afternoon we met, got off our horses, and talked awhile. When we started to re-mount, his horse was restless and Sam could not mount. His horse came sidling alongside my horse's right shoulder which put his right flank in easy reach of my right foot. When Sam let lose of the cantle, I gave the horse a swift kick in the flank and it jumped sidewise. Sam plunged right over his horse's back and lit on his back on the ground. He held the rope in his left hand and the horse could not get away. Sam got up and asked, "What did he do?"

I replied, "He stepped under you."

Then Sam asked, "What did I do?"

I replied, "You hit the ground on your back."

He said, "I believe I did by the way I feel."

When I told the boys at the supper table, they enjoyed it greatly and wondered if it would teach him anything about mounting a horse.

While the 〒 herd grazed on the range north of the Cimarron along the Eagle Chief, the cowhands ate and bunked at the headquarters ranch house.[4] It faced south, extended east-west with sides seven feet high, and was a double log house with the ends built together. It had only one outside door. Inside was a double door connecting the two rooms. The bunkhouse was in one room; the other was the kitchen. There was a window in the center of the west room on the north side

91

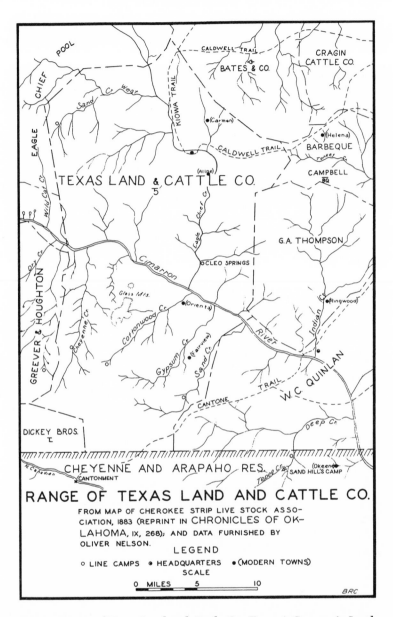

Map 4. Range of Texas Land and Cattle Co. From *A Cowman's Southwest*, ed. by Angie Debo. Copyright © 1953 by the Arthur H. Clark Company.

and one could see the creek. I believe the house was built of blackjack logs, notched and saddled at the ends. This portion of the structure was called the square. Shorter logs were used at the ends of the building above the square, cut tapered at the ends, according to the slant of the roof. They were notched and saddled by cross ties or ridgepoles which extended the length of the roof. The ridgepoles supported the clapboard roof and dirt above.

In 1878 the wagon which hauled provisions from Kiowa to the ranch house was often stranded north of the Salt Fork River because of flood conditions. Frequently two line riders, Oliver Ambury and "Cy" Davidson, ran out of food. They substituted bacon with wild turkeys in the timber along the Eagle Chief. They kept at least one staked out all the time.

When they "seen" a bunch of turkeys feeding, they rode close before the turkeys could see them, then suddenly dashed among them. The turkeys flew in all directions while the men watched to see if any flew out on the open prairie. They followed in a dead run until the bird lit; then each slackened his horse's gait, let the turkey trot, and did not disturb it enough to make it fly again. When its wings began to drag the ground and it started to look for a hiding place, they picked up the turkey while it "set" down on the ground and stretched out its neck. They lived on turkey so long they could not look one in the face for many moons.

When we were at the headquarters camp, we had a good cook who professed to be an old plainsman and buffalo hunter. Old Jim told us in all seriousness that he and two other fellows hitched a yoke of oxen to a sled and went west to hunt buffalo. Far from the settlement a blizzard struck, and a heavy snowfall kept them snow bound until their grub gave out. Since they saw no game and could get no rest, they boiled their buffalo robe to make soup. They got more hair than nourishment and decided to kill one of their oxen and consumed it before the snow melted. With one steer pulling the load, progress was slow and they were very hungry. They cut chunks of meat from the remaining steer and made him pull as well which killed the brute. The three men took and carried all the meat they could and at last reached the settlements.

When Jim finished, Fayette said, "Jim, that story is as thin as buffalo soup!" We were willing to swallow these tall stories since he always fed us good meals.

93

There were channel catfish in the Eagle Chief nearby. When the water became muddy from wading cattle or a sudden rise after rainfall, the catfish swam into muskrat or crayfish holes in the banks near the bottom of the stream. Jim would wade into the muddy stream, reach into the holes, and pull out the catfish. He tied a wire in its gills and hung it to the large, cedar-log ridgepole of the ranch house. He cut a ring through the hide at the neck and took a pair of horse nippers to skin the hide off which gave the fish a clean look. Then he cooked and served it which was good eating.

If we brought a gentle cow, which he trained to milk, he prepared puddings and other delicacies that we never had in a cow camp before. But he had no way to make butter. While we were at headquarters, he fixed a little spring house to keep the milk cool. We soon expected milk at every meal.

One noontime there was no milk on the table and we asked for it. Jim came to the corner of the room where we were eating and picked up the bucket to show us. "What's that stuff?" I asked.

He replied, "This morning as I washed dishes, I heard a peculiar noise in the Eagle Chief. I looked out and saw a wall of water rolling down the creek almost bank full."

He rushed to the spring house after the milk bucket but got there a little too late. The water had lifted the bucket out of the spring. When he grabbed, it was just turning over. The lid had flown off, he bailed up a bucket of water instead of milk.

Bill Hudson purchased a dozen hens and a rooster to furnish eggs for our table, as well as to raise some chickens to eat. One hen hatched a brood. So long as we remained at that camp, the chickens did well.

The summer of 1878 "Gus" Johnson had a herd of 2000 mixed cattle on the divide between the Salt Fork of the Cimarron and the Eagle Chief. It was reasonably wet that summer and the buffalo wallows were full of water most of the time. The young calves lay out on the high divides near the wallows, and the cows came to them to let them suck. The calves became fat lying in the hot sun without exercise and began to die. Hudson wrote to Johnson at Dodge City to bring a veterinarian. The diagnosis was blackleg induced by lack of exercise. Hudson thought dogs would cause the calves to move around. He went to Kiowa and returned with two bird dogs and one bull dog, but all he got was a general milling around. As soon as the cows saw the dogs,

94

they began to bellow and chase the dogs away. The calves lay and watched. Hudson ordered the entire herd driven each day to the Eagle Chief to drink. This gave the calves plenty of exercise and they quit dying of blackleg.

Cattle suffered from dry murrain during exceedingly dry years, caused by eating too much dry grass and drinking water too sparingly. They had drooping ears and suffered from constipation. To save them, they must be drenched with linseed oil. It was easy when a cow was down; others must be roped. A cow was easier drenched than a horse. With muzzle lifted, oil poured into her throat, and she swallowed immediately. Because of the prevalence of this disease on the great ranges, linseed oil was found in all border towns.

From spring 1878 until June 1879 rainfall in the Strip was extremely heavy. When anyone rode up a sand hill without much turf, the horse was apt to bog down if the rider did not hustle. When the rain ceased, scarcely any more fell until June 1880 with only local showers and cloudbursts in small areas. By late summer in 1879, extreme drought conditions prevailed. The big flats near the site of Cherokee, Oklahoma, had nothing growing except tall milkweeds. Huge cracks appeared in the ground. If a cow stepped into one with a hind leg, forcing the hock joint below the surface of the ground, she would be unable to pull it out. Bending the joint bound it tightly against the hard earth. Cowhands had to assist the cow as if she were in a bog.

Texas fever was a terror for the native cattle and some of the double-wintered cattle from Texas which had spent two winters no farther than 100 miles south of the Kansas line. The Texas Trail never touched the ⅂ range until spring 1879. The old trail hit Kansas a little west of Kiowa. After it crossed the ranch, the cattle began to contract the fever and Johnson lost twenty head, so we had to move our camp. Johnson accompanied us and picked out one on a high bluff overlooking a stream of gypsum water which tasted so strong that we could not stay. One fellow had worked up in the Panhandle where the Cimarron has all fresh water. Seeing the nice-looking, clear pools, he decided to slake his thirst. He took a mouthful, jumped up, and spat it out. I yelled. He saw me laughing and asked what was the matter with that water. I told him the Cimarron ran through the big Salt Plain.

I found a fresh-water spring on the south bank of a small stream in a horseshoe bend, a mile or more to the east, and there we placed our campsite, surrounded by a row of elm trees, called Elm Motte, one of the several clumps of timber along the Eagle Chief where there had been wet weather springs which protected the trees from fires. Others were called Indian Springs, Red Springs, and Big Timber.[5]

About 1 June the outfit moved near Big Timber. We did not stay because of insufficient grass for our bridle horses. We moved to Red Springs where we could stake our horses all around camp. The ranch chickens fared badly. Predatory animals ate all but two hens and a large yellow rooster. He ran into the brush and was left behind. He had faced death in so many ways that he must have lost all confidence in man and beast alike. When we sat down to eat our first dinner at the new camp, Jim told us about the terrible loss.

As I mounted my horse to ride the line that afternoon, Jim Buzard told me to ride by Big Timber in the evening to see if I could induce the rooster to accompany me. I told Jim he could issue a bench warrant; if I got there before dark, I would bring him back dead or alive. That evening I heard him make the woods ring. He seemed to be in mighty close quarters. I drew my six-shooter and rode quickly toward him. Suddenly a sharp-shinned hawk flew from the timber with tremendous speed before I could shoot. At the foot of the tree nearby lay the rooster. A stream of blood squirted from his jugular vein. I waited a moment for the hawk, then picked up the rooster, tied him to the saddle, and rode to camp.

When I related my story at supper, Buzard said, "Now, don't you fellows fall for that. He just shot that bird to keep from running him down." I said that I would let the rooster be the judge. My forty-five would make a bigger hole through his neck than the little pin-like puncture which the hawk's talon made. The explanation seemed to satisfy them.

Besides the two surviving hens, there were two dogs which caused trouble. The chickens attracted coyotes at night. The dogs slept all day, chased coyotes at night, even ran over the tent's brace ropes. Such disturbances broke our sleep, so we induced the cook to kill and cook the two hens. The coyotes lost interest in our camp, and we were able to get a good night's sleep.

One early June day Hudson came and told us to round up the entire cow herd the next morning. He wanted to earmark and castrate all the early bull calves and those which we had missed last fall. I carried in my pocket a good, white, bone-handle pocket knife to trim my finger

96

nails. I decided to sharpen and use it, but I found only a hole in the bottom of my pocket. The knife was not in camp, so I concluded it had dropped out on my line. Hudson let me use his knife.

When we started to work on the calves, we fastened one end of the rope to the saddle horn, held the other end with the running noose in the right hand, and coiled the rest in the left hand. If a rider was in range of a calf standing still, he threw the loop to drop over its head. If the calf was running, it was caught by a front or hind foot which generally threw it. If not, the rider dismounted quickly and deftly looped the horse's bridle rein around the rope. This precaution kept the horse facing the struggling calf, and the horse could not run and drag it. The cowhand must keep one hand on the rope, edge up and grab the calf firmly, then bulldog it to the ground. The nearest cowhand without a calf rode alongside, dismounted, and performed the knife act, while the first one held it.

That day Frank Tracy rode a good but slow horse. A large calf ran by; Frank threw his loop around its neck and it bellowed loud. Greatly tickled, Frank yelled, "Oh, golly!" The horse stood with his side toward it. The instant Frank finished his playful remark, the full force of the husky, running calf surged against the rope and pulled the horse full length on his side upon the ground. Frank saw what was going to happen in time to straighten out his leg to prevent the horse from breaking it.

As the day wore on, all of us had fun at his expense. When one of us roped a calf which bucked and bellowed, we yelled, "Oh, golly!" This caused Frank to use language unfit to be printed.

In time a better method of marking calves on the open range was introduced. A forked post was set solidly in the ground away from trees, banks, and even the grub wagon, so that at least six feet of it stood above ground. When the rider roped a calf, he dragged it near the post end and threw the rope in the post fork which stopped it. Two men stood by the post. When the bucking, bawling calf halted, they could work. The two prongs prevented the calf from turning right or left; the post kept it from rushing forward. The rider's horse pulled back on the rope and prevented the calf from backing away. One man grabbed the calf's hind leg; the other took the corresponding front leg. They pulled at once, and the calf fell flat on its opposite side. The rider slackened the rope. The man who held the hind leg placed his knees on the calf's shoulder and pulled the hind leg as far forward and up as possible. This prevented the calf from getting hold of the turf to cause damage. The other man used the knife.

This work required a clear open space. When the calf got up, the man with the knife stood behind it. Usually the calf caught sight of the herd and ran to it. Occasionally a calf got up with blood in his eye, seeking revenge for the damage done. When he began to prance around and look for his tormentors, the men dared not move or say a word until he started to the herd. Most of the time an animal does not discern any object until it moves. This was the only defense the two men had as they could not carry their six-shooters while dressed for work.

Hudson was present and engaged in our work. The way he maneuvered, I do not think he had ever roped from a horse. He rode around a calf a number of times, whirling the rope to throw the noose. Finally he made a good catch. I happened to be nearby, had nothing on my string, so he called me to wrestle the calf down. I got to it as quickly as possible, bulldogged, and held it. Hudson laughed heartily, greatly pleased with his good luck. He called someone to help me while he sat on his horse, smiling and bragging about his catch.

On the way to my line the next morning, I decided to look for my knife. I followed, as nearly as possible, the exact route I last rode, watching the grass and vegetation carefully. When I arrived at an alkali spot, there lay the knife. I told the boys about my good fortune.

Buzard always joked us, "Now you don't expect us to believe you could ride a half day, looking through the grass for a pocket knife, do you? It looks more like you was afraid to get that white handle soiled, and you hid it out until marking was done." This brought a laugh, but I had the knife.

When we finished marking calves, our ropes were well-smeared with blood which the coyotes smelled, and we soon found them on our hands again. We used our ropes to stake out the saddle horses at night, but they paid no attention to the coyotes. The next morning we discovered that some of the ropes had been chewed in two and the horses were loose.

That summer Dave Griffin laid over two or three days on the northern edge of the Eagle Chief. He was taking a herd of horses and mules to Canada for the Olive brothers of southern Texas.[6] After supper Frank Tracy and I rode over to their camp to see that none of the 5 mares followed them when Griffin left.

He told me he lost fifty head of horses in a stampede. He rode in front of the herd, and another fellow who followed failed to keep it bunched closely behind. Griffin happened to look back and see part of the herd turn into a hollow away from the trail. He turned to head them toward the trail. The horse stepped into a hole and fell, throwing him completely loose. The horse jumped up and started after the other horses. Griffin jerked his six-shooter and yelled, "Whoa!" The horse stopped immediately. "The most remarkable thing was that this was the second time the horse had been ridden," Griffin said.

"You would have gotten yourself into a dickens of a shape, being afoot with a big saddle on your back," I said.

"Oh, I didn't intend to kill him. I was just going to crease him!" Griffin replied. I did not know much about it then but learned later that creasing a horse or a cow was a pretty good trick if a fellow was a good shot with a six-shooter. Griffin mounted his horse and helped turn the horses back to the trail. They did not overtake the main horse herd until after dark.

Tracy and I were present when he and his stampeded horses arrived. The rest of the men had eaten their supper.

Griffin and the horse wrangler had no knives or forks, but they had some tin plates which they filled with beans and soup. Griffin pulled out a sharp-pointed dirk knife and tried to eat with it. He had a six-shooter and a Winchester. Marion Olive sat near and saw Griffin was not making much headway. Olive reached over behind his own six-shooter and pulled out the biggest, wide-bladed butcher knife I ever saw.

"Here, Mr. Griffin, take this," Olive said.

"Thank you, Mr. Olive," Griffin replied. Then he began to "fire" the soup and beans into his mouth mighty rapid.

Five Negroes accompanied the herd. They were the most ragged, dirty human beings I ever saw. They were not allowed to carry a gun, knife, or anything to protect themselves. When Griffin and Olive were in camp, they did not speak unless it was about the horses or mules. Then with a bow and curtsey with his hand, spoke to "Massa Griffin!" or "Massa Olive!"

"What is it, boy?" the one addressed would ask. The Negro told what he had in mind.

The day before the horse herd started on up the trail, Olive rode to Kiowa on an errand, and Griffin was away to see that none of the herd had escaped. Left to themselves, the Negroes sang, played, laughed, and wrestled with one another.

John Watkins came up the trail with a horse herd. According to custom, each Texas buckaroo was given two broken horses to ride with five others to break before the herd was delivered. The buckaroo must rope the horse, throw and blindfold him, let him get to his feet, saddle and mount him, then remove the blindfold.

The herd grazed in the morning; when they had eaten enough, they started up the trail in a trot. This was why the buckaroo must make frequent changes of mount. One or two men rode in front to prevent the herd from stampeding. There were no side riders. The rest rode behind the herd to keep them from stringing out too much. The Texas grub wagon followed the herd, pulled by four horses or mules. These wagons had a tread eight inches wider than our common wagons today.

During the summer we occasionally heard gunshots. We knew it was probably Indians shooting deer because white men never hunted deer in the summer. Major Miles,[7] the Cheyenne-Arapaho Indian agent, said he had the Indians under close supervision and permitted none to leave the Fort Reno reservation. Knowing how Dull Knife had outwitted the soldiers in 1878, we didn't take much stock in what he said.

Old Jim became greatly frightened. George McDonald, Fayette Thomas, and I were gone often from early morning until late night. One day George told of seeing tracks of three Indians who had taken a drink at a spring along his line. I saw the frightened cook and tried to counteract the story. How did George know there were three Indians? He replied that one wore army shoes; another, moccasins; the third was barefoot. I asked, "George, did you say one of them was barefooted?"

He said, "Yes."

I said, "Oh, I know who they were; they were poor folks."

Fayette was as anxious as I to keep the cook. We both laughed, but George did not understand our motives. He became angry and swore he would not permit anyone to call him a liar. I got him aside and explained. He got out of his angry mood but the cook left anyway.

Old Jim always had a gun and plenty of ammunition, but he was afraid to stay in camp alone. Shortly after we moved to a new campsite, Jim took his gun, the team and wagon, and started to Kiowa for a load of provisions. After he crossed the Cimarron and had gotten not more than half way from the river to headquarters, he saw a band of Indians riding from the west. He was so frightened he forgot he had a gun, jumped out of the wagon, and started to unhook a horse to ride for his life. He saw they were too close to get away so he decided to stand there and be killed. The first Indian spoke English, told him they were Pottawatomies, and asked if he had anything to eat since they had bad luck buffalo hunting. With relief Jim gave them his lunch.

The Indians wore stove-pipe hats. Plug hats were in evidence among the Caddo and other civilized Indians. The government issued them because white men's wearing apparel styles had changed. Clothing dealers hit upon the idea of selling them to the Indians who liked to wear tall hats because it made them "heap big Injun!"

Late summer when other Indian signs began to appear, Jim became uneasy and finally got an opportunity to return to Kansas. He had a claim near Garden City, and he was afraid some one might take it from him. His flight left us the delicate operation of arising before dawn, preparing our breakfast, and getting into the saddle by daybreak. We cooked our supper by lantern and firelight until Bill Dunlap came.

A few days later our camp was moved to a wet-weather spring about a mile and a half out from the Eagle Chief. Tracy and I rode the line together on 2 July 1879 across the river and found a bunch of cattle grazing in the sand hills. A two-year-old buffalo heifer was with them. I told Frank if he would ride back to camp and get the old sixteen-shooter Henry's rifle, the team and wagon, and the cook, I would ride the line and he could do the buffalo hunting. We had our six-shooters, but I felt he could get the buffalo easier with the long-range gun. He agreed and started for camp. I rode north, looked back, and saw some yearlings chasing the buffalo since they hadn't seen one before. When I saw it turn south, I knew it was leaving. I rode back toward a sand hill near which it would pass, dismounted, and walked to the top, leading my horse. In a few moments it came into full view opposite the hill and I shot it through the body. It started running. I jumped on the horse and rode after it. When I got within shooting distance, my horse became frightened and ran in the opposite direction. With a severe raw-hiding of the quirt, the horse went alongside the buffalo as I shot it through the heart. I looked around and here came Tracy, too late for the kill. He had seen the yearlings chasing the buffalo, raced ahead, and led his horse on a long rope to the brow of another sand hill when I fired the first shot. He said it "burnt" the end of his nose after it went through the buffalo.

Tracy went after the cook. I got down, bled the buffalo, and finished

101

skinning it before the wagon arrived. I discovered the first shot struck about four inches too far back from the shoulder blade to kill it. When I returned to camp at noon, the carcass had been cut up and partially cooked.

The summer became dryer and we had to watch the water supply. I saw lightning set fire to grass along the Eagle Chief in August. The only growing grass appeared in strips among the sand hills. It was difficult to hold cattle and horses on the range for they were constantly looking for green grass.

The ⅀ ranch had a mad steer which became a victim of the drought. He was large, blue-and-white with horns like a buffalo in shape and color—black. When I started riding the line that spring, the boys told me where he ranged and warned me to watch for him. He was always ready to fight and would come to anyone nearby. He remained near a large wet-weather pond near my line. One day I rode cautiously to it to see if he was still there. He was not in sight as I rode close to a thicket. Suddenly he came out with head held high, eyes glaring wildly, and sniffing the air. He was disturbed by scent and hearing rather than sight. When I saw his bristling challenge, I turned the horse directly away and rode slowly out of sight while he raged around. I reported my experience. "You got out of it better than I did. He gave me a hot chase before I got away," said Tracy.

As summer advanced and dried up the water holes in the prairie, I took another scout around the pond. I found it dry and the carcass of the mad steer lying face down. This place is still named "steer hollow."

Cowboys were fair game for outlaws in the Strip, such as the murderers of Henderson and Stockstill. Afterwards, Jim Buzard and I rode the line together along the Eagle Chief near a water spring. Work delayed us one day and we didn't get back to camp until after dark. As we neared camp, Jim said, "Look at the men round the campfire."

I jerked my Winchester and reined my horse over to the dark, heavy trees, lining the riverbank. Buzard laughed and wondered why I was afraid. I told him about a good friend who had ridden carelessly into his camp a short time ago. I didn't intend to give myself up as "cheap" as Stockstill had. We soon saw they were from another cow outfit who had finished delivering a herd farther up the Texas Trail. They were trying to return to Texas before winter set in.

We ate a late supper, said very little, and went to bed. We rose early the next day, since the cattle were trying to drift out to look for better grazing. As we were eating dinner around the campfire the next night, Buzard thought about what I had done. He laughed and told the boys how I grabbed my Winchester and rode under cover. He did not say what he did.

Fayette Thomas asked, "What did you do?" Buzard had not even pulled his six-shooter but rode out in the moonlight. Thomas said, "You, like a damn fool, rode up to the camp like that, after all we knew?" It was my turn to laugh. Jim's face turned red and he said nothing more.

A few days afterwards government scouts, C. M. Scott[8] and Mike Meagher, stayed all night with us. They had been to Fort Reno and were headed for Kiowa. Riding armed, they brought lunch as they knew there were few cow camps in their path. They crossed the Cimarron to the north side and stopped because the water was better there. They unsaddled and hobbled their horses to graze on the ⅋ range. After they ate, it was warm; they lay down but slept longer than they intended. When they awoke, their horses were missing. They had hobbled away in search of better grass. It was near sunset before the two scouts finally found them. They would have had an all-night ride but discovered our outfit lay directly in their course. We had just moved to Red Springs Camp. They told us many of their interesting experiences with Indians.

In the autumn Frank Tracy and George McDonald went to Wolf Creek in the north Texas Panhandle to assist in driving a through herd of 2500 head of steers which "Gus" Johnson had bought. Ed Farris was in charge. He was from one of Johnson's beef herds on the Ninnescah River in Pratt County, Kansas, and Barrett Buzard, Thomas, and I were left to do the riding.

The grass was so dry and short that the cattle were constantly on the move. One day George Cunningham rode into camp wanting work and we hired him. Buzard and Cunningham rode one side of the herd; Fayette and I, the other. Soon afterward Fayette and I rode down the Cimarron bottoms on the south side; a deer heard his horse and jumped up to look. It was not uncommon to find deer far out in the flats because the ear fly infested the brush and sand hills and drilled holes in their ears. Their large, sensitive ears are attuned to the faintest sound. Fayette stopped, pulled his six-shooter, and killed the big buck. Deer in this section had not been shot at a great deal. He carried the carcass to camp, skinned and dried the hide, dressed the meat, and we had venison for several days. Two or three days later he took sick and we kidded him about getting foundered on venison. He was as gritty as the best of us, but we made him remain in camp, rest, and sleep as much as possible. I rode the lines alone.

As I rode down the flats south of the Cimarron, I saw two Indians on horseback, riding toward me, nearly a mile away. I knew they were hunting deer, for they were about fifty rods apart in the grassy flat where the deer came to lie and escape the ear fly. I knew at a glance they were Indians. The sun was shining bright; I saw the glint of their old buffalo gun barrels pointed right across their saddles in front of them. White men carried their guns with the barrels pointed left and sat on horses differently. Since there were sand hills nearby, I could dodge behind them if they made any hostile moves. I continued as if I had not seen them, looking for cattle tracks across the line. I had made many good shots from a running horse and this gave me confidence. Just then three Indians rode through a buffalo pass not more than a hundred yards to my right. It nearly froze my blood when I remembered what the Indian scouts and Major Miles had told us, "If you see any Indians in the Outlet, you should shoot or run."

Since five Indians were converging from two directions, I dared not run or shoot. It was not pleasant to think about the two with buffalo guns—Long Toms or Big Fifties. They could knock a horse from under a man a mile away. The big savage in command was on a mule and gave me the high sign. I interpreted it as, "Come here! We want you! If you don't come, we'll get you anyhow!" That looked wonderfully like war to me. I never was in a tighter place in my life. I had been with Indians often enough to read many of their signs and had learned they are governed by appearances and circumstances.

I slapped spurs to my horse and rode toward the Indian sign factory, reached back to loosen my six-shooter, and sat it at half cock; it would be easy to jerk out and pull the hammer to full cock. This approach would give him an idea that I had a great deal of confidence in myself or in my backing. He stopped astonished and waited. When I jerked my horse to stop, his head was close to the mule. The Indian had a Winchester fastened to the saddle under his leg. The other two seemed unarmed. I had the drop on them for the time being, but I wondered how it would be when the two Big Fifties arrived. The old leader was hard-looking with shortly cut, scraggly, dirty hair, and face, nearly as black as an African. Had he been friendly, he would have said, "How, John!"

I knew they had not seen a white man after leaving Fort Reno. There were no cattle ranches between it and the south line of the Ƨ where I was. The ferocious-looking Indian asked in English, "You Agency?"

"Yes," I replied. I think he knew I was bluffing. I was still studying the situation over to find the best route out.

"Wo-haw [cattle] Agency?" he asked.

"Yes," I replied.

Then he looked at me savagely, "You Texan!"

"Yes," I replied; thus, I had told him two stories.

"Wo-haw Texan?" he asked.

"Yes," I answered. "Look here, Old Toppy, who are you?" I asked, pretending great rage.

"Me scout," he replied. I looked down at his mule and haw-hawed big and loud. No scout rode a mule unless he was in the mountains. He looked at me fiercely, made a grabbing motion, and said in a rasping, snarling tone, "Catch white man!"

About that time, the other two Indians came riding up the flat behind me. Without looking around I slashed the spurs into my horse's flanks. He made a terrible jump, and I reined him to whirl around left of the Indians, instead of putting me between them, so their Big Fifties pointed away from me. My horse still faced the leader but was a length of a horse farther away; this was the position I wanted. I had my six-shooter ready and I had them covered. Four were young bucks; they talked with the leader; I supposed they were planning to exterminate me. "Where are your soldiers?" I asked.

"See cottonwoods? Camped thar!" he replied and pointed at a cottonwood grove a few miles west of the present site of Homestead, Oklahoma. I had ridden there often, for it stood near the end of my line. I knew he was spoofing for there was no water near. He was giving me hot air too.

"You catch white man?" I asked, pointing a finger at him.

"Yes," he replied.

"You had better get busy; you'll find plenty to catch!" I replied and smiled.

He instantly changed facial expression and mellowed his voice, "Heap white men?"

I said, "Yes."

"Whare?" he asked.

"All up and down the river—heap white men!" I replied, pointing up and down the river with a sweep of my arm.

"Whare you camp?" he asked.

"You see that big sand hill? Just ride up on top; then you see my camp," I pointed to a huge sand hill forty rods away. The five Indians turned, rode off without a friendly salute, and climbed the sand hill rather than the flat, hard surface. I ran through the small natural pass through which they had come. I spurred my horse to a dead run into the direction of the grazing herd. Looking back I saw them reach the top of the hill. When they saw nothing but more sand hills, they wheeled to see me waving my hat as a sign that I had put one over on them. They continued on their way.

After I left camp that afternoon, Bill Dunlap drove in with a wagon, a bunch of saddle horses, and a man to assist him. He found Fayette Thomas alone. Our camp was at Elm Motte. Thomas told Dunlap we would bring in the horses when we came back that night. Dunlap turned them loose and was left afoot.

The Indians went straight to our camp. They rode in without a friendly salute and saw the deer hide. The old leader asked, "How much?"

Thomas said, "Four bits."

The Indian reached into his old poke, pulled out, and pitched a silver half dollar to Thomas, picked up the deer hide and rolled and fastened it to his saddle. "You man ride this way?" he pointed back toward my line.

Dunlap answered, "Yes."

Then the Indian said, "Little black-eyed feller, him heap mean!" [Records's eyes were blue.] "He kill Injun!"

Dunlap said, "No, he's a good boy. What did you do with him?"

The Indian answered, "We hog-tie him."

Dunlap asked, "You didn't hog-tie him and leave him out on the prairie did you?"

The Indian answered, "Yes."

Dunlap commented, "Why the coyotes will eat him."

The Indian replied, "Coyotes won't eat him. He heap mean. Me be back in three sleeps. Me get him." They started off to the northwest to cross the Cimarron above the mouth of the Eagle Chief without any friendly sign whatever.

When I returned, it was just growing dark. Dunlap was on top of the hill above camp, walking back and forth, terribly excited. He yelled, "I'm mighty glad to see you alive!"

I asked, "What's the matter, Bill?" He told me what had happened, then said that I was wanted at headquarters.

The next morning I followed the Indians' trail through the sand hills to where their tracks led far west. The signs indicated they had not stopped during the night after they left. A few weeks later we heard that a detachment of soldiers overtook this small band of Indians near the Union Pacific railroad in Nebraska. They were returned to Fort Reno.

When I reported to headquarters, Bill Hudson wanted me to help with the through herd from the Texas Panhandle. Ed Farris was sent to the line camp as my replacement and Bill Dunlap took charge of the through herd. They were being close-herded to accustom them to the range and escape spreading the fever among the native stock until cold weather came and killed the ticks.

We moved the herd south of the Cimarron away from the Texas Trail. We soon had the cattle so well-trained that we did not have to night herd, but we had to stay with them until they had quit grazing and bedded down for the night. During cloudy nights we were sometimes confused and could not locate camp. The cook hung a lighted lantern on a tall pole to guide us back so we would not have to sleep out in the grass. Meanwhile Bill Hudson transferred Bill Dunlap south across the Cimarron while he took charge of us again.

Our new cook was the most careless I have ever seen. While at the Elm Motte he was using water from the Eagle Chief. A rise brought down filthy, red-looking water, and he put on a batch of dried peaches to cook in the murky water. He served them in a crock; Dunlap grabbed the crock and threw it into the swollen river. He told the old cook if he ever set out food like that again, he would give him something to remember. The cook could have walked and carried clear water from a distance but was too lazy, Dunlap said.

One day in November after I had finished my dinner, I mounted a little saddle horse. He was gentle but had learned that camp was where he got his saddle removed. Every time the reins were loose, he would turn his head toward camp and take a nice little gait to get there as quickly as he could. This habit saved my life. I had not been out but a short time that afternoon, when I took desperately sick. Everything turned green; I just collapsed on the saddle horn and clamped my

107

arms around it. That loosened the reins and the horse turned toward camp. The old cook came, pulled me off the horse, dragged me into the tent, laid me on the edge of a pallet, went right out, and soon returned with a quart cup filled with something. With his knee under my head, he put that cup up to my mouth, "Drink that; it will either kill or cure, for you will be dead in a few minutes anyhow."

I drank every drop. He laid me down and went out. In a short time a great commotion took place in my stomach. I threw up everything except my boot heels and went to sleep right away. When I awoke the next day, the cook was the only person in camp. The boys had placed my saddle on a horse and had tied him to a wagon. I was told to come down to the branding pen when I was able. After much effort I was able to walk out of the tent. The cook had plenty of good coffee. After I drank, I was able to eat only a little food. I rode to the branding pen, but they thought there was nothing for a fellow looking like me to do. I did a little light work for a day or two before taking my place in the ranks. I asked the cook what he had given me. It was water with all the salt he could dissolve in it. I didn't care since it certainly got the job done.

The ⅀ outfit owned a bunch of mares which ran on the range but were never used for any work. The cow hands had to look after them. When they weren't seen for a couple of days, Jim Buzard took a scout around, but he could not find them.

We had seen a number of Mexicans with a small bunch of horses a few days before and reasoned they had taken them. Buzard told me to get a good horse and follow. There had been no rain for several months, but as I started up the old cow trail to Dodge City, I saw clouds forming toward the head of the Eagle Chief so I put on my slicker. I soon rode into a rain which fell harder, the farther I went. The falling rain on the parched earth created such a fog that I could scarcely follow the trail. Suddenly seven or eight Mexicans dashed up. I tried to talk to them, but they wouldn't or couldn't speak English. They talked among themselves; it appeared rather bad for me. I reached under my slicker, pulled out my six-shooter to a position of readiness but still under the edge of the slicker. I made up my mind if they wanted my outfit, I would at least try to get as many of them before they got me.

After they had talked the matter over, one said, "Adios!" They soon disappeared in the fog. With relief I followed, but it was raining so hard I could find no traces where they turned off the trail. Every gulley was bank full; the last one I crossed was so deep I had to get up into the saddle to escape being soaked. I whirled the horse around, recrossed the stream, and started back to the ranch.

When I arrived at headquarters, no one was there, for the outfit had removed the cattle to escape the contagious Texas cattle fever. It was still misting rain. I unsaddled my horse, staked him on the grass, went into the ranch house, ate some dried currants, then lay down on the bunk and went to sleep. I never awoke until after the sun was up for two or three hours.

The summer tent had been moved conveniently down toward the mouth of the Eagle Chief so we could have plenty of water for the cattle. As I approached, I heard Jim Buzard whooping and yelling along the creek not far away. As he rode in, his horse was wet all over. When he went out to the line, the Eagle Chief was just a little stream of water. The downpour was in broken country above the ⅄ range, and the hard ground caused nearly all of it to run into adjacent streams. Not a drop of rain fell near our camp. There were a few cattle which he intended to leave on the bank of the stream opposite our camp tent. He looked upstream and saw a wall of water, bank high, rolling down, which caused his loud yelling. He tried to get the cattle back across before the headwaters struck. He succeeded and narrowly escaped as the water force struck him near the bank. I told him he did not have anything on me, for I had been wallowing in swollen streams all the day before.

In a few days Bill Hudson rode into camp. Buzard told him my experiences. Hudson put up a big bluff and said high water or nothing else would have turned him back. I made no apologies; if something could have been accomplished, I would have stayed on the Mexicans' trail.

Hudson went to the Santa Fe office in Dodge City where "Gus" Johnson was passenger agent to inform him of the loss. I was positive the Mexicans had the missing mares. Johnson hired a man to watch the Texas Trail south of Dodge. The mares had been branded with a flying ⌣ that Johnson always used on his horses instead of the ⅄ brand which he considered too large. He often purchased previously branded horses and did not want them scarred with large markings.

The lookout soon located the missing mares. Johnson sent an officer to bring the leader to Dodge for an interview. He objected, but the

109

officer displayed his badge and advised him to accompany him peacefully. Even though the Mexican was visibly impressed with the surroundings, he denied all knowledge of the missing mares. Johnson said he had statements from a dozen men who would swear they had seen him with the horses, and some of us had seen them driving off the mares. He would give the leader enough time to ride out to bring them back. If not, he would have a detachment of U.S. soldiers get the whole band, dead or alive. Johnson was a man who could speak with authority. The leader carried out his instructions and seemed to be glad to get out of trouble so easily.

I worked with the ⅂ outfit until 1 December 1879. Hudson wanted me to take charge of the headquarters camp, look after the supplies, property, wagon team, and freight supplies for the ranch from Kiowa, Medicine Lodge, and Caldwell, the best for grain. I preferred to quit and join Frank Tracy in a hunting and trapping enterprise during the winter. I did not like working for the ⅂ outfit because they did not feed their hands well. They had plenty horses, but they were pretty rough old pelters.

"Gus" Johnson was a victim of lightning in 1882. He bought a cattle herd south of Dodge City. As he started back in a canopy-top, four-wheel surrey, drawn by a span of horses, a thunder shower came up suddenly, and the lightning killed him.[9]

Shortly afterwards a wealthy Easterner, Brandt, bought an interest in the ⅂ ranch. When he drove down in a buggy from Kiowa to look over the ranch, he wore a white shirt, black necktie, and shoes, instead of boots. He asked foreman Bill Dunlap for a horse to ride. Dunlap saddled an old plug but did not know the horse had not been ridden for a year. The seventy-five-year-old Brandt did not know how to ride. He mounted before he had a tight hold on the reins and kicked the horse in the side. The horse bucked a time or two and Brandt tumbled to the ground. He rebuked Bill for getting an unreliable horse; Bill blamed Brandt. When he mounted again and followed Bill's instructions, they rode off together without mishap. Brandt complimented Bill on his horsemanship. The old gentleman was friendly to all the boys and they liked him, but life on the ⅂ was so vigorous he soon returned to the east for good.

NINE

Wildlife on the
Eagle Chief Range

As I rode the line from April to December 1879, I saw the true nature of the Eagle Chief area. Not only did I see and kill some of the wild animals, I saw evidence of competition between the Indian and the white man for possession of the animals which ranged this part of Oklahoma. I have always thought that the Eagle Chief country with its springs of fresh water was a great resort for wild life. Deer, antelope, buffalo, elk, panther, coyote, lobo wolf, prairie chicken, quail, turkey, and wild horses at one time or another proliferated. The acorns in the blackjacks and the buffalo grass on the open range invited their quota of wild life—deer and buffalo respectively.

At Big Timber I recognized burr oak—scarce in the West—red oak, elm, and cottonwood. One day I saw evidence of hunter and trapper activity in this clump of timber as well as that of a fight between white men and Indians. A large unfinished dugout with barkless ridgelog and posts set under each of its ends was situated at the edge of the timber. A few steps in front lay the skulls and horns of two oxen. They had been killed and their carcasses taken away as there were no other bones in sight. Perhaps the animals were work oxen and had pulled a vehicle for a hunting party which had worked on the dugout. From evidence I later uncovered, I think Indians killed the oxen.

A few steps south was a small sloping mound on top of a shallow grave. I took a spade, dug into the grave, and uncovered the remains of a large Indian. Many bones had decayed, but the lower jaw and the teeth were in good condition. I rested the tibia bone on the ground, and the knee extended several inches above mine. The jaw also was unusually large. In the grave I found long glass beads and buttons, usually seen on Indian work shirts. Several of his ribs lay in a pile with two bullets. One was fired by a muzzle-loading rifle, the other by a cap-and-ball six-shooter. When the rifle was loaded, a little square piece of well-greased muslin was laid across the muzzle of the rifle. The bullet was put on the cloth and both were forced down the barrel

111

with a ramrod. Regardless of what the lead bullet had penetrated, it showed the impressions of the cloth's fiber. I identified the six-shooter bullet by the marks of the iron ramrod which forced the bullet into the cylinder on top of the powder. I concluded that at least two men had killed and repulsed his attack. He must have been buried by white men. In such fashion did the Eagle Chief country reveal its history.

When I told the boys about uncovering an Indian grave, Jim Buzard, who rode the south line, said he had found a grave farther down the Eagle Chief. He took a spade, dug into the grave, and found a handle and steel ribs of a parasol with the skeleton remnants. The boys thought it was a great joke on Jim and said he had dug up the grave of a squaw; no more graves were opened.

Shortly after discovering the graves, I found a tomahawk nearby. It was a calumet or peace pipe—the kind I have seen Indians use at funerals or in councils. It had a bois d'arc handle and was neatly wrapped with a copper wire. I termed it a perfect job of wrapping. I carried it to camp and placed it in my "war sack."

I was turning straggling groups of cattle into the herd in the general spring roundup of 1879 when I discovered the trail of a small bunch of cattle to their previous grazing ground. When I overtook them, there lay the metal part of a copper cow bell which farmers formerly strapped around the necks of their milch cows. What astonished me was finding that kind of bell in the Eagle Chief country. No one knew how it got there. Were Indians responsible by raiding a distant frontier settlement? I took the bell to camp but lost it.

When we bunked at the headquarters, we could look northeast and see a small hilly formation which we called Table Mound. One day I rode up on top and found what seemed to be bones of an Indian pony. Among them was the remnants of an old Indian saddle. The bois d'arc stirrups were well preserved, but the crude workmanship—there was just room for his toes—showed that an Indian had made and used them. One stirrup had a bullet hole through it which might explain how the pony died.

That summer I occasionally rode toward the southwest of the range on a limestone formation of large, flat rocks. I was surprised to find broken plates, dishes, and crockery, arranged like miniature branding pens or other shapes. If pebbles and stones had been arranged thus, I would not have thought it so strange.

Several miles up the north side of the Cimarron was small Wildcat

Creek with fresh running water in all seasons. A little footbridge was built across it with wicker banisters woven of swamp willows. No one knew who had built it.

John Sparks and Leonard went down to the Glass Mountains to hunt bear.[1] Both of them lived in Barber County; Sparks lived on a claim and Leonard's wife ran a hotel in Kiowa. As they were searching in the hills, they located a bear under a large flat rock which had broken, slid from its support, and formed a passageway from one side to the other. The bear had dug out a hollow place beneath the rock where he could be hidden from view from either end of the tunnel. Sparks and Leonard examined the signs and were positive that the bear was under the rock although he wasn't in sight. Both men were good shots with their rifles, but Leonard seemed to be the better of the two from previous tests they had made. Sparks told Leonard to stand back from the rock, and he would take a long pole to punch the bear out. He got the pole in position so that Leonard could shoot it, but the bear ran between Sparks' legs and threw him astride the bear's back. All he could do was hang onto the long hair and cuss at Leonard not to shoot. He had his mind centered on Leonard who might shoot, and instead of falling off the bear at once, Sparks rode the bear out of gun range.

I only heard of two small elk bands in this southwestern country. One was in the broken country south of the Cimarron. The other ranged along the head of Driftwood Creek in southwestern Barber County. During the winter of 1879–80 Marion Hildreth[2] worked for Dave Greever along Greever's Creek west of the Glass Mountains. This creek empties into the Cimarron from the south. Hildreth was a splendid marksman with a Winchester. While riding the lines, he found a small elk band ranging among the hills and breaks adjacent to the creek. Elk are shy, sensitive to sounds, and keen of scent which makes it difficult for a hunter to approach them. Since Hildreth was experienced, he managed to kill two elk on separate occasions during the winter. They seemed to be excellent eating and their hides were useful for many things.

A short distance east of Big Timber were the blackjacks. Here were open glades—untimbered grassy areas—gathering places for wild horses or mustangs and horses which escaped from the ranches and horse herds which came up the Texas Trail.

During the summer a large number of Texas horses of numerous brands stampeded from the main herds and gathered with the wild

113

horses near the Eagle Chief, attracted by the good water, grass, and shade. The Cheyennes found them. The signs showed that a large Indian band formed a line along the north side of the blackjacks in which the wild horses were hiding. They rode, yelling, through the timber and frightened the herd out into the open country by the Cimarron. I saw the large trail where the Indians and horses crossed. The Indians pursued them to the North Canadian above Fort Reno, then claimed them.

Frank McAlister[3] of Kiowa, a very enterprising man and a horse trader, hearing about this, got in touch with several horsemen who had driven herds of Texas horses in 1879. He secured their names, brands, and power of attorney to take their horses. He went to the commanding officer at Fort Reno, presented his papers, and induced him to send out an order for the Indians to bring all their horses to the fort. When the Indians brought them in, McAlister pointed out the branded horses which he had power of attorney to take and they were turned over.

While McAlister was waiting for the horses, other Indians showed him relics of the Custer massacre. One was a drum but the Indians would not part with it.

He started back to Kiowa with the horses and got to our camp in time to eat supper and relate all these experiences. He refused to spend the night because he had no means of carrying supplies. He wanted to keep the horses going and weary. He feared to stop in the Territory; Indians might overtake and stampede the horses again.

While I was riding the line along Pool Creek which empties into the Eagle Chief, I frequently saw a large band of wild horses watering in the pools of this creek. They did not water on consecutive days but came every other day. Wild horses had signs I did not understand. When watering time came, the stallion came as fast as he could run while the others remained in the blackjacks. He whirled around, waved his tail, and ran back into the timber. He came again and repeated the same movements. Suddenly the whole bunch came as fast as they could run. They jumped into the pools of water, pawing and rolling. I do not know how they could enjoy drinking this black water they had stirred up, but it satisfied them.

I saw this herd running, apparently for exercise, in a great circle about twenty miles in circumference. No animal will leave the country voluntarily; it invariably runs in a circle. I could see them only

114

part of the time, but the dust cloud they kicked up was in view all the time.

The only way to catch one of these wild horses was to mount a fast horse and crowd the bunch so fast that a suckling colt could be cut off from its mother. When the rider rode between them, the colt would take after the horse and rider. The rider slacked his speed to the colt's and took it to the cow corral. One of the 3 boys did this very thing. He gave it cow's milk; it soon learned to eat biscuits and became a great pet. He then sold it for $10.

In the eighties some cowboys tried to catch some of these wild horses. Men were stationed a half mile apart as they rode out where the horses ranged. The man who was to start the horses encircled the band and forced them to run past the stationed men. When the horses approached the first man, he pursued them under whip to the next man who did as the first one had. In the meantime, some of the wild horses began to lag, but the old stallion always kept behind them and forced the stragglers to keep up with the herd. As the stragglers increased in number, the stallion could not keep all of them together. When they approached hills and gulches, the stallion suddenly threw his head into the air and began to scream, and with a reserve burst of speed he split through the middle of the herd. They seemed to know what that meant. They scattered into every direction in the hills and gulches and made pursuit impossible.

Every morning for over a week in the spring of 1879 I could see buzzards circling and lighting on the ground in the edge of the sand hills. I found where panthers had killed and eaten deer during the night before. Their method of preparation for eating was to stick their claws in the center of the deer's back and strip the hide each way, up and down the back of the deer. This caused the hide to tear easily and expose all the best flesh, shoulders and hams.

I did not see a panther that summer while riding across the Cimarron every few days to look over the best grazing ground and look for strays. On one trip I saw the trail of a panther and a coyote. I followed it back close to the bank, probably ten feet high, and found where the panther had jumped off onto the sand in the riverbed. The tracks revealed that the coyote evaded his leap and ran in circles with the old panther after him. The circles, large at first, got smaller until almost twisted into a knot. Then the coyote made a straight run out, and the panther made about three long jumps, then gave up.

I rode down to the point where the bank almost disappeared into the river, then rode up the high bank to see what had happened. All I found was flattened-out grass where the panther had rolled about. The old cat certainly had a taste for roughness to go to that trouble to get a little coyote meat.

I made further observations of coyotes and other animals. Coyotes apparently play tricks on one another like human beings. Like old lobo wolves, they have various calls. I saw a coyote that seemed to be trailing something. When he came to some broken stretches of land where banks and hollows appeared, he lost the trail. He retraced his path then finally gave up and trotted up on top of a high knoll where he sat and looked about. When he failed to see anything, he set up a lonesome howl. He heard nothing so he repeated the howls at intervals. In a few moments I heard a little, short, quick "yip" in some tall grass in a hollow. The first coyote turned his head in that direction and sneaked down into the grass nearby. I interpreted this byplay to mean that his hidden mate had played a joke on him. When he heard her answer, he was satisfied that she was alive and nearby.

When I stood guard on night-herd, I frequently heard coyotes serenading. Some nights the country seemed to be filled with them, other nights I heard not a sound. One night they were howling, far and near. Suddenly, within fifty yards of me an old lobo wolf sent us his big coarse howl, and the coyote chorus stopped—never another whimper all night. Of course I could not interpret his howl, but it was obvious that the coyotes agreed—this was his night.

Ira Howell, a cowpuncher whom I met on one of the great roundups, told me his observations of a pack of lobo wolves killing a calf. As he was riding the line one day, he saw a small herd of cattle grazing some distance from him. A large fat calf was in the herd. He saw a small pack of lobo wolves run toward the cattle which started running. The wolves formed a half-circle about the cattle and packed them close together. This strategy forced the calf to the outside. Then one of the wolves dashed between it and the herd and stopped, facing it. The other wolves drove the cattle over the hill away from the calf. Then they wheeled and came back as hard as they could run, formed a circle, and closed in from all sides. They grabbed it, tore it to pieces, and devoured it in a few minutes. Howell sat and watched the whole procedure. I asked why he let them kill the calf. He wanted to see what the wolves would do.

The young coyotes were not very attractive because of their plain brown color. I observed how mother coyotes raised their whelps. They did not suckle their young. They packed dirt around the mouth of the den, made it solid and smooth by rolling and walking around on it. This enabled them to feed their young on a smooth place without getting dirt on the food. The longer they fed on this spot, the smoother and glossier it became. Whatever game was caught, the best part was carried to the mouth of the den, chewed into a fine pulp, and dropped upon the smooth spot of ground. When the meal was ready, the feast was announced to the whelps. They came and lapped it up.

The young badger was the prettiest of all the animals I saw on the range—one just old enough to get out of the den and play in the sunshine. I do not know how many comprise a litter but I have seen as many as a half dozen playing around a den.

All cowpunchers held the badger in low esteem because he failed to re-fill the holes he dug when he uncovered and ate a nest of young gophers. Numerous horses and cowhands were injured and some were killed. I suffered a broken arm, cracked ribs, and an injured knee. Despite these injuries I have long believed the badger's virtues exceed his vices. One will never find a live rattlesnake near a badger den. Even if such a snake is coiled and ready to strike, the badger uses its hard spadelike claws or front paw with lightninglike rapidity and stuns the snake with a blow on the side of its head. Before the snake can recover or recoil, the badger seizes the snake back of its head and pierces its vital organs.

If a badger is attacked some distance from his den, he relies on his large hide—four sizes larger than his body—thick hair, heavy claws, good teeth, and a sickening odor to defend himself. When a badger runs, he looks more like a tumbleweed than an animal. It takes a mighty nimble cowpuncher to keep up with one when both are on the ground.

During mating season I have seen two male badgers engaged in fierce battle because one of them meddled too much with the other's love affairs. First they rushed at each other, then circled around in a bantering manner. They finally stood on their hind legs and carried on a most scientific boxing match. When those straight spadelike claws landed on the opponent's head, it was wasted energy; but when one landed a fierce blow on the other's nose, the latter doubled up, tucked his nose under his body, moaned, sighed, and groaned like a badly hurt

117

child. To scent a nest of young gophers underground, the badger must have a delicately equipped and high-powered nose. His nose, therefore, is the one vital body spot. The conquering badger rushed back to his love's warm embrace. Since the badger is a modest, reticent creature, he slid down to his dark room below.

Once I crossed the Cimarron to the old ranch to see if any cattle had strayed back. I came to a little stream which emptied into the Cimarron. It had no running water, just pools. The first one was black as ink and the water was in motion as if boiling. I thought I saw about twenty heads popping up, sniffing for air. I pulled out my six-shooter and rode up. One animal ran up the creekbed under tall grass and I could not see what it was. Then another ran straight up the high bank opposite me. I shot and it fell into the water. I got a stick and raked out a beaver. I felt ashamed; it had such nice fur. There were only two beavers and they were fishing. By stirring up the mud, the fish would have to come to the surface to get air.

In summer I rode through a prairie dog town when the wind was high. In the middle of it was a buffalo wallow filled with a rank growth of bluestem grass. I happened to ride near the wallow and a coyote jumped out of the grass a few steps. The prairie dogs were barking at me. This town was so large that many dogs were ranging in the open on the outer edge of the town and were unaware of me or the coyote. He had slipped into the grass during the night to get a dog. As he ran, he snapped up one without slackening his speed. To keep it from biting him, the coyote threw it into the air time after time and always caught it. When he missed the last try, he ran a few yards, then stopped to look back at me. When he saw I was not chasing him, he ran back to the dog, picked it up, and loped off, doubtless it was dead.

Prairie dogs seemed to keep this spot sacred, for it was visited often and kept clear of grass. Whenever a prairie dog came to this spot, it stood on its hind legs, threw its front paws as high as it could reach, uttered a screeching cry, and then went its way.

In the center of the average-sized prairie dog town was a burrow, surrounded by a larger pile of dirt than the others. Numerous coarse pebbles and sand indicated this burrow extended to the water level. The large dog towns were apt to have two such burrows. Regardless of the distance to water, it seemed the dogs could reach it.

I have seen rattlesnakes try to enter a prairie dog burrow. A number of dogs gathered to keep him away. When he started to crawl, a dog grabbed him by the tail and pulled him back. I have seen burrows sealed tight with dirt. A man who resided near a dog town for many years told me if a rattlesnake got into one of these burrows to swallow the puppies, the adult dogs entombed the snake. It was impossible for a snake to dig out of a deep-tunneled burrow completely filled with solidly packed earth.

One morning about 4 A.M. the first bleak winter wind came blowing down. The cook arose and got breakfast. While we ate, Bill Hudson gave our instructions for the day. Three or four men took the wagon, team, and supplies and started southwest to establish a line camp in a dugout near the head of Sand Creek which flowed north into the Eagle Chief. Hudson told me to go southeast, use my judgment how far east, but get ahead of all cattle which might be drifting south. I was to go as close to the Cimarron as I thought advisable then turn up the river and go far enough west to catch the west drift of the herd. Hudson told the others to send someone to see if I needed any help down in the Cimarron country.

When I got ready to start on this trip, I put on all the clothes I had, buckled my six-shooter outside for I thought should it be needed, it would be needed badly. It had been a long time since anybody had been through the country which I was to ride that day. The cattle seemed contented and I did not see any of them until about 4 P.M. That was a small bunch of about thirty head traveling directly south. The wind roared and whipped about me all day long, but it was at my back for the most part. I turned the cattle north, facing that wind, and found a game trail which led toward a timber grove of elm, hackberry, and cottonwood near some large barren sand hills which had protected the trees from fires. These elms were the largest of this kind I had seen. The largest one must have been six feet in diameter. It had long limbs reaching in every direction making a great spread of its top but the tree was not very tall. It was so still and pleasant to be out of the wind that I slackened the horse's pace to a very slow walk, but the howling wind through the tree tops made a great noise.

When I rode opposite the giant elm, I heard a great clawing and scratching on the opposite side of the tree, but enjoying the calm so much, I made no attempt to see what had caused it. One large limb extended parallel to the game trail. I had not observed anything strange or unusual. While I was under this large limb, a dead limb, three or four feet long and about two inches thick at its base, fell and

119

struck me on the head. I looked up and less than six feet above me was the largest panther I had ever seen. His big yellow eyes were turned toward me and he was switching his tail like a cat ready to pounce upon a rat. I spurred the horse up the side of the big sand hill above the cat as quickly as possible. I grabbed my six-shooter, aimed, and pulled the trigger.

As I rode up the hill, the old panther leaped to a higher limb in an effort to keep above me. After I had fired the shot, the panther slackened his speed, and one hind leg seemed to be swinging helplessly. I beat him to the top of the tree and sat, looking at him. He uttered no screams or growls but spat like a cat. It sounded like a cow's snort. Heretofore I had often shot from this horse while running but he paid no attention. When I fired a shot from his back while he was standing still, he reared on his hind legs, quick as a flash. When the panther climbed as high as he could, which was just level with me, I put the gun down on him and fired. But the horse shot into the air and I missed so I changed tactics. The panther was slowly crawling toward me on such a small limb that he could scarcely cling to it because of his broken leg. I put the gun out as if to shoot, and the horse reared on his hind legs again. When he realized that I had not shot, he did not jump as high the second time; he just tossed his head the next time. By then the panther had gotten to where the limb forked into two smaller ones. He placed a paw on each and prepared to jump. I was anxious to get the horse quiet so I could make another good shot. When I threw the gun down for the last shot, the horse stood perfectly still. I caught the panther's head through the sights and pulled the trigger. He plunged forward and split the two limbs apart so they hung straight down. He tumbled to the earth and rolled, clawing and kicking, down to the foot of the tree.

George Cunningham had been sent down into the hills to meet me, heard me shooting, and saw me fire the last shot. He rode up and we sat there, looking at the panther.

"If you'll hold my horse, George, I'll go down to where he is," I said.

"You ain't such a fool as that, are you?" George asked.

I thought the panther would be as good as any Indian that had been shot as many times. I filled the cylinder again, cocked it, and walked to the panther. I gave him a swift kick to see if he would move. He did not seem to notice, so I took him by the tail and gave a hard pull—still no sign of life. I told George to bring the horse down. The panther looked like a powerful, dangerous animal as he lay stretched full length. Knowing how swiftly he had moved around a few moments before, it seemed we were still taking chances to be on the ground beside him. I looked where I had hit him first and why the leg was so useless. It was stretched at full length when the bullet hit the flank. The bullet came out at the bottom of his foot without breaking the skin between the two perforations. The killing shot went through his upper lip, smashed the large tusklike tooth, hit the point of his lower jaw, shattered it, and went into the hollow of his neck.

The panther was dark blue, mole-colored. The fur was the finest I had ever handled. We skinned him as we would a cow, rolled the hide up, tied it to the saddle, and took it to camp. We showed it to the boys and told them what a monster the panther was. The hide measured six feet; it must have been nine feet from tip to tip.

TEN

The Winter Trapping Expedition of 1879

Frank Tracy and I found game abundant along the Cimarron and Eagle Chief. We first established our camp south of the Cimarron, northwest of the site of present Fairview, near the Glass Mountains.

In December after shooting quite a lot of our ammunition, we decided to take off a day to reload our empty shells when it would be better to remain inside the dugout because of bad weather. We had a fire burning in the fireplace. Tracy spread a blanket smooth on the bunk and poured several pounds of powder in a pile on the bunk. We had no way to extract the exploded caps from the empty shells so we tried to pry them out with our knives which was slow work.

Tracy said, "I'll fix them."

I sat on the edge of the bunk between the fire and the pile of powder but took no notice. Suddenly there was a terrible explosion. Fire, smoke, and dust filled the dugout; coals of fire hit me. I jumped to my feet, shook off the coals, and saw the coals burning a hole in the blanket all around the powder. We got the fire off the bunk first. Tracy had filled two shells with water and had put them in the fire to blow out the caps by the force of accumulated steam. The caps were not loosened and the empty shells were ruined.

One day while both of us were there, Chief Dull Knife walked in and gave us a friendly salute, "How, John."[1]

He seemed unable to speak English. We couldn't speak his language, but we could use sign language well enough to communicate. He wanted something to eat, but I soon convinced him we also were looking for something to eat and had nothing to hand out. He wanted to know if there were many deer. I informed him they were few and far between and we were going to move in a few days.

Dull Knife was not what his name might seem to indicate. His motions were as quick and flashy as a panther in action. Sitting facing us in the dugout, appearing to be in deep study, he suddenly said, "How!" and shot out the door. That was the last we ever saw him.

We crossed the Cimarron and made our quarters in an old dugout which the ⅋ outfit hadn't used for a year or two. It required only a few shovels of dirt to patch the roof. Since it had a fireplace and chimney, we had only to gather firewood which we dragged to the dugout by a rope fastened to the saddle horn; soon we had enough to last the winter. In a comfortable dugout we did not need to burn much wood for heat but merely to cook our meals. Since it neither rained nor snowed throughout the winter, the wood was always fit to use without any special preparation.

We specialized in furs such as opossum and raccoon which was in abundance. We also tried to get coyote pelts. We had no traps so had to use poison. We took wood blocks, cut holes in them, took heated tallow, mixed strychnine with it, then placed the bait at convenient points in a semi-circular course facing our dugout. As we rode out to establish our coyote line, we carried our poisoned chunks of wood. Attached to our saddle rope, dragging behind, was the carcass of a small animal. When we arrived at a suitable place, we laid a chunk of wood on the ground with the poison preparation facing upward. It was staked fast to prevent animals from dragging the bait away.

Sometimes we would find a dead coyote with his nose lying against the block. Since he couldn't reach the tallow in the holes, he would stand and lick at the bait until the poison killed him. More often when coyotes began to feel sick from the poison, they staggered as far as they could go before death overtook them. Some went into fits and jumped high into the air; occasionally a coyote would overcome the effects of the poison and get well.

Ike Berry, an old plainsman who was in charge of the outfit awhile during that winter, rode across the range to see how conditions were and saw a coyote stand and lick at a poisoned block. Suddenly the coyote went into fits and Berry rode to it. The coyote quit kicking and lay on his side, apparently dead. He had such a fine looking tail; Ike thought it would make a good tassel for his bridle. He dismounted, took out his knife, picked up the coyote's tail, and cut it off close to its body. The shock of losing his tail brought the coyote out of his stupor. The coyote jumped and ran out of sight, but Ike sported a fancy tassel on his horse's bridle for awhile.

The coyote pelts came in so slowly that we decided to go to the Eagle Chief not far distant. There we found a number of opossum and raccoons. The opossums, seldom found in trees, had their dens in

123

brush heaps and small holes on the ground. The raccoons were fond of living in hollow trees. We would locate one large enough to hold raccoons. They appeared to have plenty to eat for all were fat.

We found one tree which was too large to fell with an axe. The hollow, about twenty feet from the ground, went down through the heart of the tree lengthwise. To reach the opening the raccoons had to climb to the top of the main body of the tree where the limbs had broken off. There were claw marks, dirt, and mud which indicated that this tree was in constant use. We decided how to proceed. Tracy said he would tie a rope around his waist, climb the tree, and if he needed the axe, he could pull it up with the rope.

When he arrived at the top and looked into the hole, he said, "If the hole has any depth, there must be a dozen in here for it is full to the top."

He wanted to shoot the raccoon which he saw. I told him not to for the blaze of the gun would ruin the fur. I asked him if he could pick up the raccoon and drop it down to me but wait until I could find a suitable club. I laid aside our shotgun and rifle and stood at the foot of the tree with club in hand. Tracy reached into the hollow, took hold of the raccoon's fur on the side of his body, and dropped him to the ground near me. He was curled up, so sound asleep he did not awaken until he hit the ground. As he raised his head to see what was the matter, I hit him across the head and killed him. Tracy reached for raccoon number two, who also was asleep, and dropped him to the ground where I also clubbed him to death. This was the fate of five more raccoons. When Tracy pulled out the seventh raccoon, it seemed to be as sound asleep as the first one. We concluded this was the proper way to hunt raccoons.

They fed on snails, fish in shallow streams, hackberry seed, and roots of certain plants or shrubs. Usually hollow trees held only two raccoons. When we used an axe to cut into a tree, the noise invariably awakened the raccoon which, if it jumped out of the tree, would start running away and sometimes escape.

When raccoons, opossums, and coyotes became scarce around our second camp, we rode farther west up the Cimarron. I saw a blackjack grove, nearly circular in shape, covering about 100 acres. It was the only grove which seemed to have acorns because of the dry summer of 1879. I rode into it to see what was there. According to the signs on the ground, I first thought somebody was herding a flock of sheep in that vicinity. I looked into the trees and saw they were loaded with acorns. The small bushes were twisted and broken by animal horns. I rode back and told Tracy I had found where all the deer were. We aimed to approach this grove about daylight each morning. If the wind blew from the north, we approached from the south and vice versa. We were able to keep ourselves well supplied with venison.

It was December and the fur traders sent representatives among the cow camps to buy furs. These agents came from Kansas, and the furs were shipped to Kansas City. Since Tracy and I were well acquainted at the Ŧ headquarters, whoever was there told the traders where we were.

Later a trader drove into our camp. We had four deer, drawn and hanging in trees beyond reach from the ground. The trader offered us $2.50 for each deer and for what we could kill by the time he returned. He bought some of our furs and I offered to sell him my large panther hide. He did not know what value to put on its skin. I told him to take it along and pay me what it was worth after he had sold it.

When he returned, he had only fifty cents for the pelt. All buyers admitted the fur was fine, yet they objected to the thickness of the panther hide which would be difficult to dress down. I had not thought about this feature until the trader had put the panther skin on the market. We couldn't get deer as fast as we had expected and didn't have any more carcasses to sell. Panthers had found the deer. Also the deer became so shy that it was more difficult to stalk them.

Early one morning Tracy rode to the grove, dismounted, and slipped carefully into it to get a good position to shoot deer as they entered. Just before he went in, he heard something running through the dry leaves but he couldn't see what had made the noise. He waited awhile, thought over the matter, and decided it could not have been a deer. He walked down toward the place from which the noise seemed to come. He found a great pile of leaves and trash looking as large as an ordinary shock of hay. He stood and looked at it a moment, cocked both hammers of his double-barreled, number eight shotgun, and walked carefully up to the huge pile, for he never had seen anything like that. With both fingers on the triggers he poked the muzzle of the gun into the leaves and began to shove them aside. He discovered the carcass of a deer. He took out his strychnine bottle, applied a liberal dose of poison, and re-covered the carcass. The next morning both of us found it uncovered with all of the bones picked clean. We rode all

125

over the adjacent country, looked for the panther carcass, but never found him.

Next spring during the general roundup of the Southwestern Stock Association, Frank Garretson came to me and wanted to know if I was the man who had hunted in this country during the past winter. I said I was one of them. He asked if we had poisoned any panthers. I told him we had tried but didn't get the job done as we had never found him. He had found a dead panther. I asked him its color and told him about the one which I had killed in the autumn of 1879. Garretson said it was evidently of the same size and color; perhaps these animals were mates.

After we had moved across the Cimarron, Tracy's brother-in-law, Hank Heizerman, a Pennsylvania Dutchman, and Wiley Cowan,[2] an old retired cowpuncher who also lived on Cowskin Creek near Wichita, brought two wagon loads of shelled corn down to sell to the ⅃ ranch. Then they came over to our camp for a visit. They had four horses and we had four. We staked out two of our horses and turned all the others loose. Heizerman and Cowan thought their horses wouldn't attempt to leave since they had been worked so hard during the day.

Heizerman was one of the jolliest men I have ever seen, ready for anything to have a little fun or some sort of devilment. While we five men visited in our dugout that night and talked over our experiences, he told us about digging a stock well. He had contracted with a man to dig it and a Negro, called "Guinea," to windlass the dirt from the well.

Heizerman's wheat field extended close to the barn. The wild geese lit and grazed on the wheat. He had a large number eight muzzle-loading shotgun with which he killed geese. One of the dogs on the hammer of one of the barrels would jar loose when the other barrel was fired. To have some fun he put extra loads of powder in each one of the barrels and told the Negro to pull the trigger which would discharge both barrels.

The geese generally came mornings and evenings. Heizerman loaded the gun, leaned it up against the barn, and went into the house to wait for the circus to begin. Directly a flock of geese lit close by the barn. The Negro picked up the shotgun, stepped out away from the barn, and turned his back toward the open well. He took aim at the flock of geese and pulled the trigger. The discharge knocked the Negro into the well on top of the well digger.

Cowan told us that in 1874 he had come up the old Texas Trail with a herd of cattle. They camped along the south bank of the Salt Fork for noon. Kit Carson,[3] the famous plainsman, was also camped there with an outfit. This was just about the mouth of Medicine River. Cowan had just gotten dinner ready when he looked around and saw a large number of Indians riding widely scattered without any formation, west-southwest, straggling through the country to the northwest. Some rode up to Cowan's camp and asked for something to eat.

The boss said, "Give 'em everything they ask for; they'll get it anyhow."

Cowan started cooking in heat. He was about worn out when another bunch rode up. He grabbed up some flour, put nothing else in it but water, threw it into a bake oven. When it was sufficiently baked, he pitched it out onto a blanket where they were squatted. One old Indian picked it up and tried to break it; that made him mad. He threw it at Cowan and struck him in the face. Wiley grabbed up an old buffalo gun to shoot the Indian, but the boss who happened to be there grabbed the gun. The old Indian jumped up, pulled his shirt open, put his finger on his heart, and pointed at Cowan. The Indians finally rode away.

That night both outfits camped together. Cowan remarked he never was so surprised when he saw that bunch of Cheyenne Indians ride up.

Kit Carson said, "Young man, never be surprised to see Indians in an Indian's country."

Something scared the horses during the night; we heard them break and run. The next morning Cowan and Tracy got on our two horses and started on their trail. They never overtook them until they got to Kiowa; they were still on the road.

Heizerman was peg-legged. He had one leg amputated about half way between the knee and hip. He had no artificial leg but used a hickory stob with an iron band at the bottom and a small spike in the center to prevent slipping on icy ground.

We knew Tracy and Cowan would be away about all day, so Heizerman said, "Let's go a'hunting!"

We got our guns and started. We walked from early morning until at least 4 P.M. He was just as jolly and full of fun as he was when we started out. As the day began to lengthen, I began to feel sorry for him and mention how tired we were.

He laughed the biggest way and said, "Just think of the fun we're having."

127

Nothing was big enough to shoot at all day. We made it back to camp all right and ate our dinner and supper all at one meal. Tracy and Cowan never got back until long after dark.

The next morning when Heizerman, Cowan, and Charley Collins, a neighbor boy who had come down with them, got ready to start back to Wichita, we told them if they went through the blackjack grove we had found, they might get a shot at some deer. Tracy gave Collins his number eight shotgun and I took my rifle. Collins and I rode around to the opposite side of the grove. I showed Collins one place where deer might leave the timber and rode around to another place where deer passed in and out. We dismounted to watch for deer at both places.

After awhile we heard the two wagons coming; then I heard Collins shoot. I knew then there was no use to stay and watch any longer. I mounted my horse and rode back to Collins.

He saw me coming, jerked off his hat, and began to wave it in the air and holler, "I killed the biggest buck I ever seed!"

As the wagons came up, Heizerman motioned to me to come to his wagon, "What was the first thing he said when he shot the buck?" I told him. He took a big laugh, "That's all I wanted to know." Then he began to torment Collins.

Men who had been in cow camps long found it difficult to adapt themselves to the conventions of the settlements. Many funny stories were told and they were received with loud, hearty laughs. When Frank Tracy and I dissolved our hunting and trapping partnership in February 1880, we went to Medicine Lodge and Tracy went to the Heizerman home near Wichita. Tracy met his future wife there and they attended church services at times.

One Sunday the preacher was trying to illustrate that contentment was the main thing in life, not the acquiring of wealth. He told a story of a widow with several children to support. When cold weather came, three of the children were on a bed with only one quilt. They complained about it being too light, so the mother laid some thin planks of lumber over the quilt. They commented how much more comfortable they were.

One poked his head from under the cover and asked, "Mother, how do poor folks get along who haven't got any planks?"

At this point Tracy exploded with loud haw-haws, not realizing his cowpuncher training had gotten him into a social blunder until he felt his lady's elbow jabbing him in the ribs.

"My, but I was ashamed. You could have lit a candle with my face," he later told me.

While in Medicine Lodge I worked for Charley Curry,[4] who had a small ranch on the eastern edge of Medicine Lodge on which he built a large house, barn, slaughtering pen for hogs and cattle, and a catch pen. The pens were back of the feed lots. He bought fat cattle to butcher, along with a few hogs. He never scalded nor scraped the hogs but skinned them.

He had a butcher shop run by his father-in-law, Mr. Petit, on Main Street in the north part of town. The butchering was done on Charley's farm. The animal was driven into the catch pen up a narrow chute. A large hempen rope was dropped over its horns, fastened to a windlass, and it was dragged into position to be struck on the head with a heavy hammer. When the beast fell, its throat rested over a slanting trough. Its throat was cut and the blood ran into the hog trough.

Curry had come up the Texas Trail in 1869 and settled in southeastern Kansas for a few years. In August of 1876 when the last herd of buffalo passed through Indian Territory to the edge of the settlements near Kiowa, Curry conceived the idea of starting a buffalo herd of his own. He roped six buffalo calves and took them to camp, but the weather was too hot and all of them died.

One day Curry told me he had a fine black mare to sell me from a herd of thirty horses he had purchased from some Mexicans for speculation. He believed they were "wet," which meant they had been stolen and driven across the Rio Grande.

We went to the corral; he pointed out the horse, "There she is. Isn't she a beauty? Her name is Mag." When she heard Curry call her name, she ran to the fartherest point of the corral, acting wild. He said, "Mag, come here," but she acted wilder than ever. Then Curry popped his whip on the ground, "Mag, come here, I tell you!" She ran to him. He held out the bridle and she took the bit in her mouth. He put the bridle over her ears, dropped the reins to the ground, petted her, and picked up one of her feet. She acted like a worn-out horse. I told him I was not in show business and could not use her.

Curry and I rode to the Triangle T, better known as the ⧾ ranch, in March and bought some beeves to butcher. The foreman, Sam Fling, told me I could soon get employment on the ranch. During the first week of April when the grass greened considerably, I rode to that ranch and went to work.

129

ELEVEN

Working for the ⇑ Ranch

Frank Bates was the owner of the Spade ⇑ ranch.[1] It lay south of the Salt Plains; the northeast corner was in the Salt Plains. The headquarters dugout was very small, and one of my duties with the other cowhands was to enlarge it to keep step with the growing outfit. Bates did not yet have a large herd; he had but one regular man besides me, Tip McCracken.[2] Tip, Sam Fling,[3] Fayette Thomas, and Jerry Frey had all come up the Texas Trail together in 1878 with the first and only herd that Bates brought from Texas to establish the ⇑ ranch. In the spring and summer of 1879 I saw these men frequently. Thomas quit the ⇑ ranch in October 1879 and returned to Texas to see his widowed mother. Frey returned to Texas in 1878 after he delivered the herd. Thomas came up the trail again in 1880, then went to work for the ⇑ outfit with me.

I had worked only a short time when I took sick and was down for at least two weeks. I could scarcely eat and became weak and thin. Sam Fling, the foreman, became uneasy about my condition. He asked if I was using my real name for many a cowhand was using an alias. He inquired about my parents' address.

Fling was trying to teach a young fellow from Kansas City how to cook. Just across a small stream of water from our tent, a shepherd bitch had a litter in a hole in the creek bank. I had just gotten so I could sleep; one day when all were on herd, I was asleep on a pallet in the tent with the edge raised a little to let in fresh air. The cook came in, sat on a box, and began to call that slut as loud as he could yell. I was badly in need of sleep; this dog-calling awakened and made me mad. Worse still, the dog, hearing his call, ran through the water, and seeing the tent flap raised at the head of my pallet, ran across my face. I yelled at the dog to get out; being gentle, she lay down beside my pallet. The cook then roared at me to let that dog alone.

He had said if I ran the dog out of the tent, he would "beat my head off." My six-shooter lay within reach; my heavy Stetson lay over it. I slipped my hand under the hat, grabbed the pistol, and cocked it. I drew both next to me. He saw only the hat moving. As I raised it, I tucked the gun behind the blanket. I brought the hat down with all my strength against the dog and yelled, "Get out of here!" She left in a hurry. The cook jumped to his feet, looked at me for a moment, then turned and walked out. He had not seen my gun with my finger on the trigger.

That night McCracken came to camp. While I was ill, he always called at the tent when he came into camp to see how I was getting along and bring water and other conveniences for me. The next morning he would leave me whatever he thought I would need. I told him we lacked just one step of being without a cook. I told him what had happened. He cut loose with a volley of oathes, "Why didn't you kill him anyhow?"

When Fling came in, Tip told him about my trouble. Fling assented he would take up the matter with the cook, for he wanted to get rid of him anyhow. The next morning Fling saddled up a horse and told the cook to gather up his belongings. Fling took him to Timberlake's camp. This left me alone during the day, which was better than before.

A few days later a southwestern desperado, Bill Anderson,[4] came along and stopped overnight. He wanted to know what was ailing me and how long I had been sick. He was cured by a similar illness with the patent medicine, August Flower. He rode to Kiowa, about thirty-six miles distant, to get a bottle for me. The next day he came back with the medicine. I, too, seemed to improve and it was not long until I was able to go to work.

In the meantime, the horse which I had bought from "Gus" Johnson wandered off. No one knew where he was. I told Anderson and he said, "As I was coming up the Texas Trail, I met a fellow I knew, and he told me he had a stray horse that came from the north down the trail."

The fellow told Anderson if he found anybody who had lost such a horse to write what he would take for the horse and he would send a bank draft. I had paid $25 and Johnson had given me a bill of sale. I wrote that I would take $25 and enclosed my bill of sale. Soon I got the return for the horse.

Frank Bates was friendly with all of us but did not enjoy camping out. He liked to be with us when we were cutting out beeves. On one occasion he hitched Bob and Dirk, his favorite horses, to his top buggy and drove out where we were at work. He motioned to me, "Don't you think I could drive Bob and Dirk into the herd and pick out a beef just as good as you?"

131

"Frank, you know what would happen if you made a dash at a steer with the team and buggy; you'd have a stampede!" I replied.

Realizing he still wanted to cut out and could not ride my horse, I agreed when he suggested, "You ride in and pick out a beef and drive him out to the edge of the herd. Then I will dash in behind with Bob and Dirk and drive him on out."

He followed the steer out and did a good job, but the next time it frightened some of the steers and the herd became uneasy. The boys began to grumble and "Texas Dave" Thomas said Bates ought to be stopped. I told Dave, John Watkins (a boy who came up the trail with this herd), and some of the others to let him proceed for we were working for him; he was paying us. Soon Bates saw that he was not doing much good and quit.

We got the beef herd out off the range before time to camp. Bates drove up to the grub wagon, unhitched and unharnessed Bob and Dirk, and turned them loose among the saddle horses. "I'll have to lay my bed under the wagon to keep off the dew so I won't catch cold," he said when bedtime came.

I suggested, "We'll make too much noise and wake you up. You had better sleep under the buggy." He agreed; I arranged a wind-break and helped fix his bed so he would be sheltered.

When I returned to the wagon, Watkins remarked how funny it would be to pull the buggy away and leave it among the nearby sand hills. "You will not," I warned him. "You are apt to lose your job. Out of respect to my employer and a desire to see you continue your job, I refuse to let you."

"I'm entitled to a little fun once in awhile," Watkins complained, but he dropped the prank idea.

When Bates crawled out of his den the next morning, he stretched, twisted, got up, walked around, and felt himself. He remarked with evident pleasure, "I never took a particle of cold last night. I was terribly afraid I would."

Bates stayed with us until we got across the Salt Fork, then said, "I'll drive on ahead and make a kind of party of it. I'll tell the people in Caldwell you are coming with a herd of beeves. Several of them will drive out with buggies and teams."

"Now look here!" I said. "I'll have perfect control over the steers and my men but you'll not control the mob. Some will get in the way and cause trouble." He changed his mind.

Bates always delighted in great displays. Once I met him at the Arlington Hotel in Wellington, Kansas. When we finished our conference, he picked up his ornamental cane, put on his silk hat, "Let's walk up and down the sidewalk a little bit; you walk a step or two behind and to one side so everybody can see us!" We walked a block up the street, crossed over, and came down to his brother-in law's real estate and land office. "Bill, this is one of my 'punchers!'"

"Yes," McDonald said and went on with his writing.

I played into Bates' hands. Noticing some large turnips and pumpkins lying on display in front of the office I asked, "Were those apples raised in this country or were they shipped in?"

"Why they're not apples," Bates pretended amusement.

"I was just wondering what kind of trees they grew on."

By this time the agent and his customers began talking among themselves. Bates told them he had sold his Wellington property and invested in a small ranch in the Strip.

"How large is it?" someone asked.

"It contains only 75,000 acres with 5000 cattle," he replied.

I returned to the ♁ ranch and told Sam Fling about the fun we had. "That's old Frank," he laughed heartily. "He's great on the display."

In June 1880 I was riding the line with Tip McCracken. As we came out from dinner one day, we saw a heavy cloud moving toward us; the storm struck the cattle and drove them out on the Salt Plains before we could get to them.

As we were riding north, Tip at my left, a bolt of lightning passed just over our heads, struck the ground right beside his horse, and made a tremendous report. His horse reared straight up on his hind legs and appeared to be falling backwards until McCracken placed both hands on top of his head; then the horse came down again on his four feet. McCracken felt as if his face was on fire. He turned toward me; it was very red.

We overtook the cattle far out on the Salt Plains and turned them back, but the storm soon passed over. Thereafter, rains came regularly and streams began to fill with water.

This June the southern cattle began to arrive on the Texas Trail. Bates sent word for Fling to buy a herd of young cattle as the grass had begun to grow. One day while Fling was watching the trail, he saw a herd driven by Kingsbury[5] and Dunson, 1400 yearlings from Fort Worth, Texas, and he bought it.

133

We had to night herd for awhile to keep them from mixing with the winter herds. Later the rains came so often that we had a tough time trying to herd day and night. We were close-herding—John Watkins, John West,[6] Sam Fling, and I. Whenever it stormed of nights, Fling and I were usually together as long as it lasted. Watkins and I herded during the day and bedded them against a high bank. The high bank was caused by another bend in the creek which deflected the water.

On top of this bank was a pair of owls, white as snow and pretty as could be. I showed them to Watkins and told him we should take care of them if they needed any help, should the bank cave in. They had small horns like a horned owl, large yellow eyes, and a bright red ring around each eye.

One day we were near this bank when Watkins, being close to the owls, pulled out his six-shooter, and shot one of them. When he picked it up and saw what a lovely bird it was, he became terribly ashamed. The mate left immediately; I never saw it again even though I was in that part of the country for some years thereafter.

I was sent out to ride the south line, watch for through herds to keep them from coming through our herd, and turn them into the new trail, which was established in 1879 and led northwest, up Eagle Chief Creek.

One day I saw a herd coming, rode down to meet it, and told the boss to turn it up the new trail. I told him where there would be plenty of water at Pool Creek and other watering places farther up the trail. The old trail was now blocked at the Kansas line by new settlements, fenced in pastures, with numerous small herds.

Another day I met a herd of big beeves coming up the trail, went to the foreman, told him my story, and directed him. He began to tell me his troubles. When they arrived at the Washita River in Southern Oklahoma, they camped for the night. He set out double guard because he had observed that rain was threatening. Instead of an ordinary rain, a "cyclone" struck. He saw four-year-old beeves forty feet in the air, whirling around like leaves. He could not understand how any of his men or cattle could live in such a storm.

When daylight came, the cattle were rounded up as well as could be, and he discovered he had lost forty head. Some were killed, others crippled, some unaccounted for. He sent a man back to report to the ranch where the herd had originated to get an outfit to come gather up the beeves that were able to travel and take them back to Texas.

I asked why he didn't stay over another day, gather up the beeves that were able to travel, and bring them along.

He replied vehemently, "We stay there another night? No! Supposin' another one of them things come along. It'd wipe us all out of existence." I told him it was unlikely another such storm would pass along that same route in a thousand years. He would not live to see another one like it.

John West and I were on herd one afternoon when it was approaching time to turn the herd toward the bed ground to get there before nightfall. I saw he was not pushing against them to turn them, so I rode around to see what was the matter. I found him lying on the ground and saw his end of the herd was grazing out toward him away from the bed ground.

I said, "John, it is about time to turn them back to get them in on time."

He said, "Let them come a little closer and I'll show you something; we'll have a little fun."

When the cattle got within about twenty-five yards of him, he raised up and began to swear. In a moment after some really loud oaths, the whole line of steers had turned around and were walking in the right direction. Then West had a hearty laugh. This was the first time I had ever observed the manner in which swearing affected and controlled cattle.

West was a happy, good-natured fellow but found it convenient to have more than one name. When I met him in the spring of 1879 on the ₮ ranch, he went by the name, John Dugan. He had come up the Texas Trail in 1878 with "Red Neck" Brown who had married an Osage Indian and was the father of Charlie Brown, later a prominent man in Osage country.[7]

I met "Red Neck" Brown after I quit the range. I asked him if he remembered John Dugan, now John West. He replied, "Yes, he was a good cowhand but was very peculiar."

A freak accident happened on the ↑ ranch in November 1880 with a small black horse which was good for all purposes, nice and gentle. This horse's specialty was to fall in such a way to throw his rider loose, then jump up and run back to camp. The farther from camp, the better it seemed to please him. Tip McCracken was using this small horse as one of his regular mounts. He was riding the north line of the range, six or seven miles from camp. The cattle had begun to crowd out farther on his line which kept him out sometimes until after dark.

135

Near night a norther came up, he was a long way from camp, and the horse was anxious to get back. McCracken knew what would happen if this horse managed to fall and throw him off.

The practice of a cowpuncher when his horse fell was to allow the horse to throw him as far away as possible to prevent being struck by the horse's feet. McCracken made up his mind to stick right tight to this little horse if he did fall. The horse made two or three attempts which McCracken frustrated.

When the horse finally made his tumble, he picked the wrong place. His back was a little downhill and McCracken's leg was under him. McCracken thought he was getting the worst of the bargain after all as things began to look pretty blue. The horse couldn't get up, McCracken couldn't move, and a blizzard was coming. He would prefer to be afoot and walking to camp rather than lying with a leg under that horse in a blizzard. If he could make that horse kick by catching its upper hind leg, the horse would roll his body, and McCracken could work himself out. So he made a sudden grab into the horse's flank with one hand, the horse kicked forward, McCracken grabbed the leg with his other hand, then threw both arms around its leg and pulled it as far as he could into his arms, but the horse wouldn't kick.

This put another idea into Tip's mind. He doubled down with his mouth and teeth set in the horse's shin bone and began to gnaw. The kicks began to come pretty free and fast. He reached around and finally got his arm through the bridle rein, then resumed gnawing on the horse's shin. As the horse jumped to his feet, he found McCracken was holding the bridle rein. McCracken got to ride to camp after all and he had something to tell his grandchildren.

In November Sam Fling, another fellow, and I took a wagon and span of horses apiece, which was the custom on the range, to get supplies and corn to feed the few saddle horses which we kept to ride during the winter. On our return journey we stopped at McPherson's camp, about half way back to the ranch, and stopped on a high knoll for the night. We spread our blankets under the wagon because the weather was so mild and we were used to sleeping in the open. It was so warm while we were in Caldwell that I forgot to buy a pair of overshoes.

About 4 A.M. a norther struck; I was practically barefooted. The high wind drifted snow into the low places and traveling became difficult, but the snowfall stopped in the forenoon. We did not attempt to travel until afternoon.

136

Before the snowfall stopped, a boy about fourteen years old came riding up on a big work horse and said his mother, a widow, lived in Kansas where corn was only twenty cents a bushel. She, according to the boy, had heard that corn could be sold for fifty cents a bushel in the cow camps. He and his little ten-year-old brother were coming to McPherson's camp with a load of shelled corn. They had gotten within about a mile of the camp when night overtook them. We asked how the little boy was standing the cold weather. They had taken plenty of bedding with them and the little boy was comfortable. This was a rather severe test for boys of such tender years to be sent down into this country at that time of year. I had known of grown men freezing to death on such trips.

Our next stop was at Timberlake's camp. I rode with my feet wrapped in blankets. I had to get into the snow to unhook, feed, and water the horses. By that time my feet were frozen so stiff I could scarcely walk up a small rise to the dugout.

When I entered, I told Ervin Timberlake my feet were frozen. He had a bucket of fresh spring water which he poured into a large pan, then helped me pull off my boots. He told me to put my feet into the water.

I said, "Erv, I can't get my feet into that cold water." Timberlake, a large fellow, reached over me, took me by the legs, and stuck my feet into the water. I sat there and it was a pleasant sensation. I thought my feet looked peculiar; however, I felt them and found a thin scum of ice.

I said, "Erv, come here and feel my feet."

He put his hand down into the water, felt them, then said, "That's sure getting the job done."

In a little while I felt my feet again and there was no ice. I continued to hold them in the water but they began to feel cold. I believed they had been in the water long enough.

He asked, "What do you do when your feet get cold?"

"I go to the fire and warm them," I answered.

He said, "You have reached that stage so try it out."

When we awoke the next morning, we had ten miles yet to go to get to the ✞ camp. I got a couple of burlap sacks, wrapped my feet, and did not suffer any bad effects.

We left Timberlake's camp as early as we could because we had several bad places to cross. We did not know how deep some of the drifts might be. We did not encounter any serious difficulty nor have to

137

use double teams. We arrived at our camp before night but we had to travel slowly. We exchanged positions whenever a good stretch of road appeared, so one team would not have to break the road all of the time.

Young Short,[8] who brought up a small Texas herd during the summer of 1880, made arrangements on the 우 ranch to winter. He established his camp on the south line and was riding that line when the November snowstorm came. Shortly after the storm Short saw a strange-looking object aside from the line. He rode toward it and found a man doubled down in a peculiar shape. He never noticed until Short began to talk. He told Short his feet and some of his fingers were frozen when the storm first struck. He traveled as far as he could go and had to crawl most of the time. He had given up all hope of finding assistance and was trying to write in a little memorandum book who he was and where he resided. His name was Bates and he ran a restaurant in Anthony, Kansas.

Short lifted him onto his horse and took him to his camp where he had a two-gallon can of kerosene. He laid the man on a bunk with his feet sticking out over the edge, wrapped burlap sacks around them, set a pan below to catch the dripping kerosene which he continually poured on the man's frozen feet. I do not know whether this was the first treatment of this kind or not; at any rate, it was successful. When I saw him next June, he showed no effects of his terrible experience.

Bates had merely decided to take a vacation trip without having any definite object in mind. He traveled in an old-fashioned, open spring wagon with a good horse and mule. When he came near the blackjacks in the breaks of Turkey Creek, night overtook him. It was warm; he tied the mare to the spring wagon and turned the mule loose.

When the storm struck, he ran up and down a hollow to keep warm. He unwittingly ran farther out and lost the location of his team and wagon. A fire broke out and burned the wagon, harness, and all his effects. The mare was badly burned but the mule escaped. The snow put out the fire before it burned much of the range grass.

Bates returned to get his mare the next June. She had run on the range so long that she could not be caught. There happened to be enough men present to round up all the horses and hold them until we could rope her. Bates tied her to the side of his driving team. We turned him around and showed him the timber grove at the mouth of Medicine River where it emptied into the Salt Fork at Major Drumm's ranch.

We rode off but Sam Fling looked back, "Look where that blamed fool is going." Fling turned to me, "Go stop him, show him that grove, and tell him to keep it in sight."

I overtook Bates and repeated Fling's instructions. As far as we could see, he seemed to be going right. That night about 10 P.M. he drove into the camp of Bill McMillan, one of Major Drumm's foremen,[9] about seven miles up Salt Fork from his headquarters. When Bates told him his plight, McMillan sent a man with him down to headquarters and put him on a road that led directly to Anthony. We later heard that Bates took nearly two days to get home, though it was only a half day's drive from Drumm's headquarters. He vowed never again to cross the territorial line by himself.

It was no uncommon thing to be caught out after darkness. Fling told me he got caught on the wrong side of the river. There was no timber, but he found enough driftwood to keep a little fire going between his knees all night. He knew the way to camp; but there was too much snow in the gullies to ride, get his horse down, and be in a worse predicament than to sit by a little fire all night.

On another occasion Fling and Wheeler Timberlake rode down the Cimarron as far southeast as the present Dover, Oklahoma. They stayed one night at a cow camp and got a late start the next morning. It had snowed and drifted badly. When they couldn't make headway or arrive at their destination as they had calculated because their horses were exhausted, floundering through the snowdrifts, they decided to stop and rest their horses until morning. There was a large dead tree at the spot with other dead limbs around. They cleared off the snow, built a fire, and when it subsided, they raked away the coals and ashes and laid on the hot ground. They left their saddles and saddle blankets on their horses and tied them in a sheltered spot among the trees. Before morning the ground had cooled and they were awakened. They got up and made an early start.

Later brother Frank came down to the ⚕ ranch from Medicine Lodge to get my help. He had taken 800 head of cattle to winter besides the cattle which he and I owned. He had sold the yearlings which we had driven from Chautauqua County in 1879. I went with him because Young Short was riding the south line for the ⚕ ranch and my foreman could get along without my help.

TWELVE

Medicine Lodge and Ranching in Barber County

The first time I saw Medicine Lodge, the county seat, was in 1878. I found the public well in the middle of main street with a good wooden curb over it. The water was pulled up by a long rope around a pulley wheel fastened to a crossbeam which rested on two supporting upright timbers, firmly fastened to the curbing below. The two rope ends were tied to wooden buckets. One rested at the bottom of the well, the other at the top. As the filled bucket was pulled up, the empty bucket descended to the water. A large wooden water trough stood close to the well curb so livestock could drink. The person who drew up the water could empty the bucket into the trough without untying the rope.

Before drilled wells were used, an open-dug well was usually the first public enterprise in early-day settlements of the Southwest, usually located as central as possible so all citizens could be served. The well in course of time had to be cleaned out as silt and refuse collected in it. It was a great inconvenience for those who had failed to have a supply of water on hand.

The wind was blowing a gale as I rode up to water my horse and drink. A fine looking young man came out of a nearby house with a bucket in his hand. We talked awhile and then I asked, "Does it blow this hard all the time here?"

He replied, "I don't know; I just got here from the East, yesterday. If I thought it would be blowing this way all the time, I would leave tomorrow."

In 1880 a man came to Medicine Lodge with a well drill which made a hole eight inches in diameter. He drilled wells as near the residents' doors as they desired.

Tom A. McNeal was editor of *The Medicine Lodge Cresset*[1] and boarded at the McCanless restaurant. McCanless was a tall, slender man. His wife was a well-built woman, a good cook, and a tidy housekeeper. McNeal's paper told about the new well driller and the eight-inch hole which it made. He added that McCanless would have a monopoly on cleaning the wells, as he was the only man in the city who could descend into these wells to clean them out. This issue was in Mrs. McCanless's hands before McNeal came for his evening meal. Just as she finished reading the well story, McNeal walked in to get his dinner. He was met with a shower of cups and saucers. Mrs. McCanless said, "I want you to understand you cannot put slanderous remarks about my family in your paper."

In the next issue of the *Cresset* appeared a humorous article, "War between China and the Scots. China won a smashing victory and the Scots have fled in great disorder." Other funny expressions, coupled with the thought that her hasty action caused the loss of a steady cash boarder, caused her to let him know the war was over and peace was restored.[2]

In March 1882 an agitator drifted into Medicine Lodge and started his mouth running to anyone who would listen to the rattle of his empty head. Some of the boys decided they had enough of his prattle, so they laid plans to get rid of him. Some wanted to tar and feather him, then ride him on a rail. Businessmen opposed the plan for fear it would injure the city's reputation. They were told to see editor McNeal who considered the proposal seriously, then suggested Frank Records could chair a meeting and challenge the men to a debate. If advertised as a political meeting, women and children would not appear. McNeal then asked Barney Mann to be present to give help. Mann, a Swiss bachelor and great lover of children, was well-educated and always participated in religious and educational matters.

Brother Frank called the meeting to order. He presented the rules to govern the debate and asked the agitator to lead off with the subject of foreign immigration. The time allotment was given. At the end of the speech McNeal was to speak and neither speaker was to interrupt the other during the debate.

It was held at the outskirts of the town in a building which was lighted by some old lamps that some of the boys had furnished. The evening was warm and the windows were open. The agitator took his time limit and advocated the removal of restrictions against all nationalities. McNeal, who took the opposite side, made the most ridiculous statements as to what would happen, how this country would be filled with things we couldn't use. He happened to know the year when Mann came across the Atlantic. He began to give the dimensions of a huge ship, a mile long and a half a mile wide, loaded to near sinking

141

capacity. This was too much for the agitator who said, "I don't believe it; I never heard of such a ship."

Tom turned to Mann and said, "Isn't that so? That's the year you came to America." Mann replied that it was.

The agitator asked, "What was it loaded with?"

Tom replied, "With Dutch and kraut."

This caused such a laugh, the moderator thought it was time to let the meeting blow up. He arose and spoke in a loud voice, "I command disturbance here!"

Three or four men picked him up and slipped him through a window as the agitator looked on. The boys began shooting out the lights. With the moderator gone, the agitator became so nervous he made a quick get away through the door. Just then one of the boys began crying out that he had been shot. Then the others began to yell, "Stop that fellow, he was the cause of the shooting of this fine man, hang him to a limb!" This gave wings to the agitator's feet, and no one was able to catch sight of him again. Everyone seemed to be well-satisfied with the debate. I couldn't see much difference between this procedure and the one which the merchants had disapproved.[3]

McNeal gave rather humorous lectures in various parts of Kansas. He sent word to Adrian Reynolds, editor of the *Sedan Times-Star*, that he would be in Sedan and asked Reynolds to publish a notice of the lecture in his paper. Brother Charlie attended this lecture and he thought it was amusing and instructive. Reynolds did advertise it and referred to McNeal as the "funny" man which did not suit McNeal. He wrote to Reynolds the definition of a funny man as someone who had a silly grin on his face, trying to attract attention and did not know when people were making fun of him. Reynolds put McNeal's definition in his paper, then added, "Well, Tom is a funnier man than I thought."

McNeal was associated with the Capper publishing company of Topeka, Kansas, for many years.[4] He traveled extensively for the company, both at home and abroad. He appeared in Cuba, Haiti, and the Philippine Islands and wrote interesting, descriptive articles about the habits and customs of the citizens of each country. He had more vision and concern for the future than other young men who came from similar environments and wrecked themselves or sank into obscurity. By his own efforts he made a marked impression on his fellow men and was a model for others.

The regular gathering place for visiting cowhands was the saloon.

The Medicine Lodge saloon building was long. The bar in front at the left of the entrance had the usual brass foot-rest. Back of the bar was the dance floor and the dance orchestra occupied the balcony above. In 1884 I entered the saloon and a loud voice greeted me from the balcony. I looked up, saw, and heartily greeted "Terrapin Jim" Wilson and "Cap" Johns. I was with Wilson both in 1878 and 1883. They had been with Henry Brown and Billy the Kid in the Lincoln County War[5] of the seventies. They had their arms around each other and held a mug of beer in their hands. A large schooner of beer rested on a small table in front of them.

"He is a good friend of mine. Give him anything he wants!" said "Terrapin Jim" to the bartender.

"Just for that, I'll take a glass of beer!" I agreed. I held up my glass and they raised their glasses. "Long life and happiness to both of you!" I said.

"The same to you!" they replied.

We poured the vile-tasting stuff down our necks. I walked out and never saw them again. Johns secured a claim in the Cherokee Strip near Kremlin[6] and lived there until his death.

Stanley Parsons was a ranchman in Barber County in 1878. His neighbors, Hocraft and Russell, had a large ranch.[7] One day Parsons said to Hocraft, "If you'll come over and eat Thanksgiving dinner with me, I'll give you something you never tasted before."

Hocraft said, "All right, Parsons, I'll come over." Parsons got a big dinner comprising beef, potatoes, and other things. After they had eaten and were visiting, Hocraft said, "Stan, you got me quite a good dinner but I didn't notice anything I hadn't eaten before."

Parsons replied, "Well, did you like the beef?"

Hocraft answered, "Sure, it was well-prepared."

Parsons then said, "I told you that I would cook something you had never tasted before, didn't I?"

Hocraft said, "Yes."

"That was one of your yearlings!"

Hocraft exclaimed excitedly, "Stan, you don't aim to say you butchered one of my yearlings, do you?"

Parsons replied, "Sure, I promised to give you something you had never tasted before."

Then Hocraft said, "Well, I see, I think you ought to have sent me a quarter of it anyhow."

143

Every slicker or maverick, and there were many of them straying about, usually was slated for destruction; it was the custom in the cow country. Hence Hocraft could afford to take the joke in good humor.

After selling our two-year-old steers in Barber County, brother Frank went over into the Cherokee Nation south of Coffeyville in late 1880 and bought 125 head of yearling steers from Abe Mills who had originally bought them in the Choctaw Nation. Tom Jones had come up the eastern trail with a Texas herd and was working for Mills. When he sold this herd to brother Frank, Mills decided he would not need Jones any longer so Frank hired him. It was not permitted to cross the Kansas border. They stopped at farmhouses for meals and slept with the yearlings.

The only unpleasant incident occurred west of Caneyville. While they were eating supper with a settler, Dick George came and asked who they were and where did the cattle come from. "Don't you stay here tonight," George said when Frank told him. "Move right on. We have lost enough cattle with Texas fever. If you don't start right now, there will be twenty-five men with shotguns to visit you. They will hang you and kill all the cattle."

"I know all about you and your dirty bunch!" Frank replied. "You hanged innocent men in the early days! You tell those murderers I have the same saddle gun which was issued to me to shoot wild Indians. I will be ready when you come!"

The farmer's wife heard what was said. "That is the way with him, always trying to stir up trouble but he won't come back," she said as George rode away. Her prediction came true.

When Frank and Jones arrived at Jonesburg, they bought twenty cows and the herd was harder to handle. Brother Charlie, who had just returned from Manhattan, Kansas, where he was a student in the state college, joined them and made the trip to Barber County. They also took 500 head belonging to P. H. Chapin.[8] They established their camp on the east bank of the Medicine River south of a range of sand hills and cottonwood trees. When they arrived, fine weather prevailed, and the cattle were contented with the plentiful supply of grass and water. Frank and his two helpers rode to a point south of Cedar Mountains and began to repair an old abandoned camp for their winter quarters, while they occupied a summer camp where the herd grazed. A snowstorm came before they finished.

When Frank and I arrived at Kiowa that November, I bought a pair

144

of arctics for snow still lay on the ground. As we rode out of Kiowa, Frank showed me where his camp was.[9] At the first river crossing I turned off the Kiowa-Medicine Lodge road, and Frank rode on to Medicine Lodge to let Mr. Chapin know he had help. Frank, Charlie, and I had contracted with Chapin to use part of his range and care for his herd during that winter.

Whenever I came into the neighborhood of P. H. Chapin's large, pretentious home 1½ miles east of Medicine Lodge, I rode in, put my horse in his barn, fed, watered, and took care of it as I would at any cow camp. Very few ordinary cowhands would do this. I was welcome as a member of the family. They always invited me to sleep at their house, but since they had a well-equipped bunkhouse in their large barn, I slept there. Chapin's boys slept there, too, save during the winter.

Chapin, formerly of Illinois, dealt in fine horses and bought the cattle herd as a side line. His brand was a backwards L connected to a D ₋D. He was well-equipped with lots, corrals, and snubbing posts. If he wanted his stock handled, he would have me attend to them. He had one $1100 stallion which he brought from Illinois, along with several good driving horses, which he took to Wichita and other cities to exhibit at fairs.

Chapin kept his best horses in close pasture where they could be handled every day. The stock horses for sale were allowed to run in a larger pasture and these, I was obliged to rope. My method of roping these young stallions was pretty rough for I would rope their front feet as they ran by. As the horse fell, it would kick forward with its hind feet and throw one of its hind feet through the front feet. Then I half-hitched this upper hind hoof with the front feet which threw three feet in a bunch well-bound together. I was free to use the knife easily and in a few minutes the young stallions were changed to geldings.

Every cow outfit always had someone who could use the knife in an experienced way to change young bulls into steers. This job was not as serious or risky with cattle as with horses, but many cowpunchers never learned how to castrate or brand cattle. The owners of those herds or their ranch foremen who could depend on employees to perform these operations entailed a considerable saving when they need not hire so-called experts.

In branding cattle most anyone could take a red hot iron and slap it against an animal to make a scar or a blotch, but it took experience and

145

knowledge to make it perfect. When a person set a red hot iron against the animal, it would smoke. When an experienced person placed the hot iron against the animal, he would watch the change of smoke, then quickly remove the branding iron. An inexperienced person might hold an iron until it had burned through the hair and hide both without noticing any difference in the smoke, causing a blotch and scar. One later could not tell what the brand was. The color of burning hair was different than that of burning hide. The hide would not be burned or scarred, but the hair roots would be killed along the stamped form of the letter or device. This caused a sticky substance to collect around the face of the branding iron. To guard against that we kept a thin side of bacon lying beside the fire which heated the irons. When the material was observed on the branding iron, it was pressed against the side of bacon, then transferred to the fire which burned the branding iron clean again. This procedure, plus the knowledge and judgment of the branding man, was not only a quick but clean method. The animal hide would make as good leather as did the one which had never been branded.

Some of the cattlemen decided to spay their heifers, for they discovered such animals would usually bring more on the market than steers. Their flesh seemed finer-grained and more tender, according to the experience of the packers and butchers. The spaying of the female cattle was not new; it had been practiced in the settlements with domestic herds.

Early that summer Chapin had bought 800 head of cows and heifers, a wagon, and a span of gentle mules from Arkansas from S. W. Lard.[10] He had driven leisurely west across the Arkansas River through timber country to the prairie. He released all but two of the drivers. Lard, a quiet, shrewd man, knew a small force could handle a grazing herd which would pick up weight. There was no need for bridle lines to drive the grazing mules which hauled the wagon behind.

One day a fellow dashed up and demanded, "What do you mean by grazing over my land? Why haven't you got an outfit capable of driving them along?"

"I didn't think there was much need to hurry," Lard said in his usual mild manner.

"I'll show you whether you will hurry or not! I'll give you to understand I'm a son of a bitch from Texas!" the man roared.

"I expect you have given your pedigree all right, but I am from Arkansas and my mother was a woman!" Lard replied.

146

This mild shot caused the fellow to look him over. When he saw Lard holding his six-shooter in his hand, he wheeled his horse and dashed away faster than he came.

Tom Jones had agreed to stay until I came from the ranch. He rode to my brother John's residence in southeastern Kansas and became ill of pneumonia. Realizing he could not live long, he gave John his mother's address. John notified her that her son was at the point of death but she could not come. Father visited and talked to him many times about his soul's salvation and he confessed Jesus as his Savior. He told Father to write to his mother that he had accepted her faith and hoped to meet her in heaven.

The camp was most uninvitingly situated. In front of the pup tent a huge pile of logs was burning which looked as if it would temper the wind to a shorn lamb as well as a cowpuncher. After the snow melted, the dry sand sifted like gritty flour around the east side of the sand hill. When we turned our heads west, a more vicious puff of fizzle dust struck our faces. I was determined to get out of here at once. When asked where, I replied we could not find a worse place and suggested we go to the dugout on the south side of the range. There we could catch the drift of the cattle as we worked on the winter camp.

We found a large wooden keg, filled it, drove to the winter camp site, looked over the surrounding range, and found a deep washout in Cedar Mountains filled with water which a small flock of wild ducks was using for winter quarters. When I rode into and up some of the canyons, I observed why the hills were so named. The farther I rode, the more numerous were the cedar tree stumps. Some were so close together that there was danger of a horse getting a foot fastened between two of them. All the trees had been sawed off close to the ground; the stumps were six to ten inches in diameter, some even a foot. The earliest settlers told me that in the heyday of cedar-post cutting, men drove forty and fifty miles to cut them. Some cutters had been ex-buffalo hunters. During my survey I do not recall seeing a single live cedar. It is strange how destructive that civilization has been, but they were enjoyed and used. Farmers used them to fence their claims; others sold them to feed and clothe their children.

We soon got our winter camp shipshape and established our lines with respect to adjoining cow outfits. We boiled the gypsum water, let the lees settle, and poured it into the water keg for drinking and cooking. When gypsum water is frozen to the streambed, one can see a

147

mineral substance layer between the ice and mud. When the ice melted, we discovered water, pure as rain.

On the west side of Medicine River was a settler named Reynolds with a small herd of shorthorn cattle. They crossed the river, tasted the fine buffalo grass south of Cedar Mountains, and refused to stay on their home range. Reynolds sent for my help. The morning I rode to meet him, his wife, and two boys, I found the cleanest dugout I had ever seen. The fair-faced Reynolds came to the door wearing an apron; his hands showed that he had been making bread. He asked me to dinner which was the best I had faced for some time—roast beef, sweet potatoes, fresh butter in nice-looking rolls. Reynolds came from the East for his health, couldn't ride a horse, so did the house work, milked cows, skimmed milk, and churned butter while his wife and young sons farmed and took care of the livestock. He was worried about his cattle running on our range, but I told him not to worry about it. They just walked through and grazed to the south. They seemed to know they were better than our common stock and did not go to water two days in succession. If stormy weather prevailed, they returned in a trot!

That cold winter I wore a skeleton cap, pulled down to cover my face completely. I had made-in eye holes to give perfect freedom of sight. The snow remained on the ground from November until late February. The cattle wintered well because the wind swept snow from the buffalo and winter grass. One day while the snow was melting and when a stiff breeze was blowing from the north, I rode through a prairie dog town and saw a large rattlesnake curled up in the mouth of an old abandoned dog burrow. The sun was shining and within a few inches of the snake lay a pile of snow.

Although we believed our water was absolutely pure, Frank became seriously ill with a bad kidney infection and we took him to the doctor in Medicine Lodge. Mr. Chapin took him home for several weeks.[11] When he was able to travel, he returned to Peru. There he met Addie Kelso, the girl he subsequently married.

Chapin was wealthy and his wife was interested and participated in all social affairs of the town. They had three boys—Frank, Luke, and Neal. The family subscribed to magazines and more than one newspaper. When Neal was five years old, he sat down alongside his mother and read the newspaper headlines while she sewed, knitted, or did other work which would not make any noise. When he read a headline which appealed to her, she said, "Read that article, Neal." Once in awhile he struck a rather large word which he couldn't pronounce and she told him to spell it.

The Chapin's oldest son, Frank, worked in the Medicine Lodge bank when Henry Brown and Ben Wheeler raided it in 1884.[12] He had just gone to the post office with the mail, consequently, he escaped. The Chapins had a piano which Mrs. Chapin and Frank played. If cousin John was present, we listened to music as good as an ordinary orchestra as he had formal musical instruction. John Chapin had a well-modulated voice and was a splendid singer. He sang nearly all of the popular tunes without any score sheet or word, but his singing moods were like his drinking moods. He might not drink a drop of liquor for a month, but once he began to drink he did not stop until he was completely out. He sobered himself by coming to his cousin's home and working at hard labor. They admired his good qualities.

John had been prominent in Illinois politics as a member of the state legislature. A bachelor and former Union soldier, he stopped in Arkansas for a few years on his journey west, but he was out of his element there. He later operated the store at Red Fork on the stage coach line crossing on the Cimarron River.[13]

He got into heated discussions at times, and one hot-headed fellow got wrought up and challenged him to a duel. John was accomplished in the use of firearms with three years' practice in the Union army. His judgment prevailed on him to keep out of a duel. He tried to argue the fellow out of it, but nothing else satisfied him.

Finally he agreed to the duel. They would be bound by the duelling rules of the day—one was to choose the weapons; the other, the distance. The Arkansas man was to select the weapons, Chapin the distance. The Arkansan called for Navy Sixes.

When Chapin was asked the distance, he replied, "800 yards." These guns were effective only at 100 yards. This brought a loud protest from the Arkansan. He suggested they reverse the order; the seconds agreed.

When asked the distance, the Arkansan replied, "Ten steps."

They called for John's weapons. He said, "Squirt guns!" This brought a roar of laughter from the crowd, much to the discomfort of the challenger.

John told me another story of some fun he had with a full-blood Cheyenne Indian who could talk a little broken English. The Indian

149

came into Chapin's store at Red Fork and told him he wanted a tablespoon to take a dose of quinine and a cup of water to wash it down. Chapin told the Indian to put the quinine into some other ingredient to overcome its taste.

The Indian replied, "No! Doc. Noble say good!" Chapin let the Indian put a heaping tablespoonful of quinine into his mouth then stood in front of him to see the effect. The Indian spat it out, "God damn, shit! Doc. Noble, heap big lie!"[14]

THIRTEEN

The Roundup of 1881

Green grass began to appear along the Chikaskia and Frank returned just before we held a neighborhood roundup. We cut out and counted the strays; thirty of our cattle were missing. Since there were no settlers along the stream, the first cowman to appear got first choice.

In the March 1881 meeting of the Southwestern Cattlemen's Association in Caldwell, Abner Wilson, Major Drumm's foreman, was elected general roundup captain with numerous duties. He was to map out the country, tell where and when to begin to work the Strip to the best advantage, prepare a diagram of each one's holdings, and decide which way to go, once the roundup was started. He was to watch the progress of the cattle as they rubbed or licked off their winter coats. When brands could be easily discerned, he was to announce the time to start the roundup.[1]

Frank was still weak from his illness and unable to ride. He and Chapin decided I should take the two mules and wagon, along with my regular mount, and attend the general spring roundup. I was to ask five or six cattlemen near Medicine Lodge to go with me. One would be the cook and drive the mule team. Our Barber County outfit included Fred Bunker, Fred Dudley, Henry Goddard, Charlie Meigs, Jim Springer, and Jim Wilson, a group of fine men, with the exception of myself.[2] We met in front of Lon Little's store in Medicine Lodge, filled the wagon with grub and feed for the mules. They had sold out of stake rope for the mules, but supplied me with hobble rope which was heavy, hard, and disagreeable when tied about their necks. I was given a vote of thanks by the crew when they saw how nicely these previously stubborn mules led.

Outside Medicine Lodge we followed the road to Old Kiowa, drove south into the Outlet, crossed the Salt Fork below the mouth of Driftwood Creek, then followed the old Texas Trail to the military road that led to Fort Cantonment.[3] We camped along Spring Creek and after

151

dark John Melrose and Fred Little, two other Barber County cattle-men, joined us.[4]

We turned all the saddle horses to graze until after supper. The two late-comers unsaddled and tied thirty-foot ropes around their horses' necks to turn them loose. When they walked among our horses, the dragging ropes caused a stampede which left us afoot, except for the hobbled mules. The next morning Jim Springer and I saddled them and followed the horses' trail. It crossed the Cimarron to the south, turned west near Deep Creek, and we overtook them near the present site of Homestead, Oklahoma, returning late that afternoon with no losses.

Since none of us knew where the roundup outfit would meet, Jim Wilson and I rode to Fort Cantonment and arrived around noon. It had been erected in the spring of 1879; there was no hotel or restau-rant but there was a government store. We purchased some cheese, crackers, and sardines for lunch and rode back to camp since no one else appeared. The outfit finally came and we began our work.

The young Cheyenne Indians there were still sore about the treat-ment they had received from the hands of the government, and it did not take much agitation to stir up trouble between them and the whites. A young Indian claimed a horse which a Texas cowpuncher, George Jones, was riding. When the argument had ended, the young Indian was badly beaten over the head by Jones's quirt. Word scat-tered among the Indians. They began to put on their war paint.[5]

As we started up the Canadian River, a small detachment of soldiers escorted Amos Chapman, a government scout, upriver to the Chey-enne war council. The soldiers were mounted but Chapman was afoot. He had been shot through the thigh in the battle of Buffalo Wallow a few years before.[6] His thigh bone was never set and it stuck out so far from its true position that he was unable to ride a horse. Although he had a bad list, he walked at a good rate of speed. They were moving along the south bank of the North Canadian opposite us; we were just pulling out from our camp.

Chapman saw us. Without slackening pace, he yelled, "You fellows had better be pulling out of there. We're going up to the Indians' war council to try to talk to them. If I can't persuade them to keep the peace, they'll be right out killing every white man they can."

Just to have a little fun, I yelled back, "Bring on your Indians; we'll kill all we can of 'em."

152

There was no Indian outbreak and that was the last time I saw Amos Chapman. He was a good interpreter and had married a Cheyenne. He died a few years ago near Cantonment.

When we worked the Cherokee Strip, instead of taking one general cut, each wagon represented a smaller territory of only two or three ranches. The cuts then were not so large and hard to handle. As these cuts increased in number, the actual number of cattle was kept down because they were being dropped out to the ranches where they belonged.

We followed the Canadian River as far south as Fort Reno, looking for the cattle drift from Kansas and the Strip. I saw one of my associates, John Smith, ride into the deep current and drown his horse, but he swam to shore. I asked what the matter was. He said the horse couldn't swim.

When we left the Canadian, we turned north toward the Cimarron, through as rough a country as I ever saw. As we began to leave the high, rocky hills and approach the Cimarron, we found traveling much easier because of small streams that emptied into it from the south.

Charley Curry of Medicine Lodge and I were riding together. We saw a black bear come out from under a big flat shelving rock and start running ahead of us. Curry said, "Let's rope him."

I told him I hadn't lost any bears. I yelled to Bill Mills, a reckless fellow, to help Curry rope the bear. They soon had their ropes on it and took it along to the point where we stopped for noon. They linked four trace chains together, long enough to stake out the bear. If they had used ropes, the bear would have bitten them in two.

Curry and Mills took the bear to the wagon to which Mills was attached and butchered it and a yearling, as it was their day to kill a beef for the entire wagon train. When I went to Mills' wagon to get our share of meat, they asked me if I wanted bear or beef. The bear looked too much like a dead dog so I took beef. The boys who took bear meat said it was good.

Clem Powell from our outfit had been in bear country and knew something about their habits. He said, "Come on boys, let's go up to that flat rock," from which the old bear had run; he believed there were cubs there.

The noise of our horses' feet on the rocks and turf near the rock frightened the four little cubs, which were the size of a grown house cat. They climbed up a big, dead cedar tree which stood at the back

153

part of the rock. Powell told all of us to get around the foot of the tree; he would climb up and drop the cubs down. When he started to climb, they began to squall. When he got in reaching distance, he took them by the back of the neck, like a cat carries its young, and they let go of the tree. He reached them down toward us as far as he could before dropping them, for fear of hurting them.

The first one dropped to the ground and the nearest fellow picked it up. When he tucked it into his arms, it snuggled up contentedly as a kitten. After this the boys would catch the cubs as Clem dropped them; they neither bit nor scratched.

These four cubs were the loveliest pets I have seen. We took them to camp; they would play and wallow on the ground. They were distributed among different wagons; Sylvester Flitch's outfit got two.[7] Powell was with Flitch and each had a cub. They did not lose much so far as food goes when they lost their mother, for they were fed sourdough biscuits and plenty of beef. They were gentle as kittens until they were thrust alongside a wagon, or anything they could climb. Then they became wild as ever, screaming and fighting.

While we were cutting the herds along the North Canadian, we threw all of the Strip and Kansas cattle into one big herd and brought them over to the Cimarron River. One man was sent from each wagon to take one two-hour watch on night herd. The wagons were strung along at about fifty-yard intervals. I went from the Barber County outfit and took one guard. We met at Sylvester Flitch's wagon.

The fellows who had no assignment would come to Flitch's wagon to play with the bears. Once in awhile a fellow would pick up one and put him where he could reach the wagon wheel and it would begin to squall, bite, and scratch. Then Flitch would halloo, "Hey, you fellers, let them bears alone."

On the way north to Barber County we crossed the swollen Salt Fork. Smith had no trouble here because the horses waded mostly, and only an occasional hole would cause our horses to swim. The next stream was Driftwood Creek.[8]

I told the boys we should hurry to cross before it could pass fording for we could see a heavy rain up toward the head of the creek. The rest thought there was no need to hurry, but I rode ahead to see what the prospects were for a good crossing.

At the highest point I looked upstream. The creek was out of its banks and coming fast towards me. I took off my hat and waved for

154

them to hurry. I rode downstream ahead of the flood and crossed to the north side. I was then in a position to stop the horses in case they got scared and wanted to run after they crossed the swollen creek.

The other fellows hurried the horses and got them across in time, except Smith; he got into deep water. I then saw he could not ride a horse in a swollen stream. When he got a little past the middle, he raised up into his saddle and jumped over his horse's head into the deep water and swam ashore. This frightened his horse which turned completely around and swam right back to the wrong side of the creek. I took the rope from my horse and walked back to the bank where I thought Smith would come out. When he plunged in with all his clothes on, I thought surely I'd have to rope and pull him out. When I saw he was making it safely, I pretended I was going to rope him.

It made him mad to see my heavy, water-soaked rope. As he got in reach of an elm limb, he pulled himself to the shore and yelled, "Don't you dare hit me on the head with that wet rope!"

When he got out, I told him we had better catch his other horse, its mate. It neighed to the mate across Driftwood with the horse herd. We got a rope on his other horse and started to leave. The horse with the saddle jumped into the stream. By that time the water was running nearly over the elms which we had "rode" under. As he got there, the saddle horn caught on one of the limbs, but he was on the downstream side of the tree. The force of the water carried him clear and he swam out safely.

Continuing northward, we worked all of the ranches in groups. After Barber County we stopped in Pratt County which was being rapidly settled. When we approached a ranch, we scattered to round in all the cattle to work the herd. Those which did not carry any of our brands were left. If any of our brands appeared, we took charge.

Branding longhorns was always dangerous. Pat Gallagher of the Comanche County Pool was branding cattle one day on the L U ranch on the open prairie.[9] He was holding down a cow while others branded her. As a cow fell to her side on the ground, it was usual for the man who was to hold her to grab the tail, pull it through between her hind legs and up through her flank in front of her hip bone, then place his knees in the center of her back, and pull with his weight and strength. This prevented the cow from catching her toes in the turf and getting on her feet. While Gallagher was in this position, another cow "come" running out of the bunch and charged to gore him. Someone hollered;

155

he turned to look just as the cow struck him. She "run" a horn in his mouth through the cheek just below the cheek bone. It did not kill him but it left a bad scar on his face. This made the boys mad and they roped the cow which had done the hooking and "throwed" her with the branded side up. Since she was so interested in the L U, they branded her on every available space from neck to hip with L U brands. The next spring when I was on the general roundup, I "seen" this cow and asked what that meant. They told me that was the cow that had hooked Pat Gallagher.

In a similar accident elsewhere about the same year, Sam Fawcet was holding a cow the same way. Another cow charged but no one gave Sam any warning. The cow's horn struck him before he knew that he was being attacked. The horn entered his vital parts and eventually resulted in his death.

Abner Wilson managed the roundup so satisfactorily that a vote was taken at the March 1882 meeting to see what the members could give him that would be useful to show their appreciation for his worth to them during the previous roundup. A majority voted to give him a $100 saddle. They took up a collection and got a few dollars. Wilson was to order the saddle and the association was to pay for it. He ordered it but the contributions did not roll in very fast.

One of the solicitors approached Ike Pryor, told him how things were going, and asked him for a contribution. Pryor reached into his vest pocket, pulled out a quarter, and said, "There, take that to buy a horn string for the $100 saddle." And thus the contributions rolled in. I think Wilson paid at least 75% of the cost of the saddle.[10]

FOURTEEN

Ranching in Pratt County

After our stop at Medicine Lodge I took my own cut up to Sand Creek in southern Pratt County along the Chikaskia River to be with brother Frank who had moved our herd where there was plenty of water and a good range. Since the Texas Trail had been pushed farther west, there was no danger that southern cattle or beeves would be fattened here for the eastern market. This made an ideal spot for the small cowman.

Charles and I drove both our cattle and Chapin's herd from the winter range south of Cedar Mountains in Barber County where we spent the spring and summer. Chapin's herd numbered 800 in the winter, but most were heifers and calving in the spring. Because nearly all were experiencing difficulty, we were busy looking after the ones which were heavy with calf. Charles was especially helpful since he had taken veterinarian courses at Manhattan. We needed help so Chapin sent Frank, his eldest son, a splendid cook. We occupied a combination tent and dugout. It was half dugout, half sod. The tent sat inside it.

In June Charles and I separated our cattle from Chapin's herd which had sold. Near evening a man drove up to our camp in a farm wagon drawn by a span of horses. When he asked about Chapin's camp, I told him it was farther east down the Chikaskia River. He had left Medicine Lodge that morning and had not seen a human being or a place of habitation until he arrived at our camp. He would not continue alone and wanted me to go with him. I told him that it was a short distance and if he kept his direction, he could not miss Chapin's camp. He related how he had followed a highway which finally became a mere path, then a ground squirrel trail which he followed until it went into its hole. Then he knew he was lost.

I agreed to take him over to Chapin's camp. I mounted and started across the prairie in a cow horse trot and he followed. As I came to a small canyon with a slanting approach angling into the bottom and an equivalent ascent on the opposite side, I met George Smith coming

157

from Chapin's camp. Since I was some distance ahead of the man, I stopped to talk with Smith. When the man drove to the edge of the small canyon, he stopped and asked what we were doing. I replied that I was waiting for him. Still he showed no signs of driving any farther. I remarked that if he was not going any farther, I would return to my camp. He replied that he would resume travel if I would ride along. I rode on and George met him but never stopped. When we arrived at Chapin's camp, he was the best-pleased man I have ever seen.

I turned to go when he stopped me. He had a large amount of money which he was to deliver to Chapin that day and had become alarmed when he saw us talking in the canyon. He wanted to pay me $5 but I refused. He said it was hush money to take it but promise not to tell what an awful predicament and how worried he had been. Since it would do him so much good, I took the $5. As I returned to camp, I saw lightning in the southwest.

We had a few big domestic cows but the balance of the herd were two-year-old steers. I had just sold the cows and since banks were few and far between, I transacted on a cash basis. I had more than $300 in my pants pockets. We had offered to sell the steers; a man named Moore heard about it and came to look over the herd.

He arrived late in the evening and decided to stay all night, intending to make the deal in the morning. The same evening George Smith came to stay all night. We had a light camp wagon with bows and sheet; in the back was a cupboard with dishes and cooking utensils enclosed by a door, hinged at the bottom and fastened at the top. When opened, a leg strapped to the door served as its support when we let it down as a table for our meals. Our wagon stood on a knoll north of our tent. Brother and I took our grub box out and set it inside our half-dugout, half-sod house to escape the wind. We let our guests sleep in our wagon.

Our dugout faced a small canyon whose banks did not exceed twenty feet. Brother and I slept on the buffalo grass, the best bed in the world. As we went to bed, we noticed signs of rain. During the night a heavy clap of thunder and a roar of wind awoke us.

As I raised up, the wind hit; a flash of lightning revealed my pants making a hasty getaway. I grabbed a pants leg just in time to save the money. We picked up our bedding and ran for the tent. Scarcely had we gotten inside when a tornado struck. George Smith came dashing from the wagon. In a moment I heard a strange gasping yell between the tent and dugout wall. I stood for a moment, wondering whether it was man or beast. I poked my arm under the tent, felt a man, and knew it must be Moore. He was not moving. I dragged him into the tent. We pumped and rolled him around with difficulty because the storm's force had broken the ridgepole and only one end of the tent was left standing. He began to breathe again but we did not know what caused his problem. When he was able to talk, he told that he was afflicted with asthma and had come to this country for his health.

When morning came we took invoice of our effects and discovered our wagon was missing. We supposed it had been carried east or northeast, as the storm came from the southwest, but we could not see it. The storm was a regular twister, for we found the wagon southeast in the bottom of the canyon. If the wagon was moved in a direct line from where it stood to where it fell, it would have passed directly over our tent.[1]

We found sheet, bows, bedding, and clothing which our two guests left in the wagon unmolested. It faced up the canyon but the left hind wheel was smashed to pieces. A hole in the ground indicated that the wagon had been dropped some distance.

Moore drank some coffee but ate little breakfast. He was to ride down to his brother's claim. He must have decided this country was too healthy to suit him for we never saw him again.

One day while on herd along Sand Creek, I saw a man driving in a wagon from the settlements northeast of us. He was looking for a big cattle bedding ground which had been in use by different herds for a number of years. He inquired if it belonged to me. I told him it did not belong to anyone. I asked why he wanted to know. He said that cow chips comprised all the fuel the settlers had. In his settlement the price of cow chips had increased so that he could not afford to buy them. He was out searching for cheaper fuel. I asked him what he had paid. The prices had been twenty-five cents a load but had advanced to seventy-five cents. I told him a man ought to be paid a dollar a day for sitting around such a fire. He could help himself and it wouldn't cost him a cent. He was so astonished at my seeming big-heartedness, at first, that he demurred. Finally he drove over to the grounds and loaded his wagon. I sat on the ground watching him, but he seemed to be very uneasy for he kept turning around to look at me. He took only half a load and started back. This is a sample of some of the hardships which confronted the pioneer settler in the prairie country as late as 1881.[2]

159

I decided to go to Peru to buy another herd and use $300 as down-payment. When I arrived at Caldwell, I met Sam Fling and nothing would do, but I must go out to a herd of 700 mixed cattle which Frank Bates had bought from Col. Colcord.[3] When I told Fling my plans, he said to put my money in the bank until I returned from the ⊕ ranch.

I found another young man and got him to go with me. We went to "Big George's" livery barn[4] to get a saddle horse for the boy and arrived at the herd first. Colcord had hired Theodore Baughman to drive him out.[5] While we were waiting, Baughman told some of his tall stories and Daddy Colcord was greatly amused. Baughman was a thorough-going bum who thought the world and the fullness thereof belonged to him. He never missed eating a meal nor paid a cent. One of his stories went as follows:

When he was bringing a herd of longhorns from Texas, a storm struck as they were stopping for the night. The cattle became uneasy and stampeded but at last the cowhands got them back on the bed grounds. Baughman found time to ride into camp to "show the boys what an old seasoned cowpuncher could do." They were complaining bitterly because of nothing to eat. Baughman jerked out his knife, cut off a slice of raw bacon, grabbed a handful of dry flour from a sack, and rode back to the herd, eating the bacon and taking a bite out of his handful of flour.

Colcord looked at me and winked, "Boff, that's what I call a dry meal on a wet night."

Fling said he would overtake me as soon as he could. I should take the cattle and start them southwest towards the ranch. I sent the boy's horse back to "Big George" by Mr. Colcord. I caught a young, inexperienced, but gentle horse, about which I knew nothing, for the boy to ride. We scarcely got the herd under way, the boy and I on either side when going down a small hill, his horse stepped into a hole, fell, and threw its weight and the boy on its neck. I heard it crack like a dry stick. The boy jumped to his feet and began to bemoan his fate. He had not wanted to undertake the trip in the first place. Now he would have to pay for a horse. This seemed to be so ridiculous that I laughed and told him that there would be no charges against him, just unfasten the dead horse's saddle girth and take off his bridle. We turned the horse over and picked up the saddle. I told the boy to work a little afoot until the wagon came up and place the saddle in it. He and the cook took turns at scaring forward the stragglers at the rear of the herd while I pointed it in the right direction. We couldn't afford to stop for such a little thing as a horse breaking its neck.

Soon Fling overtook us. As he followed our trail, he found the dead horse. We had a few other loose saddle horses with the herd but lacked hands to get hold of one until Fling arrived. After the herd was delivered safely at the ⚕ ranch, I left by stage coach for Medicine Lodge, then back to our Pratt County pasture.

FIFTEEN

Back to the ♁ Ranch

I rode the south line of the ♁ ranch when I returned in the fall of 1881 and met the Timberlake outfit's rider. Their cattle company at first comprised of Jim, Wheeler and Ervin Timberlake (the cook), John Corbin, and Allen Hall. These men were new to the range business and did not take to hard riding. They preferred to hire someone who would not cost much.[1]

One fine morning when sounds carried far, I was riding to meet their rider when I heard whoops and yells, a dog barking, and cows bellowing. They seemed to be fighting off the dog. I rode a little faster. Soon I saw about fifty head of cattle running back into the ♁ ranch, and in a few moments I met a fellow wearing a sport cap and riding a pacing horse. He pulled tightly on the reins and kept the horse's head high. It would be unable to see prairie dog holes and apt to put a foot into one. "I am in the employment of the Timberlake Cattle Company, and they said I would meet someone that was riding for the ♁ Company," he said.

"Well, you have met him," I replied, looking him over. "Where did you get that horse?" I asked a moment later.

"Oh, the horse and dog belong to me. The dog's name is Jack," he answered.

Just then a jack rabbit dashed by us. The dog took after it and his master began yelling. "Let him alone," I said. "It's all right for one Jack to chase another!"

He turned his pacer loose at top speed, and it was laughable to see the horse sling his legs around. The dog soon stopped and the rider came back. "Did you see what a fine pacer he is?" he asked.

"Yes, I was scared almost to death for fear he would get his legs plaited together, fall, and hurt you." I answered.

He told me what he had paid for the horse; the salesman assured him the horse was but six years old.

"Yes, but he meant it was six years old when Noah turned it out of the Ark to get a bite of grass!" I commented.

162

"Oh, no! It cannot be that old," he replied. "But don't you think it will last?" he asked.

"Yes, it will last as long as your job will," I said.

"Well, I just wanted to ask you, for the horses you fellows ride act like they will eat a man up!" he commented.

"Oh, yes, they used to. But they found we were such tough chewing—most of us taste like tobacco juice—that it left such a bad taste in their mouths. All sensible Texas cow horses have quit such filthy habits." I reined my horse toward camp.

He rode back east but I kept turning in my saddle to watch him. When I arrived at camp, Fayette Thomas had ridden in. While Fling, Thomas, and I were eating, they saw me smile. "Well, what is it?" Fling asked after a few moments.

"He sure has been seeing things!" Fayette prompted. "So just begin telling it."

I laughed and told them. Fayette roared with laughter; Fling barely grinned and said, "That thing has got to stop."

"Sam, I would like to see that sight, too. We could trade lines. Be a good sport!" Fayette begged.

"We are seeing too many funny things now!" Fling answered. Sometime afterward I met one of the firm members, or something that looked like a cowman.

The Cragin Company, an eastern outfit, later bought out Wheeler Timberlake. This syndicate did foolish things such as discarding his old dugout; it was not good enough for them. They built houses and moved in some of their relatives to stay the whole year round. They built a long hall for them to entertain the eastern members of the company when they came West. They had an annual affair with a hunting expedition.[2]

The first time I ever saw Galloway cattle was when this company shipped a carload of them from the East. They were fat enough to put on the block. Some looked to be eight or ten years old. They had been pampered and fed in stalls all of their lives. I was riding past the ranch when I saw this herd of ten or twelve—some weighed 2000 pounds—standing at the gate where they had been driven in. I presumed they had been shipped to Anthony, Kansas, and driven down. It was afternoon, the sun was blistering, they were thirsty and starving for a bucket of water and a bale of hay. One was dead and the others looked as if they would not last long. No one was around.

I took time out and rode down to the cowhands who were lolling around in the shade of the house and told them their Galloway bulls were badly off, "One is dead and the others won't last long." They became alarmed and went out to the cattle. I resumed my journey and never learned what happened to the rest of the Galloway bulls.

This year I lost one of my favorite horses, Nigger Baby, because of a rattlesnake bite while we were gathering up late calves and their mothers to brand. Sam Fling told us to go out one afternoon and work the north end of the range. We made a roundup and cut out about twenty head of calves with their mothers. Fling told me to start down toward the ranch pens where we were to brand and mark the calves. He and the others scattered to look for other bunches of cattle while I took the cut. The cattle went through a ragweed patch where gophers had been working up the ground surface. I was following directly behind.

When I got into the middle, I heard a snake rattle; the horse made a quick move and began to limp. I looked down and "seen" the rattlesnake coiled, ready to strike again. I got off my horse and killed it with my quirt. Blood was dripping from the horse's ankle on his left front leg as if the snake's fangs had struck a small blood vessel. I thought it was a hopeless case, but took out my knife and scarified the hide where the fangs had entered, then cut off the snake's head and tail, split its body, took my dollar silk handkerchief from my neck, put the snake's body around the horse's ankle, and bound it with my handkerchief. I watched for the others; presently I saw Fling and waved my coat. He came riding fast to see what was the trouble, the others followed.

Fling told me to remove my saddle; we would throw the horse and burn the spot where he was bitten. This was the cowboy's sure remedy for snake bite if you could get to it in time. Fling said, "Everyone of you smokers got no matches in your pockets; how do you light your pipes?" He told me to put the saddle on the horse and ride him towards camp as far as I could for he wasn't going to last very long.

The farther I rode, the worse he limped. I "seen" he could not make it, but I did not like the idea of carrying my saddle on my back. I turned up into a winter grass flat where an old worn-out horse was grazing and rode up. Since no one had been interested in him for so long, he paid no attention until I "throwed" the rope around his neck. I pulled my saddle and bridle off Nigger Baby, put them on the old bone pile, and rode him back to camp. When I got there and pulled the saddle and bridle off, he turned and started walking back to his grazing ground.

The next morning after breakfast Fling said, "You'd better go see if Nigger Baby is dead." When I got there, he was stretched out. It was a horrible way for such a nice horse to die.

When Tip McCracken and I were riding the western lines of the ⚹ ranch, we would meet about half way between the headquarters camp and the line camp that was established on the northwest corner of the ranch. Often I had seen an antelope lying close to the line which I rode; sometimes it wouldn't get up unless I rode pretty close, then trot off, never much afraid.

One day I met Tip and told him how tame the antelope was. Since he didn't have many cattle on his end of the line, he rode back with me to get his dinner. He had his little shepherd dog with him. When we started back, we "seen" the antelope lying on the ground with its head turned around as if enjoying a good rest. Tip said, "Let's get down our ropes and run on to it and rope it." He always carried a small saddle rope which was easy to throw.

I told him, "No, we'll ride down close to it; you can get off and take your rope and walk right up and throw it onto the antelope."

Tip told me to watch the dog and not let it follow him. I got to watching Tip and forgot the fool dog. The first thing I knew, it got around in front of the horses and started trailing Tip. He was getting so close to the antelope that I did not try to stop him. When he was ready to throw the rope, the dog saw the antelope for the first time, ran, and jumped on it. The antelope leaped to its feet and almost hit Tip as it ran by. He was so startled he never "throwed" the rope at all.

I yelled, "Rope it! Rope it!" He never got himself pulled together in time to attempt a throw. I never "seen" it on my line again.

Bear were occasionally found on the ranch. Jim Denton, a line rider, saw a bear on the small stream. He usually carried a Winchester, a six-shooter, and a butcher knife; but this time he had left all his hardware at camp except his butcher knife. He roped the bear and took him to a big cottonwood tree which had a large limb sticking out. Jim rode under the limb, passed the rope over it, pulled the bear clear of the ground, and caused him to hang in the air until he was dead. Then he got down and skinned the bear. Jim was very proud of his bear skin on display at headquarters.

One morning in late fall I was temporarily in charge of the ranch

165

while Sam Fling was away on business. John Watkins was driving up the saddle horses; as usual, he was running them. I went outside and told him to stop because we wanted to separate those which we were going to use on the line during the winter and give them grain. It seemed so funny to John that he took another dash or two.

Before he stopped, his horse broke behind. I saw his head snap forward in an unusual manner, and the horse stopped with him sitting motionless in the saddle. He was as white as a sheet. I walked up and helped him from his horse; he believed his neck was out of joint. He walked slowly into the dugout, lay down on his bunk, and was not able to ride for several days.

Bill McMillan, one of Major Drumm's foremen, was holding a big herd of four- and five-year-old beeves between three and four miles up the Salt Fork on the south side of their headquarters. Of mornings I would ride south until I got to the breaks, then turn east on a line between the breaks on the north and the blackjacks on the south. These breaks were along the heads of Clay and Wagon Creeks which ran through both the ♀ and Timberlake ranches. Wagon Creek emptied into the Salt Fork; Clay Creek spread out into the salt plains near present day Cherokee, Oklahoma.

One morning before I got to the head of the breaks, I met twenty-five or thirty of "them" big steers from Bill's herd coming from the south. One big ranch cow and one big ranch bull were with them. I got behind them and gave them a good old shove toward the north where they belonged. Since I had no cattle on the west side of the ♀ ranch, I thought if I gave them a big send off, I could get back to my line to see if any of our cattle had trailed them out.

I went on through between breaks and blackjacks, following the old cattle trail. I could see their fresh tracks up the new trail from the southeast. I followed them to the old trail. I "seen" where they had come down the old trail from the north to the point where the new trail branched off to the west. They followed it to a little road which we had made by hauling blackjack timber out to make branding pens and sheds. It must have been about a forty-mile trip. Somehow they had never picked up any other cattle along the way because they had made most of the journey at night.

When I "come" in to headquarters, Sam Fling said I ought to have followed them right through the range. Since they had come through and then started back again, I was afraid they might have picked up some of our range cattle which might have gotten tired following them and turned off some other way. Fling said we would take their trail.

We found they had gotten tired and had scattered among our herd. Fling rode over to Drumm's headquarters to have them send a couple of men over the next morning for us to round up that end of the range.

Next morning Tip McCracken and I went to the north end of the range; it was nice and warm. I was wearing a light knitted blouse. When we got to the herd, the wind came out of the north, as if it were coming off from ice. We could see the air was filled with butterflies, millows, grasshoppers, locusts, and many summer birds flying south, trying to keep ahead of the cold wave. We were holding the herd, watching the cut, and trying to keep from freezing to death at the same time.

Tip rode around the herd, then ran back to a big bunch of tall grass and lay face down. I "seen" a chance to have a little fun, ran over, put my face close to him, and began to snort like a big animal, smelling of him. He reared up, struck with both hands, and let out a yell, as always, whenever anything startled him. He cut in after me. We both were afoot and soon got pretty well warmed up. When we got ready to go back to camp, we were pretty badly chilled. Usually the autumn weather came by degrees, but this time it seemed to have come in one cold wave which caught us napping.

When I returned to the ⚡ ranch, one of my fellow cowhands was Frank Stephens whom Sam Fling hired shortly after I left. He was assigned to the north-line dugout, and his companion was a large, black shepherd dog which he talked to as if he were a man. In time Frank confided in me that his real name was Bill Counts. He had a shooting scrape in Ogallala, Nebraska, and changed his name.

He was having a hilarious time with some other fellows when a saloon keeper shot him through the body below his heart. He lay in the hospital until his funds were exhausted, then sent word if the keeper would give financial aid, he would consider the quarrel ended.

The saloon keeper sent an emphatic, "No! Let them that dance pay the fiddler!"

Counts was furious and vowed revenge. He had a friend whom the bartender mistreated, and the two agreed to shoot it out with the saloon men when Counts was able. They rode to the saloon, observed through the window that there were no customers, pulled their hat brims low, walked to the bar, ordered, and drank two whiskeys. They reached back as if to get money but drew their guns instead. Each fired at his man who dropped to the floor, apparently dead. The concussion of the shots extinguished the lamps. They left, mounted their horses, and started down the old cattle trail. The town officers were notified the following morning. No one knew which way they had gone. Both injured men recovered. They had recognized their assailants and a reward was offered for their capture.

During that winter Counts left the ranch and gave me his shepherd dog. When he was ready to mount, he pointed to me, "Shep, go to him and he will take care of you." The dog walked soberly to me, I patted him on the head, and he lay down at my feet as Counts rode away. Whenever I rode away from camp on my line without asking Shep to accompany me, he merely sat and looked at me. If I told him he could go, he promptly followed.

One morning the sun shone bright, and a north wind blew the loose snow into drifts in the hollows. The area covered with buffalo grass was swept clean. After feeding the horses and eating breakfast, I decided to ride across the range to see what the cattle were doing. Instead of riding one of the regular horses, I selected Roach, the black-maned, stout, gentle bay horse, raised in the settlements near Fort Worth. He was with the horse herd that Bates purchased from Kingsbury and Dunson the spring before at Caldwell.

When I was ready to go, I noticed Shep looking at me very earnestly, "Come on, Shep," I said.

He fell in behind. As we proceeded down the imaginary trail, the snow was about six inches deep on level ground and belly-deep to Roach in the hollows. We stayed on level ground as long as possible. The deep snow in the hollows did not bother Shep as much as the coyotes when they struck our trail. Soon these wily, hungry fellows trotted up close to us and Shep showed his displeasure. He chased them but could not catch any. One coyote kept about a rod ahead, looking back at Shep as he ran. So the coyote did not see the deep drifts until he plunged into one of them. Immediately a game of snap-grab-and dodge ensued for a few seconds. It was a fifty cent circus while it lasted but the coyote made his get-away.

When Shep got some distance from me, he suddenly realized he might meet his waterloo for coyotes sometimes combined against their enemies. When he turned back, the coyotes invariably followed again. I told Shep not to chase them anymore for we might find a big job farther up the line. He quit and walked close behind.

168

I approached the washouts and gullies carefully; some were several feet deep with perpendicular walls. If a horse or cow fell in, it might be killed or crippled. By riding slowly, Roach had a chance to test the depth before plunging in. When he felt the snow giving, he stepped back and tried another place. Soon we reached level land on top of the breaks and were able to travel faster. These breaks drained north into Clay Creek and Twin Springs on Timberlake's ranch. During the storm some of the cattle grazing in the flats adjacent to these streams found shelter behind these banks, others lay in the tall grass.

As I rode along my line, I began to think the cattle were still content to lie in their grassy beds. I was in a canyonlike draw when suddenly 1000 head of longhorns came over the bluff rim in a column of about twenty abreast, traveling in a fast walk. I had to act at once. From about 4—10 P.M. Shep and I bent every ounce of energy to turn back a seemingly endless column of cattle. I never got to see how long it was, but I knew it was too big a job for one person.

I immediately thought of Shep. I saw a bluff in front of the column and knew we could hold a point on it and turn the fast-moving column north along another canyon so I told Shep, "Go get them!"

Shep took his position and barked furiously while I dashed up to the head of the column, yelling and pounding on my cowhide leggings. The great herd started back towards the north on the side of the canyon which they had followed south.

While our attention was directed at the herd, the great column of cattle had formed a new point back of me; I saw it in time. I could not leave our original point, so I pointed to the column back of me and yelled, "Shep, go get them!"

He ran back and tore into them like fury. The column turned back north and formed a complete U-turn. From our two points Shep and I kept the column in motion until the last one passed.

During the day the sun softened the snow, but when it sank low in the west, a crust formed and hurt Shep's feet so badly he could scarcely walk. I told him to sit down at the U-turn and bark at the cattle as they passed, he did so. The sun set in a cloudless sky and the roaring wind subsided.

Night came. Shep's barking caused the coyotes to howl and they gathered closer to us. I was afraid to ride too far from Shep so I told him to lie down and not bark anymore. He obeyed but the silence made more work for my horse. When I rode too far away, Shep would set up a bottomless pit howl which tuned the coyotes anew. They understood and began to give short, sharp, bantering cries which all plainsmen recognize as a forewarning of attack. I told Shep not to howl; again he obeyed but barked at the few bunches of cattle that came less frequently.

When the crunching of the cattle's feet died in the distance, I sat on my horse for a few moments to see if there were any more stragglers. As I record these incidents, I recall the almost overwhelming sense of loneliness and helplessness that came over me. Gone was the roar of the crushing of frozen snow and the bellowing of cattle. Shep barked no more and my shouting and beating on the leggings were silenced. I lifted my eyes toward the beautiful dome of heaven; it was studded with a myriad of sparkling stars.

Suddenly within a few rods I heard the most unearthly howl that was ever throated by a coyote. A short distance beyond, another sent up the vicious call to kill, repeated again and again. The sneaking, old rascal near me had heard Shep's cry for help. He found he would need help to dispose of Shep so he called the whole pack. I was determined not to leave Shep to be torn to pieces, even if I had to lie by him in the snow all night. He had worked so faithfully for me. I decided to carry him on the horse.

I rode close to Shep and stopped, "Shep, let's go home!" He got to his feet feebly and looked wistfully. "Give me your paws!"

His hind feet were so sore they could not bear his full weight. He arose on his hock joints and raised his tender front feet as high as he could. I took hold of his front legs, then lifted and swung him astride behind me. His hind legs rested on the horse's hips; he tucked his front paws under my arm.

I said, "Hold tight, Shep!"

When Roach started his usual cow horse trot, I felt Shep's front legs grip my body. Roach followed the little trail he had made that morning; we expected no trouble. I do not know if Shep had ridden before, but I am sure he would have straddled a bucking bronco with me rather than stay where he was. There must have been some greatly disappointed coyotes when they found Shep was not there. As we rode along the homeward trail, Shep dozed. When I felt his paws slip and his hug loosen, I said, "Brace up, Shep, and have some style about you." His hug tightened again.

We arrived at camp about midnight. I rode close to the dugout, took

Shep's front legs, let him down lightly, told him to go to the door, then rode to the bank stable. I watered, unsaddled, and found feed for Roach. When I got to the dugout, Shep was lying at the door. I opened it, pushed him inside, and there sat Sam Fling, dozing by the open fireplace. He awoke as I was helping Shep to the fire, "What in the world kept you?"

"There has been a hot time in the old town tonight," I said.

Fling called the cook, "Dutch George," and asked if he had any hot coffee.

"You 'shust' keeps late hours!" the cook hurried out of his little annex. While he was preparing supper, I told him to prepare a good meal for Shep, for he certainly had earned it. When Shep heard this, he began to struggle to his feet. "No, Shep, 'shust' stay where you are. I brings it to you."

Shep lay down and ate by the warm fire. I greased his feet which caused him to lick them. By morning he could walk but he remained around camp. I told Fling about our experience then. Fling said, "I was afraid of that. I ought to have gone with you."

I told all the boys that Shep saved the day; the large herd would have smashed me, had it not been for him.

The sun shone bright and clear the next morning and softened the snow. Fling saddled Bob, one of his favorite horses; I had my other regular mount. We took the same trail, single file and more carefully at the gulches with deep washouts. We did not want to ride into a gulch even though there were two of us. When Fling saw where Shep chased the coyotes, he laughed again and again.

At the bluff Fling looked at the wide trail which was worn bare of snow, stopped his horse, and remarked, "My gracious, I did not expect to see such a sight as that." We discussed the longhorn's coming-out party for a while. Fling added, "Ride on to the end of your line, and I will scout around to see if any came out after you left." He rode in a wide circuit and met me at the end of my line, "Well I found nothing. As there is nothing to do, I will ride to Timberlake's camp and see what they know about this storm."

As I rode back to camp, I observed spots where buffalo grass showed through the snow. The snow melted soon, the big storm became history, and good weather prevailed.

We fenced the ranch in 1882 and there were no more drifting cattle for Shep to herd. In the following spring a former acquaintance and admirer of dogs drove to our camp in a spring wagon and took dinner with us. The farmer, whose name I have forgotten, was from southern Kansas and had a small herd of cattle. He asked about Shep. I told him about his intelligence and good deeds and he wanted him. "All right," I said.

When the man got ready to drive away, I said, "Shep, you can go with the man." Shep walked to him and he helped Shep into the wagon. "Shep, get up in the seat," I said. He promptly did so.

When Shep's new master saw this, he laughed. "I thought you had been stuffing me, but seeing his intelligence now, he will be worth more to me than a hired man!" he exclaimed.

As he drove away, I took my last look at Shep. This man's farm would be the best place for good old Shep's last days.

During the previous spring and summer a number of horses stampeded from the north-bound herds and collected in the blackjacks north of the Cimarron. Someone caught and sold a gentle pony with two small road brands on its left shoulder to "Dutch George." Fling tried to prevent it.

"I 'shust' needs him!" "Dutch George" replied, ending the argument. Very proud of his new pony, he kept it staked on good grass and gave it plenty of water. He placed his saddle on it, led it around, but did not ride it.

Fling had two excellent horses which he forbade the cowhands to ride. Because they were gentle, someone stole them. Paint, an attractive, white-spotted bay, was a good cutting horse, a willing worker. Bob was an attractive, finely-built sorrel with a short tail, but not a good cutting horse.

That winter Frank Bates went to "Big George's" livery barn in Caldwell for his buggy and driving team but one horse was lame. He hired one from "Big George" and drove to the ranch. As was his custom, he turned both horses loose with the saddle horses. That night the cook's pony got loose and a strange thing happened. There must be a way dumb animals communicate. Since the pony had once run free in the timber, somehow he got the idea of perfect freedom stowed away in that good old driving horse's system. The two left the ⚲ range. The next morning all the other horses were where we left them.

Fling took his horse, Paint, and followed the trail to the thick timber but came back. He knew it would be tough; I think he didn't want to use his nice horse.

172

"Dutch George" fairly threw fits, wringing his hands, "My $8 has gone into the blackjacks and I never see them no more!"

"It is good enough for you," said Fling. "I tried to keep you from buying that thing in the first place. If it was not for the driving horse, I would not waste a minute looking!"

The next morning Fling told me to take his other favorite mount, Bob. I had George fix a lunch for I well knew that I could not get back before night. I put on my cowhide leggings and old ducking coat, for riding at full speed through the thick brush and timber would be hard on clothes.

When I arrived at the blackjacks, I soon found tracks of two horses—one set small; the other, larger. By noon I had not found the horses but had picked out a good place for Bob to graze. I lay down in the shade of a tree to eat my lunch. When I finished, I saw Bob was satisfied. I mounted him, picked up the trail, and followed it until near sundown, then rode over to Smith and Lee's camp on Big Turkey Creek to stay all night. The cowhands admired my mount but seemed to be curious about my rough clothing until I told them what I expected to do. They laughed at the idea.

After breakfast I mounted Bob and rode to where I had dropped the trail. I followed it to a large glade but too many tracks confused me. At a large sand hill west of the glade I tied Bob to a small tree and walked carefully to the top. About 10 A.M. I saw the two horses; one lay on its side, apparently sound asleep; the other grazed and lifted its head often to look around. Keeping under cover of trees and hills, I rode to a point in the open between the horses and the thick brush. I turned Bob straight at them, whooping, yelling, and pounding on my cowhide leggings. They did not have time to look for any way to escape. Terror stricken, they ran north through the opening in the timber to the Texas Trail. Bob entered heartily into the spirit of the race. He pulled so hard on the bit I thought he would run over them. He kept them at full speed until they settled into a slow cow trot with their heads down. Their only interest was to keep away from the quirt.

When the horses entered the ⅄ corral, "Dutch George" saw me. He ran as fast as he could, "When we want them, we 'shust' send you after them. You get 'em!"

"If Bob could talk, he would have a different story to tell," I replied. "Sam, that is some horse you have. I will trade Little Dog for him," I added.

"I got enough riding your mount while you were gone," Fling laughed. "You go in to dinner while I unsaddle and feed Bob."

Fling soon came in, and when I told him how mad Bob seemed because the pony and buggy horse could not take any more abuse, he was pleased. "It was but one shot in a 1000; that was why I let Bob go for he was the only horse on the ranch who could do the job."

He laid down on his bunk to take a nap. I intended to do likewise, but "Dutch" wanted me to help him plan some way to fix his horse so he could not get away. I told him to get a bell; then he could bell, stake, hobble, or crosstie and sideline him.

"Let up on that crazy stuff! You'll have the Dutchman going crazy! That will take more rope than we have on the ranch!" Sam said. He had been listening more than sleeping.

"Dutch George" put two ropes on his pony; one on its neck, the other, a hacimo [hackamore], on its head. He tied it to a log, hobbled it, got a bridle, and placed the bits in its mouth. Each day he saddled it, placed a small pack on it, increasing the size daily, until he could place all his earthly possessions on it and lead it with perfect safety. Then he called for his time and walked away leading his pony, loaded with a coffee pot, frying pan, flour, bacon, salt, bedding, and some extra clothing. He was the happiest Dutchman on earth—and the most laughable moving van I ever saw.

SIXTEEN

The Talbot Raid

I was still with the ⚓ ranch during the fall or early winter when the Talbot Raid on Caldwell occurred.[1] Jim Talbot was one of the most powerful men I had ever seen. He could take hold of two ordinary men and handle them easily.

Anderson Hance told me once when Talbot got full and noisy, the town marshal told him to keep quiet or he would be put in the cooler. Talbot said he could not do it, so the marshal deputized two other men to help. They took Talbot and got about half-way there when he turned, threw his escorts to the ground, and sat on them. Talbot jumped up, ran back a short distance, then stopped and told the marshal if he would put a cot up for him, he would go back. He didn't want his wife to see him drunk. The marshal got the cot.

During that summer Bob Bigtree, Bob Munson, Jim Martin, Doug Hill, and Jim Talbot had come up the Texas Trail with a herd of through cattle to Caldwell. When the men were discharged, they had a considerable amount of money. They went into town to stay for awhile, have a good time, and protect each other. They knew gamblers would be after them. So when one of the five began to drink and lose his judgment, the others would take him out of the game and put him to bed to sober up.

The boys had looked after one another's interests so well that the gamblers got together and began to prejudice citizens of Caldwell against them, saying they were a bunch of outlaws. No one investigated but thought the accusation was true. Some of the gamblers started a fight with the cowpunchers who easily routed them.

The town marshal, John Wilson, a gambler, himself, stood in with them, called and armed some deputies, including Mike Meagher, an old government scout, who thought that everything was on the square. He had trouble with Jim Talbot on a previous occasion and was willing to aid the town marshal.[2]

Talbot advised the others to get their horses and leave. He was

175

standing the crowd off in front of a saloon. Hance told me Talbot stood in the center of the cross streets to watch the town, see the livery barn, and keep the enraged populace from shooting the boys who were trying to saddle up. The marshal had ordered everyone who would go in with him to York, Parker, and Draper's hardware to get guns and ammunition.

B. W. Key, the store manager,[3] had gone to dinner and just sat down to eat when the firing began. He jumped and started for the door and his wife grabbed him. He later told me he had no idea his wife was so stout. She hung to him until he got to the front gate where he broke loose. When he arrived, he saw a string of men coming out with arms and ammunition. He told them he was running this store and nothing could go out without the money. He began to search for those who had guns from his establishment and take them out of their hands.

Talbot had a buffalo gun at his house. He told Jim Martin to go get it with the cartridge belt. Martin found the gun but the belt had fallen behind a trunk and he couldn't find it. He left the gun since he had no ammunition and the mob found both gun and belt.

Talbot and his men prepared to leave town. Some of the Caldwell men got on top of buildings and Talbot couldn't see them. George Spear was hit while saddling a horse. A bullet pierced his body and killed him instantly.[4] Talbot started to the livery barn through an alley and met Mike Meagher. Mike knew Talbot had a quick, deadly aim, so he went down the alley to get the drop on Talbot. Both raised their guns but Talbot was quicker and killed Mike. Talbot later told me when he got the signal to come to the barn, he saw Mike raising his gun to shoot but Talbot said nothing else.

"So that is the way you got him."

He replied, "Somebody did, as sure as God made little apples in the summertime." This was his favorite expression.

Talbot's bunch started for the Territory with the crowd after them. As they came into sight, Talbot saw a man dismount. He said, "Scatter boys, they've found my gun and ammunition!"

Talbot's outfit was outnumbered. They rode into the first hilly terrain and took their stand to hold off the crowd until nightfall. It was a deep canyon with two other hollows coming directly toward each other from opposite sides of the main canyon. One man was sent up the right-hand hollow, another up the left-hand side to protect each other. The other three in the main canyon could protect them.

The crowd soon had them surrounded and began to try to find a way to get into the canyon, but whenever a head appeared above the brow, a bullet came their way mighty quick. W. E. "Short Horn" Campbell thought he had a way figured out to rout them, but he exposed himself and got two flesh wounds for his trouble. Thereafter, the pursuing mob was mighty careful about showing themselves above the bank.

They yelled, "Come out now for we're comin' in after you!" Then they stamped the ground in unison and pretended they were coming to overwhelm the men. But the Talbot group never appeared, and the crowd soon saw they had no chance to force them into the open.

When darkness began to form, they set guards all around who were to work together in pairs to keep in communication with each other. They would meet, talk awhile, then walk in opposite directions to the end of their beat.

Meanwhile Talbot began a birdlike chirp to call his group together and arrange how to get out. They slipped up close to the line at the highest point to get some skylight and saw how the sentries patrolled. They decided that each one could go on all fours as the two sentries walked away from the central point of their beat while the other four would watch with their guns. When each one got safely outside, he could fire on the sentries if trouble started. Soon all were out of the canyon and on their way afoot, as the mob had their horses.

It was a clear night. They started west, eventually struck the old cow trail, then turned south toward Pond Creek. After awhile they saw a campfire and found some freighters. They approached, ready for action if the freighters should fight. They hadn't heard anything and made no disturbance. They told the freighters they hadn't had anything to eat since morning—the fight had started just at noon—and they were given supper. Then Talbot told the freighters who they were and what had happened. They were not used to walking and needed five horses. The freighters were to select the horses for them, remain two days, say nothing, and by that time, the horses would be returned safe and sound. But if they told the pursuing crowd and they should follow, they might get their horses shot to pieces. They didn't propose to be taken alive.

Talbot and his men rode all night to Timberlake's camp for breakfast. Then they came over to our camp and stayed with us all day. Late in the evening Talbot and Frank Stevens took the freighters' horses back to Timberlake's and stayed all night. Stevens rode his own horse.

The next morning they delivered the horses to the happy freighters who thought they might not see them again.

Timberlake returned to his own camp. Stevens went on to Caldwell and got ammunition for the Talbots. When he arrived at Caldwell, the Talbot Raid was the talk of the town—the killing of Mike Meagher and George Spear. Stevens dared not stay in Caldwell, so he rode out to Hall's camp on the state line about fifteen miles west of Caldwell and spent the night.

After Stevens returned, all the cowpunchers on the ⚢ and Timberlake ranches began to investigate to see how many saddles and horses they could dig up so the Talbot bunch could ride out of the country. I had five horses but gave only one; Stevens, one; and Tom Cave furnished a saddle. We got them mounted and started off that night. Since Bob Munson seemed to be a rather straightforward sort of fellow, I let him take a $60 horse with the understanding the horse would be returned as quickly as he could. I haven't seen the horse since.

We were willing to help them because we had the same opinion that "Short Horn" Campbell had. After he had gotten the otherside of the story, he said, "Any man ought to be killed, who would get out and fight for the cause of a gambler."

"Short Horn" Campbell was the man who introduced Hereford cattle in the Southwest. Why he was called "Short Horn" Campbell is more than I know. If he had been called "Hereford" Campbell, I could have understood.[5] The first time I saw this breed of cattle was in Caldwell at a livestock show. Campbell had some men leading around his fine, gentle cows and bulls at the fair from his Strip ranch. One wild yearling had been turned over to a boy to lead. The animal became frightened and started to run, dragging the boy after him. Some cowpuncher in the crowd grabbed the rope and saved them both. People laughed and asked him why he put a wild steer in the care of a mere boy while the gentle Herefords had 200 pound men walking around with them. Campbell walked up to a big fellow, took the rope out of his hand, and told him to tell the boy to come there and take charge of the gentle cow. The next run the steer made, he didn't make much headway with that heavy man hanging on the rope.

Jim Talbot got a job with a friend in the Texas Panhandle and sent Hank Smith to Caldwell with a covered wagon to get his wife and household effects. Smith drove into Caldwell during daytime and said nothing about his mission.

178

GOVERNOR'S PROCLAMATION.

$1700 REWARD!

STATE OF KANSAS,

Executive Department, Topeka, Dec. 9, 1882.

I, JOHN P. ST. JOHN, Governor of the State of Kansas, by virtue of the authority vested in me by law, do hereby offer a reward of FIVE HUNDRED DOLLARS for the arrest and conviction of one Jim. Talbott, as principal, and THREE HUNDRED DOLLARS each, for the arrest and conviction of Jim. Martin, Bob. Munson, Bob. Bigtree, and Dug. Hill, as accessories, to the murder of **MIKE. MEAGHER**, in Sumner County, Kansas, on or about the 17th day of December, 1881.

[L. S.] In Testimony Whereof, I have hereunto subscribed my name, and affixed the Great Seal of the State, at Topeka, the day and year first above written.

JOHN P. ST. JOHN.

By the Governor:

JAMES SMITH,

Secretary of State.

Wanted poster for the Talbot gang. From *Why the West Was Wild*, by Nyle H. Miller and Joseph W. Snell. Published 1963 by The Kansas State Historical Society.

The officers had kept close watch on the house for awhile but by the time Smith arrived, they had become inattentive. Smith stayed a day or two and rested his team. One night he drove to Talbot's house; he and Mrs. Talbot loaded the wagon and drove away. She was not missed for several days and the officers never knew what became of her.

Doug Hill, one of Talbot's men, showed me his badly disfigured left hand. The little finger had been cut off, the finger next to it badly scarred. He had worked on a Texas cattle ranch where there were as many Mexican as white cowhands.

Hill was assigned to a line camp and dugout with a Mexican. The outside work was the usual riding in opposite directions. The inside work consisted of getting wood, building fires, getting water, cooking, and washing dishes. When they got to camp, the Mexican sat down, rolled a cigarette, and began smoking. Hill said nothing but prepared the meal for both of them; then they sat and ate. The next meal Hill asked the Mexican to help. He told Hill he was above such work.

Hill replied, "All right, I'll cook what I want and you can do the same." Hill had his six-shooter strapped on, the Mexican had a knife. The Mexican became angry and ordered Hill to cook for both of them. He kept his eye on the Mexican. When he was not observing, the Mexican leaped against him with such force that he fell into the wood box with his six-shooter pinned beneath him. The Mexican stood over him trying to knife him. He tried to reach his gun with his right hand and keep the Mexican from stabbing him with his left hand which was almost ruined before he could draw his gun. When he did, the fight was soon over.

Hill mounted a horse and rode to headquarters badly smeared with blood. The owner of the ranch didn't blame Hill as much as himself because he knew there was bad feelings between Texan and Mexican cowboys. He sent the Mexican hands to care for their dead comrade and saw to it there was no more mixing of cowhands.

Hill saw it would be better to leave that country so he rode away. If Hill had aspired to be a two-gun man, the Mexican's knife spoiled all such hopes. He could not hold a gun in his left hand, but he was certainly swift with his right hand. I saw him hit a fellow with his fist and have his fully cocked six-shooter under his nose before he could pull his gun from its scabbard.

A few years after the Talbot Raid, Charlie Siringo,[6] the retired cowhand, restaurant owner, and sideline private detective, had made quite a reputation for himself. He arrested Jim Talbot, who was charged with killing Mike Meagher.

Bill Stobaugh, my Oklahoma claim neighbor, was at the trial. Talbot was disguised as an English Cockney, immaculately dressed, wearing a monocle, and affecting the manners of a well-bred Englishman. When the trial was held, there were very few people left in Caldwell who had known Talbot. No one could positively identify him and no one had seen him kill Meagher.

I have always believed there may have been an understanding between Talbot and Siringo, for Siringo was also an old Cowhand from the Rio Grande.

SEVENTEEN

Neighborhood and General Roundups of 1882

I had been away from the ⚔ ranch for a good part of the 1881–82 winter but returned in early spring of 1882. Frank Bates and J. D. Payne, his uncle, were busy with the reorganization of their affairs. Until then Payne and Bates had a partnership in the ranch with only one brand. Now they "was" trying to have two separate brands. Payne chose **JD P**.[1]

A neighborhood roundup was held. Since foreman Sam Fling was absent from the ranch, I took charge of the small roundup between the ⚔ and Drumm ranches. I put Wade Spears, a twelve-year-old lad, wrangling horses for us. Another lad, George Leonard of Kiowa, had a great desire to be a cowboy. When he was about fourteen, Abner Wilson of Drumm's outfit hired him to wrangle their saddle horses.

Our mare herd ran on the flats along the north end of the range. It came up close to where the boys were holding their saddle horses. Leonard wanted to see the colts so he rode after the herd and undertook a roundup. His horse stepped into a hole and fell with such force that it rolled over George and crushed in his breast. He was taken to his mother's hotel in Kiowa where he lingered for a month or more without proper surgical treatment and died.[2]

Bates had a bunch of mares to raise his own saddle horses and had bought a good Morgan stallion which he turned loose among the mares in the summertime.

When heel fly time came that spring and chased the cattle into the bogs, George Short and I rode to pull the cows out since we knew the range so well. I decided to ride old "Morg." He had been tied and fed well. No one knew whether anyone had ever ridden the old stallion, and George was greatly amused at me for wanting to ride him.

He thought I'd be fired for taking old "Morg" out on such an expedition. I saddled him and he walked along as if he was used to it. He took such long steps and walked so briskly that Short's horse had to take a cow trot to keep up. His back was so broad my legs stuck out like pins in a pin cushion and he was tiresome to ride.

182

We rode up to one bog and there was an old longhorn Texas cow stuck in it. She was ready to fight when we came in sight. She wanted to use her horns, so we took our ropes from the saddle horns and tied on to her and started out for high ground.

Old "Morg" pulled like an old plow horse, and we soon snaked her out to high, dry ground. We knew she could not get up by herself so we dismounted and removed the ropes. I told George to take "Morg" and lead him up on a high bank where he could see me. We knew when the cow did get up, she would be fighting, and we did not want the old stallion within reach of her long horns.

I made a quick jump at the old cow and frightened her. She put forth her best efforts while I tailed her up. As she started to get to her feet, I pulled back on her tail and held her in balance so she could steady herself and get her front feet squarely under her.

Before I dismounted, Short asked me how I was going to get away. Nearby was an old willow stump about ten feet high and two feet in diameter. I had planned this for my refuge in the event the old cow should attack. When she got to her feet, I turned, ran to the stump, and crawled up. She charged but I had gotten to the top. She stuck up her nose but could not reach me with her horns.

Short could see all that was going on. He began to call to me to kick at her, for he knew she would continue to stalk me if I showed signs of fighting her. I kept perfectly still. When she heard Short, she started in pursuit of him.

I waited until she got several rods away, then yelled, "Keep still up there or she'll come up and horn old 'Morg' yet." Just then she whirled and came back. Of course I could have stopped the fight mighty quick with my six-shooter, but I did not think that would be nice to haul her out of a bog, then kill her. We both kept still and she walked away. The farther she walked, the better she moved. I got down, went up the hill, and we were soon on our way.

In the general roundup of 1882 Fayette Thomas and Hank Smith were trying to force strays from opposite sides into the same cut. Both were mounted on good cutting horses, and the yearlings were trying to get back into the herd. They came running toward each other, chasing the strays. Thomas's yearling ran against the front legs of Smith's horse with such force, it knocked off its horn and turned his horse on top of him. I was just outside the herd helping to hold it. As I saw the big horse fall, I didn't see how on earth a man could come out alive. I rode

183

up quickly and jumped off my horse to help Smith, thinking he was dead. I asked if he was hurt.

He said, "Not much," but I could see he was. I caught his horse and led it back but Smith couldn't get up. I helped him up onto his horse and he started for camp. It was some time before he could do much work.

On the same roundup as I was trying to cut out an animal from the herd, it dodged behind a large cow. Instead of keeping after the animal, my horse attempted to leap over the cow before I noticed. He caught his knees against her side, turned a somersault over her, and fell on me. That raised such a commotion, the whole bunch started to run. My unhurt horse got up and started off. Dick Wilson caught my horse and led him back to me where I lay on the ground and asked, "Are you hurt?"

I said, "No," then reached for the bridle rein but did not know where I was. I ran clear around the horse, trying to find the rein. Dick jumped from his horse and told me to lie down. I was hurt worse than I thought. I sat awhile, then asked him to look at my neck because it felt as if it had been injured. He didn't think anything was broken. In a few moments I got on my horse but was unable to work further that afternoon. I rode back to camp and laid up for the night.

The next morning my neck was terribly swollen on one side and so stiff I couldn't turn my head. The work was light since we were moving to another ranch. I fell in with Bill Wilson, an awful fellow to have fun, and told him about my accident. I couldn't turn my head without turning my whole body. Presently I observed that I was riding alone. I could hear some of the boys riding behind but they didn't seem to be trying to overtake me. Directly Bill began to yell, "Look, here, look quick and see what's happening here!" I had to turn the horse half way around before I could see. Bill laughed fit to kill. He thought it was a good joke.

We finished the Strip roundup. I transferred to Major Drumm's wagon under Henry Johnson, the captain. In our cut were cattle belonging to Major Drumm, W. E. Campbell, D. R. Streeter, and all the strays of the Barber County Association.[3] We had worked hard all day in getting together the cuts for each wagon. All wagons "was" camped along Turkey Creek, far enough apart to make it convenient for each wagon to hold its cut and horses without interfering each other.

Our camp site was on a level piece of land along the south bank, surrounded by a high bank on three sides. A deep water pool in the creek lay around the foot of this high bank. When we bedded the cattle for the night, there was a line not over twenty rods long to ride. Someone foolishly staked a horse so it could graze across the line we "was" to ride on night herd.

Johnson saw it was going to rain and he thought it best to have two men. One could ride across the flat alone and meet the other at the middle of the herd. He told Ad Martin and me to take the first guard.

Soon rain began to pour; then came a heavy hailstorm with stones as large as prairie chicken eggs, half the size of domestic hen eggs. It caused the cattle to jump and run. Martin and I had just met; he could have headed them easily away from the ford and turned them toward the high bank. When the sheet lightning began to play, it was almost like noonday. The staked horse had drifted across our line, pulling its rope high enough to catch the front feet of Martin's horse and "throwed" it onto the ground. I ran back and saw what happened.

About twenty-five cattle beat me to the crossing but the others were stopped. I ran out onto the high ground after them. Then hailstones as large as my fist began to fall. One hit me between my shoulders on the spine. Another penetrated the heavy wagon sheet close to a bow and dropped into the bed of our camp wagon. When I overtook the cattle, they were drifting with the hailstorm, but when the big slugs began to fall, one of them struck a cow in the back of the head and knocked her down. The cows turned and ran up around my horse as close as they could. They were trying to get their heads under shelter and were so badly scared they were bawling as if they were being killed. My horse and I were as badly scared as they. If one of "them" slugs hit me in the head, it might kill or knock me off the horse but we escaped all the rest of them.

The wind was blowing terribly hard, sheet lightning was playing, and the roar of the hail was terrifying. Suddenly in the midst of this turmoil and fright Martin "come" dashing up behind me with a wooden water bucket on his head. It was made of cedar staves and held together by brass hoops, considered a mighty good bucket in "them" days. A slug hit the bucket; another hit Ad's horse and knocked it to its knees. I was certainly glad to see him coming for he always wore a million dollar smile and he brought it with him. Together we held the cattle stationary as they continued to poke their heads around us for shelter.

The force of the wind soon drove the storm past. As soon as I could make Ad hear, I said he was the biggest fool I ever saw. Surprised, he wanted to know why. I told him he should have stuck his head under the wagon and stayed there.

He said, "Oh, I couldn't think of you having all this fun to yourself. I had to come out and at least enjoy a part of it."

We turned the cattle about and drove them back to camp. We hadn't paid any attention to our saddle horses and found they had run into the blackjacks for shelter. Soon we met Henry Johnson, the captain of our wagon, coming out to hunt for us. He didn't know whether we were dead or alive. Seeing the cattle, Ad, and I were all right, he told me to take the cattle on into camp, and as Ad had the bucket on his head, he could go with Johnson to hunt the horses. They overtook them soon for they had stopped behind the trees to escape the big hailstones.

It was near morning. Johnson told the cook to get out and fix breakfast. We would see what was the order of the day. As soon as daylight "come," we changed horses, "eat" our breakfast, and put two or three men on herd with the cattle and horses. Johnson told Ad and me to lie down and get some sleep. He didn't think there would be much doing that day.

Three or four men rode up to the wagon about 10 A.M. and told us they were a delegation sent from the other wagons to see what had become of Henry Johnson and his outfit. They wanted to know where his cattle "was." Johnson told them the cattle were under herd just over the hill and we hadn't lost a cow or horse. They wanted to know how that was.

Johnson said, "Two men held them through all that storm."

Quince Hunter inquired, "I want to see them men."

"They're lying there asleep," said Johnson. Hunter insisted, "Wake 'em up, I want to look at 'em."

Johnson hollered, "Wake up!" He told us Hunter and his delegation wouldn't believe that we had held the herd during the terrible storm. We told them we "done" the job.

Hunter replied, "And you still got your hides on, that's what I wanted to know." Then he rode off.

Although we had everything ready to start, Johnson told us to hold the cut while the others rounded up the blackjacks and separated their cattle which took all day. Johnson exempted Ad and me from further duty until we got onto the road. The others didn't object, for they thought it was a great deal better to work in good weather than to be out in such a storm.

Everybody heard about how one outfit had held the cut without losing a cow or a horse. Some of the would-bes began to tell they "was" one of them. One day I was in a bunch of fellows including "Missouri Dave" Thomas. He began to tell how he and another fellow held the cut during the terrible hailstorm without losing a cow or a horse. He couldn't recall who the other fellow was. That tickled me and I began to laugh.

I said, "I can tell you who the other fellow was, Dave. It was Ad Martin and me. That's who the other fellow was."

It changed the expression on Dave's face like that of the Cheyenne Indian after he took the dose of quinine.

In traveling from one range to another we naturally became acquainted with each other and there is where I first met Charley Colcord.[4] Our habits, tastes, and interests seemed to be in accord and we formed an attachment for each other.

Colcord went through to Barber County with us. After we had worked the whole country in the general roundup, we then worked the several cuts and those cattle that were to remain in Kansas were left there; those that belonged to Indian Territory ranches were taken there.

The general roundup that spring finished at Medicine Lodge. It was the boys' custom when they came to a town to stop, get a shave, haircut, and clean up before walking about town. After visiting the barber, I walked down the sidewalk toward a long store-building with a lean-to along the side, equally long as the building. The ceiling was low; all the inside walls and ceiling were plastered. There was a long bench on each side of the gallery where anyone could be seated. It was an ideal place for a shooting gallery which was in operation.[5]

I heard shooting and stepped into the door. Charley Colcord and two other fellows who had been doing the shooting, stood and leaned against the shelf where they kept their guns. They were talking.

Colcord saw me. He had taken a drink or two, too much, which rather clouded his judgment and made him feel funny. He yelled, "Hey, fellows, look what's coming and I've got a gun this time."

At least one of the guns was loaded. He picked up one with no idea it was loaded, pointed it at me, and made a line shot, just a trifle too high to hit my head. Being a low ceiling, my head was very close to it. The bullet tore a strip in the ceiling, eight or ten inches long, over my head, then glanced away from the ceiling in a downward course into the front wall. The marks indicated the gun's powerful force. It would have passed entirely through my head if Colcord had gotten a fine bead on it. Suddenly realizing what he had done, he let the gun drop with a loud noise.

The proprietor yelled, "You'll ruin that gun, dropping it that way!"

Colcord said, "My God, I might have killed you." He started to me, tears rolling from his eyes, hands extended.

I thought he was going to fall. I jumped, grabbed him in my arms, assisted him to one of those long benches, set him down, and sat beside him. I spent some minutes trying to console and convince him that he was such a poor shot he couldn't hit me, but he was so unstrung that it was some time before he got to his feet again.

His great feeling in regard to my life and welfare after that foolish shot caused me to have great interest in him. I have often seen his pictures in the *Daily Oklahoman* and have read some things he wrote concerning the range and the early days. I was glad to see the success he made of his life and sorry to read the published accounts of his death.

The cattlemen from the Territory had all of their cattle in one cut and were ready to start back to the Strip. The boys took a notion to have some fun in town. They drove the wagon out on Antelope Flat southeast of Medicine Lodge and camped where there was plenty of grass and water. I went uptown to get a shave and a haircut. When I was about ready to go back to camp to arrange for night herd, Nate Priest,[6] the town marshal, told me he understood the boys were going to shoot up the town that night. I didn't think there was anything to the rumor.

Nate said, "You know all of the boys from the Strip, and I want you to tell 'em I've organized a gun club of twenty-five businessmen. If they start shooting up this town tonight, we'll be right there with twenty-five breech-loading shotguns, loaded with buckshot."

I told him that sounded bad to me and was poor judgment of the businessmen to get out and kill the cowpunchers because they wanted to have a little fun after they had spent all of their money there. All the cash business done in town was with cowpunchers and cattlemen.

Nate was on his horse, headed north to his country home a short distance from town, when he stopped me. I was on my horse, headed south to camp. I asked where he was going. He was going to do his chores, then return to take charge of the gun club. "I want you to stop long enough in town to get the word scattered out among the boys what is going to happen to them if they start shooting up the town." As he rode on, I thought he wouldn't be back. I told one or two fellows what he said.

There was a town ordinance, probably in force in all Kansas towns at that time, that saloons had to close promptly at midnight or their licenses would be revoked. So, just at midnight the saloon owners shoved everybody out; their clocks must have been set alike. All at once without any warning, we could hear from our camp shooting, yelling, and a continuous roar like one solid shot. They must have emptied their six-shooters at least twice around, judging from the length of time the battle raged. In a little while the Territory boys came riding into camp, rolled up in their blankets, and went to sleep. Everything became quiet.

About daylight "Happy Jack" Shepherd came in and reported that a girl had been killed during the shooting. Bill Wilson and Frank Streeter came to where I lay asleep, woke me, and wanted to know if I would take care that their stock was brought down to the Strip with the rest of the cut. They wanted to get across the state line into the Strip before a warrant could be served. I told them if they would wait a minute, we would have breakfast before they started. They said "Happy Jack" had told them they had killed a girl, and the town marshal would be down with a posse to arrest the whole outfit. Everybody knew they were in town during the shooting, and I was out with the cut when it occurred. It was my opinion that it was one of "Happy Jack's" tall stories. He had said to me the day before, "they're going to make me marry 'Red' Connor's girl."

I had said, "Jack, we'll stand by you; I'll gather up the boys and we'll show 'em you don't have to marry her."

He was about "half-shot," but he acted so in earnest, I thought he meant what he was saying. He had said, "Oh, don't do that, I want to marry the girl!" Just as I surmised, it was one of his big stories; no one was hurt.

A few years later I met a traveling man who was in Medicine Lodge that night. He had eaten a late supper, lit a cigar, stepped to the sidewalk in front of the hotel, and stood there alone, smoking, looking around. He heard no sound. Suddenly without a moment's notice, volleys of shots, shouts, and yells broke loose. His mouth flew open and he never knew whether the cigar fell in or out, he was so badly scared. He started to run into the hotel, but in his excitement he missed the entrance, ran around north of it, and fell into a pile of boxes and barrels where he lay still until the battle was over. He didn't know how anything could escape being struck with so many guns being fired and the air so full of bullets.

EIGHTEEN

Cowboy Pranks in Caldwell

Several unusual incidents occured in the streets of Caldwell, Kansas, in the early 1880's. The streets were unpaved, and the dust was controlled to some extent by a large street sprinkler, pulled by a span of large horses. One man drove the team and controlled the flow of water by a long brake which he adjusted by his foot.

Hitching posts were in front of every business house to accommodate the customers, whether on horseback or with teams. Often the horses became impatient and pawed the earth. In time this caused holes and ditches in front of the posts and when rain fell, they filled with water. One of these pits was unusually deep in front of Louie Segerman's restaurant and hotel which was a favorite spot for certain cowpunchers who often tied their horses and left them standing at the posts a good part of the night.[1]

An attractive feature of this place was an awning, supported by posts about five feet apart which shaded the front of Louie's building. There was a bench made with a 1' × 12" plank and fitted between the awning posts. It was further supported by a narrower plank resting edgewise. This made a strong and comfortable bench.

Louie was confined to his work inside during the daytime in hot weather. When it became cooler in the evening, the short, fat German often went to the bench, laid down on his back, and sometimes fell asleep. A rainfall had filled all the holes in front of his hitching posts. That night Louie went to his bench and laid down to cool off.

Ben Wheeler, the town marshal,[2] came to the doors of a saloon where a bunch of us cowpunchers were assembled. The saloon stood a door or two north of Segerman's hotel. Ben motioned his hand to us and said something to the boys next to him. They rushed out and I followed.

As I came out, Louie was getting up from a water pool and was the maddest German I have ever seen.

The marshal ran up and yelled, "What's a' going on here, what does this mean?"

Caldwell, Kansas, 1888. Courtesy of The Kansas State Historical Society, Topeka, Kansas.

Louie was ranting and telling him in his broken English what had happened. When he finished, the marshal put on a big demonstration of authority. I happened to be standing next to him; he grabbed his six-shooter, pointed his finger at me, "Did you do that?"

I promptly told him, "No!" He continued his investigation as Louie stood looking on. Then Wheeler cut loose and gave us a big lecture on somebody's abominable conduct of disturbing the rest and slumber of an honorable citizen while reclining on his own dunghill. This greatly encouraged Louie, and he put in his six bits worth to "shoot 'em mit a bullet."

Then the marshal said, "That's the idea, Louie, shoot 'em mit a bullet!" This made the marshal stand in thick with Louie and it amused the boys wonderfully, for all of them knew that the marshal had rolled Louie into the mud hole and had run into the saloon next door.

Another funny experience happened to a fellow who stopped at the Leland Hotel. He had a habit of coming out in front of the hotel and leaning back in his chair against the side of the building and falling asleep.

Johnny Blair took some matches, tied them together, and fitted them on the bridge of the fellow's nose with the match heads pointing upwards in front of his eyes. I happened to be directly across the street and saw Blair strike a match to light the rest. A perfect success, it made a big flame and smoke. Blair yelled, "Fire!"

The fellow's eyes flew open; he started to run, fell over the curb, jumped up, and started up the street as hard as he could run. All he could hear was people laughing. He stopped, looked around, and found they were laughing at him.[3]

In back of the Leland Hotel someone had a full-grown black bear chained to a post. There was a livery stable nearby. The owner of the bear warned the owner to be careful about standing any of his vehicles in reach of the bear for he would claw everything to pieces. But someone carelessly backed a spring wagon so that one wheel came in reach of the bear, and he tore off one hind wheel before anyone discovered it.

The owner of the bear had a fifty-gallon wooden barrel sunk into the ground, leaving the top of it level with the ground. Every other day the man who ran the street sprinkler would drive down and fill the barrel with water. It was fun to see how cautious the bear was. He always

193

approached the barrel in the same manner, walk around it several times, look into it, walk to its edge, claw the water with his paw, jump back, and look, strike it with his paws, then jump back and look again. The next time he approached the barrel, he reached down into the water and stirred it awhile, then jumped back to look once more. Then he came to the barrel, thrust his front leg to the bottom, and felt all around. Finally he turned around and backed down into it, leaving just his head sticking out with a great big bear grin.

The owner always fed the bear from the rear end of the hotel. His food was placed on a tray and whenever the bear saw it coming, he always went the length of his chain away from the fellow, no matter how hungry he was. He wouldn't return until the man left, then cautiously gave it a thorough inspection before touching it. If it passed, he sat on his haunches and ate all of the food.

When watermelon time came, that was another thing. The bear always met the man with the big watermelon cut into halves. The bear came as far as the chain would let him, stood on his haunches, and held out his front paws with the palms up for the man to lay a watermelon half on them. Then the bear sat down, rolled on his back, got his hind feet up to slip the watermelon on their soles, and hold it steady with his front paws. He began to eat, look around, and grin as if performing a great feat.

In December 1878 at a stopover in the Wendel Hotel, I talked with the proprietors until almost 10 P.M. before going to bed.[4] We heard a wagon and team running down the street. I told Mrs. Wendel that a team must be running away with somebody.

She said, "No, it's them Mitchell boys."

They would come to town, stay late, and proceed to disturb the peace as they drove away. Mrs. Wendel had three boys and hoped they would never do such things. She seemed to be a mighty fine woman. Wendel, himself, was rather careless about drinking and sometimes got entirely too much.

The Mitchell boys soon went to work on the range. One was working south of Caldwell three years later. One afternoon while he was riding the line, a light thunder shower swept over the range. When he didn't return that night, someone rode out to look for him the next morning. Both Mitchell and his horse were found dead but neither had any marks. His six-shooter belt buckle was melted—proof that lightning had killed them.

194

Whenever a shipment of beeves arrived at Caldwell, the town merchants stationed men in front of their stores to induce the cowpunchers to trade with them. I saw a cowboy riding from the south up main street. Just then Sam Harris, who was in front of Unsell's store, saw Charlie Siringo and ran out into the middle of the street to greet and escort him into the store, calling him Charlie. I asked Harris who he was. He replied, "That is Charlie Siringo. I thought everybody knew him."

I remarked that I had not heard of him since 1879 and did not know that he was in this part of the country.

Siringo was married and operated a restaurant in Caldwell which became a popular place for the cowboys.[5] He was writing a book of his life and was going to give each of his cowboy friends a copy. I left Caldwell before the book appeared. I purchased one in 1886 from a news butch on a train as I was returning from Kansas City where I had sold a load of cattle.

Jim Buzard and Ike Berry first told me about Charlie Siringo. He had worked a month for Bill Hudson at the 3 ranch in December 1878. Hudson had to make a business trip and employed Siringo to work during his absence. When Hudson returned, Siringo began to trap and hunt on the ranch. He built a small dugout in a bank along the Eagle Chief a short distance downstream from the ranch house in a small elm grove. He did not get the roof high enough and one night during a rainstorm, a large steer walked upon it and broke through. He nearly kicked the life out of Siringo before both could get out.

Rain was followed by sleet, and the storm terminated in a snowfall which left Siringo in a bad plight. He packed all his personal belongings on Whiskey Pete, his horse, and arrived at the 3 ranch house at about daybreak. Buzard said Siringo was a forlorn-looking specimen, spattered with mud, with bruises and skinned places scattered over his body.

After Siringo rested a few days, he and Berry turned to the subject of horse racing and made a bet. Siringo bet $20 that Whiskey Pete could outrun a company horse. He won and started south with the money in his pocket—$25 for his December salary and his $5 trapping outfit.[6]

Pat Carnegie had a ranch about thirty miles southwest of Caldwell. He was popular among the cowmen, for he always carried his ready Irish wit with him and used it on all occasions. At a neighborhood roundup Carnegie was cutting out a big native cow which had no mark or brand. The owner of the herd hollered to Pat, "What are you cutting her out on?"

Pat replied, "On her general appearance, just like you cut her out when you throwed her into your herd but I'll not do like you did. When I turn her loose on my range, she will have Pat Carnegie's brand and ear mark on her."

Pat was at the annual meeting of the Southwestern Cattle Association, having his usual good time. The association adjourned about noon; Pat ate dinner, mounted his horse, and started for his ranch with his shirt collar flying open in his customary way, facing the north end of a south wind which is always cold in winter or early spring.

When Pat arrived home, he was so hoarse he could hardly speak. He lay down on his bunk, told one of his riders to get a fresh horse, go back to Caldwell, and get Dr. Noble, who arrived and found Pat had a desperate case of double pneumonia. He soon passed away.[7]

Word scattered rapidly about his death which was the main topic of conversation among all the camps of the association. The cattlemen couldn't believe it, as they had so recently seen how jolly and rugged he appeared to be.

I had known Tim Birmingham several years before his wedding. I had seen him at the general roundups about once a year with Oliver Ewell's outfit.

One day I was in Caldwell and "seen" Ewell, "Crate" Justis, and others who always attended the annual stock association meetings. Since I never had attended these meetings, I had no chance to see them in Caldwell. I wondered what they were doing all dressed in their Sunday best. They seemed as glad to see me as I was to see them. They wanted to know if I had come up to the wedding.

I told them, "No, I didn't know anything about the wedding." I asked whose it was. They said it was Tim Birmingham. Since Tim and I were always joking each other, I said, "Who is the unfortunate lady?" Her first name was Lizzie. She used to wait tables in the hotel at Kiowa where Tim had met her.

Ewell and Justis were going upstairs in the hotel on the east side of main street where the ceremony was to occur.

Just then Bill Parker came rushing up and asked, "What does all this mean? Where are you going?"

I told him I was going up to Tim Birmingham's wedding. Then I noticed he had been drinking too much and was awfully ashamed I had said anything about it. Parker must go up and take charge of things, as he put it.

Mr. Ewell said, "I'm awfully sorry you said anything to Parker. We were trying to give Tim a nice little wedding. Now we don't know what we'll do with Bill. He's getting too boisterous and slack in his language. Since he followed you in, we'll have to delegate you to get rid of him."

I said, "I believe I can manage it if you can get Tim out of sight for awhile."

Ewell said he would get Tim behind some curtains so Bill couldn't see him. Then Bill began to gawk around and talk boisterously, trying to find Tim. I said, "Bill, as I come by Phillips's saloon, I seen a lot of cowpunchers in there. I expect that would be a good place to look for him."

So down the steps we went. He swore he'd make Tim set 'em up to the whole crowd. There was quite a bunch of fellows toward the back of the saloon. As we came up to the crowd, I told Bill to go one way and I would go the other way. When I got enough men between us, I ducked and dodged out the door. I went right back to the hotel where the wedding was and told Ewell I had given Bill the dodge at the saloon. He would get a plenty to hold him downstairs.

A Presbyterian minister was there to perform the ceremony. The bride carried a bouquet and wore a veil with an attractive bridal outfit. Tim looked very well in his wedding suit.[8]

After the ceremony we offered congratulations. While we were doing that, the minister was displaying an assortment of nice marriage certificates and wanted to know if Tim and his bride wanted to buy one.

I said, "Tim, by all means, for you will want to show it to your grandchildren."

That being the case, he bought one. I stepped back slightly behind the crowd I thought I had done my duty. Then the preacher said he would have to have at least two witnesses to sign the marriage certificate and asked Tim whom he would have. Tim said he wanted Oliver Ewell and me. I ducked out of sight while Oliver was signing, thinking he would pick somebody else. He was determined that I should sign it and no one else would do. I suggested he get "Crate" Justis but he said he wouldn't feel married if I didn't sign it. So I went forward and Tim was pleased a great deal.

197

We were a little late getting out the next morning. As I was walking along, I "seen" Bill Parker. I didn't care to see him but I just had to go along and meet him. I didn't know how he would feel about my giving him the dodge. He "seen" and walked straight toward me. He ran his arm straight out and up and began to work his fingers. Just as he got to me, he got his hand drawn to his head and he began to scratch it. I asked him if it felt that big.

He said, "It sure does and roars like thunder." I told him if he didn't quit swallowing such stuff, he would wake up some morning and find himself dead.

In 1886 I saw John Eaton at the Leland Hotel in Caldwell and he told me how he and Tom Turner ran a railroad train. They were working for Ed Hewins of Hewins, Kansas,[9] and took a trainload of cattle to Kansas City. On the return they got off at Independence, Kansas, missed the train, then boarded the next one. They were traveling on passes but the conductor on the first train had taken them up. They told the second conductor their fare had been paid. Of course he couldn't take anybody's word and was going to give the signal to put them off the train.

Then they took charge of the train and ran it themselves. They forced the conductor to run past the first station and intended to keep the train in motion until they got to their destination. But the conductor wrote a telegram to the marshal at Elk City and dropped it to the next station agent they passed. The marshal was directed to meet the train and arrest two men who were holding it up.

Even though Eaton and Turner had ordered the engineer not to stop at Elk City, he halted. Eaton ran to the door to see why the train had stopped and looked down the muzzle of a double-barreled shotgun. It looked as big as two rain barrels loaded with tombstones.

"The marshal ordered me to throw up my hands," Eaton said.

I asked, "Did you throw 'em up, John?"

He replied, "Just ask me how quick I did throw 'em up!"

They took their guns, placed hand-cuffs on them, and took them back to Independence. They were fined, but couldn't pay, so were obliged to lay out in jail.

Eaton started up his awfully loud, foghorn voice, keeping people awake for blocks around. The jailor thought he would play out in time but he seemed to grow stonger as time passed. The jailor tried to stop him but Eaton kept on yelling. So the jailor fixed up an iron rod which could reach every part of the cell. He jabbed and punched Eaton when he yelled. Eaton said that contraption beat him so he kept still.

Eaton got the sheriff to send a telegram to Ed Hewins to come bail them out. Hewins "come" over, paid their fine, took them to his ranch, and put them to work again. That was the first and last time that Eaton tried to run a railroad.

NINETEEN

Stagecoach Travel
on the Frontier

Exciting travel experiences occurred all along the frontier. Preston Norris, John Morris, and Jack Jones of Peru had been subpoenaed to attend district court in the county seat, Sedan. The court adjourned on a Saturday at noon, and these men wanted to go back to Peru, their home, seven miles down the Little Caney River. They met "Nate" Bessey, an old friend who lived near Peru. He was an old plainsman who had "drove" stagecoaches through the western mountains. They asked him how he had come; he said in a one-seated top buggy which could not take three. Bessey thought he could trade it for a two-seater at the livery stable. He came back shortly with a two-seated spring wagon. They arranged to eat dinner and go with him.

They knew Bessey was rough as the Rocky Mountains and would do most anything for fun. Before they got to Peru, they learned more about him. A short distance east of Sedan is Wolf Creek which had no bridge and steep banks. To cross this stream required a long turn in the shape of the letter "S." Bessey drove one span of well-broken Indian horses who had good wind and could run long distances without fatigue.

As he came to the brow of the hill above Wolf Creek, Bessey said, "Gentlemen, I'll show you how I used to drive a stage through the Rocky Mountains." Before they could get an idea of what he was going to do, he "throwed" a line out on each side, let out a big yell, and cracked his whip over the backs of the horses and the race was on. Morris began to curse, trying to get Bessey to stop, then plead with tears. He was entirely too late for Bessey had started something which even he couldn't stop.

Morris, not much of a hand at prayer, put up the best appeal he could under such circumstances. Jones occasionally swore six-inch oaths at Bessey but they seemed to glance off. "Pres" Norris, highly educated and refined, sat straight as if he had swallowed a ramrod and never said a word.

200

If one of the horses showed any slackening of its speed, Bessey would touch it up with his whip to make it hold true to position. If the team began to swerve towards a side road or turn into a farmer's driveway, he would give the horse nearest that side a keen cut with the whip on its shoulder and cause it to place its feet in the straight and narrow way again. Thus Bessey drove the full seven miles.

When they arrived at Little Caney about half a mile north of Peru, which also had no bridge, Bessey used the same tactics to guide the team across as before. Then he had a straight course into Peru.

When they got into the town square, Bessey, having no guide lines, yelled, "Whoa." The team proved they had plenty by stopping immediately.

Jones and Morris got their feet on the ground as quick as possible and left. Norris, with his usual dignity, stepped to the ground and said, "Gentlemen, this wagon was made when men were honest!"

At various times from 1878 to 1886 I observed stagecoaches as they traveled from Wichita to Fort Sill, Indian Territory. I never rode one except between Medicine Lodge and Harper, Kansas, so most of my observations were not made from the boot of an omnibus but from the hurricane deck of a Texas cow pony. I was the only passenger that morning from Medicine Lodge. As I started to climb into the coach, the driver said it would be more comfortable in the booth with him.

The weather was cold. Two tandem teams of mules, wheelers and leaders, pulled the coach. One large wheeler was mean and wanted to run away or to tear things to pieces. The driver had already told me about its disposition. He managed to get about four or five miles without mishap. Suddenly the large mule clamped his teeth on the bit and took things into his own hands. The team broke out into a dead run down the road for awhile; then the driver pulled them off the road on to a level piece of prairie and drove in a circle.

The coach was making such a roar I shouted into the driver's ears, "Put 'em on the road and pour the whip to 'em for you can't get 'em there too quick to suit me."

But he held them in that circle until they slackened into a trot; then he let them take the road and never urged the mules to go any faster than a trot. Presently we came to a downward dip or slope, a regular hairpin turn, and in the bottom of the depression was a deep washout. The driver swung his arm toward that huge hole and said, "That's why I wouldn't do what you said. Take the lines and drive awhile for my hands are dead." He had gripped and pulled the lines so long that he had lost all sense of feeling in his hands. I was accustomed to driving four horses, so I took the lines and drove while the coachman pulled off his gloves and rubbed his hands until the feeling came back again.

I asked if the road was fairly good from there onward. He said it was. I asked permission to take the whip and pour it on to that old mule until we could get satisfaction out of him. He did not know how much the mule could stand and did not care to test his capacity just yet. The mule seemed satisfied that he had done enough for one trip.

When I arrived at Harper, I took a train to Moline, then a stage line to Sedan. This line had no regular stagecoach. The conveyance was a large spring wagon with three spring slats fastened across the wagon bed; three persons could occupy each seat. The driver sat in the front seat, making it an eight passenger coach. The wagon had good brakes, controlled by the driver's foot. The harness had heavy tugs but no straps to check the momentum of the carriage.

On the trip the hack driver told us some of his experiences with passengers. One time when he met the train at Moline, a woman named Fitzpatrick took the hack for Sedan. She was a fine-looking, well-dressed, intelligent-looking woman. She had been to Kansas City, it seemed, for the purpose of buying clothes as she had suit cases and hand boxes. The woman and hack driver had formerly lived near each other in Sedan and had cordially hated each other. They recalled all of their former difficulties. The driver began to study some plan to get even.

When they reached a shallow rocky stream, it was slightly swollen from a recent rain. He could have driven close to the little falls just below the crossing and the water would not have been over hub deep there. But he stopped and told her that the stream had risen which would be difficult to cross.

A farmhouse stood in plain sight. The driver advised his passenger to get out, go there, and stay all night; he thought the stream would be down by morning. She asked, "What will you do?"

He replied, "I'll take a chance and cross if I can."

"If you're going to take a chance, I'll take one with you."

He admired her courage. If she did cross, she would have to fix for it. He took her luggage and fastened it high up in the seat. If she wanted to keep her skirts from getting soiled, she would have to stand in the seat and hold on to the bows which held the hack cover. The

202

driver knew perfectly where to drive so the water would come up to the seat and no higher. He drove into the water very carefully to the other side without accident. She began to praise him and expressed her regrets for the way she had treated him in former years. From that point on, both driver and passenger were sociable.

On our trip we had one large hill to ascend and one stream to cross. The road was rough and rocky all the way. The north slope of the big hill was covered with ice because of thawing snow which made it difficult for horses to retain their footing. We thought we would have no trouble with only two passengers. Near the top of the hill one of the horses struck an icy patch, slipped and fell flat on his side, slid back under the carriage, and stripped all the harness off.

We passengers jumped out and helped lift the carriage around to get the horse to its feet again. After we got it harnessed, the horse did its share of the pulling and we arrived at Sedan without further mishap. The other passenger asked me if that was a sample of Chautauqua County. I told him it was.

He said, "I'll just take your word for it." When he got to Sedan he said, "Here are $2; one for delivering me to Sedan and the other back to Moline."

He warned the driver not to leave him. In later years I made another trip from Medicine Lodge to Sedan, but in the summer. Just one other passenger was with me in the mail hack. He stated his business, which was identical with the previous story, then asked me the same question about the country. I related the previous story.

At Sedan he said, "I've seen enough" and pulled out two silver dollars for the driver, "Don't you leave this town without taking me for I've paid my fare to Moline."

On one trip from Harper to Medicine Lodge by regular stagecoach, there were five men and two women. They were business men and women who lived in Medicine Lodge and had been attending a fraternal convention as delegates. I was personally acquainted with only one man. I was the only cowpuncher; no one seemed to notice except the man who knew me. The women acted as if a cowpuncher was an inferior person. When we arrived at the first sand stream, it was covered with ice. The water pressure had not cut through the ice but had made it thin in the middle of the stream. The four-mule team and the front wheels of the stagecoach got safely across the center of the stream. But owing to the coach construction and the load, great weight

203

rested on the hind wheels which broke through the ice. The team, still on the ice, couldn't get footing to pull. The driver hollered down that we would all have to get out to make the coach as light as possible. Some men suggested different things. One thought of taking the axe to cut the ice in front of the hind wheels but that would have been almost an endless job.

I told the women it would not be necessary for them to get out; we would soon have the coach out of the stream. The driver was going to try to make the mules pull the coach out. I told him not to start the mules until I had given them better footing. A considerable amount of loose, dry sand had drifted into low places near the stream's edge. We men lined up along each side of the team and threw sand on the ice under the mules' feet.

When the driver saw what we were doing, he said, "That's a new one on me but it will surely do the job."

I told him not to start until we had given him the word. We got behind the coach on the ice to lift the coach. When we gave the driver the word, he cracked the whip and the mules, having good footing on the sand, began to pull as we helped. The hind wheels rolled up onto the ice and the driver drove out on high ground.

When we got to the second stream, the coach did the same thing, but we all knew what to do. As quick as the hind wheels broke through the ice, the driver told us we would have to get out and get busy with sand. It didn't take the men long to get out. The women got out and helped. Soon the ice was sanded under the mules. The men got behind the coach, as we did before, and we soon drove out upon the bank.

This was the last stream we would have to cross. As we drove away, one of the women turned and gave me full credit for getting them out of the ice. We soon came to the big washout which caused a hairpin turn in the road. I told them about my previous experience with the runaway mules and showed them where the coach driver circled the running team out on the level prairie. All said they would take their chances with a coach stuck in the ice rather than ride in a coach over frozen ground behind a runaway team. The women were pleased to think we had consumed so little time in getting out. It was nearing sundown then and it was after dark when we got into Medicine Lodge.

When the railroad came to Caldwell, the northern end of the stage line was established there and the coaches ran regularly. Stage stations were usually about twenty-six miles apart. The original route went due south to the state line, then southeast twenty-six miles to Pole Cat station. The second station was Pond Creek; the third, Bison; the fourth, Red Fork, where present Dover stands; Kingfisher was next; Fort Reno was the last one I recall.[1]

Usually four mules pulled a single coach but when the roads were bad, six were required. The vehicles were heavy and cumbersome, but stoutly built. The driver rode in what was called a boot, a seat reinforced with an iron frame at the ends of the seat. A long iron rod at his left, extending to the running gears of the coach, was operated by his foot to apply or lessen the brake pressure. Around the top of the omnibus was an iron railing into which all freight or express could be carried. There was a catchall at the rear of the coach in which the driver carried an axe, spade, or anything that might be needed in an emergency.

Passengers could enter or leave the coach through two doors, one in each side. Seats were arranged lengthwise of the coach, but there were no straps like those in street cars of today. When the southbound coach was ready to leave Caldwell, a number of people would assemble to see who was leaving. The manager of the stage line, Henry Todd, was usally present to see that the passengers got away on scheduled time.

One day I recall seeing at least one woman passenger rushing from the Leland Hotel to the open door of the bus which faced the hotel. At the same moment a man hurried to enter the opposite door. As they ducked their heads to get into the coach, they collided like two battering rams. The woman read the riot act to that poor fellow; he stood back and meekly took the tongue lashing, then quietly climbed into his seat.

During a lull in business when not many men from the cow camps were in town, Todd came to me and wanted to know if I would drive the stage, as one driver was unexpectedly missing. I wanted nothing to do with the coach driving business, for I had been in "them" things for the last time. I pointed out a man on the street who had asked me a few minutes before where he could get a job. Todd asked him if he would take the job. He did. They went to the barn, harnessed four mules, led them to the front, and hitched them to the coach. The driver got into the boot and picked up the lines to start.

The city of Caldwell had dug a drainage ditch in front of the barn but had not refilled it properly. Todd had not noticed the condition of

205

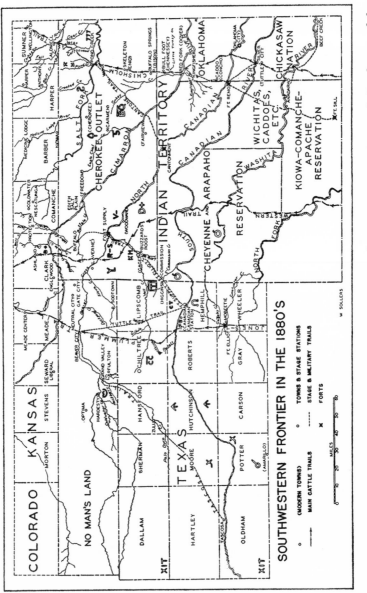

Map 5. The path of the Stage Line through Indian Territory in the 1880s. From *A Cowman's Southwest*, ed. by Angie Debo. Copyright © 1953 by the Arthur H. Clark Company.

the ditch. The awkward new driver did not set the brake firmly enough and permitted the team to start too quickly. When the coach struck the ditch, the driver's foot slipped from the brake, and he fell down in front of the omnibus. Two of its wheels passed over his body, killing him; someone stopped the mules. Todd climbed up and drove the stage, himself.

The Southwestern Stage Line also built boats to be used in high water. Across Pond Creek the company built a bridge from cotton-wood trees, growing nearly on the banks. A chain was fastened across one end of the bridge to prevent freighters and others from using it. There was a notch in the tree cut high above the ground in which the padlock key for the chain was hidden. No one could see it unless he stood on the bridge railing.

Salt Fork was the next stream which required a boat during high water. If it was too high to cross by coach, the passengers and mail were placed in the boat at about the time the other stagecoach appeared from the opposite direction. Each coach would take the other's passengers and mail. The same procedure was observed at the Cimarron.

I have crossed both Canadian Rivers but have never seen any boats. Sometimes the stagecoaches did not connect on schedule when the Salt Fork or the Cimarron were at flood stage. I recall one instance. The northbound coach arrived at the south bank of the Salt Fork. The manager of the stage line, Henry Todd, was on an inspection tour as a passenger. He was so confident that the coach from Caldwell would eventually come that he permitted the driver to turn back to Bison. Thus Todd, Bill Dunlap, "Boff" Baughman, and a big fat boy in his teens were left afoot. To while away their time they looked for some-thing to interest themselves.

They saw a raccoon run across the prairie, surrounded and killed it with sticks, dressed it, built a fire, and roasted it. It was rather flat tasting for they had no salt but the boy was hungry and made a meal of the raccoon. It was so fat the boy got his face and hands greasy. That gave the talkative Baughman a subject for discourse.

He talked about the beauties of nature and pointed to the boy as a perfect picture of health, how he fitted into the glories and grandeur of nature. Dunlap said Baughman was useful for once, as they needed all his stories to while away the long hours that night on the open prairie. The southbound coach did not arrive until the next forenoon.

In the early 'eighties two deputy U.S. marshals arrested Wes Fay, a

207

notorious desperado of the Southwest, and his associate. They boarded the stagecoach at Caldwell to take the outlaws to Texas to stand trial.

There was a general order: if drivers had women passengers, to stop near a swampy, thick growth of small timber through which the stage line passed. All passengers must leave the coach, the men in one direction and the women in the other. This stopping place, as I recall, was just north of Bison. Mrs. George Haynes and Henry Todd were also passengers. When the coach arrived at the thicket and stopped, all of the passengers were ordered out. The two officers left their guns in the coach because the prisoners were handcuffed.

When they returned to the coach, Fay, because of his unusually small hands, had removed his handcuffs and held the officer's Winchester in his hand. He ordered the officers to unlock the handcuffs of the other prisoner. When that was done, the outlaws said they would kill the two officers, but Mrs. Haynes made such a plea that they decided to let them live.

The outlaws took all the officers' firearms and asked Todd if the mules were broke. When he didn't know, the outlaws ordered Todd to mount each one and show their gaits by riding them around. Todd did, the outlaws selected two, and rode off. They were left with two mules to pull them to Bison where the coaches always changed teams.

Henry Todd offered $50 for the mules to be delivered at Bison. One day a so-called "cowpuncher" came leading the mules and claimed the reward.[2]

After Fay's escape, John Chapin of Red Fork Station, where Dover is now located, sketched the account of this affair and sent the drawing to the *Police Gazette*. He told me when the drawing appeared, it had been censored. Chapin had drawn pictures of the men, portraying them indecently exposed. Todd was riding the mules with their heads low, between their knees and bucking, while his coattails flapped in the breeze.

TWENTY

Working on the Skeleton Ranch

When the fencing was begun in 1882, I was holding a through herd of 3500 cattle for J. D. Payne at Skeleton ranch on Skeleton Creek where North Enid now stands. He wanted the herd kept there until frost killed the ticks and chose this unoccupied range because of the abundance of grass and water.

I had five men, including a cook. They were John Beck, an illiterate consumptive; Myron Cleveland; "Little George" Frear, Payne's stepson; Charlie Ritchie, the cook; and Steve Carr, a cross-eyed Negro. The cook and I were the only ones who were right-handed. When a visitor asked me about it, I answered, "We can all get around a pot of beans with a spoon in each hand and do effective work as anybody."

Throughout the summer I had to make a number of changes among the men. John and Myron were on herd one afternoon. Myron, with his Winchester rifle, attended one side of the herd; Beck, the other. Myron rode up to Beck, "John, the cattle are working too close to the breaks leading to Bear Creek. You had better turn 'em back, for we'll have to be starting for the bed ground pretty soon."

John replied, "Let me have your Winchester, Myron, I'll show you how I can turn 'em back with it."

I presume he believed if he skipped a bullet alongside the herd, they would turn back. He took the rifle, pointed it, fired, and killed a cow. He mounted his horse, came to camp as hard as he could ride, and told me he had shot a cow out there. I asked if he had killed her.

He said, "Yes, I killed her dead."

I said, "What did you shoot her with? You didn't have anything to shoot with that I know of."

He explained and I told him to return and help Myron get the herd to the bed ground. I wrote to Sam Fling that I was sending John Beck back to him. He had killed a $25 cow and his work hadn't been satisfactory. I felt sorry for him; perhaps Fling could give him some profitable employment on the ✟ ranch.

In the morning I told Beck to catch a horse which I wanted to get rid of and put on his saddle. I gave him the letter and told him to take it to Sam Fling on the ⚕ ranch about fifty miles west.

I wrote a letter to B. W. Key at Caldwell to send a man down on the morning stage. He sent a big sixteen-year-old fellow. I told him he could take first guard.

He was between the herd and camp when a small tornado struck. The cattle ran straight from him; he ran directly across the bed ground to get into the lead of the herd. I jumped onto my horse and started after the rampaging cattle. A big flash of lightning revealed the running herd strung along a quarter of a mile. The boy was riding alongside the cattle at top speed. When we got them stopped and quieted, I asked how it was that they had such a lead against him. He told me as he ran across the bed ground, his horse couldn't see because of pitch darkness and struck its head against a post which was set there to locate the bed ground. The horse dropped to the ground as if dead. Beck lay on the ground momentarily, then got to his feet. He led the horse a few steps, saw he was recovering, then mounted him, and was in full pursuit when the lightning flash revealed them to me. I told the boy he had done fine since he was so young and had never worked cattle before.

As summer advanced, many cows became infected with screw worms from screw fly egg deposits. Since these parasites feed on live animal flesh, I wrote to Key to send us a case of cresylic ointment. The glass jars were so thick and heavy that the ointment had to be taken out by knife point. We placed it in a large soup spoon, melted it over a small flame, and poured the hot liquid into the worm-infected wound. This served as both curative and preventive for the scent drove away the screw flies.[1]

In the spring of 1881 Frank Bates had bought a herd of saddle horses at Caldwell from the Kingsbury and Dunson outfit, including Bob and Dick, his private driving horses for a number of years—Black Spanish, Nigger Baby, and Roach. Roach and old Shep helped me stop the great cattle drift in the winter of 1881–82. These horses were all gentle and easily handled. During this summer I rode Little Cream, the best roping horse I ever rode, from this outfit. If he liked a fellow, he behaved nicely. If not, he was apt to kick or attempt to bite him. He worked well on the open range, for he felt the pull of the cow's weight at the saddle horn while it was running. He dashed in close to the animal's left side to force it to the right and stepped over the slack rope with its front feet. Little Cream then braced himself for the spill.

A lone rider stopped to stay all night. I "seen" he was in bad shape but had no idea what was the matter. His eyes were terribly bloodshot. He rolled his head in a peculiar manner and wanted to know how far it was to Caldwell. About two nights before, a thunder shower had come up while he was on night herd and a bolt of lightning killed his horse. When other cowpunchers found him, they at first thought he was dead. They carried him to the wagon and he began to revive. They put him in the camp wagon and took him with the outfit the next day. The following day he said he could ride and the boss told him to go to Caldwell to get medical attention. After staying all night with us, he said he slept and felt better, but his eyes were in bad shape. He rode on towards Caldwell and that was the last I saw him.

To show the value cattlemen placed on wild horses, I recall an incident which occurred after we had made our change of horses at noon. I generally rode out in the afternoon to see how the cattle were doing. If the riders let the cattle go too far out towards Black Bear Creek, they might follow the draws leading to this stream and the men lost sight of them. As I rode through the grazing ground, I "seen" something a' coming straight towards the herd. I rode towards it to make out what it was and to turn it away from the herd. There is no telling what it would have done if it had taken a notion to free itself from its torment. It was either a mustang or an outlaw horse which someone wanted to get rid of. An old, full-grown, flint cowhide had been tied to its tail. No telling where it came from and no one knew where it went or cared. I turned it clear of the herd and watched until it went out of sight, nothing was disturbed. It was actually funny to watch the animal run. Sometimes the dry hide was sailing straight out behind the horse; again the hide turned on its edge; its legs caught on the turf which caused the hide to bounce onto the horse's back. He lowered his head and began to buck. As the hide slid down his side, the horse kicked it with his hind feet. I heard its hoofs hit that dry hide several hundred yards distant. It didn't look so funny when I "seen" it coming toward the herd but after I got it past the herd, I enjoyed the sight as well as the fellows who had tied the hide to the horse.

In the fall when I went to deliver this herd fifty or sixty miles west to the ⚳ headquarters ranch, a three- to four-day drive, we could not make a direct drive because of the appearance of cattlemen's new fences. The fellows who were contracted to build them used well-seasoned posts. Kegs of fence staples were set along the line at intervals. The heads had been knocked out. The upright kegs were filled with the staples ready for use.

It was difficult to drive a herd across country without a marked trail. We struck one fence and were obliged to turn the herd around it, which delayed us. As we followed the fence, the boys found some of these kegs. They dismounted and filled their saddle pockets with staples. Whenever a steer began to lag, the fellow near it took some staples and threw them at the beast. The points invariably pierced its hide and caused the animal to quicken his pace to the great amusement of the boys. This saved them from making so many runs to make the herd string out and trail. It was also much better than to wake up the straggler by swearing at him. Whenever a cowpuncher swore at a steer, it was always done in a loud, keen voice, and it seemed to stir the beast to action more quickly than any other device. The moment it started, the steers began to turn their ears toward the swearer and change direction.

Later that fall I went to Caldwell after a load of wire, flour, bacon, etc. When I went in to see Key at the Yorke, Parker, and Draper store, he seemed greatly pleased. "Do you know how much trade you brought us this summer?" I had never figured it up but I knew it was a pretty good bill. He said, "We have just settled up with them and it amounted to $1200."

There was a small single-shot Ballard rifle in the ⚹ camp. I had shot prairie chickens with it and we had plenty to eat. At that time there was nothing much to do around headquarters. One morning I looked across Sand Creek and "seen" a flock of turkeys walking single file upstream. I took the rifle and went toward them but they "seen" me and hid in the grass. I decided they had slipped away and was about ready to return to camp when a big gobbler jumped up and started to fly up the creek. I jerked up the rifle and took good aim; when I fired, a big bunch of feathers flew. He never flapped his wings again but used them to balance himself to sail ahead. As he drew near the ground, he changed course a little, kept sailing over one bank, and finally disappeared behind a bank along the creek bed. I expected to find him about where he went out of sight. I had about given him up when I looked still farther up the creek and "seen" where he had struck the top wire of the gap. I slipped up behind the water gap,

212

raised up, looked over, and "seen" him lying flat on the ground with his eyes watching me. I took aim and shot him through the head. When I picked him up, I discovered the first shot had struck him in the thigh and left him only one leg to run on.

I took the old gobbler to camp. Bates and Payne were there alone. They got a pair of scales, dropped their work, took his measurements and weight; they said people back home would be amazed at the size of turkeys which "growed" wild in the country.

TWENTY-ONE

The Last Big Cherokee Strip Roundup

The last big roundup was held in 1883. The Comanche County Pool decided to send a wagon outfit to attend the spring roundup on the South Canadian River. Sam Fling sent me from the ⚕ ranch and Abner Wilson sent "Texas Dave" Thomas from Major Drumm's ranch to join the pool outfit. We were instructed to fall in with them on the Texas Trail.

Because the Indians seemed to be subdued, there was no need to go armed. Many cowpunchers quit carrying six-shooters by 1880; those who did were considered tenderfeet. But we knew this southern roundup would be met with opposition from rustlers so we strapped on our six-shooters.

I took five horses and my bedding and met Dave at the appointed place, but we never "seen" anything of the pool wagon. It looked as if it would rain as it was already misting, so we stopped, took off our packs, and put them together on one horse; thus, we had enough horses bunched before us which made it easier to drive them down the trail. We overtook a wagon, but it was the Barber County wagon with Lee Bradley[1] in charge. The wagon had good bows and sheet over them. We told him we would like to unpack our horse and put the pack in his wagon on account of the weather. He had plenty of room. Our horses with theirs made a fairly large bunch.

Dave and the Barber County boys started on ahead. Bradley and I, behind. As we rode along, we heard a turkey gobble in a small brushy hollow off to one side of the trail. I said, "Let's go over and get that turkey." Lee thought it would be useless to go; I told him if we worked it just right, we could have turkey for supper. We rode around to the opposite side of the thicket; when the turkey flew, Lee shot with his six-shooter but missed. I had not drawn my gun.

Lee said, "Let's chase him." We rode rather fast until he lit in the trail, which I wanted him to do. We rode around him to turn him back toward the wagon. Lee wanted to give chase; I told him not to excite

214

the turkey and make him fly but let him trot. I suggested if he turned out on Lee's side of the trail, Lee should ride out slowly to turn him back. If he turned on my side, I would do the same. He was taking the "turkey trot" down the trail and gradually tiring. Lee became greatly interested in the chase when I told him that was the way we had always caught turkeys. Directly we could see his wings beginning to droop.

By the time we overtook the wagon, he was dragging his wings clear to the ground. He didn't seem to notice the wagon until he got almost to it. He had been looking for a chance to turn back. He tried to break past us but could run only a little and couldn't fly at all. Lee hollered to the cook to look out behind. The cook poked his head up over the wagon cover and looked back but couldn't see what we were doing yet.

I hollered, "Come and get your turkey for supper."

He "seen" him then, jumped out, ran back, gathered him up in his arms, and wanted to know where we got him. I told him he was a mighty tired turkey now, but he would be rested up considerably before we arrived where we would camp for the night. So we had better tie him carefully if he wanted to cook him for supper.

We crossed Turkey Creek west of where Hennessey now stands before we stopped for the night. We wanted to get to higher ground lest the stream rise during the night and cut us off from our destination. We ate all the turkey before we left camp.

That night Dave told of a most peculiar accident that happened to George Gordon when Major Drumm sent him to look over Gordon's range. I had known Gordon several years as a single man. His small range was on Preacher Creek southwest of where Hennessey now stands. I think Major Drumm had staked this young fellow, for he had given financial assistance to several other cattlemen, some who were prominent. I arrived at this conclusion because Dave was his outside man.

Dave found Gordon with his young wife and a baby less than a year old, living in a one-room log cabin. It had one door and a half-window to let in sunlight. He stayed all night with the Gordons. Nothing of note happened until they were at the breakfast table. Then like a flash, things began to materialize. Gordon made some awful strangling noises, leaped to his feet, and fell out the door onto the ground, rolling and gasping for breath, black in the face. Dave and Gordon's wife rushed out to where he lay on his back, gasping for breath and working at his throat with his fingers. Dave asked, "What's the matter with him?"

Gordon's wife observed that his two front false teeth were gone, "He has swallowed his teeth!"

Dave told her to take him to Fort Reno and put him in care of the military post surgeon. They found he could breathe, lying in a certain position. Gordon kept a span of mules in a little shed close to the log house. He also had a spring wagon in which Dave and Mrs. Gordon fixed a bed. They hitched the mules to the wagon and she took the baby in her arms.

Dave told her to drive southeast and cross the Cimarron above the mouth of Turkey Creek. She was to continue in the same direction until she struck the old cattle trail and stagecoach route to Fort Reno. Dave closed up the house and started back to Major Drumm's ranch.

When Mrs. Gordon reported at Fort Reno, she found a competent surgeon. He said this was the third case that the medical journals recorded in which the patient survived such an ordeal.

Gordon's wife was less than twenty years old, driving through a wilderness country which she had never seen with an infant in her arms, and her husband, who might die any minute, not knowing what to expect or what would happen after she got to Fort Reno. This was grim courage and heroism of a high order.[2]

After Turkey Creek our next stop was the Red Fork ranch on the Cimarron. John Chapin was in charge and also ran a small general merchandise store in connection with the ranch. I hadn't seen him for a few years so we had quite a visit.

We went down to see if we could cross the river, but it was so high we "was" afraid to go in right away. Since this was the regular stage line crossing, the company had a row boat, but Chapin had orders not to let anybody have it. He would let me have it if I would take good care to bring it back. I told the Barber County outfit I could get the boat if we could get somebody to row it. Ad Pardee knew how.[3] I "seen" he was a stout fellow and decided he could row the boat alone if he had to. There were only two oars, but there was room enough on the seat for two men. I pretended we had two men to operate the boat and went to get the key to unlock the padlock which held the chain that fastened the boat. I told Pardee to bring the boat around so we could load it with our bedding and whatever else we had to carry.

While we "was" loading it, seven or eight Indian boys came up. They were under supervision of a German who had gotten a contract to deliver them to Caldwell. There, they were to take the train for the

Carlisle Indian School in Pennsylvania. Some of the boys were nearly full-grown and spoke good English. One of the big boys wanted to know if they could get that boat to carry his parents across to the north side.

He pointed to the south bank, "That's my father and mother sitting over there. They want to find a way to come across so they can go with us to Caldwell."

I couldn't let him have the boat, "If you'll take our empty wagon across the river to the south bank, I'll give you a dollar and a half in silver and bring your father and mother when we come back for this load."

This tickled the boys immensely and they went after the wagon at once. In the meantime the German drove into the river and started across to where we were. He had a brand new wagon and a span of large mules, long-legged and good travelers. We stood watching to see how he would make it. The mules kept coming; first one would drop into a deep hole; as he came up, perhaps the next one would go down. The German stood up in the wagon and held the team steady until he got about forty yards from the north bank. Suddenly both mules went out of sight. He stood holding on the lines, looking, but there wasn't a thing in sight.

All of a sudden they popped up like a flash and made such a sudden jump that the force of the deep water "throwed" the wagon bed right out of the standards; the driver let go the lines as he floated downstream. The mules walked right out onto the bank. Some of the boys caught and tied them up. The Indian boys just stood looking without a smile or an appearance of fright.

The German was hollering, "Help! Help!! I want help!!!"

I said to the Indians, "If you expect to get to Caldwell, go and get that fellow."

They all started in a rush; some had to swim all the time while the tall ones could find places where they could wade. They soon caught him, shoved him close to the bank, and brought him up to our wagon.

Pardee came to me, "I can't find a man who has ever rowed a boat before."

"I'll just have to go myself," I didn't tell him I had never rowed a boat.

We got in and started up close along the north bank to get a good chance to cross before the current forced us below the crossing on the south side. We hadn't gone very far when he began to inquire what was the matter with me. At times my oars missed the water or plowed toward the bottom.

"Ad, I'll just tell you the truth; I never have handled an oar in my life but we've got to cross this river."

He said, "If I had known that, I never would have gotten into this boat, but go ahead and do the best you can until we hit the current." When we did, he said, "Let me have your oar." He leaned back as far as he could with both oars and took that boat as fine as I ever "seen." When we got through the current, he said, "Take the oar."

I laid hold of it and we soon shot up "again" the bank. The old Indian came up, grabbed the prow of the boat, and helped pull it on to the bank. We unloaded and motioned to him and his squaw to get in. I tried to get him to take my oar. He shook his head vehemently. When we struck the current, Ad took both oars as before and we soon crossed and unloaded the Indians.

By that time the Indian boys had gotten the old German and his wagon box safely ashore and had taken our wagon across to the south bank. The boy with whom I made the deal was waiting for his money. I handed it to him and we got ready to start back across with our second boat-load.

The German came rushing up, "These boys want their money." He turned and talked to the boys, then came back, "They say you never paid 'em."

I replied heatedly, "You're a dirty liar; they never told you any such thing. You start right out of here or I'll build a smoke under you." He wheeled, started right off, and never said another word.

We took the second load just as the first one. Pardee thought I had improved right smart. If I kept up, I would learn to handle a boat.

When we came back, Pardee took the boat around, chained, and locked it. I took the key to Chapin. We mounted our horses and crossed the river as we had done many times before, either wading or swimming, when the water was deep. We reloaded our wagon, hooked up the team, and started for the North Canadian.

Just before we arrived at the river crossing, Pardee killed a large buck and the whole outfit had enough venison for several meals. The deer were numerous in this part of the country because the government had begun to issue beeves to the Cheyennes. Since they had plenty beef, they did not do much hunting.

Now all the rest, particularly the young, wanted to chase deer.

Young Jim McDonald hadn't been out on such a trip; he wanted me to go with him to try to kill some deer. I told him I hadn't lost any deer and had enough with my string of horses to attend. So he went by himself. After awhile he came riding in with the most sorrowful look on his face. His horse was bleeding at the nose and he wanted to know what could be done.

I asked what had hurt his horse. He had jumped a bunch of deer and was pursuing them through the timber when a dead limb ran into one of its nostrils. The limb broke off and a piece was left in the flesh. McDonald dismounted and pulled the stick out and the blood gushed which gave him a terrible scare. He thought a great deal of this nice, gentle, company horse. If the horse bled to death, he might have to pay for it and probably lose his job.

It was so far up the nostril we couldn't see where the wound was. I told him if we had a hot iron to run up the nostril to hit the spot, it might cauterize the wound. He took an iron stake pin about eighteen inches long and heated it red hot. Before the horse knew, McDonald thrust it up the nostril. I suppose it hit the right spot for it stopped bleeding immediately.

My horse, Little Cream, fell out with Clem Powell, a member of an eastern cow outfit in the Strip. Of nights we turned our saddle horses loose to graze. In the morning we made a corral out of our ropes by tying them to the grub wagon wheels. We usually walked in with our saddle ropes and roped the horses we were to use that day. The morning I decided to ride Little Cream, I picked up my bridle instead of the rope. As I entered the corral, I met Powell running out and Little Cream, with his ears laid back, was after him. "Whose horse is that?" Powell yelled. "Take him out of there. He'll kill somebody!" I merely walked up and put his bridle on. Then Powell laughed, "What's the matter with him anyhow?"

"Why he is the best horse I ever rode. He runs so smooth I can rope a steer as accurately as if I were standing on the ground," I answered. He had more respect for Little Cream thereafter.

We found the North Canadian running over its banks. There we overtook the Comanche County Pool wagon with Tom Pettyjohn in charge. Tom Doyle and Jim Wilson were the other representatives. They "was" wanting to cross to the South Canadian just as we. They had finished working on a raft to set a wagon box on to cross because the Canadian is deep.

Tom said, "Now we've got the raft made, we've got to get a rope stretched across from a tree on this bank to one on the other bank." Someone asked how he was going to get it across. He said if he could get someone to play out the rope, he could swim across and tie it to the other tree. Doyle and Wilson both objected. If Tom could get the right kind of man, he would show us. He looked us over, then said to me, "I want you to take the rope and play it out to me."

I replied, "All right, I'll do the best I can. I want to cross that river myself."

"Let's go upstream. I've got to have the advantage of a current to make it to them trees," he observed. He pointed them out and found a place which seemed to be far enough upstream.

I placed a rope coil around my arm. He took the rope frazzle between his teeth and passed it over his shoulder so that the rope pressure would tend to pull his head up from the water. Then he got in and started to swim straight until he struck the current. It carried him down and I walked to keep opposite him as I was afraid we might run out of rope if I stood still. As good luck would have it, he came out on the opposite bank at the trees where he wanted to fasten the rope. Soon we had it stretched up and tied solidly at each end.

We pinned together a bunch of dry logs and put the pool wagon box on the raft. Noah Mills stayed on as ballast; he could pull the raft back and forth across the stream. When one side appeared too heavy, he shifted position to keep it from dipping water. We loaded everything into the wagon box which we wanted to take across.

Powell said his horses couldn't swim. I told him that he was to blame, not the horses. I was riding old Buck, a big dun, bald-faced horse, a good swimmer. I had him take my horse and I'd take his horse. He started first and I rode behind to watch. He leaned to one side. I yelled at him to straighten up, not turn over old Buck and drown him. Old Buck had belonged to mailman, Charlie King, who sold him to Sam Fling. A good ranch horse, he swam swollen rivers like a duck. This quality was especially appreciated in a country where there were no bridges across creeks and rivers. Powell's horse swam as good as any horse. He acknowledged he had learned more about riding a swimming horse from me than he had ever known.

When the pool got ready to take the running gears of their wagon across the North Canadian, they tied a rope to the end of the tongue but forgot to tie down the front bolster. When they pulled it up on the south bank, they found the water's force had lifted it and the king bolt. Somehow the coupling pole stuck fast in the wagon hound and all they lost was their bolster. This outfit carried more tools than I ever saw in a cow outfit. They cut a young solid tree, bored a hole through it, and made a wooden king bolt and standards. I didn't know common cowpunchers could become such good wagon makers.

Our empty wagon box was easily taken across on the raft. That left Bill Parker and me with all the saddle horses. The bank was steep on the north side and it was difficult to get the horses to take to the water. We had to fasten ropes to form a chute to force them in; then they readily swam across. We both understood how to swim horses.

All my horses were good swimmers, but I had forgotten the peculiarities of the one I rode. When he took to the water, he let down to see how deep the water was first. That left me about ten feet above him, waiting for him to come up. He always came up and swam as pretty as a duck when he got ready to go.

When I came out on the south bank, the other fellows had a big fire burning and on a log sat Tip McCracken, "Barbecue" Campbell's ranch foreman. I hadn't seen him for several years. He said there had been an awful sight of cattle rustling between the two Canadian rivers.

Rustlers were usually old cowpunchers who had been thrown out of work because of the range fencing. They changed brands by reapplying a branding iron to change the original mark. Some were very successful, but cattle inspectors usually caught up with them. Frequently a rustler mutilated the original brand and added one of his own elsewhere.

When I was working for the ♀ outfit, I always tried to make them all the money I could, which is to say, whenever I was cutting a herd of cattle on general roundups and found brands so blotched that no one could recognize them, I would run them into the ♀ cut. I also ran in stray animals which had perfectly plain brands but were not claimed by anyone. By being familiar with Kansas and Territory brands, that gave me a good chance to pick up a good deal of stock for the ♀ outfit.

Henry Johnson was stationed at Kansas City by the Cherokee Strip Live Stock Association.[4] He knew every brand that came into the stockyards and was certain to point out any irregularities. Inspectors always asked shippers about them. Some rustlers then resorted to driving cattle to Darlington or Fort Reno to sell to the government agency for Indian beef issue. In time this became a flourishing business for the cattle rustlers. The blanket Cheyenne Indians soon saw through this system. Whenever they wanted a beef, they rode out and shot one from the rustlers who could say nothing. Anyone who happened to cross the reservation was apt to have cattle killed; horsemen were apt to lose horses when Indians appeared and demanded a toll for crossing their reservation. This led to the killing of Running Buffalo at Cantonment in 1884.[5] After Old Oklahoma was opened to settlement, Chris Madsen[6] took charge of the government issues at Fort Reno. He caught some but was unable to convict them. This rustling practice was soon broken up.

The rustlers who heard that we were coming down from the Strip to round up that country said they wouldn't allow us to cut out any "burnt" cattle. They had branded a number of strays during the previous winter. McCracken saw several of Campbell's cattle with winter brands as he rode through their range. Since their threats, we were more determined to round up and cut out anything we could claim.

The next morning before we started south, a Texan came to our camp and told us he was driving a herd of full-fed beeves across the Territory on grass to Caldwell to ship to the eastern markets. Many others were doing this because of the high freight rates on the M. K. & T., the only railroad through the Territory. He didn't have a man in his outfit that would swim a horse across swollen streams and he wanted some of us to swim back across with them.

I told him he must have a dickens of an outfit, they needed a good firing. We had our jobs and were not doing swimming for other parties. His men were sitting there listening; they knew we had been swimming and had not considered it difficult. One man spoke up and said he would swim it if we would tell him how. We all rounded up his herd and pointed them down into the river. They plunged in. I was on the right-hand point, downstream. I told him since the cattle were swimming well, he should swim alongside, downstream, to keep them from turning with the current and let his horse swim without interference.

He did well until he got within a few rods of the north bank when he got excited, lost control, jumped to his feet on the horse's back, then leaped right over the its head and started swimming for the north bank. He was a good swimmer and beat the horse to the bank. Since no one else had taken to the water, the cattle kept crowding downstream until they got to a large tree with spreading branches dipping into the

222

swollen stream. It seemed the cattle were going to break at this tree and cause trouble, but just then a big longhorn steer went under a big limb, his horns hooked on the limb and the current swept his body into the tree. He was on his back, heels up, struggling for life. It made such a noise that he turned the herd upstream again. The balance swam across in good shape. The old steer finally slipped loose and followed the herd.

The men of the Comanche County Pool told the Texan he could use the raft and take the rope too if he would give them as much rope as they had in the cable across the river. He did, gladly. He couldn't swim a horse and never had been across such a stream. He didn't blame the boys for not wanting to swim.

We started for the South Canadian where we had our first roundup, a regular rustlers' roundup. They had about 4000 head in one roundup which was difficult to find stray cattle, so many different brands did the rustlers claim.

Bill Parker was outside, helping hold the roundup; he worked for "Fine" Ewing whose brand was an appropriate **UN**. I saw two big four-year-old beeves with the **UN** brand and earmarks. I noticed five rustlers, claiming the cattle, had bunched between their roundup and our cut. "Bill, here are two of 'Fine's' big beeves," I aimed for the rustlers to hear.

Bill said, "All right, I'll help you get 'em out."

As we started them out, they yelled, "Hold on there, you can't take them out of that herd." Bill carried a Winchester on his saddle and I had a six-shooter. We drew our guns and started the beeves out to put them in our cut.

Tip McCracken and the rest of the boys began to come over to our side of the herd. They stopped and never said nor did anything more. After we had gotten the beeves into our cut, Bill and I rode back to the rustlers.

There was one fellow with them who had stayed overnight with me on Skeleton Creek in 1882. I said, "Puckett, I'll show you why we were so cocksure about these two steers." I took out my brand book which had the brands and ear marks of all cattlemen in the Strip. I turned to the page which showed Ewing's brand and earmark. I told him the steers had only Ewing's brands and earmarks. Bill Parker's horse had the same brand on its left shoulder. "What have you fellows got to show for your claim?"

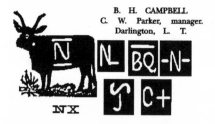

B. H. CAMPBELL
C. W. Parker, manager.
Darlington, L. T.

EWING & POTTER
Postoffice, Caldwell, Ks.
UI– on either or both sides.
Horse brand same left hip.
Range in forks of Cimaron
river and Cottonwood creek
Indian Territory.
W. P. Ewing in charge
OTHER BRANDS

DICKEY BROS.

Cantonment Ind. Ty
Ranch North and
South Canadian riv
ers. Cattle branded
with same brand on
either side or hip &
same on both sides.
Horse brand TL on
left hip or sholder.

HEWINS, TITUS & WILSON
Post-office address.
Indian Springs, I T
Left side mallet, parallel
bars and Roman cross.
Both sides ——and
8. Right side VT.
on left side.

right
side

left side. The above are additional
brands.

DICKEY CATTLE CO.

Range on North and south
Canadian rivers, near Cantonment. Indian Territory
Home office 17 .243, State
Street, Chicago, Ills.
cattle branded as per
cuts on left and right sides.

Some cattle branded on either side or hip
and some on both sides.
L7L on right side and
LLL on right side.

T. F. WORTHINGTON
in charge.

W. E. MALALEY.

Crop off left ear and
a hole and slit in the
right. Running W
on both sides imme-
diatley back of the
shoulder. Horse
brand, running W
on right shoulder. P
O range and ranch
Pnalt Creek, I. T.

Also Sweetwater, Wheeler Co. Texas.

Carnegie & Fraiser
Range on Coldwa-
ter, I. T. P. O. Pond
Additional brands
(prinipally on left
side or hip) : 55; Z;
7; II; JII; and H;
⊖ and II; over
cross; OR. Horse
brand same as on
cut without the T.

**KANSAS CITY
CATTLE COMPANY**

STOCK RANGE   STOCK RANGE

Eagle Chief and Cimarron Rivers.
P. O. Kiowa Kas & Kansas City Mo.

Brands on either side or both. known as the
T5 brand, old m F. shallow fork in right : now
wd under bit in left
ADDITIONAL BRANDS
Both sides. Mark, crop and under bit in
both.
Horse brand same as cattle, on right hip.
A. H. JOHNSON, Manager.
Kansas City, Mo

E .M. Ford,
Hunnewell,
Kan. Ranch
on Red Rock,
I.T. 4D right
side. F right
jaw. Also ⌒
& reversed D
on right side.
G; P and ⌒on
left side; JY
on left shoul-
der and hip. 4D left shoulder and hip; heart
on left hip. John Miller, Manager

Cattle brands of Kansas and Cherokee Strip cattlemen. Adapted from advertisements in *The Cheyenne Transporter*, by Clay Maxwell.

They had no claims but had orders to hold all **UN** four-year-old beeves. Bill said we would still hold possession of them.

Puckett came and asked me what I thought of Parker's ideas, if he was usually correct on such things. I said he was an old experienced cowhand, had worked for Ewing for several years, and ought to know all about them. Then Puckett wanted to know about Tip McCracken, how long I had known him, and if he was a bad man. I told him that Tip came up the trail in 1878. I had been with him ever since. He was down along the South Canadian hunting "Barbecue" Campbell's cattle, would take them whether they had winter brands or not, and we would stand by him. This was the first time I had seen McCracken riding heavily armed. He carried a Winchester, six-shooter, and dirk knife which the rustlers had noticed.

After we finished working this range, Parker and Dave started up the South Canadian with the pool wagon. Noah Mills and I went south with the Đ wagon to the Caddo Indian reservation.[7] They had lots of horses and cattle but no individual brands. Their tribal nation brand was a T on a stool, Ꞓ.

I did not see any hogs or chickens in Caddo country although these Indians were civilized. Most men wore plug hats, ornaments around their necks and in their ears, white men's type of pants, gaudy shirts, and beads. They paid no attention to us as we rode through.

The Indians had just begun to use houses instead of lodges. There were some nice-looking frame houses; most were log houses. The Caddoes were a clean race. The ground around their lodges was cleaned of all grass and vegetation about a rod in every direction. When they built their houses, which usually faced the south, the ground was cleared in like manner about two rods wide in front. The squaws kept the ground clean daily, using a maul—a log about four feet long, square at the bottom, and tapering to a hand-hold at the top. When it was dry, they sprinkled the ground, then tamped it with the maul. There was no erosion there; the ground would neither blow nor wash away. At the side of each door was a mortar, a log about three feet tall, standing on end. On top was a smooth, hard hewn-out basin.

The reservation had small corn fields, but we did not learn how the Indians planted and tended their white soft-kerneled corn. We called it flour corn. The little sample we got proved to be fine bread. They kept their corn in the house. As they arose in the morning, they took the corn for breakfast, poured it into a mortar, and pounded it with a

225

pestle, four inches in diameter, two feet long, made from hard close-grained wood on the same principle as was the maul. They always had a neat-fitting cover made of native wood for the mortar to keep out rain or dirt.

The Caddo country was fine-looking as most of it had never been disturbed by the plow. It rained nearly every day we were there which kept the streams flooded. There were no bridges or roads. We had to swim the streams every day as we looked for cattle. This included the Washita River and Sugar Creek which seemed so crooked. The south bends of all these streams nearly always struck a blufflike bank. The north bends were usually low. I think this caused such floods along the Washita after the white settlement.

When we first began to swim the streams, the weather was cloudy and cool and we kept on our clothes most of the time. When the clouds began to break and the sun to shine, we rolled up our clothes in our slickers and rode all day in our underclothing which usually dried out rapidly. When evening came with camp duties to perform, we got into our clothing again.

One night we came to a corral which was built to serve the surrounding community. We put our cut there and did not have to night herd. I saw a new log house, complete, just ready to hang the doors and windows. It would be a nice place to sleep that one night. Three of us took our bedding inside. The old lodge was standing in front of the new house and I put my saddle there. I thought it would remain dry and safe inside. We noticed a storm coming but paid little attention.

About the time we were making our beds, two young nearly-grown Indians came in, said it was their house, and they were going to sleep in it that night. They didn't have any bedding but that didn't seem to bother them. They lay on the floor. The storm struck with the proportions of a hurricane. The two Caddoes were scared nearly to death. They screamed, howled, and threw themselves in all sorts of shapes. Finally they dashed outdoors and that was the last we saw of them.

The next morning we saw the results of the storm. Some of the tree tops broke, other trees were uprooted. When I got out to look for my saddle, I found some of the poles which supported the roof of the round lodge had rotted, and the pressure of the storm had mashed the roof on top of my saddle. The building didn't appear to be very heavy, but when I attempted to get the saddle out, it was a big task. I decided to take my chances out in the open.

226

The next morning we scattered out to gather up cattle. I went southeast and came back toward our cow camp when I met George Dean, who belonged to a cow outfit along the Washita River. He had worked with us and had a cut of about thirty head. I found one which belonged to the Strip. He objected because other fellows of our outfit were present when he cut it out and didn't claim the cow. I showed him the brand and told him I'd have to have her, that was why we were down there. I cut her out and started back, she was wild and made a terrible run, but that suited me for I kept her running in the right direction.

Suddenly she whirled to the right and seemed to be frightened nearly to death. I thought she was trying to turn back for she was running toward a round grove of large trees. I raised a yell and began to pound on my leggings to frighten her, rode through the trees, and turned her back. It was a large arbor, nicely arranged, and in it was a gathering of Caddo Indians. They seemed to be religiously inclined, exceedingly peaceful. I could see one man standing before the crowd and concluded he was a missionary addressing them.

When I overtook our cut, Noah Mills was driving it along. We had not gone very far when I saw a bunch of Osage Indians, wearing blankets. I knew them by their hair cut. I stopped and asked in Osage where they lived; they answered, Pawhuska. I found out they were going to visit the Cheyenne Indians. They wanted to know if I was Osage. I told them when I was a little boy, I was with the Osages and they came walking to me much interested. They had just stopped for noon and were unsaddling their horses. I told them I would have to go with Mills for the cattle might get away.

We had to night herd because it was still raining. I was on until midnight. When I got into camp, every suitable place was occupied. Since I had a good slicker, heavy leggings, and a good Stetson hat to cover my face, I lay down in the mud and went to sleep. When I awoke in the morning, my right shoulder was resting in a small pool of water and felt dead. I have been bothered with rheumatism in that shoulder ever since.

We kept on going north. That night I told the boys I wasn't going on night herd as I had been doing more than my share. I was going to sleep late and let somebody else do something. I slept alone; we usually doubled our beds and slept in twos.

Upon waking the next morning, I heard Mills say, "Who is that laying over there asleep after sunup?" The fellow sleeping with him said it was Records. I was dry, warm, and having a pleasant time. I opened my eyes, looked around, and saw the heavy dew on grass blades sparkling in the sunlight. Noah said, "Let's get him by the feet and drag him around in the dew awhile and see how he likes it."

The other fellow said, "All right, let's go."

I jumped to my feet, holding my old forty-five, "You'll never get to me. I like fun but there's no fun in anything like that."

They both stopped. Noah said, "He won't shoot us; come on let's go." As they started, I fired into the ground directly in front of their feet. The mud and sand peppered their faces. Noah said, "Oh come on, he won't kill us."

The other fellow said, "I don't know, but I'd kill any fellow before I would let him drag me around in that dew or sand." He turned and went to his bunk.

"Well, I guess that's about right," Mills turned to put on his clothes.

When the cook got breakfast, he used up all the flour, fried all the sow bosom [bacon from the belly of a hog], and made a big pot of coffee, more than we could use. He counted us, counted his biscuits, and found we had a biscuit and a half apiece. "Let's do this on the square; bring your tin plates here and I'll ration it out to you." He also gave each one a slice of bacon and told us to help ourselves to the coffee.

One fellow among us worked on a ranch about a half day's drive away. His camp was on Deer Creek on the Arbuckle Trail.[8] The country was exceedingly rough or broken to cross with no roads. But he knew how to follow the divide to get through with his wagon without much trouble. He rode ahead on his horse and the cook followed with the wagon.

We started with the cut and the horses and tried to follow him, but he soon passed out of sight in the cloudy, misting rain. Soon we lost the wagon trail and consequently got into trouble going up and downhill continually. We didn't mind for it was cool and the cattle would not suffer from heat. Finally we reached a section where the soil had been washed from the soft sandstone rock, wasted away in the bottoms.

As the horses climbed the banks, their footing would slip and they would fall on their knees, badly damaging them. We decided not to continue but had two choices, we could follow a divide leading southwest or northeast to the south bank of the South Canadian River. We chose the latter and found a bluff as far as we could see. We found a place to descend to the riverbed nearby, crossed to the low north bank, and found it smooth and easy travel most of the way.

Sometime before night one of Milt Bennett's cows which had run wild for several years decided not to leave that country. She broke out of the cut and started back. Two inexperienced young fellows attempted to head her off but she soon discovered they didn't know what they were doing. She turned, charged, and bluffed them. I saw they were not doing any good so I rode back. They said, "You better keep away from her, she'll gore your horse."

She saw me coming and charged. I stopped, turned my horse broadsides to give her a good show, and pulled out my old six-shooter. When she got within about ten steps from me, I put a forty-five bullet where I thought it would do the most good. One of the boys said, "Why, you have killed her!"

"It looks that way to me." I asked if either one of them had a knife, they didn't. I told one of them to ride ahead and overtake the outfit to see if they could get a knife or two. He returned and said there wasn't a knife in the bunch.

I had a small pearl-handled knife which I used to clean my finger nails. Dismounting, I took it and bled the cow. I cut the hide just above one of the hock joints, split it up to the hip bone, and peeled it off on the hip to expose the round steak. I began to cut out chunks, filled my saddle pockets, and had the two boys roll up all they could in their slickers. We rode on, overtook the outfit, and told them we would have steak for supper.

Toward night we began to look for a suitable place to stop. Finally we came to a place where a large cottonwood tree had been half-burned by a prairie fire. A recent storm had broken the tree about ten or twelve feet from the ground and formed a good place to build a fire.

The inquiry went out, "Who has any matches?" There wasn't a match in the crowd. Presently one fellow who was wearing a heavy coat under his slicker began to feel of the lining in the tail of his coat where he found some dry cottonlike material. He took my knife and split the lining to get the lint. The rest of us found a considerable amount of thin, dry wood fiber between the bark and the body of the tree. We put the lint and fiber together, fired a six-shooter into it, and soon had a roaring fire.

We gathered around with our chunks of meat to roast. We had no salt but no one objected. We lay down contentedly to sleep, scattered among the big dry limbs without bedding for it had gone with the wagon.

When daylight came, Jim Hudson, John Eaton, and I got out and began to roast some more beef. No one else could even stand to smell it, much less to eat it. So what little we got to eat, we ate raw.

We went on up the South Canadian. There was only one fellow who knew where the Arbuckle Trail crossed the river. He told us a sharp butte, which stood out prominently and could be seen at a long distance, marked the crossing. There we could recross and go up Deer Creek to the cow camp.

The first sign of habitation appeared when we saw a curl of smoke in some timber along the north bank. I told the fellows I would ride over to see what it was. It was an Indian teepee and a squaw was standing in the doorway. At the edge of the thick timber was an Indian with a rifle. We guessed when he saw us coming, not knowing who we were, he decided to be safe rather than sorry. I asked her in Indian sign language if she had anything we could eat. She shook her head. I asked if there were any white men's houses near, again she shook her head.

We had an awful time keeping our cow outfit together. About seven or eight were grousing and wanted to ride to Fort Reno nearly fifty miles away. I don't think they could have made it in a day. If it hadn't been for Hudson, Eaton, and me, they would have left the cattle. We told them they could go if they wished; some cows in the herd had calves; we could milk the cows, eat land terrapins, and get along fine without them.

Finally we saw the sharp butte; that revived hope in the complainers and they even helped us drive the cattle. When we got to the Arbuckle Trail, we stopped and changed horses. I caught my best horse. Mills stayed until we got the cattle located on good grass and near water. They were tired and would stay several hours without roaming about. Eaton took two men and all our horses, crossed the river to the south, and took the trail along the high ground which overlooked Deer Creek Valley. Eaton had the poorest bunch of horses I had ever seen on a roundup but was one of the best cowhands with whom I have worked. He had grit and determination.

Noah and I started after the outfit. My horse was so anxious to get with the other horses that I was having difficulty holding him down to a decent gait. Directly he jumped into a deep water hole and kicked water all over me. That made me mad so I turned him loose and away he went. I began to pass the others who were slouching along as if suffering all sorts of misery. I overtook Eaton and his men trotting along behind the horses. I began to whoop and yell, pound on my leggings, and stampeded the whole bunch down the trail.

Eaton hollered, "Come on boys, he'll eat up everything in camp before we get there."

They began to pour it to their horses and came at top speed. I was so busy fighting the horses to keep them going at break-neck speed that I had not noticed the camp.

Eaton yelled, "Throw 'em off from the trail, them fellows will beat us to the grub pile yet!"

I rode in front and turned the horses down the little bluff bank into Deer Creek Valley. I never stopped until I got in front of the door of a log cabin. I jumped off, threw the rein over the horse's head, dropped it on the ground, walked up to the door, and looked in. I saw a big pile of biscuits and a big platter of bacon. I grabbed a biscuit in one hand and a slice of bacon in the other, then looked to see who was there. Five men were sitting there grinning and at first glance I didn't recognize anyone.

Eaton appeared, put his hands on each door jamb and looked in, "Say, fellers, he don't know much to begin with and when he gets hungry, he ain't got a lick of sense."

The owner said, "Come on in and help yourself, we was looking for you."

I was starting on my second round of biscuit and bacon when the other fellows began to come in. I saw a fellow whom I knew, "Hello there, I hadn't noticed you before."

He replied, "I know you but can't remember where I saw you."

I answered, "You stayed all night with me in the Strip a year ago."

"I remember you now; you fed me good and I'm glad to see you able to feed yourself, yet," he said.

The cook had driven our wagon behind the cabin but I hadn't seen it until I finished eating. When he saw us coming, he started cooking.

The sun was shining rather warm; I lay down under the wagon and went to sleep. After the fellows finished, Eaton told me to get up, eat some more, and take the wagon and outfit back to the cut; he would stay at the camp that afternoon, then come back to the herd. I was to kill and dress a beef. I took Mills and the cook with me. Our cook who drove the wagon had lost a job in the Washita country. Left afoot, he was trying to work his way back north.

Eaton had a fine, red yearling steer in the cut, which he had swiped. Since he did not know whether he could make away with this stray, he thought I had better kill it. He described it. The five fellows in the log cabin were waiting for their wagon to come. He would have them bring their wagon to our cut and get all of the beef we didn't want in exchange for flour and salt. He told us we wouldn't have any bread but to salt and roast the kidneys. We would find it as good as any bread we ever ate.

I shot the beef and we began to dress it. When we finished, I told Mills one of us should ride back to a little hill where we could see some distance along the Arbuckle Trail for fear the wagon might miss us. He turned to the cook and said, "Get on my horse, ride back, and see if you can see them."

The cook asked, "Which is your horse?"

Mills pointed at my dun horse and said, "There he is."

I said, "Don't you start off with that horse." He looked around, saw I was going to empty the saddle if he didn't, and slid off. Mills told him to get on his bay horse. He did and rode off. I said to Mills, "Do you ever expect to see your horse again, Noah?"

He replied "Why?"

I said, "He's just a transient without a job, wanting to get out of the country. Now he has a good outfit."

"My gracious, I never thought of that!" Mills dropped everything, set out afoot to the top of a high sand hill, stood looking, then turned, "Here they come."

Next morning we started north on the Arbuckle Trail. A Caddo Indian, White Bead,[9] had several hundred cattle but had never allowed anybody to cut his herd. When we got in sight of his ranch, we saw he had quite an outfit for a blanket Indian and decided to stop and look through his herd. We observed his cattle were all in one corner of the pasture. He sat on his horse out on a little knoll, holding a big buffalo gun, Indian style.

Several boys rode up and looked at the herd from the outside but none would go in. I was a little behind and asked why they didn't go in.

They replied, "It's dangerous to go in there, he don't allow anybody to cut his herd."

I told them I was going to look through his herd just as if it was anyone else; if he attempted to turn that old gun around to point at me, they were to let me know. I rode through White Bead's herd four times, two round trips, and the last time I came out near him. I gave him a friendly salute as I went out and he bowed his head in a very important manner. He wore complete Indian regalia, including an eagle feather stuck into his hair.

Farther up the Arbuckle Trail we saw some large two-story stone buildings—the Mennonite Indian mission school. They had a fairly large herd of Pole Angus—black hornless cattle. It looked strange to travel for so long through unsettled country then find large buildings with such improvements out on a bald prairie.[10]

We stayed all night at Cantonment, the next important place. Mills and part of the fellows left us there and followed the North Canadian; we turned northeast towards the Cimarron.

Eaton, Hudson, two or three others, and I were together. Eaton and his outfit wanted to cross the Cimarron and follow the Cantonment Trail up Indian Creek. I wanted to cross above the mouth of Eagle Chief, so I caught one of my horses to serve as a pack horse and loaded him with my ten years' collection of personal effects. I cut out my cattle, took them and my saddle horses, and started north in a "crowd to myself."

I rode up the west side of Eagle Chief after crossing the Cimarron. The sun was shining; the cattle were hot, tired, and hard to drive. The horses led out pretty strong as they sensed they were close to their old accustomed range. When we got near Big Timber on the ⅃ range which joined the ⚕ ranch on the southwest, I left the ⅃ cut there, rode on with the horses, and got back to the ⚕ camp in good time for supper.

Boss Sam Fling told me he and Timberlake had arranged with Major Drumm for John Smith of Timberlake's camp and me to go with Drumm's wagon to attend the roundups in Barber and Comanche counties in Kansas. Frank Streeter, "Texas Dave" Thomas, John Smith, and I comprised the outfit. We were gone another month and I did not return to the ranch until 4 July. This was the longest roundup I ever attended and I lay in the shade ten days before beginning to work again.

TWENTY-TWO

Neighborhood and Kansas Roundups

A neighborhood roundup was held in early spring on the ranches of W. E. Campbell, the Crooked Creek Pool,[1] and Maj. Andrew Drumm. The first two lay partly in Kansas and partly in the Strip. Sam Fling told me to take my string of horses without a wagon and attend.

As I started out, I rode one horse and took three others. The ⊕ outfit had bought a large black Norman stallion to run with the mares for they wanted to raise their own horses. As I was going through the north end of the ranch, that stallion "seen" me and came running as hard as he could run. He frightened my horses and I had a hard time holding them. I didn't want to kill the stallion but I didn't want him to kill me. As he approached, I took down my saddle rope, doubled it three or four times, and twisted the shortened lengths of the rope to use as a club. He stopped with his head two or three feet from me. I knew he would soon begin to paw and bite or whirl and kick. I took the rope, hit him squarely in the face, and yelled at the same time. He was so startled that he wheeled and ran back to the mare herd as fast as he could.

Bill Wilson and I were the only outsiders. When we finished the roundup, we took our two strings of horses, rode to Kiowa, and stopped for dinner at the hotel. Mrs. Chatham, the proprietor, was one of the single women. Shortly after we arrived, she sent word to the other four girls to come.[2]

After dinner we went into the parlor. There was an organ and the girls invited us to sing. Since that was out of our line, we expressed our regrets. I told them I had been a good singer before tunes came into fashion. They seemed to understand my awful condition. Bill said he had such an awful voice that whenever he started to sing, every teamster within a city block got down to search for a dry axle. These explanations seemed to be satisfactory.

The girls sang and played for awhile; then we told them since we had a long ride to make, we had better get our saddle horses. I told

234

Bill to saddle the horse that would cut up the worst and I would pick a similar one. This was our way of entertaining the Kiowa girls in return.

Wilson's horse was a plain bay with black mane and tail. Mine was coal black with a bald face and one white glass eye. We usually looked for such animals as being hard to handle. Bill mounted first. He cinched his saddle tight to get all he could out of his horse. For awhile I thought it was going to dump him. All that saved him was that he happened to get his hands full of enough leather to hold himself in the saddle. The girls squealed. Some told him to hang on for if he fell he might get stepped on.

The girls had been admiring my horse and hoped he wouldn't do anything bad. Of course I hoped he wouldn't be bad enough to throw me. I understood him well for he had taken such spells before. I let him have his head down well but knew he would not buck long. When he began to pitch, the girls thought it was a pity such a nice-looking horse should have to cut up like that.

Bill, an awfully devilish fellow, liked to get jokes on other persons. When we started off, I told him I was ashamed of him for taking an armload of leather to hold himself in the saddle. The girls were literally ashamed of him for he looked more like a baboon that a human being.

He said, "I don't think you done much better; you wouldn't let that horse get his head down or do anything."

I told him how straight I sat in the saddle and how the girls were bragging about the manly appearance I made. Of course I made no headway kidding that fellow.

The last general roundup in Barber County was held in the middle 1880's. Jim Elston was the captain of the county cattle association. By this time the settlers were so numerous that it was hard to round up the country. The people, mostly from the East, did not know what it meant to see so many men riding together. We came to one farm with house, barn, and a recently-built poultry house. The whole farm was fenced and cross-fenced with a four barbed-wire fence, forty acres for farming, the balance in pasture with fifty or sixty head of cattle. A fenced lane led from the main road to the house. We rode through the big gate into the pasture and found no strays.

We were ready to ride to the next bunch of cattle. Back at the gate sat a big man, demanding $50 damages. Elston explained this had been

235

the custom ever since the beginning of the cow country and this was apt to be the last roundup.

I noticed Gene Pardee, Bill Wilson, Frank Streeter, and some others nearby. I told them the ground was soft; the posts were not solidly set as yet; we could dismount and lift four or five posts, then lay the fence with the wire next to the earth with the posts on top. We did, then mounted and rode out.

As we came to the gate where the man sat, we noticed an elderly lady and a young woman, supposedly his wife and daughter. They seemed to be well-pleased at what we had done. They had tried to prevail on the man to let us out. As we rode past the house to the main road, they were laughing and talking. We gave them a friendly salute and they nodded.

Elston said, "Hadn't we better set that fence up?"

I answered, "No, let it lay, he'll have something to remember us by."

"It may look kinda funny to you fellows down in the Territory, but I live in this county and may meet that old fellow some time," Elston remarked. "It might end in a foot race."

I said, "Didn't you notice how fat and short-legged he was? He can't catch you."

The next bunch of cattle was in the sand hills to the northeast. We noticed a little boy riding around and keeping them pretty well together. When he saw us, he wheeled and went over the hill as hard as his pony could run. Gene Pardee said, "Look at the boy, he's going places, now!"

I said, "When we get the returns from that pony race, we'll see something come toward us."

As we were pushing the herd together, a man came riding bareback on a big workhorse with a blind bridle and carrying a heavy rifle, "What does this mean?"

I replied, "This is a general roundup, probably the first and last you'll ever see."

He laughed, "I heard about you fellows, but I didn't know what you looked like! My little boy come running and told me there was a bunch of Indians over here killing my cattle. I unhooked this horse from the plow, grabbed my gun, jerked the harness from him, climbed on, and since these cattle are about all the property I had, I decided to come die with them."

Next was Mr. Wisner's ranch with Pole Angus cattle and Percheron

236

horses, a large farmhouse, barn, and other buildings in proportion.[3] It was a well-improved farm with a large pasture. He had come from New England and his son, "Al," was with him. As we rode up, we thought no one was at home. We pushed the big gate open and started to ride in.

When we got to the pasture, Wisner came rushing out of the door and yelled, "What do you mean by trespassing on my place without any authority?"

I had met him before so I turned and gave the usual salute, "This is the general roundup."

He had heard but did not expect us so soon. "Just ride right in, gentlemen, and look the cattle over."

He told us about the fine Percheron horses and wanted us to look at them, too. We told him we wouldn't stop, as we had other points to make, but congratulated him on the appearance of his herd of cattle.

We wore our slickers and leggings because showers fell one day. It was so wet the cook could not get supper and we all went to Kiowa in search of grub and amusement. Some cattlemen whose ranches were near sent their outfits home. Some of the rest of us found a corral and put our cuts in it. All the Kiowa restaurants and hotels were full so we went to A. W. Rumsey's store and got crackers, cheese, and sardines. After I had slipped myself outside of this, I found a number of the boys who said they were going to look at the new town hall.

When we arrived, we found about seventy-five cowboys wearing their slickers and leggings. Among them was McNabb, formerly of Peru. He was more than six feet tall, wore a heavy black moustache and goatee, was a good fiddler, and a jolly fellow. He sat on the box in the middle of the hall, removed his slicker and leggings, and played for the boys. A row of benches stood next to the walls all around the hall and all the fellows, excepting myself, were seated on them. The hall door was wide-open and a light shone out the door.

At that time there were only five single women in the town. Bert Crew, Frank Streeter, and Bill Wilson went up town to see if they could get them and have a dance. Suddenly McNabb felt the need for exercise. He jumped to his feet, gave a yell, and started directly for the door, kicking nearly to the ceiling. He held his bow in one hand and his fiddle in the other. His big hat was pinched to a sharp point at the crown. He wore a tight-fitting jacket, and his pants were so tight he

237

looked as if he had been melted and poured into them and the legs of his high-heeled boots. He looked more like the picture of Satan with the exception of the barbed tail.

Meanwhile the boys succeeded in rounding up all five girls. I was the only one who saw when they arrived at the doorway of the hotel. They saw McNabb and stampeded, ran over their three escorts, and headed back to town, so badly scared they fought like furies. The boys gave up the unequal struggle. Bert came into the hall and yelled, "Get them war garments off and look like humans!" he demanded.

Of course none of the fellows knew what had caused his demonstration. Some decided Crew needed a good cleaning up right then. I stepped in between them, "Bert is right about getting the girls to the door for I saw and heard them squeal."

"Why didn't you come and help hold them?" he asked me.

"It would have been like taking a mad bull by the horns to jump out among them. I would have scared them worse than ever," I replied, "Come on, we are headed for bed!" I jumped out the door, made a bee line for the livery barn, climbed up the steps to the hay loft, stretched out on the nice new hay, and slept like a log.

Next morning I went to Mr. Rumsey's store. He exclaimed, "Well, young man, you look rather clean and fresh. Where did you stay last night?"

"I stopped at the hotel de horse!" I replied seriously. This brought such a hearty laugh that I had to wait a minute, "How about another round of cheese, crackers, and sardines?"

"Just step this way." Mr. Rumsey fixed a place at the counter. "Eat all you want as it is on the house and it won't cost you a cent!"

"How is that, Mr. Rumsey?" I asked.

"A fellow that can take it and get a laugh out of it is rather scarce. I have known you for six years and you have always been the same."

The new hall that McNabb dedicated in such an uncouth manner with his Highland Fling was later sold and moved a short distance northwest. It was remodeled and used as a country school house. Frank Streeter married one of the stampeding girls, Miss Fanny Blanton.[4] Dennis Flynn married another one less than a year later.[5] I do not know what became of the other three.

While I was on the 1884 roundup, Brother Charles went to White County, Arkansas, and bought 300 head of one-, two-, and three-year-old steers and heifers. The drivers tied sticks to the horns of the wilder ones to drive the herd up the road through timber country to a railroad station to be shipped to Ft. Smith. I hired Boyd Bartholomew, George Bradley, and Bob McClure as drivers to meet the herd there. Elisha S. Records, with his team and wagon, was the cook. They stopped in the Territory south of Jonesburg to hold the herd until late fall. Then Charles hired Bradley and Charlie Claussen to drive the herd to the Lane south of Caldwell where they wintered.[6]

TWENTY-THREE

Driving the ↑
Cattle to Caldwell

Early in April 1884 Bates made a business trip to the ranch in his two-horse buggy. On his return trip to Caldwell he decided to cross the Salt Fork at the Wagon Creek ford which was used by several ranch outfits. He found the Salt Fork had more water than usual. Bates drove into the river near a sand bar that extended downstream from a point where he left the riverbed. There was a cool north wind and he crossed without mishap until he reached the north bank. As the water rose into the buggy bed, he remembered a suitcase was in back, filled with all his valuable ranch papers. He looked out and saw it floating downstream. He hurriedly tied his team in a cottonwood grove, removed all his clothes, ran down a sand bar, waded out into the stream, and recovered it. Then he ran up and down in the sand until his body heat counteracted the chill. He dressed and drove on without any bad effects.

The next time Bates came to the ranch, he humorously remarked, "When I saw all of my tally sheets floating off, I thought of you and wished you were with me."

I asked, "What good would I have done?"

He replied, "You would have got it for me, for I was sure I would have gotten a bad cold riding in a buggy so far."

Driving herds of beeves to a railroad point seventy-five miles distant is not always easy. In 1884 the ↑ ranch made three shipments of beeves to Caldwell, I had charge of two.

In July Bates sent Real Hamlet,[1] a former cowpuncher, to tell us to drive a herd of beeves to the Caldwell stockyards by a certain date. I raised a roar since Sam Fling, the foreman, had gone to his own ranch in southern Kansas. It was hard to get extra help that time of year. We would need three or four more men besides the cook, Charlie Ritchie, who was willing to go for that would secure him another round of drinks at Caldwell. Ike Berry was there along with Young Short who decided to throw in several of his good beeves. "Missouri Dave"

Thomas, Myron Cleveland, and I comprised the crew. Everyone knew what to do so everything went like clockwork.

Berry had served as a mule skinner in the regular army in the Southwest and had a great deal of experience working on large ranches. Short was a great race-horse and saddle-horse man; he had one little bay, bald-face horse which was one of the finest saddle horses that I ever "seen." Dave wanted to buy it and Short agreed to let him have it for $75. Dave told me what a good trade he was making! I thought it was the most foolish thing he could do; the company furnished him more horses than he could ride. I asked him what he was going to do with it since he would have no use for it. He wanted the name of having the finest saddle horse in the Southwest.

When Short and I got the herd ready to start, we saw a thunder shower approaching. We agreed not to attempt to move until the shower passed. When the worst was over, I rode around the herd at full speed until my slicker looked like a big balloon as the wind caught it. Short made fun of my appearance to the others, "It's a good thing the herd was looking the other way or they would have stampeded. I have never seen such a ridiculous sight in my life."

It was so muddy in crossing Pond Creek Flat, the steers could hardly make it. I looked to the northwest and could see a funnel cloud letting down to earth. I said, "Look at that cloud, Ike!"

He watched, "We'll hear from that when we get up to Caldwell."

As the point of the cloud neared the earth, it began to weave and swing around but didn't last over half an hour. Then it lifted and the long ropelike portion of cloud disappeared. Everything was normal again. There were mighty few settlers in the part of Kansas where the cloud was performing so it may not have done damage.

We could have stopped the herd to let them rest and cool off; but Pond Creek Flat produced more large, hungry, voracious mosquitoes than any other section in cow country. Short related how he had spent one night there the previous year when the buffalo wallows were filled with water. They fought mosquitoes until 2 A.M. when a wind came up out of the north to drive them away. The next morning the men's faces were swollen and they could hardly see. So we pressed on.

When we neared the stockyards, we rounded up the herd and cut out Short's steers. I reported to Bates and went to town. I found Berry in a saloon, playing cards with Dave Spears. Dave's capper, Fred Swigert, was loafing around behind Berry and signaling what Ike's cards were. At noon Spears took Berry to a restaurant, gave him a good dinner, and jollied him by telling him how hard it was to keep up with him. I followed and warned Berry, but he paid no attention and didn't stop until all his money was gone.

We usually stayed two or three days at Caldwell, rested up, and went to York, Parker, and Draper Wholesale and Retail House where we "done" our trading. Besides B. W. Key, Albert Witzleben was the bookkeeper.[2] This firm had a list of all the hands who worked for the cattle ranches that patronized them. Key carried it with him to the post office. He called for our mail and placed it in his ranch post office beside Witzleben's desk. The bookkeeper kept a complete list of all our dealings. We went there to draw out our money so we had no need of a bank or post office. Key always knew where we stood with the company.

Dave had a program already mapped out which I didn't think much of; it looked mighty bad to me and worse for him. When he "drawed" out all his wages, he bought his horse and a few clothes. Then he started on his program by going on a big drunk until his wages were gone. I "seen" very little of him excepting a little trouble which he had with two other fellows. But he got out without any bruises. When I got ready to go back to the ⚐ ranch, I told Dave we would start the next morning. That afternoon I was sitting on a bench in the shade of a building on the west side of main street. I "seen" Dave staggering, just able to walk out of the wholesale house a little distance up the street. Most of his steps seemed to be pointed toward me. As he drew near, I "seen" tears rolling down his cheeks and he was sweating like a harvest hand. He handed me a letter from one of his married sisters. I told him under different circumstances he might not want me to read his mail but he insisted.

The letter had arrived two or three days ago. I "seen" the name of a girl or woman who was dangerously ill and she was wanting Dave to come home. The doctor said she might not recover. I told him I "seen" nothing so unusual except the reference to the sorely afflicted woman.

Dave said the woman was his oldest sister. She was the only mother he ever knew since his mother had died when he was born. He loved her as mother and sister. He gave me another letter which stated she was gradually sinking and talking about Dave all the time. She wanted to see him before she died. He said, "Now I've come to ask you what to do. I'm so drunk I can't take anything into consideration."

242

I said, "I'd go, Dave, I wouldn't stop a minute."

He replied, "You know I've acted a fool and spent all of my money, I can't do anything."

I told him, "Let's go over and see Witzleben and Key." I started and he followed me across the street.

As I stepped into the door, Key said, "Well, what can I do for you now?" I didn't want anything but said Dave Thomas was in a pretty bad shape. I "seen" I had touched a sore spot, for Key had a habit of chewing his moustache when he began to confront a hard proposition. I told Key the story. "We'll go see Witzleben and see what we can do," he said.

Witzleben opened his big ledger, looked into it a little bit, and said, "No, we are held responsible for these goods and we can't afford to take such chances."

I wanted them to get Dave a new suit, hat, handkerchief, tie, and a few other things. He needed enough money for the round trip. I turned and asked if I had any credit.

"Yes, you can get anything you want."

I told them to outfit Dave for travel, get him a little hand bag, and have a little to spend for necessities. We got him equipped and I went with him to the depot. He was as sober as a judge by the time he paid for his ticket. When the train pulled in, he shook hands with me and said he never would forget my kindness; he wouldn't stay but a day or two in Missouri but come right back to the ranch to repay me.

I "seen" him after he came back, and he said he got there in time to see his sister before her death. He was certainly glad he had gone back home for it seemed to do his sister so much good. Just as soon as he got some money, he went to Caldwell and paid the account.

Later in July Bates sent word to drive another herd of big beeves to Caldwell. My outfit was comprised of Dave, George Frear, Bud Moore, and John Watkins. "Little George" had come from New York to his stepfather's ranch. He told me that he read dime novels which stated that cowpunchers rode horses until they dropped dead. He later learned not to run a horse in this manner and was becoming a fairly good cowpuncher.

We had to round up the range and cut out the beeves from the other grades of cattle. A good system in starting a cut prevents all sorts of work and unnecessary trouble. There is as much difference in the dispositions of animals as there is among human beings. The person

243

who does not know or attempt to learn is certainly laying hard lines for himself in the cattle business.

After we had gotten the herd rounded up and were waiting for them to settle down a little, two of the boys who wanted to show how they could cut beeves out of the herd rode in. Each one picked on a high-headed and wiry-looking steer and tried to chase them out which made an awful disturbance.

I "hollered" to wait a minute; I would show them how to start a cut. I "seen" a big pot-bellied steer standing near the edge of the herd, about half asleep and chewing his cud. I rode in between him and the herd and started walking him out. He walked slowly along and I drove him out to a convenient distance. I saw another steer with a similar disposition and walked him out the same way. As quickly as I "seen" him throw his ears ahead, I knew he had seen the other one, then I returned to the herd. I was not so particular about the third one, excepting that he was of proper age and fat enough. This one moved more rapidly and didn't want to start, but I "seen" him throw his ears ahead and knew he was going on out. I told the boys not to chase the steers after they "throwed" their ears ahead, they would go on out. By the time we were ready to start, it was so late we thought we couldn't get farther than the Salt Fork above the mouth of Wagon Creek.

I rode ahead to Timberlake's camp. "Erv" Timberlake was the only man there. He wanted to know where I was going. I told him we had started to Caldwell with a beef herd. He said, "You just turn right around and go back to the ⚓ ranch with your beeves for old Salt Fork is running right over its banks and you'll never make it."

I said, "You don't know us, 'Erv,' we're going to hit that river and go right across it."

"Why Jim Lee was three days in trying to cross. He got 'em across once and they come back on him," he added.

"'Erv,' he don't know how to cross a river and he don't know how to keep 'em across. He proved that when he let 'em come back."

Timberlake said Joe Hargreaves, the best cowman in the Southwest, had more sense than to try to cross. He was just drifting down the river along the south bank, waiting for the river to go down.

"'Erv,' he's showing bad judgment by going down the river, he ought to go up so he could cross after the flood crest had gone down." I told Timberlake I was going back to get "them" steers, put 'em across the Salt Fork on the first drive, and we would hold them on the north side.

He said, "If old Frank Bates knew you was going to do such a trick as that, he would fire you in a minute."

I told Timberlake we would go cross the river immediately after dinner. As I rode back to meet the herd, they were moving along nicely. I rode in front, stopped them, and motioned to the fellow on the west side to come over. That would let the cattle scatter out over the fine buffalo grass which would suit the steers mighty well. They could get a good fill and "lay" down.

The sun was shining and the wind was out of the north. This would be favorable, as the steers would smell the water and want to go to it. I went back, stopped the wagon, and told the cook to get dinner; we wouldn't cross until afternoon. I told the boys to tie everything in the wagon, tie the wagon box down to the coupling pole, then tie the front bolster down.

While they were all around the wagon, I gave them the program to follow so we wouldn't lose anything. They were to hitch the team to the wagon and follow the herd in regular order; cattle first, loose saddle horses next, and the wagon last. I put each one in the place which I thought was best and asked them to stay put. When we got the cattle going across, two of the boys should tie their ropes to the end of the wagon tongue and fasten them to their saddle horns. Two more on either side of the wagon were to tie their ropes to each side of the wagon box and fasten them in like manner. This would make six horses on a very light wagonload. The fellow pulling on the upstream side would be especially helpful in the current if he could keep his horse up and going. I told Watkins to take the left-hand point upstream; I would take the right-hand point downstream, the worst side. Dave would take the second position behind Watkins; "Little George" would be second behind me. Moore would attend the saddle horses and team to keep them from getting mixed up with the herd as they might get gored.

I told the boys if we got the herd started into the river and they "seen" me holding my hat up in the air as high as I could reach, not to crowd the herd so hard on the sides. If they "seen" me swinging my hat in circles, they were to pour it on to the herd and make them come as fast as they could.

I told Watkins we should crowd the point tight until they went into the water for we didn't want the leaders to slacken their pace. If they did, it might cause the herd to mill. It is natural for the steers in front

245

to get frightened and begin to set back and not want to go on across. Watkins was to ride into them on his side, I would ride into them on my side. We must beat them and yell as loud as we could. They were used to that and would know they were not doing things to suit us.

As we rode among them, the herd was packed all around us. Occasionally one would swing his head and rap us across the back with his big long horns. Of course he couldn't hook us for if he tried, he would run his nose under water. At times we had to hit them over the heads with the butts of our quirts to keep them from trying to jump onto our smaller saddle horses. I told Watkins if his horse happened to go down in a sand pocket not to fall away a minute about the horse but jump up into his saddle and leap straddle a steer. He would be so badly scared he wouldn't know about it until he got on land again. If we succeeded in getting the herd half way across, Watkins was to watch their ears. If they "throwed" them ahead, he was not to say another word but get out of the bunch and to shore as fast he could. When he got out into the open country, he could begin to sing to them.

We both got across the river at about the same time and went through the sand hills as fast as our horses could run. When we got out on the open flat prairie where there was lots of slough grass and water everywhere, we both began to sing as nice as we could. I looked back and saw the big steers pouring through the sand hills at top speed, terribly frightened. As they saw the leaders grazing and drinking, they settled down in a hurry.

This was the first time "Little George" had seen swimming a herd across a swollen river. He didn't see how we could live while we were packed among "them" beeves with thrashing horns. We told him we were fighting for our lives. A fellow feels mighty proud to come through all of that and not lose anything but it soon passes and he forgets.

When we camped for the night, I put on a double guard as the steers seemed to be so uneasy and were liable to stampede. "Little George" and I took the first guard; we rode in opposite directions, met, passed without stopping, whistled and sang so the cattle knew what the noise was as we rode around. We had our slickers and leggings on for it looked rainy.

We happened to meet on a little sand hill opposite our wagon. All of a sudden as if there was an electic shock all over the herd, the cattle started right toward us. "Little George" asked, "What will I do?"

I answered, "Go that way!"

That was the last I "seen" of him until the next morning. His horse stepped in a hole and "throwed" him loose. The horse jumped to his feet and ran to camp. "Little George" jumped to his feet, pounded on his leggings and slicker, and yelled. That turned the whole herd into one body. I was in front of the stampede, trying to hold the herd in check until the other boys could get there, by causing them to run in a circle. Soon they came. We got the herd stopped but they wouldn't lie down. The whole force had to stay out until daylight.

Our old cook, Charlie Ritchie, a great fellow to have fun, laughed the next day at "Little George." He said after the thunder of the stampede had died out, he heard something coming through the grass going, "whit, whit, whit." He wondered what sort of animal would make such a noise. He grabbed the lantern, held it up, expecting to see anything loom up. It was "Little George!" The cook had heard his leggings and slicker flapping together as he came running into camp. Richie said, "If them steers had heard such an unusual noise as that, I wouldn't have blamed them for stampeding." The next night the steers felt like bedding down and staying there after they had walked another day.

It required three to four days to make the trip from our ranch to Caldwell, seventy-five miles away. Traveling depended on the condition of the ground. When it was dry, the herd walked right along without any trouble. When it was wet and muddy, we had to drive slowly because of hot weather. The beeves in the lead wouldn't be so badly off, but in crossing such places as Pond Creek Flat, the tail end of the herd were sinking into mud to their knees. It took considerable pull to get their feet out of the gumbo soil which caused them to get hot and make mighty slow progress. Often their tongues were lolling out.

We arrived at Caldwell after the big stampede without further mishap. On the return trip we went due west. As we had nothing but saddle horses and the wagon, we could go through settlements without much trouble.

A man named King lived about three miles west of Caldwell and always had a lot of watermelons to sell. I had seen him for several seasons. Because of his great weight and height I could recognize him at a considerable distance. He weighed more than 300 pounds and was between six and seven feet tall.[3]

247

Watkins and I were riding together behind our saddle horses. When we came in sight of King's farm, he was hoeing in his watermelon patch. Watkins had taken a few drinks before we left Caldwell which made him feel a little funny. When I saw King, I told Watkins we might find some ripe watermelons there. We stopped to ask King about it and he said it was a little early for the melons. He wouldn't guarantee they would be ripe or fit for eating. Then Watkins noticed the great size of King and asked how tall he was and how much he weighed. Watkins got off his horse, walked over to King, pulled up his pants legs, and gave him a thorough inspection. He tried to measure King's ankles, calves, and thighs. He told King that proper training would make him a world champion prize fighter. King said he didn't want to go into anything like that.

We left at that point and resumed our journey. Presently we passed a house which stood 300–400 yards from the road; a nice driveway led to the house. They had a shepherd dog which liked to chase people as they passed, but it didn't seem to notice us until we had gotten pretty well past the driveway. It came as hard as it could run down to the road and turned toward us. Watkins turned in his saddle and took an off-hand shot at it. As the gun cracked, the dog dropped dead.

The country seemed to be unsettled and we could turn southwest to the state line. It seemed other outfits had been going across the country in that direction. Thomas, Moore, and "Little George" were coming at a distance behind us. When they overtook us, I noticed Dave had drunk a little too much for his own good.

In front of us was a creek with a narrow horseshoe bend and a close passage between a high bank at the heel of the bend. Just then an old farmer came running out with a pitch fork in his hand, stood in that narrow place, and told us to turn back. I rode up and told him we were strangers, had gotten here by mistake, and wanted to go to the state line quickly. He seemed to have heard this story a few times before, "But you can't go through here."

Dave came prancing up and began to tell the old man what he must do; if he didn't get out, he would give the finishing touch to him right now. As he was reaching for his six-shooter, I said, "Dave, that's an old gray-headed man just like your father."

He said, "Yes, I'd kill the s. o. b. who would kill him! That being the case, we'll just turn around and go back the way we came." We turned around.

Soon Moore overtook us, "Which one of you fellows killed that nice shepherd dog back there?" he asked. I told Moore I didn't want to tell him who "done" it until after I had found out the number of the mourners and what they "was" going to do about it. He said, "No one was in sight but the dog is still dead." I told him it was one of John Watkins' wild shots. Moore replied, "I put it about there as soon as I seen it." We continued to the state line before we camped for dinner. We could then turn our horses loose without having them stuck with pitchforks.

After dinner we started down through Ben Garland's ranch.[4] Ranchmen at that time had the happy idea they could feed their men cheaper on pork than beef; it was common to see hogs running around the ranch headquarters. We "seen" a sow with a bunch of pigs.

Watkins said, "Let's catch a pig!"

Several dismounted, slipped up close, caught one, and placed it in our grub wagon. When we came close to Wheeler Timberlake's ranch, we stopped for the night. The boys thought they ought to have some milk to feed the pig. Since I was so well acquainted with Timberlake, they said I would have to go after the milk. I knew they always kept a milch cow or two, so Dave and I got on our horses and rode over to the camp to get enough milk to feed the pig until we could get to our ♀ ranch camp.

As we were riding in a high lope from Timberlake's camp, I heard a rattlesnake rattle under the horses. We didn't know whether it hit one of the horses. When we turned back, we found that Dave's horse had stepped on the snake's head and killed it.

When we got back to our wagon and gave the pig its milk, it seemed to take hold right from the start. It being a male pig, I told the boys we had better change him into a barrow. Since I always handled such cases among cattle or horses, I performed the operation. When we got him to camp, he was so contented, nice and easy to handle, and rooted for his own living. The boys gave him pieces of bread and some of the grain we always kept for the work horses. This pig had everything his own way.

That summer a black cloud formed in the northwest and came southeast. At first sight it did not appear unusual but as it came near, I could see it was not an ordinary rain or wind cloud. There was not much wind during its brief stay. It came shortly after noon and lasted until sundown. At its worst stage the visibility was less than fifty yards.

I was about twenty miles south of Caldwell. When I arrived, I was told that all lights in the city were necessary to transact business.

It was not a dust storm as we did not have such things in those days, save in a local area. Many theories were advanced as to the cloud's probable origin. Because it was so dense and black, some said it was volcanic smoke, but there were no ashes or other visible objects nor did it smell like smoke. Where it originated and what became of it, no one seemed to know. The cultivated mind may easily produce some reason for its coming and going and the clear sky with bright sunshine which followed.

Frank Bates usually fed us well and never objected to anything which we got; we did not impose upon him or take advantage of his generosity. "Little George" was sent to Caldwell after a load of provisions or camp supplies; Bates was there when George was loading at Yorke, Parker, and Draper's. George slipped a number of cans of strawberries and blackberries into the load because he would have to camp out one night on the road. He planned on some extra eating before he returned to camp. He told Key not to tell Bates about it; if he did, Bates would raise hell. This amused Key so much he told Bates who replaced the cans with tomatoes and corn. When George camped for the night, he looked for the choice fruit for his supper. He soon came to the conclusion that someone had played a trick on him which he laid immediately to Key. The next time he saw Key he asked him about it. Key explained that he had to carry the account just as it was delivered and did not want to have any trouble with Bates. Frear was satisfied. Later I also made the same sort of trip. When the load was completed, I told Key that I had to camp out for the night and wanted some quality fruit to eat, put it on the general bill. He did so and nothing was ever said.

In late 1884 I had a serious injury shortly before I left the ↑ ranch for a two-year period. Sam Fling had already quit and Frank Bates asked me to take over but I declined. I told him that Bud Moore, who had been with us quite awhile and was a good worker, might do all right as manager.

We had several head of two- and three-year-old bulls to brand and change into steers. I supposed Moore would order us to round up the herd, cut the bulls out, rope, mark, and brand them on the open range. But he ordered the bulls put into the corral, and we had to ride in and rope them on the slick ground.

250

I was the first one in the corral and roped a bull in spite of what I had told him beforehand, that the insecure footing was apt to throw the horses. When the rope tightened, I turned my horse with his tail towards the bull to pull him away from the fence, so Dave Thomas could get behind the bull and heel him in order to stretch him out. We were in such close quarters; before I knew what was happening, about a dozen cattle surged against the rope between me and the bull. This threw the horse over backwards so straight that my head hit the ground. It felt like a light tap on the top of my head. I couldn't see anything but I could hear everything that went on. Moore hallooed to the boys to carry me outside and lay me under the shade of the fence. I lay there quite a bit before I could see. The horse had fallen on my leg and bruised it slightly. My ankle was severely sprained and I was not able to walk for several days.

In a few days I went to Caldwell and met two other crippled up cowpunchers. Cal Smith was walking on one crutch. A horse had fallen on him. The other fellow worked for Ed Hewins. A horse had fallen on him and had broken his thigh bone. When we met on the street, we would say, "Hello, Crip."

TWENTY-FOUR

Crime Comes to Cow Country

Dodd, an Albino, was the type of fellow who wanted the world to know he was bad. He was foreman of a ranch along the Washita River. Once he cut out a cow from Colson and McAtee's herd which they had claimed. He said if they got the cow, it would be over his dead body. So the boys put up a job to get her without hurting anyone. Someone cut her out but Dodd ran to turn her back. Bill Larkin[1] rode alongside him, reached over his horse's hip, and jerked his gun out of its scabbard. George Davis rode directly in front of him with his six-shooter in his hand. Dodd discovered his gun was gone and made a dash at Davis to get it. Davis fired his gun so close that I could see the smoke roll out from the armholes of Dodd's vest but he was not hit.

We were all busy cutting and holding cattle. By the time the smoke had cleared, about seventy-five men were gathered around Dodd and Davis, looking at them. That left Dave Hargreave and me to do the work. I said, "I don't see how a bullet could slip through that crowd without hitting someone."

He replied, "I've got more sense than to risk my frame there." I laughed; he was one of the largest men on the range.

I happened to ride close enough to hear Dodd say, "If it hadn't been for that s. o. b. Bill Larkin, I would have got that cow or killed somebody."

Larkin laughed, "We got the cow, though." He extracted the cartridges from Dodd's gun then handed it back.

Sam Fling was acquainted with Dodd and met him at the cattleman's convention at Caldwell in the Spring of 1884. Dodd told Fling he was going to send a wagon down to the Red River on a cow hunt. Fling told me to ask Dodd when and go with him.

While in Caldwell Dodd became enamored with a "soiled dove." When he was ready to return to his Washita ranch, he thought he would go see her. He sent his wagon and cut back to the ranch with the cowhands who were working for him. He found she had gone to Hun-

252

newell with Pat Hanlon. Pat wore his long, curly hair flowing down his back. Dodd "tanked up," hired a team and buggy from "Big George," and swore he would come back with Pat's head tied by his long hair to the hind axle of the buggy. "Big George" had experience with such fellows and made Dodd pay livery expenses in advance. Dodd did not return that night. George went in search of the team and found them in a livery barn in Hunnewell. They said Dodd had been killed in a fight in a dance hall by Pat Hanlon. Since Dodd was shot in the back of the head, George believed it was the female who did it. I did not get to make that trip down to the Red River for another bad man had gone up "salt river."[2]

John Potts was born and raised in Texas but I have forgotten his real name. It was reported he had killed a man in Texas. A reward for his arrest and conviction was posted. He was a surly fellow with few friends. When he was drinking, he became abusive. He never stayed long at any cow camp.

Finally in 1884 he was working with the 5 outfit and staying at the headquarters on Eagle Chief Creek. The teamster who was hauling freight for the 5 that winter bought a jug of whiskey and brought it with him in his load. Potts drank freely and became abusive. He and Ben Franklin, another 5 man, quarreled and Potts wanted to shoot it out. Ben told him he was drunk and to wait until morning when it would be settled.

In the morning they met and Ben asked Potts if he had sobered up. Potts said he had. Franklin then said, "You owe me an apology for the things you said last night."

Potts said that he did not apologize to anybody; he would back up what he had said last night. Both had six-shooters and Ben told Potts if he didn't apologize, they would shoot it out. Potts was a quick fellow to draw but he fired before he aimed and missed. Ben was a little more deliberate and dropped Potts with the first shot. He lived only several hours.

There was another fellow in the camp who had known Potts in Texas. Potts told him to tell their acquaintances there that he had died gamely with his boots on. He was buried on a little sand hill close to the ranch house, and four posts were placed around it with three or four strands of wire stretched around.

I was on the way from Caldwell to the ♀ ranch the morning of the killing. I stayed that night at Timberlake's camp and Fayette

253

Thomas, who was in charge of Timberlake's ranch, told me about the shooting.

Ben Franklin was there the afternoon I arrived. He hid out because he did not know who was with me. Curtis Cadwell, a cousin from Chautauqua County, and I had driven out from Peru via Caldwell. When I told Fayette that Curtis was my cousin, he must have signaled to Franklin who appeared in a little while and asked me who my partner was. He told me why he was hiding out for a few days. He didn't want the federal authorities to arrest him as he would have to go to Fort Smith. He preferred to be arrested by Kansas authorities and tried at Medicine Lodge, which he was. All the witnesses swore he had killed in self-defense.[3]

In 1884 I was in Caldwell and heard that the Bates and Beals cow outfit had arrived at the stockyards to the south.[4] They had driven a herd of beeves to ship to the eastern market from their Texas Panhandle ranch.

A cowpuncher, Oscar Thomas, considered bad, came with them. After he drew his pay, he began to drink and gamble. When he saw that he was being fleeced, he went on the warpath. As a gambler reached for his winnings, Thomas drew a dirk knife and tried to stick it into the gambler's hand but missed by a slight margin. It cut a foot-long gash on the table top. The gambler was telling me about his narrow escape. I told him Thomas was just fooling. He replied, "Just come in here and see." There was the large gash.

After Thomas spent all of his money at the saloons, he went to York, Parker, and Draper's. Witzleben saw that Thomas had drawn out all of his money so Key would not let him have the goods. Whiskey had taken his reason and he began to abuse Key who sent for the marshal. Both marshal and deputy, Bedford Wood and John Philips, came, one to the back door, the other to the front. They ordered Thomas to put up his hands but he was so drunk he did not understand, he merely stood and looked. Thomas was a small man, and the marshals were both large. They could have handled him easily but they appeared to have no confidence in themselves. It had become the popular practice in Caldwell to have open season on cowpunchers. It was a harmless pastime to shoot them. Both men shot and killed Thomas.[5]

Cowpuncher Bob Cross of the Crooked Creek Pool decided to quit cowpunching and go into "decent business." He fixed up a dugout in the Strip and went into the business of robbing country stores within a

254

radius of twenty-five miles as well as stores in Hunnewell and Caldwell. He wore a mask, got all the money he could, took what groceries he needed, then retired to his hideout.

C. M. Hollister, the marshal of Caldwell, began an investigation. Since Cross was not working for anybody and seemed to have plenty of money, Hollister decided he was guilty and arrested him. Cross did not resist and seemed to be so amiable that Hollister did not ask anyone to help him nor did he handcuff Cross. Hollister took Cross to jail until he could arrange a preliminary examination. The wind was blowing hard and as Hollister attempted to open the jail door, his hat blew off. He whirled to catch it which threw his six-shooter within easy reach of Cross who jerked it out of its scabbard and shot Hollister dead.

Cross made his escape but was apprehended, tried, convicted, and sentenced for life in the penitentiary. Hollister was a good officer but did not last long.[6]

In the 1880's Henry Brown and Ben Wheeler were marshal and deputy marshal of Caldwell. Nobody knew where Brown came from or whether he had an assumed name. A two-gun man, he could take a six-shooter in each hand and make one think a battle was on. He had killed at least seven men while in office.

"Ben Wheeler" was an assumed name. After he had been deputy for some time, he let the word out that he was to be married. No one knew but what he had a legal right to "commit matrimony." I was in York, Parker, and Draper's store one evening when a man entered. Mr. Key said, "I thought you were at the wedding."

The man replied, "It was called off." Key wanted to know why. The last train brought Wheeler's wife from Texas and they were at the Leland Hotel.

Brown and I had worked together on the ⚹ ranch and his work didn't suit me. I told Sam Fling. He discharged Brown and that made him sore. Brown didn't know that I was the source of his downfall. He was so mean to his horses; he had no mercy. I never could stand to see a person abusing a dumb beast.

Whenever we took a herd of beeves from the ⚹ ranch to Caldwell, word spread about. Brown knew I would be with them and came to hunt me up. He seemed glad to see me.

Brown never took a drink of intoxicating liquor nor accepted any kind of a drink. He was always on the lookout for enemies; there were plenty of men who would kill him any minute. One day I saw him at a saloon. Several fellows urged him to take a drink at the bar. He tried to talk them out of it but they wouldn't take "no" for an answer. They lined up at the bar, and he was the last one to step up to the bar at the left. The slop jar in which the glasses were rinsed was setting on the floor directly under his left arm. When they raised their glasses to drink, he raised his glass, then turned it bottom side upward and emptied the liquor into the refuse jar. He set his glass on the bar at the same time as did the others. I don't think that even the bartender saw what he had done.

I said, "I was just wondering what you was going to do." He laughed.

In May 1884 I was holding my cattle in the Lane south of Caldwell in the Cherokee Strip. I saw Oliver Thompson coming down the trail with a bunch of saddle horses, going south. I rode along and he asked if I had heard of the attempted robbery and the mobbing of Brown, Wheeler, Bill Smith, and John West. I was so astonished I did not sleep a wink that night. I had known them so long and had been with them so much; I didn't think it was possible for them to do such a thing.

Brown and Wheeler had asked for a few days' vacation. They left Caldwell on horseback and rode down into the Strip without telling anybody where they were going. Somewhere in the Strip they had made arrangements to meet two Texas cowpunchers, Bill Smith and John West. They headed toward Medicine Lodge, got there about 10 A.M., rode up to the bank in drizzling rain, tied their horses, and went inside. Ben Wheeler pulled out his gun and told vice-president George Geppert to open the safe for they were there after the money.

Rancher Wiley Payne, president of the bank, had been over to Medicine Lodge the day before and didn't like the appearance of the books. He stayed all night at his camp and came back into town. He had just arrived at the back door when the hold-up was taking place. Payne drew his six-shooter but Brown killed him at the first shot.

Wheeler said to Geppert, "You s. o. b., you gave us away!" and killed him instantly.

They had to get out in a hurry for the shooting had attracted attention. The town was full of old buffalo hunters and cowmen with guns. Rain had drawn the horses' ropes so taut to the hitching posts that it was difficult to loosen them. By then the townsmen were ready to take up the chase.

The four men rode west to get into the hills and rough country.

256

Since Wheeler was a heavy man, his horse soon played out. The other three had to ride slowly to keep together. They saw they couldn't reach the hills, so they stopped in the first deep gulley and took refuge in a washout. It had water in it so they stuck up a white flag and wanted a council. Lee Bradley went up to where they were in the cold water; they said they would give up their arms and surrender if Bradley could guarantee they wouldn't hang but would give them a fair trial.

Bradley motioned to several other fellows to approach; they agreed to the proposition. The four men surrendered and were returned to Medicine Lodge where there was no substantial jail. They were hand-cuffed, leg-shackled, and placed in a log house under heavy guard.

Joe McNeal, the Barber County Attorney, went alone to hold a council with the prisoners, got their names, and other facts to prepare legal proceedings against them.

In the meantime the town's rougher element worked up the people; it was decided there would be a neck-tie party that night in spite of McNeal and Bradley. Bradley got word and told some of the mob leaders if these men were hanged, it would be done over his dead body. He had given his word they would get a fair trial. The mob took Bradley and hand-cuffed and locked him in a room. When night came, they went to the log house to open the door. The men were all loose.

Brown and Wheeler both dashed for liberty. Wheeler broke through the crowd; fools near him began shooting at such close range they set his clothes on fire which made a good mark in the darkness. The shooting continued until he fell. Bill Kelly was there and told me Brown hit him in the back so hard he thought it was broken. Brown grabbed for John Moore's six-shooter, but he was so big and tall and held the gun so high that Brown couldn't reach it. Brown was riddled in the milling crowd but none of the mob was injured by the bullet fusillade. As Brown fell, he let out such a gasping yell that they ever heard from a human being.

Smith and West could have gotten away while the mob was so engrossed with Brown and Wheeler but they just stood and waited their turn. They were hanged. Wheeler was carried back. He didn't want to be hanged, but wanted them to wait until 10 A.M. the next day and he would tell them the whole story. But the mob didn't stop; he was strung up with the other two. When they started to hang Smith, he told them his mother was a widow. He wanted them to write to her what had become of him.

The mob did not know who the men were, but someone remarked that two of them looked like Brown and Wheeler from Caldwell. A telegram was sent there to tell of the robbery and killings. It asked for someone to come identify them. The Caldwell people called a meeting and appointed John Blair to go.

He told the assembly how badly things had gone under Brown and Wheeler's rule, stating a number of bad things. He paused a moment, "If it doesn't prove to be them, what I have said goes for nothing. I want you to be witnesses that I never said it." When Blair returned to Caldwell with the confirming news, he felt free to stand by all he had said.

A number of years later Joe McNeal published an article in an Oklahoma paper to set matters right. He thought the reasons for the robbery had been kept in the dark long enough. Wheeler had told McNeal that he and Geppert were boyhood friends who graduated together in a Texas institution of learning. Geppert, a defaulter, had no money in the bank and had cooked up this foolish scheme to save his reputation. He had told them just how to maneuver and when to appear as Payne wouldn't be there. They could pull a fake robbery and save Geppert's standing.[7]

TWENTY-FIVE

Billy Malaley's Pole Cat Ranch

I have met many fine men in my time but I do not believe I met a finer man than William Malaley. I met him in his home in Caldwell, worked with him on his ranch and at the general spring roundup and after coming to Oklahoma, I met him at Hennessey. He has been in my home in the Cheyenne-Arapaho country. I have had many business dealings with him. He was always honorable and obliging. He told me some of his experiences when we were in camp on his ranch.

He was the deputy U.S. marshal who pulled Pat Hennessey from the burning remains of his freighting wagon and buried him in a shallow grave.[1] On a later trip from Fort Reno to Caldwell, he was driving a span of fine horses, hitched to a top buggy. He carried a six-shooter and Winchester rifle. About half-way up the trail he met two riders who turned out to one side so he would have to pass between them. Knowing what that meant, he threw back the top of his buggy, placed the lines over his shoulders to keep his hands free, picked up his Winchester, and motioned for them to get back on their side of the trail. They immediately knew he was no tenderfoot and knew how to protect himself so they got back. This put them in a position so Malaley could open up before they could draw their guns; they did not molest him.

Major Hood and Senator Plumb of Kansas were Malaley's Texas Panhandle ranch partners until late 1884.[2] Malaley was the superintendent of all the holdings. Frank Newcomer, a consumptive, was their foreman and later a line rider. I thought a great deal of Newcomer, a banker's son. His parents, acquaintances of the major and the senator, prevailed them to employ Frank with a view to restoring his health.

Newcomer and "Hamp" Meredith, a regular-type cowpuncher, camped together in a dugout and "done" their own cooking. In the rear corner of the room was a bed of regulation height, solidly attached to the wall. They kept a lantern hanging to the support of the ridgelog

259

where they could reach it from their bunk. When they wanted a light during the night, they could strike a match and light the lantern.

They kept three dogs in their dugout. I thought that one dog was one too many. One night Meredith and Newcomer had gone to bed; the dogs were sleeping outside close by. All of a sudden a terrible fight started among the dogs and from the outcry, they knew the dog had gone out of one of them mighty quick. Since another one was doing more howling than barking, they guessed it was badly wounded. The third was still barking good. Suddenly something dashed in and darted under their bed. Both had grabbed their six-shooters when the commotion started. When they realized the dog-exterminator was under their bed, they needed a little light on the subject.

They lit the lantern and set it down at the foot of their bed to shine on the dog-killer. They began to turn up the bedding with one hand with their guns in the other. Whenever they "seen" anything that looked like an animal, they gave it a forty-five bullet. Such animals will fight instead of running away when wounded. The animal was on its back under the bed and tore their bedding and anything else it got its claws into. They kept pouring the lead into it until it lay still.

They reached under the bed and pulled it to see if it had any more fight left. When they were assured it was peaceable, they stepped onto the floor and pulled it out. It was a large panther. They had one dead dog, one with a big patch of hide torn off, and one dead panther—the fruits of the chase. Meredith and Newcomer had quite a bit of patchwork to do so their bedding would stop the north wind.[3]

When they dissolved partnership, Malaley and Hood owned the Pole Cat ranch south of Caldwell on Pole Cat Creek where the Southwestern Stage Company made its first stop out of Caldwell. We referred to all who worked for this company as Malaley's men.

Later Major Hood shipped a trainload of beeves to Chicago. When any person shipped livestock on a railroad, both parties signed a contract that the animals would be delivered safely at the designated point. Furthermore, the contract allowed as many as four men for a round-trip ticket from the shipping point. An injury to a shipper as a passenger on a freight train would hold a railroad liable to damages.

If the market reports showed there was a difference of five or ten cents a hundred weight on the day, the stock should have been sold, but if the stock were sold at a date later than the contract called for and at a lower price, the shipper was also entitled to damages on that account.

As the train approached Chicago on a curve, the major was in the caboose. There must have been a defective rail for the latter half of the train left the track, smashed a number of the cars, and killed or crippled many cattle. The caboose and major were scrambled with the pile-up; he suffered a fractured hip and thereafter used a cane. Major Hood brought suit against the railroad for his injury and the loss of cattle. But he wasn't particular on one point; he received all of the able-bodied stock where the wreck occurred. He asserted that his injury was permanent. I never heard how he fared in these law suits.

Soon after, the major came down to the Pole Cat ranch. He and Malaley cut out all of the big beeves and shipped them to Chicago. While they "was" driving them to another pasture for the night, a big beef began to play and jump around. He came to a narrow, deep gulley and started to jump it but ended in the ditch, caught his lower jaw on the opposite bank, and broke his neck. Malaley "seen" the whole performance and said his spine snapped like a dry stick. The steer was jammed so tightly in the little gorge that Malaley could only skin one hind quarter. He cut out a large piece of round steak and carried it to the cook, "Nate, here's $50 worth of steak." That is what this four-year-old steer would have brought on the market.

Major Hood had hung his cane on a nail in the ranch dugout and did not use it the day of the ranch roundup. Not being used to camping out, he drove his buggy back to Caldwell to spend the night. Malaley stayed and got the herd started toward Caldwell. When he got in his buggy, he stopped at the dugout, talked with me a little bit, and drove on.

I went inside, saw the Major's cane, grabbed it off the nail, and ran out, yelling at the top of my lungs, waving the cane. Malaley whirled his team around. "The Major may need this in his business," I said as I handed the cane to Malaley.

"Yes, the hook on that stick is supposed to hold about $10,000! I think I can get it to him before he gets too far away," Malaley said as he drove away. The injury was another reason why his cane was so valuable.

In the fall of 1884 I left the ⵣ ranch and took charge of my cattle interest in the Lane ranch. A fellow named Clark became foreman, and in a short time he and Bates had a disagreement. Clark shed tears when Bates released him. Bates drove over and asked me to serve as his foreman but I declined and suggested Bud Moore. A year later

Bates came again. Moore had created much dissatisfaction because of his mismanagement. I told Bates I could not serve nor do him justice for I had my own business. He then suggested I let him make a public statement that I was foreman and would go down once or twice a month to look over the ranch. He offered to pay me $50 a month for the winter of 1885–86 but I refused. He finally prevailed on Tip Mc-Cracken to serve. Tip took his wife and small child with him but this was unsatisfactory.

In the summer of 1885 we had shipped to Kansas City all cattle that were fat enough to go on the market. I went with them, then returned to Peru where I got a buckboard and a span of horses. I hired two boys to accompany me in September to go to Malaley's ranch and get the cows and calves. One drove the team hitched to the buckboard and was supposed to do our cooking while the other one and I rode the saddle horses.

Late that fall Charlie and I placed 100 head of steers and some barren cows on Billie Malaley's range. During the winter of 1885–86 heavy snow and sleet covered ranges and obstructed roads. I was residing in Peru where brother Charlie and I had taken all of our heifers and cows to feed. In January Malaley wrote that all the cattle were starving. He wanted me to come see what I could do about mine. Charlie drove me to the north-south road, the only one open that would reach the railroad at Elk City to Caldwell. I sent my saddle as baggage to Wellington, then changed trains to Caldwell.

I went up to Malaley's house. He told me I could either get on my horse, ride up Bluff Creek, and buy stock fields as there were plenty at a reasonable price. Or I could take his brand new grain wagon, fine driving horse, and stallion; find plenty of harness in the barn; take the wagon to haul a load of shelled corn to my cattle; and feed them on the grass. There was so much snow and ice I could not get the cattle to the stock fields so I went to his barn; got the team; drove up to Yorke, Parker, and Draper's; and loaded up with forty-five bushels of corn.

Malaley told me to drive down to his Pole Cat ranch and tell Frank Newcomer to send this team and wagon back to Caldwell in care of a fellow at the ranch, named Jack. Newcomer was to permit me to use Malaley's horse, old Hippy. I could feed him my corn and Malaley's hay.

When I got the corn out to the ranch, I piled it out in a pasture which Malaley was not using and rode old Hippy out among the cattle with a sack of shelled corn. I poured out a couple of quarts of corn on a smooth solid spot of ground and when the steers smelled it, they immediately came up as I rode away and ate every grain that lay on the ground, along with a good deal of grass. Afterwards I sent word to George Mayes in Caldwell to bring out two more loads which cost twenty-five cents a bushel.

He drove the wagon facing one direction and the other the opposite direction with the tail gates together. When the corn was run to the ground, he scooped the remainder from the front ends of the wagons into a cone shape which gave maximum protection against rainfall. There was little or no waste and I saved all but one of my cattle.

An old man named Fort was there; Malaley had merely given him working interest in a bunch of mares on the ranch. Fort was seventy-four years old and getting to be mighty cranky. He thought I was imposing on Billy and was so grouchy he wouldn't call me by name. The nearest he ever got was **AF**, the brand which I had on the cattle.

The deep snow made it difficult to get around afoot. Fort and John Gross were hauling hay for the stock and saddle horses, scattering some among some of the poorest cattle. The hay stack yard was about four miles down Pole Cat Creek from Malaley's camp. The mare herd ran loose among the stacks where they fed and sheltered themselves.

One day Fort and Gross planned to haul two loads of hay so they left the gate open. Something interfered and they did not return for a second load. Fort never thought of it until after supper when it was dark. He said that gate must be shut but Gross made much light of it. The more John talked, the madder Fort became, more determined to go.

I said to Newcomer, "Frank, he can't make it. I don't think he can get half way down there."

Newcomer replied, "Let the old fool go."

Since John couldn't stop him, I knew it was no use for me to say a word. I went to the barn where the horses and saddles were. The old man had a gentle saddle horse, his favorite. I took his saddle, placed it on the horse, and led it to the door of the dugout.

Just then Fort came out and met me. He looked and saw who it was and what I had, then said, "What in thunder are you doing here with my horse and saddle?"

I answered, "I brought it up here for you to ride."

He snapped, "Take that horse and saddle back where you got them. I don't want you to be fooling with my stuff."

263

I said, "See here, Mr. Fort, you're going to ride this horse down there or lick me. We'll just fight it out right here."

He looked at me a moment, then said, "Well, I'll ride the horse." He mounted and started off. I could hear the horse's feet creaking in the frozen snow. It was a cloudless night but a breeze was blowing from the north.

After awhile the dugout door opened. The old man came in, pulled off his glove, walked up to me, stuck out his hand, and said, "Well, Mr. Records, you are the best friend I've got. You proved that by saving my life! I'd have frozen to death if I had went afoot. In fact I don't think I could have got half way there." Afterwards I was always "Mr. Records."

Mr. Fort told me about Fred Brooks, a cowpuncher, who made a particular effort to show how bad he was. Fort and Brooks stayed together one winter. All Brooks could talk about was gun plays, shooting up towns, and running things over other men. Fort could hardly stand to be with him. They were camped in a dugout, set back into a bank. Leading to the door was a trench or runway in which one had set a box.

One day Brooks walked out the door, began cursing, and emptied his six-shooter into the box. Fort asked what was the matter. Brooks replied he had not had a fight lately and was practicing up.

I saw Brooks in action only once at a general roundup at the Lightning Rod ranch where he was. Someone started to cut out a steer; Brooks stopped him. They talked and the other fellow acknowledged he was mistaken. Brooks said he better be careful about cutting out cattle from his herd. In a few moments someone else started to cut out the same steer. Brooks came swearing worse than ever, turned back the steer, and declared that someone would get killed over that steer yet. Young Short and I were sitting on our horses near enough to see and hear all.

Unknowingly, "Hi" Sheridan[4] started to cut out the same steer. Brooks came with more violence than ever. It took Sheridan so by surprise that he said, "You must be bad."

Brooks replied, "I'll show you whether I'm bad or not." He pulled his six-shooter and began striking at Sheridan with it and hit him at least once. Then some of the other cowhands rode between Brooks and Sheridan to stop Brooks.

Short said, "If I had been in Hi's place, I could have put a bullet up under his chin while he was swinging his gun over."

264

I never had seen Short with a gun until I was sent to his camp the next winter to help hold back Drumm's cattle from the range. I learned he was never without a six-shooter. He had the gun barrel sawed short so he could carry it in a scabbard in his leggings where no one could see it. He could get at it quickly, which in most cases is more than half the battle.

Brooks didn't stay long in one place because of his quarrelsome disposition. He returned to Texas but unfortunately took the same disposition with him. He got into trouble, killed a man, and got a life-long post office address. Outlaws infested this part of the country for many years. But at last they were given a "perfect cleaning."

The snow and ice lasted nearly two months, the ground was frozen hard. "Gus" Hegwer, an experienced trapper from Kiowa,[5] had a string of traps along Driftwood Creek which empties into the Salt Fork above the mouth of Medicine River. When he did not return home after one storm, searching parties found him dead.

Tom McNeal wrote in the *Cresset* that range cattle lived during the first half of the winter on recollections and the second half on anticipations. This was one winter when they did not get as far as the anticipation.[6] Fenced ranges caused great losses to the cattlemen.

Tom Morris, one of Oliver Ewell's cowhands, had bought a through herd of 200 yearlings and put them on Ewell's ranch along the Eagle Chief. When winter approached, Ewell advised Morris to take a business college course at Wichita for his future benefit. Since the stock were with his own herd, the 200 could be handled as well as if Morris were on the range so he followed Ewell's suggestion. He was in Wichita scarcely a month when Ewell wrote him to buy a gross of skinning knives and some whetstones, come down, and begin skinning his cattle. Elijah Morris, Tom's brother, told me Tom lost all his cattle.

Cowhide dealers made money from the loss of so many range cattle. "Red" Conner of Medicine Lodge took his family down to the Crooked Creek ranch southwest of Caldwell, lived in a dugout, and skinned the carcasses during that winter and early spring. He sold $800 worth of hides.

Other cattlemen had scarcely any losses. One cattleman who lived in Caldwell had about 400 head. He rounded them up without a single loss. They were used to rough treatment.

There were high banks and timbered spots on Malaley's range and bluestem grass appeared above the snow. Grass also appeared on the hills where the wind had blown. Cattle did not suffer so much on his ranch. He had shipped out most of his beeves and had planned to restock his ranch the next year. Cattle prices broke to such a low figure despite the unprecedented losses all over the ranges, so Malaley decided anything would be better than cattle business.

Next spring I helped Malaley conduct a local roundup of neighboring ranches. Thousands of dead cattle in every direction were piled where they had bunched and attempted to keep warm. As they stood near banks, those pushing from the rear knocked them down; others piled on top where they perished. If they had been open, the cattle could have drifted to the sheltering blackjacks and other natural wind brakes.

I contracted to sell my two-year-old steers to J. D. Payne of the old ♀ ranch. He told me to cut them out of Malaley's herd and hold them so he could look at them before he decided to buy them. I cut and drove them just outside the ranch's western gate and into the Lane which was reserved for herds coming from Texas bound for Caldwell for shipment. Payne decided to take the cattle but couldn't drive them for a few days as he was planning to ship some beeves. Afterwards he would send his cowhands to get my herd. He wrote me a check for $250 and would pay the remainder when he received the herd. While waiting, I herded the steers. I trained them to come to a certain point to bed each night. Water was plentiful in a stream nearby and the grass was excellent. When dinner time came, I rode to Malaley's ranch, ate, then returned. When they were bedded down, I left and rode to his dugout and stayed the nights.

One day while returning from my noonday meal, I saw a fellow chasing something toward the breaks in the direction of Caldwell. Becoming suspicious, I counted the steers and found one was missing so I redoubled my vigilance. One day three strays belonging to "Barbecue" Campbell came to my herd and I let them stay. My herd was one short, these three made two too many.

Ten days later Payne's nephew came with Myron Cleveland to get the steers. We strung out and counted them; I showed him the three steers. He paid me the full amount and took my herd.

In 1886 I shipped out a carload of steers from Malaley's ranch to Kansas City and rode with the load. I went to Chautauqua County; hired two saddle horses, a span of horses, and two drivers, Raymond Dodson and Charlie Polson; and returned to Malaley's ranch where I had left some cows in his pasture.

266

We started back to Chautauqua County with my sixty head of cows and calves early in the morning and camped for dinner near the Chikaskia rock falls. When I heard some persons talking above the falls, I walked up and discovered two young men using clubs to kill large fish which were on their way to spawning grounds. The boys belonged to a camp of Oklahoma Boomers[7] which was in great need of food. The first real distress that I had seen in my life was in this camp. This influenced me to stay out of the Oklahoma land run of 1889.

TWENTY-SIX

Foreman of the **JD P** Ranch

In 1886 while Charles, Frank, and I had our cattle back in Chautauqua County, J. D. Payne wrote and asked if I could come take charge of the old ⚜, now the **JD P** ranch, as he had purchased Frank Bates' interest. I agreed to meet Payne at Kiowa on a designated date but heavy snowfall blocked roads and stalled trains. They had to be opened with snow plows. I had to go to Elk City, the first open road which was mostly north-south.

When I arrived at Kiowa, no one was there to meet me. I went to L. C. Farris' Livery barn to get a horse; I had my saddle. He had only one horse, an old outlaw. If I could ride him, it would not cost me anything and I could bring him back when I got ready. I mounted and he did all he could to get rid of me but he wouldn't leave the barn.

While I was mauling him around, Frank Streeter came up the street on the run, "I knew that was you as soon as I saw you." I did not believe the old pelter could carry me very far anyway so I pulled my saddle off. Streeter then said, "If you'll stay all night, I'll take you down to our ranch. You can get a horse there to ride to the **JD P** ranch and send it back from there."

I took him at his word, and the next morning we drove down to his ranch in his spring wagon. I got the saddle horse and rode to the **JD P** ranch. A few days later I sent it back in care of Payne who was going to Kiowa.

The ranch looked desolate; the mare herd had not been kept under control and was running with a Texas stallion with no thought of improving the stock. The fences were in need of repair. I looked at the pens which had just been finished and told Payne they should be torn down and their positions reversed. The catch pen was on the north side, the corral south of it. Since the prevailing winds were from the south, we were compelled to work in the dust.

Frank Stevens came and wanted to buy some of the saddle horses for a cow outfit that he was planning to join in Canada to seek new cattle ranges. Payne put such a high price on them that Stevens and I were unable to make any bargains. I suggested that Payne sell a number of his old saddle horses to the settlers in Barber and Comanche Counties. I broke a number of them to work, hitched them to a wagon from which I had removed the top box, and drove them around over the range until they were broken to pull but Payne did not act on my suggestion.

I hired "Erv" Timberlake as cook. When Payne and Bates found how cheap they could raise hogs, they bought two or three for the ranch. When I returned, they had quite a bunch of hogs. When Payne came down from Kiowa, we had a regular butchering day. The hogs were nice and fat. The pork was pickled in a barrel; Payne made sausage and headcheese. I never had liked headcheese but this was the best I ever ate. The sausage was also good. The meat fed the outfit throughout the following summer. If one of us had to be gone all day, he would take slices of the well-pressed, well-seasoned headcheese for sandwiches.

In early March we noticed smoke rising in the blackjacks south of us. We didn't pay much attention until late in the evening when we "seen" it heading our way. The following morning we still saw smoke. I suggested we backfire against it. Payne had just finished working up the meat. I took the boys over to the creek east of the ranch camp and started firing back toward the ranch house. I decided to let the south end of the range burn off.

The wind came up earlier than expected, and the fire was coming at a high rate of speed before we could stop it. It looked as if we would lose everything, but we managed to get it checked and saved several hundred acres of unburned grass between the two creeks. Since there was a high bank along the east side of the creek, we went across, took water and burlap sacks, and fought the fire along the sides. The fire-head swept on toward the Salt Fork. We carried water in a barrel in the wagon and used our burlap sacks again to keep it from backing into the camp. Since we couldn't stop for a noonday meal, we really appreciated the headcheese sandwiches.

When night came, the grass became slightly damp from dew and the wind lulled considerably. We sent someone to camp to get Mr. Payne's driving team, spring wagon, and plow. We hooked it to the rear of the wagon and made a little furrow alongside the fire which was threatening to back in. Afterwards it was much easier to whip out the fire as it usually died out when it struck the little furrow. We followed the course of this side fire until we struck a tonguelike formation of the Salt Plains; there was little here to burn. It was about 2 A.M. We had fought the prairie fire continuously for at least twenty hours. We saved enough grass to last until the spring grass came on.

On the spring roundup Dick Larkin, a cowpuncher I had known several years, asked me whose steers bore the **AF** brand. I told him they were mine and where I had close-herded them. He was very much concerned and told me about a cowpuncher who had been out of work and had been rustling fat beeves from the big cattlemen and selling them to butchers in Caldwell. He was sorry rustlers had taken my steer, for they aimed to make the big cattlemen bear the loss because they had put up fences, turned off so many old hands, and hired tenderfoot fence riders in their places. I told him they need not feel too bad, for I had shifted the burden on to J. D. Payne by using "Barbecue" Campbell's three stray steers in completing the delivery. Larkin accepted this as a good joke. He told me the fellow who took my steer was a good friend of his and mine but declined to say who. I was suspicious his name might have been Dick Larkin.

Many years after the Oklahoma settlement, I hauled a load of wheat to Kingfisher and saw a familiar-looking fellow who had just carried a slop jar from the saloon to the street where he emptied it. I asked if he were Jim Lee, an old cowpuncher who had been with the Cragin company, adjoining the ⚹ ranch. He replied, "No, do you know Jim Lee?"

I said, "Yes, but who are you?" He was Dick Larkin. He asked where I lived. I told him and said that the two boys with me were mine.

He remarked how neat they appeared, then said, "Just look at me. I have gone completely to the dogs. I am working in this saloon for a living."

That summer Payne hired Van Leven, an expert from Kansas City, to spay the heifers. This "new deal" was handled in a peculiar fashion and was the only experience I had with this type of work. It was tedious and difficult to perform on wild cattle. They were first driven into a catch pen, then roped and thrown on a platform with their heads and shoulders considerably lower than their hips. Ropes were attached to their hind feet to keep the animals from sliding down the platform, then snubbed to a snubbing post. Both front feet were tied by another rope, also snubbed, to draw the body taut at full length. The expert

270

stood alongside the platform with the animal's belly toward him. He used his spaying knife with cutting point curved upward. The slanting platform caused the animal's paunch and intestines to slide forward out of the way so the flank incision could be made. He made the incision wide enough to slip two fingers under the pride and lift them out to snip them off with a pair of sharp calipers. He closed the incision with needle and thread to prevent infection, then placed a disinfectant on it and turned the animal loose.

The sun poured down disagreeably and we did not get to benefit from the wind. Had I known Payne was going to spay his heifers, I would have insisted the catch pen and the corral be reversed. The longer we worked in this spaying pen, the more anxious we wished it to be discontinued. Even the Kansas City specialist, who had been induced to come because of the prospect of an extended job, was glad to quit before it was finished. Later when Payne began to buy, sell, and ship stock to Kansas City, I met Van Leven. He was working in the stockyards for a commission company.

One day at the yards he felt something in his teeth, reached over to a nearby post, took off a splinter, and picked his teeth. He caused his gum to bleed, was infected with the foot and mouth disease, and died.

When the second Cleveland administration came to office, the tariff against foreign cattle importation was removed to such an extent that incoming cattle, hides, and horns brought foot and mouth disease and the horn fly. This was one important phase of a Democratic administration which we remember. Not only did it cause millions in losses to cattlemen but also the loss of two friends—one in Kansas City, the other in Oklahoma.

Black Spanish was a powerful coal black horse. A good roper was required to rope him, even in a corral. Hard to hold, a man must have some energy and ability of action to mount him. The horse always made a show—he snorted, pranced, and wheeled around, putting on great display. I liked to ride him because he was fine-looking and able to do things well. He had good wind and endurance and could be ridden long distances without fatigue. I did not take him on roundups because he stirred up the other horses too much and was not a good cutting horse. When I returned as foreman, the boys had almost outlawed him by letting him run free. I soon found him some pretty hard jobs.

Frank Bates had a driving team which he would take to "Big

271

George's" stable in Caldwell when he was not using them. Once another horse had to be teamed with his buggy horse. This horse was gentle, had been worked, and we thought we could turn it loose on the range. A wild mare found and took him over close to the salt plains in marshy land where vegetation was fresh and green. When we found them, he was just as wild as she. I told the boys we had to take that horse back to "Big George" the first chance we had. We knew we couldn't get near enough to rope the mare and the old horse would stay with her or die.

I took three men and started out. I told one fellow to take the first station but keep away from the course which I proposed to make the horses follow. I put Myron Cleveland, a red-headed lad, on the second station. I told each fellow, as the horses came running by, to ride in close without turning them and dash after them, whooping and yelling. I took the third station and was riding Black Spanish. The fourth man was instructed to slip up close to the horses and crowd them as fast as he could to keep them on route which he did. He was riding a good horse and was a fellow who always did his best. I got on to low flat ground to keep out of sight until he had crowded the horses past me. When Black Spanish "seen" them a coming, he began to put on such a show I had to take the horses a little sooner than I wanted to. I poured it on as hard as I could until we approached Cleveland's position. But he had gotten on to a high hill instead and got interested in the race. He thought it was the prettiest one he ever saw. He never offered to take his turn. I knew it was too late to make any changes then. I just poured it to old Black Spanish as far as he could go. I thought it would be better to shoot the mare than risk killing a good horse like Black Spanish, so I slackened his speed to a walk to rest and permit Cleveland and Marion Simeonson to catch up. We all rode back to camp.

I told Marion to clean his rifle. He was a good shot and had often killed deer for us. In fact on one occasion when he jumped a bunch of deer, he fired and dropped one of them. Without stopping to reason about what he would do with so much meat, he killed a second deer.

The next morning I told him to ride over where we had found the horses and take his rifle. If the wind was from the north, he must come into the marshy land from the south and vice versa. The wind happened to be from the south. From his northern approach Simeonson was able to look lengthwise up a number of sloughs without doing so much riding, as they flowed to the Salt Plains from the south. He was a cautious hunter and knew he would have to take great care to get close enough to make a dead shot. I didn't want him to be "bringing them in alive." Once he had told me a funny story about that so he had a good laugh when I used those words.

It took him an hour or two to locate the horses. He shot the mare according to the old buffalo method. She "throwed" her head down between her forelegs as if trying to throw a rider and began to buck. With the last jump she lit right on her back, dead. The other horse broke into a run as the gun cracked. When he found the mare wasn't with him, he began to neigh. Simeonson went to his saddle horse, stood around and waited while the horse ran around looking for the mare. He came closer to Simeonson's horse. Simeonson took down his rope and "throwed" it around his neck. Since he was close to Timberlake's camp, Simeonson went over and took dinner with them. They asked him what he was doing there. He told them he had come over to get the horse he was leading. There was a mare but she laid down, so he left her.

Shortly afterwards someone went up to Caldwell, and I sent the old buggy horse up to "Big George."

My last hard fall came this year. One stallion and a herd of mares were running loose on the range so long that they were getting to be as wild as mustangs. I told the boys we would get them up once in a while and corral them to domesticate them. I knew it would take hard riding to corral these animals. I selected a powerful, yellow saddle horse with yellow eyes and with the meanest disposition I had ever seen in a horse. If he ever got a chance, he would not hesitate to kill a man.

When we went after the horses, I found some were wilder than I thought. It took mighty hard riding to keep them headed toward camp and the corral. When we got pretty close to the corral and thought we had them about ready to drive into it, a few horses broke through between two riders and started right up the creek. There was only one place where they could cross and get back on the range. I was on the opposite side when I "seen" it happen. They had a lead against me in the race for the crossing. I poured it on the old yellow horse and he delivered the goods.

I passed them and thought I would have an easy task to turn them back as they were badly winded. I was watching ahead and "seen" a wolf's den but had not noticed that there was a second hole three or four feet to one side of it. I was ahead of the horses and ready to turn

273

in front of them to start them back toward the corral. It was terribly dry and dusty. The old yellow horse didn't see the second hole but "run" both feet down into it to his shoulders. I turned loose, catapulted over his head, and landed on the hard ground on my right elbow and left hand. This kicked up so much dust that the horses just stopped and looked; they could have run on and escaped.

I jumped to my feet, grabbed the bridle rein, threw it over my horse's head, mounted him but he could scarcely move. Each step he took, I could hear a strange grating in his shoulder. When he jumped into that hole going full speed, his shoulder was so badly injured that he never was a good work horse after that.

My right arm was so numb I couldn't do anything with it. My right forearm bone broke close to the elbow but there was nothing I could do about it then. No one within seventy-five miles was capable of setting it. I let it heal as it was but a knot formed on the bone and it was a great annoyance. The lightest contact with any object was painful. In later years I got into difficulty with a horse and in the scuffle, broke the bone in the same place. When it knitted again, the knot disappeared and it scarcely ever bothers me anymore.

All ranch foremen were empowered to draw checks against cattle company funds. On a trip to Kiowa I went to A. W. Rumsey's bank and found that Payne had left only $35, too small a capital. Had I discharged a cowhand, there would not have been enough money to pay for his services.

While I was in the settlements, I became engaged to the girl who later became my wife. After I got things in motion, I wrote to this "only girl on earth." In due time I received a reply. She seemed to be greatly surprised for she thought "out of sight, out of mind." In my reply I said that distance lent enchantment to the view.

Payne brought our mail to us as he came down every week or two from Kiowa. As he was handing out our mail he said, "You are the only one who seems to have a lady correspondent."

I replied, "That's a fellow I got acquainted with up in the state."

He said, "You tell him he can certainly write a lovely hand."

This country now looked empty without her, so I stayed only six months and returned to Peru in August 1887 to be with Dora Belle Barker, the only girl I ever wanted as a life companion.

TWENTY-SEVEN

Cattle Shipping Business in Kansas

I went to Kiowa in August to tell J. D. Payne I was quitting. That was my last work on the range. Dick Male and I drove a spring wagon which he took charge of when we arrived at Kiowa. He worked at the ranch from time to time. In 1884 he took a claim in the Medicine River valley opposite old Kiowa in Barber County. He built a stable and residence on a range of sand hills on the south side of his claim. By 1885 he had two young horses, two old mares, and a few cows.

A cloudburst occurred one evening about 10 P.M. over the headwaters of Elm Creek, a small stream which emptied into Medicine River near the southern edge of Medicine Lodge. Frank Shepler, his wife, and small baby lived in a small house in the creek flat in a little elm grove. They were in bed when they heard a peculiar noise like running water. Frank stepped out to find water nearly to the top of the bed. He grabbed the baby and climbed a ladder to a small room above, his wife followed. The water followed them. He handed the baby to his wife and attempted to punch a hole through the roof so they could get on top of the house. Just then the house went to pieces. That was the last he ever saw of his wife and baby. He was thrown into an elm tree, caught hold of a limb, and hung on until the flood passed by. His wife's body was found in a drift but the child was never found.[1]

The crest did not reach Kiowa, eighteen miles from Medicine Lodge, until 10 A.M. the next day. Male had a cow lying out in the flat, heavy with calf, and he had been carrying feed to her. After he had breakfasted and had finished the chores, he went out to feed the cow. As he was returning, he heard a rumbling noise up the Medicine River flat. He saw a wave about four feet deep coming down the flat. Every cow or horse took just one look and broke into a run for the sand hills.

Dick didn't take the oncoming torrent of water seriously until it struck his cow. It threw her in the air as if she were a little chip. Male ran toward his house as fast as he could but the water cut him off. He turned toward his barn, was cut off again, then turned toward the largest sand hill. A swiftly moving point of water struck him as he grabbed the brush which grew at the foot of the hill. When he got out of the water on top of the hill, he discovered he was a mile from the shore. He had two companions, a cottontail rabbit and a land terrapin. The rabbit seemed to realize their common calamity and soon permitted him to pet it like a house cat.

Male saw people gathering around on the bluff opposite him across the river. He took off his coat and began to wave. Soon someone took off his coat to wave back. Male assumed some of them were his parents from Kiowa.[2]

He noticed the water's crest had begun to recede. He began to wade into the current which separated him from the sand hill on which his horses and stable were. He soon found he could wade safely. They were in water up to their midsides. Apparently the water had reached the tops of their backs, but fortunately their halter straps were long enough to keep their heads above water. He untied, led, and held them for awhile. They seemed to be quiet, so he slipped the halters from the two young horses. To his amazement they jumped into the swollen river.

Since the river was full of floating objects as barbed-wire fences, he never expected to see them again. He finally saw one of the horses emerge, walk out, and stand motionless for some moments. He thought he had lost only one horse, but still he stood, looking. After several minutes the second one came out, stood awhile, then walked off.

He held his two old mares for some time, seeing that they grazed before he turned them loose. They had no desire to take to that water. He wondered how he would get along without anything to eat. He thought nothing would be left in his house which was on a smaller sand hill than the ruined barn.

There was a chained boat by a big cottonwood tree directly east of Kiowa at a road crossing some distance above his claim. To his amazement the flood brought him the big tree and boat with its oars intact. They lodged against the sand hill on which he had taken refuge. But the flood didn't bring the key to unlock the padlock that held the boat to the tree. He had to expend a considerable amount of labor to break the chain. Male, born and reared in Maryland, was familiar with boat handling. Once the chain was broken, it was not long before he was able to cross the river and get something to eat.

In 1887 Dick Male heard of a fellow who lived up the Medicine

River from his claim and had some mares which might be bred to his stallion. Male discovered a fellow living in a new frame house on that low bottom along the river.

Male asked, "Ain't you afraid of high water here?"

The fellow answered, "No, the river never gets up here."

Male said he didn't want to cause any uneasiness, but he had seen water over ten feet deep where the man's house stood. He looked at Male as if he thought a man who was such a liar wouldn't be safe to do business with. No one could recall a flood like this before 1885 nor has one occurred since.

Dick and I stopped at Drumm's ranch and got dinner. Alpha Updegraff was there. He and I had worked the Cherokee Strip together. One day as we were riding along together I had said to him, "Alpha, did you know that we were old blood relations?"

He said, "No, I notice that we look a good deal alike and about the same size." (Alpha weighed 220 pounds and I weighed 130). I told him the story about our fathers working on the Mississippi River together. His father had told me the story when I stayed in his hotel in Medicine Lodge, Kansas, in the latter part of November 1878.[3] Alpha seemed to get a great kick out of it. He would tell the boys that we were blood relations for we looked so much alike. Thirty years later Updegraff's son and daughter and my oldest son attended Northwestern State Teachers College at Alva, Oklahoma.

At Kiowa I met Scott Cummins, the Pilgrim Bard of the Southwest, who published a continued story in *The Medicine Lodge Cresset*.[4] I also saw Fayette Thomas and told him I was going back to the settlements to stay. He asked me to intercede for him to succeed myself. I told Payne I would have to quit since we disagreed on so many different things. He was worried about my intentions. I told him there were plenty of men and recommended Thomas as a good cowman who would attend strictly to business. Payne did not look upon him with much favor and he did not care to take any suggestions from me.

In the six ensuing years, I went into the shipping business and operated a meat market and an ice house in Peru. I bought and shipped cattle, hogs, and an occasional load of grain. I had one beef contract for the construction gangs along the Denver, Memphis, and Atlantic Railroad. DeFord and Wackman were the Contractors. I sold the beef to sub-contractors who had contracted to build road beds and tear down hills.

Brother Charles and I usually had about 150 head of stock cattle on hand at all times. We generally sold dry cows and two-year-old steers. Since we had to feed the stock at least three months, we could sell them for feeders in the fall when market prices were favorable.

The railroads was rather liberal to shippers in the 1880's. Caldwell attempted to hold all the cow country trade, but the adjacent rough country and lack of water was so objectionable that trade in time moved to Hunnewell where the country was level and well-watered.

In 1884 when I was taking a herd from Frank Bates' ⚕ ranch to Caldwell to be shipped, I had one carload of my own stock which went with Bates' trainload. He billed these cattle to the Kansas City market. I told Bates to get on a good saddle horse and ride alongside the herd. I wanted to show him some steers which inspector Henry Johnson might challenge at Kansas City. They were strung out so we could look them over good as they passed. I began to show him the beeves I had put in at different times which might be challenged. If challenged, I advised Bates not to say too much, for he couldn't prove them by any of his road brands or earmarks.

Bates met a man who lived at Belle Plains, Kansas, who wanted to full-feed about that many steers. So Bates sold this trainload of steers to him. Of course I never inquired about his business. I think he figured it would pay him to sell to somebody else rather than put them on the open market at Kansas City. When the train arrived at Belle Plains, the cattle were unloaded, including mine.

Expecting to hear from my cattle in a day or so, I stayed in Caldwell four or five days but never heard a word. I told Harry Hill, the commission man, about it. He soon located them at Belle Plains, then sent word to the commission house in Kansas City to get "them" cattle. That "throwed" them several days late for the market for which the contract called. I asked Hill how much damages I should demand.

He said, "If we put the damage too high, it may cause delay by an investigation." I told him there were so many things to consider, such as difference of market days, shrinkage in stock weight, etc. Then he said, "If I say $100, they'll stop to investigate. If I say $50, they will pay it without a word." I consented; the claim went through without protest. When I got the returns from the sale, I was agreeably surprised to see how well they weighed.

A few years later I met a fellow in Chautauqua Springs, Kansas, who was having trouble with a liveryman who had forbid him to dehorn cattle near his barn. I tried to convince the liveryman there was no harm in dehorning cattle in the adjacent lot. I helped the fellow move his dehorning chute elsewhere. In the meantime I told him what I thought of the liveryman for doing such a foolish thing.

The fellow began to warm up and asked my name. Then he asked me if I used to operate out at Caldwell and if I had a carload of cattle jumped off at Belle Plains in 1884.

I told him, "Yes." He asked me what I thought of the weights of my cattle when they were finally sold in Kansas City. I laughed and told him I was surely pleased, "How did it happen?"

He said the commission company sent him out to get the cattle. He found them in the Belle Plains feed yard. The man seemed to be similar to the liveryman who had just caused him so much bother. He insulted the commission agent when told who he was and what he wanted. The agent reasoned since there was but one load of cattle, the owner must be a small shipper—I had thirty-one head. The agent got the exact number from the feeding pens and fought for the biggest ones. Since he was dealing in small business, himself, the agent naturally favored me. Furthermore, since the feeder insulted him, he had another reason to favor the small shipper. They had some pretty hard-fought arguments which nearly came to blows.

I got a substantial benefit from the weights—$50 for shrinkage when there was none. Some of Bates' big steers weighed almost twice as much as the small stuff which I was shipping. Luck was with me, thanks to the insulting manner of the feeder at Belle Plains.

I used the cowboy's remedy on my father in the late 80's when a snake bit him as he felt for potatoes among his potato vines. I "seen" him walk toward the house, carrying a snake on a stick. He asked, "What kind of snake is that?"

I answered, "That's a copperhead."

He asked, "Are you sure about that?"

I said, "Yes, I'll just show you." I took a stick and pried its mouth open and showed him the fangs. I did not know until then that the snake had bitten him.

He held his right forefinger out toward me to show where the two fangs had cut through the skin and into the flesh.

I said, "Come on into the house and I'll fix that." I found only one coal of fire in the ashes in the stove. I told him to hold out his finger. I held his hand and laid the coal on the marks of the fangs on his finger.

279

Dora Belle Barker Records (1860–1943), the third of ten children, moved to Kansas from Illinois with her family in the 1870s. Her son Ralph (1889–1957) attended colleges at Edmond and Alva and received his B.A. from the University of Oklahoma, where he returned to teach history and was voted "Most Popular Professor" in 1930. His Ph.D. was from the University of Chicago. Courtesy of Western History Collections, University of Oklahoma Library.

He said, "My gracious, your remedy is worse than the disease."

I told him that if it was a success, all he would have to treat, then, would be the burn.

Steam generated under the coal; presently it popped into the air and fell to the floor. As it did not swell a particle, he knew that the cowboy remedy was effective.

In 1886 young twenty-four-year-old William A. Shanklin held a meeting in Peru. He was stationed there by regular appointment of the Methodist Episcopal Church. He was a university graduate and had entered business at Chetopa, Kansas, where he was converted at a meeting and felt called to the ministry. He sold his business, went to Peru, and held a revival meeting. After he was licensed to preach, Peru was his first appointment where he organized and built the first Methodist Church.[5]

He preached with persuasive, convincing power and influenced more than 100 people to confess Christ at his first meeting. It was there that I first saw the emptiness of a worldly life and accepted the Gospel of Christ in its fullness. Most of the converts joined the Methodist Episcopal Church, others joined other denominations. Among them was Dora Belle Barker, the girl whom I married 28 December 1887.[6] When we removed to Oklahoma, we had two boys who were born in Kansas; we later had one boy and two girls born in Oklahoma.

TWENTY-EIGHT

Frank Records among the Pawnee Indians

Brother Frank worked in the government service about thirteen years, from 1872 to 1892.[1] When Generals Caddison and Gatchell established the Pawnee Indians in Indian Territory, the freight for all the Indians was still hauled from Coffeyville, Kansas. The Osages were east and the Pawnees west of the Arkansas River, so the government decided to build a ferry across the river and Frank was put in charge. The ferry site was located by the two generals.

Government employees stretched a cable with guy ropes across the river under the instruction of General Gatchell. After they finished, they found the boat was upstream from the cable; the rising river brought the boat too close to the cable for anyone to stay on it.

Just then the current started the boat; the general leaped off the boat to the bank and yelled, "Let her go boys, let her go to hell. She'll eventually go there anyhow." Some of the boys had thrown the guy ropes over the cable before they jumped which caught and stopped the boat. The general said, "Good work, boys, I would rather have lost the boat than one of you. The government could soon make another boat, but it takes a long time to produce such fine men as you."

They operated the ferry about a year when an unusual rise in the river brought water so close to the cable that a large tree with a large hook-shaped root came down near the middle of the stream, caught the cable, and pulled it in a V-shape before it broke. The government began to haul the supplies for the Pawnees from Arkansas City.

While brother Frank was running the ferry, he saw something coming down the river at a high rate of speed which proved to be a large catfish. It was doing well in the current but it swam into shallow water behind a point of a sand bar. Because of its momentum it slid out onto the dry sand. Brother told his helper to catch the fish while he anchored the boat. He took no club but thought he could hold it. When he jumped onto it, he found that was what the fish needed—a little more weight—to start right back to the water. Frank came running

282

with a pole which he had used to propel the boat, knocked the fish in the head, and killed it. They had no scales to weigh it but it measured more than six feet in length.

When brother Charlie was hauling logs for the government, he usually carried a cap-and-ball six-shooter. This was before the extensive use of metal cartridges. He often got a chance to shoot turkeys and prairie chickens. These birds frequently alighted in trees to feed on acorns.

One morning as he was starting out to work from the bunkhouse, he noticed a flock of prairie chickens lighting in trees nearby. He drew his six-shooter and began to shoot at one that was nearest him but it was partially hidden by twigs and leaves. The boys called Charlie, "Dad," because he was so serious and particular with everything that was placed in his care. He fired two or three shots at the chicken and had not knocked it out of the tree.

General Caddison came along and said, "What's the matter, 'Dad,' can't you hit it?"

Charlie replied, "No, I'm just trimming away the leaves and limbs so I can kill the chicken."

This greatly amused Caddison. Charlie killed the bird with the next shot and Caddison said, "That certainly proved that your statement was true."

Brother Frank was appointed government farmer for the Pawnee Indians in 1889.[2] He taught them how to farm and harness their ponies by getting the proper-sized collars to keep from making their necks and shoulders sore.

The Indians who had government-built houses had to see to their care and up-keep. If they could be induced to use stoves, he showed them how to set up, where to locate, and how to build fires in them. He explained the use of the stove pipe, the damper or draft regulator, for many had never seen a stove. It was a complicated piece of machinery and difficult for them to operate.

Carpenters were building a house for an Indian and had it completed except for hanging one door when they were called to another job of more importance. They showed him how to hang the door and left. The Indian tried to get the door to fit but could not get it to fill the opening. Since he spoke good English, he came to my brother to fix the door. Frank asked him what was the matter. The Indian replied the door was too short at one end.

283

Frank asked which end was too short. He replied, "the top end."
Frank accompanied him and when they arrived and looked at the
position of the door, he told the Indian the door was too short at the
bottom end. The Indian said, "No, look at the big hole at the top." It
seemed the Indian had set the door on the ground instead of setting it
on the door sill. Frank set the door on the sill. The Indian took a hearty
laugh and said, "I thought it was too short at the top end when it was
too short at the bottom." Frank then hung the door.

The carpenters were building a house for another Indian. When
they got ready to shingle the building, the Indian told them to go to
their next job, for he and some other Indians could take care of it. So
the carpenters left. The Indians soon had the roof on and all their
lumber under the roof. That night a big rain fell, literally drowned
them out, and ruined all their food supply. The next morning the
Indians came to get Frank to see what was the matter. He soon saw
they had begun at the comb of the house and had shingled down to the
eaves. This caused all of the water which fell on the roof to run into the
house instead of running off at the eaves.

There was such a heavy demand for rock because the government
built stone buildings that Frank had to open a new stone quarry. He
took several Indians to assist him. Some were cutting away bushes and
removing small stones so teams and wagons could get there. There
were scorpions and a few rattlesnakes but more copperheads than any
other kind of snakes.

As Frank was removing some surface stone, something stung him on
one of his fingers. He jumped and attracted the attention of an Indian
close by. The Indian made close examination and found a copperhead
which he had killed with his pick. The Indian called to the others who
began to run about in all directions, looking about the grounds. Frank
put his foot on a scorpion and mashed it. He inquired of the inter-
preters to learn what the Indians were looking for.

The interpreter said, "They're looking for a certain type of weed to
cure snake bite."

Frank told him it was a scorpion which had stung him. The interpreter called to the other Indians and told them it was not a snake bite
but a scorpion sting. They came back, laughing, as if it was quite a joke.
Frank wished he had let them search for the weed to see how they
would apply it.

Adolphus Carian was a half-breed Sioux Indian who was a member

Francis Asbury Records (1850–1917) with Adolphus Carian, a half-blood Sioux who was a member of the Pawnee tribe. Through Frank's influence, Carian became an effective Christian missionary. Frank worked with the U.S. Indian Service at the Osage Reservation for thirteen years, then served as Pawnee subagent, ferryman on the Arkansas River, Indian farmer, and chief of police. In 1909 he settled his family in Ochiltree County, Texas. Courtesy of Western History Collections, University of Oklahoma Library.

of the Pawnee tribe. He was large, rather reckless, but very popular with the Pawnees. Brother Frank began to talk to him about his influence with the other Indians and how he was leading them the wrong way. Frank influenced Carian to attend church and Sunday school. Carian soon became interested in religious affairs, accepted the faith, and began leading his people to the straight and narrow way. He studied for the ministry and caused many Pawnees to accept Christ as their Savior. He remained in the work and kept his faith until his death.

There was a Pawnee Indian named Running Eagle. As was the custom of the Indians, he named himself or his tribe named him. After his escape from death he became a great believer in prayer. The Pawnee and Sioux Indians were at war with one another when he had this experience. One March, Running Eagle had just reached manhood. He had started afoot, unarmed, on an errand that seemed important to a young blanket Indian. He was far out on the open prairie in western Nebraska when he saw six Sioux Indians, also afoot. They saw him at the same moment. Since he was a good runner, he started at full speed. They pursued. Glancing back, he observed some were gaining and he knew he would be killed for it was a war party out for Pawnee scalps. He began to pray to the Great Spirit to save him from such a tortuous death. Just then a cloud came over him, and snow began to fall so heavy he could see but a few feet from him. He changed course and, as he related it, he thought he had attained the swiftness of an eagle until he came to the center rim of the snow flurry. Then he dropped into a buffalo wallow in the tall grass and remained there until nightfall. When he returned to camp, he related his story and was then called Running Eagle until his tragic death. He always gave the date of his miraculous escape as the beginning of his Christian life.

As a member of the Pawnee police force, it was an Indian's duty to see what the white man's business was. Running Eagle saw a heavily-armed white man, lying on the ground, letting his horse graze. The Pawnee had his six-shooter but it was not loaded. Being friendly, he walked up to the stranger, and extended his right hand to shake hands. The stranger grabbed Running Eagle's hand with his left hand; at the same instant drew a revolver and shot the startled Indian three times in rapid succession. Running Eagle drew his gun and fell dead.

Another Indian appeared, picked up Running Eagle's gun, aimed, and snapped it at the white man as he rapidly rode away. The stranger escaped and was never arrested.

A short time before Running Eagle's death, the Indian department issued an order that all government farmers should also be made chiefs of police for the tribes that they served. Brother Frank, as chief of police, took the trail which was made in the mud but darkness prevented him from following any farther. Frank could see a light ahead; he rode to it and found a cow camp. There were no extra men there excepting Bill Doolin. The other men said he had been there all day. Doolin said he had not seen anyone answering to the description of the killer. That was as far as the investigation got.

One day in 1889 Major Woods, the Pawnee agent, told brother Frank that he had heard of two white men at a Pawnee camp and told him to investigate. If true, the men must be escorted to the outskirts of the Pawnee reservation. If they returned, they would be placed in the guard house. When he found the men, he recognized Bert Dobbs who was considered a disgrace to a blanket Indian. His relatives were our neighbors in Chautauqua County. The other, Gordon Lillie, a young man who had ambition to be something, was getting first-hand material for a book which he was writing. Brother Frank took them to the border as instructed and we never heard of Dobbs again.

Gordon Lillie met such opposition in the Pawnee reservation because of the Ghost Dance. It was an invention of some rascals or renegade white persons who were shrewd enough to put in operation the theory that the mind was superior to matter. The Indians were instructed to face the east, stamp the ground, mark time, and chant, "White man go; buffalo come." This they did until exhausted, then fell to the ground. They were supposed to see a large white buffalo coming from the east, followed by vast herds of black buffaloes. In a physically spent condition they would see what seemed to be reality.[3]

When they revived, the Indians were in a mood to exterminate the white race. They considered the renegade whites to be their best friends. The Pawnees agreed to give the scallawags so many ponies if the vision should come true. The unscrupulous whites took the ponies, drove them away, sold them, and were never apprehended. This criminal racket was extended to other Indian tribes. The scouts were sent out because the Indians had become so uneasy.

Bill Dunlap told me when Lillie got his book completed and ready for the press, he did not have money to publish it. He asked Dunlap to furnish the money and he would let him have half the sales of the book. Dunlap asked him how much it would cost. Lillie replied $5,000. Dunlap did not like to put so much money in a venture without seeing it. Lillie permitted him to read it and he told me it was the most foolish stuff he had ever read. He advised Lillie to build a fire with it.

I asked Dunlap if he remembered any of it. Lillie wrote that he and another fellow had gone up the Cimarron River on a buffalo hunt in 1888 and were attacked by a band of plains Indians. Dunlap said, "Why that was long after you and I had throwed our six-shooters away." Lillie found someone to help him get it published, sold it to the publishers, reserved a small part of the royalties for himself, and was paid $30,000 for the manuscript in addition to the royalty. Then Dunlap remarked, "If my foresight had been as good as my hindsight, I could have cleaned up quite a bit of money." He concluded, "But I never thought people would read such stuff."[4]

I never saw Gordon Lillie's first book, I merely recall Dunlap's account of it. I have read accounts of his being a buffalo hunter and a plainsman but I doubt whether he ever saw a wild buffalo; I have seen some of his tame ones, also his imitation of a frontier town built of cottonwood logs and a council house, all the results of his boyhood dreams. This should be an inspiration to the youths of this country; that in spite of his humble start in life, he at one time was considered the greatest Wild West showman in the world—Pawnee Bill.

TWENTY-NINE

Cowhands and Trail Drivers

The cow country was cosmopolitan; it was no place for sectional differences. It was governed by its own ethics. Whether cattlemen came from the great cities or elsewhere, they were friendly, understood, and slept in the grass with us. Many cowpunchers had fought in the conflict between the States. In the Union army were Bill Dunlap, Sylvester Flitch, Bert Griffin, Nate Key, and Ike Berry. Fifteen-year-old Bill Malaley, a former Alabaman was a dispatch-carrier.

"Erv" Timberlake was a confederate soldier. He was short, heavy, could not ride well, so he chose to cook. When he quit the ♌ ranch while I was foreman, I took him to Kiowa. He went to cash his check, and I went into Rumsey's store. After we had talked awhile, Rumsey, seated at his desk facing the door said, "Just wait a minute. I want to have a little fun with 'Erv.'"

He reached behind the safe, picked up a low-crowned, wide-brimmed cotton hat with little notches all around the edge of the brim. He put the hat on and stepped behind a high counter. "Erv" walked right past the tall man without noticing him. He stepped behind "Erv" and bumped him with his elbow. "Erv" whirled around. "Here old Yank, I captured you once!" said Timberlake as he grabbed Rumsey's hat.

"Yes, and that was the same hat I had on when you captured me!" Rumsey replied.

"You bet it was!" "Erv" agreed.

They were pleased to see each other again and had a jolly conversation about their war experiences. They told me about their original meeting in Dixie. Rumsey had enlisted in the Chicago Mercantile Battery which went up the Red River with General Banks to capture Shreveport, Louisiana. He was captured by Timberlake's group at Sabine Cross Roads and imprisoned at Camp Ford, Tyler, Texas. There he traded his Yankee cap for a Confederate hat. At Lee's surrender Rumsey and other released prisoners started north. Timberlake and other Confederate soldiers headed south. The two groups met almost at the same spot where Rumsey was captured.

Bill Dunlap was a friend of long standing. Both of us worked for "Gus" Johnson on the 5̄. I saw him many times on roundups, at cowmen's gatherings, my farm, and in Hennessey. In 1880 he was camped in the Cheyenne Motte and had a boy cooking for him, tending camp, and wrangling the horses while Dunlap rode the line for Bill Quinlan.

One morning Dunlap found that coyotes had cut their stake ropes and all of their horses were loose. He told the boy to catch and saddle the gentle horse to drive in the other horses while he got breakfast. The horse was gentle but if the saddle girths were drawn rather taut, he would buck.

Just as Bill got his hands in the dough, mixing the bread, the boy came in and said he had gotten the horse but he couldn't ride him. Bill let his temper get the better of him. Without stopping to remove the dough from his hands or to take any precautions, he jumped on the horse which the boy had cinched up taut. The horse threw his head down between his knees, began to buck, and ran under the little elm trees. He threw Bill into the top of one and Bill whirled over with his back down, hanging onto a limb above him.

The boy looked up at him, "Now, get smart."

That tickled Bill so he got over his mad spell and began to laugh. He got down and told the boy to follow the horse out where he had stopped to graze and loosen the cinches before he attempted to get on. The boy did and rounded up the horses by the time Bill had gotten breakfast.

The last time I saw George Short was in 1918 when he was on the police force at Lawton, Oklahoma. My family and I went there to attend the first armistice celebration. My son, Earl, was in the Medical Corps at Post Field, Fort Sill. I had heard that brothers George and Young Short were living in Lawton.

We spent the night after the Armistice with Harvey Black, the man who staked the claim east of mine in the Cheyenne-Arapaho Run of 1892. Years later he bought land ten miles out of Lawton toward Elk City. He told me George was on the police force.

On Sunday we drove near the police station and stopped. As we were walking along a narrow board walk and talking, I saw a policeman coming from the station with a small rifle in his hands. The nearer the man walked toward me, the more he looked like George Short. Black stepped behind me purposely to see if I would know Short, who noticed we had slackened our pace and were looking him over mighty close. As he stepped in front of me, I was positive it was Short. I said, "The longer I look at you, the more you look like George Short to me."

He replied, "Yes, that's who you're lookin' at but who are you?"

I said, "As long as you and I were together and you don't know me. That's funny."

He commented, "If I ever seen you before, I don't know where it was. I know Black."

Black said, "That's why I stepped behind you, to see if you would know George when you met him." I told Short who I was.

He replied, "You had the advantage of me; you was lookin' for me and I didn't know you was on earth. Which way are you going? I'm in a hurry."

We three walked together back toward our car and talked. Short told us he had just got a call to go up town to shoot a mad dog. His brother had died about two years before. He wanted me to stay over a day. I told him we were down at Fort Sill because our son was in the army. We had one of the teachers from the Hitchcock schools with us and she must report for duty the following day so we would have to return.

He was astonished, "Has it been that long since we was together on the range?" He started ahead but suddenly turned around, "I want to tell you about a letter I got from Major Drumm." The old major had reached his ninetieth birthday; his many friends and business associates gathered at his residence in Kansas City to honor him. Others wrote congratulatory letters. George's letter was read at the celebration. Short said, "I told him he probably wouldn't remember me but he would remember my brother, Young." The major replied to George's letter that he remembered all of the boys he associated with on the range. He wrote such a fine and complimentary letter throughout that Short had framed it. He wanted me to see it but we left that day and I never saw it.

Tip McCracken was born near Ashville, North Carolina, 2 October 1855. Four years later his parents moved to Montague County, Texas, where the older school boys carried guns to protect themselves from Indians who stole livestock and murdered some settlers. As a child, Tip walked four miles to school and had little opportunity to secure an education. He began working with cattle when he was quite young. In

1881 he was a cattle pool foreman near the present site of Enid, and in 1882 he was "Barbecue" Campbell's foreman in the North Canadian range. The Cheyennes killed many of Campbell's cattle. Tip married Anna Smith of Barber County, and for three years he was such a failure at farming that he returned to the range as J. D. Payne's ranch boss until 1887.

Henry Lafayette Thomas was born 15 January 1859 near Montgomery, Alabama, and his parents moved to Texas in 1860. At age seventeen, Henry came up the trail as horse wrangler and made two trips in as many years. He rode the line for the $\bar{5}$ and ⚔ ranches and in 1883 became the Cragin Cattle Company manager. Subsequently he and Tip brought a small bunch of cattle to Barber County and raised cattle but no crops. He married Della Smith in August 1887. His formal education was limited but he loved to read history. He died 30 January 1911.

In the summer of 1877 Oliver Ewell had a herd on a range along the Cowskin Creek near Wichita. Not far from there lived the Morris family who had recently taken a claim. Ewell hired their son, Tom, and he proved so reliable that Ewell kept him until the opening of Oklahoma in 1889. I first met Tom in 1878 and saw him at numerous roundups.

Morris was so powerful he could ride alongside a cow at full speed, reach down, grab her by the tail, and when her hind feet left the ground, throw her on her side. If he wanted, he jumped to the ground and easily planted the cow's horns which is what we called embedding the horns in the turf. I had to give the tail one turn around the saddle horn to throw a cow.

Shortly after I took my claim in 1892, I asked Hennessey banker, John Smith, if he knew Tom Morris. He did and spoke highly of him. In 1894 I met Morris on the road near Hennessey. He was one of the old cowpunchers who took land along Turkey Creek. He lost nine head of horses from eating mouldy buffalo grass. He then bought twenty-five head of two-year-old heifers with calves but killed nearly all of them when he over-fed them ripe German millet. Then Tom turned to raising hogs. Two car loads of his wheat-fed hogs except ten died from cholera. "You see I lost both my wheat and hogs," he said. He later bought a fruit farm in Arkansas where he resided until his death.

There were few musical instruments in the cow camps; however, nearly every camp had someone who was a fiddler. Old John Chapin of the Red Fork ranch was an up-to-date violinist. Wilson played violin by ear. Nate Keys, Billie Malaley's Pole Cat ranch cook, a fifer, was a member of a fife and drum corps during the Civil War. Occasionally there were cowpunchers who played a harmonica.

All of the cowhands with whom I worked had at least one favorite song which they sang to the cattle. At this distant time I recall only a few lines. Tim Birmingham's was "Tim Finnigan." George Spofford's was "Mrs. McLaughlin's Party." Ben Franklin's was "Sadie Ray." Bill Dunlap had two—"The Days of Forty-Nine" and "Grandfather's Clock." Charlie Ritchie's was "The Home of My Boyhood." Frank Tracy's was "The Dying Cowboy." He told me that this fictional theme refers to the Tom Sawyer saloon in Wichita, Kansas.

Ike Pryor came up the old Texas Trail in 1870 and became a wealthy cattleman. From a homeless orphan in his early youth, Pryor rose to become the president of the American National Live Stock Association in 1917 and 1918.

King and Kenedy of the great King ranch in Texas sent horses through the Strip into southern Kansas in 1881. These bore the brand "K" on both jaw and shoulder and a Lewis Polk PLO brand on the hip.[1] One of the horse wranglers broke to ride a bright sorrel horse with a flax-colored mane and tail. A Kansan bought him and my brother, Frank, obtained him in a trade. A year later I purchased this horse, named Flax. I rode him in the Strip Run of 1893 and had him fourteen years when I sold him to Jim Jones, an ex-cowpuncher.

Anyone who saw "Shanghai" Pierce could truthfully say he had heard him, also. I saw him in Dodge City in the summer of 1878 and I also heard him. He was widely known in the cow country and received his nickname because he was a slender, tall, long-legged fellow with a thin, high-pitched voice that could be heard at a considerable distance.[2]

George McDonald told me about a roundup at which Pierce appeared. He attempted to direct the actions of a granger whom he had hired to convert into a cowpuncher. The fellow with a heavy, black mustache was riding leisurely through the herd. Pierce yelled, "Get some action on yourself, 'Mustache.' You ought to have a'hold of them plow handles right now." This caused a laugh among all of Pierce's cowpunchers who were in hearing distance; few could fail to hear that familiar voice. The effect on "Moustache" caused him to make an unusual effort to qualify as a cowpuncher. Then came "Shanghai's"

293

keen voice, "Cool down there a little, 'Moustache.' You have run over a cow, knocked down a yearling, and killed a calf!"

When Frank Bates went down into Texas in 1878 to buy the herd to start his ⚛ ranch, he ran across "Shanghai" Pierce.

He wanted Bates to buy 1000 of his heifers, "They are the finest bunch of two-year-old heifers in the state of Texas and I've got 'em well trained. I'm grazing 'em on an island out in the bay. I swim 'em across the lagoon every morning and swim 'em back to the mainland to corral 'em at night. They can outrun a deer and swim like a duck. You needn't to be afraid to invest money in 'em for you'll never drown any of 'em, taking 'em to Indian Territory." Because of his extravagant description, Bates was afraid to put a dollar into them. He was afraid a stampede might cause the loss of the entire herd. When Bates declined, Pierce said, "If I can't sell you the heifers, let me give you a little advice. If you go to buy a herd and the man appears to be in a good humor, you get mad and stir 'im up. If he begins to get mad, why you get in a good humor. That's the only way to work up a successful deal." Bates often laughed about this experience.

I saw Pierce in Caldwell a number of times and incidentally, heard him. During one of my stops, where I got my mail and bought supplies, I saw one of the Southwestern Stage Line coaches loading up with passengers and mail in the summer of 1882. S. S. Birchfield, a big Texas cowman,[3] was on this particular coach. Just as it was ready to start, "Shanghai" came out of the Leland Hotel with his home town newspaper in his hands. He and Birchfield were from the same Texas town. In his high-keyed voice he proceeded to read an account of the death of an old settler whom both knew. I could see people coming from all directions on the street toward the coach to see what the excitement was about.

The driver attempted to start but Pierce yelled, "Hold on a minute!" Then he continued to read from the obituary notice at the top of his voice. This was one occasion in which the stage coach did not pull out on time.

In 1881 cowhands were scarce. Pierce had a herd not far from Caldwell. He hired a sixteen-year-old boy who came up from Texas with a herd and went to Caldwell to take a train back to Texas. Pierce induced him to work for him until he could dispose of his herd. The boy consented to go down the next morning but when he awoke and saw a steady downpour of rain, the boy decided to return to Texas. He happened to meet Pierce on the street. Pierce recognized the boy and wanted to know why he did not go out to his camp as he had agreed to do. The boy replied it was raining.

Pierce asked, "What would you have done if you was out in camp when the rain came?"

The angered boy replied, "I would have went to camp and crawled up in the wagon under the sheet and stayed there until the rain was over."

Pierce did not want such cowhands around who would not stay out and take care of the stock. This was the same boy whom I hired to help take the Colcord herd to the ⚛ ranch.

THIRTY

Cherokee Strip Ranchers

I met many of the cattlemen of the Southwest. Some had little under-standing of the cattle industry. Others like Andrew Drumm, Ike Pryor, and Tony Day made fortunes. Many men carried large quantities of cash with them in the cattle country. Young Short told me that on a spring roundup in northern Texas in the late seventies, he had seen S. S. Birchfield carrying a maral filled with twenty-dollar gold pieces. When night came, he set it outside of the wagon so it would not be kicked over. He handled it just like his saddle.

Once in the spring of 1880 when Kingsbury and Dunson came up the Texas Trail, Kingsbury had $600 stuck in his hip pocket. There were days at a time when he did not recall having the money. But when he paid off his hands, he pulled out the huge roll and paid them off in cash.

I met Oliver Ewell and "Crate" Justis at "Fine" Ewing's ranch. Both men came from Parksley, Virginia. In 1872 Ewell; his brother, a doc-tor; and "Crate" came west to Texas where they bought some cattle. In 1874 Ewell and Justis drove a Texas cattle herd through eastern Indian Territory to Chanute, Kansas. This partnership continued until 1909. They established their ranch above the ƚ ranch on the Eagle Chief in 1878 and occupied it for fifteen years.

Mr. Ewell disliked government scouts. I attributed this to the fact that many of them drank and caroused, while Ewell was a total ab-stainer. "Texas Dave" Thomas was like Ewell. "Crate" Justis was tem-perate in every way but occasionally drank a glass of beer. I saw them at Caldwell in the eighties and met Justis in Kansas City after I became an independent shipper in Chautauqua County. I saw Mr. Ewell at Kiowa in 1928 and Mr. Justis at his home in 1937.

Frank and Roy Streeter were born in Youngstown, Ohio. Their father brought the family to a ranch home south of Kiowa in 1879, later called Streeter's Springs. The family lived with the family of Jack Crewdson, Major Drumm's first foreman, for ten days after their arrival.[1] I met Frank at numerous roundups and when I left the range, I saw him last at Kiowa.

F. Y. "Fine" Ewing had his ranch on Driftwood Creek slightly southwest of Kiowa. He came from Missouri and was a reckless sort of fellow with an awful temper. I recall a story he told about the first man he ever shot in Missouri. He got as much of a kick out of telling it as I did listening.

Ewing and a neighbor had a falling out and they threatened to kill each other when they met. "Fine" armed himself with a small seven-shooter, about five inches long, which shot small round pellets, no larger than an oversized pea. Thus he was in shape to kill and be killed.

One day Ewing took some grain to have ground at the neighborhood gristmill. Just as he stepped inside the door to look for the miller, he saw his sworn enemy. He drew his gun and shot the fellow from the rear. He plunged headlong into a barrel and "Fine" thought he was dead. Since no one had seen him drive up, he stepped into his wagon and drove on. When the neighbor got out, Ewing was not in sight. He never knew what it was that stung him.

W. C. "Bill" Quinlan's range was north of the Cimarron southwest of the present site of Enid. His headquarters on Indian Creek had plenty of water. When Old Oklahoma was settled, Quinlan built a nice cottage for his family and remained in the Strip until it was opened to settlement. He had two sons and a daughter.

Tom Waters and Cal Smith worked around his camp most of the time. They hauled all the lumber, household supplies, furniture, feed grain, and other things from the Rock Island section station which became Enid after the Cherokee Strip opening. Waters told me Enid received its name from Mrs. Quinlan's sister, a deaf mute, who lived with them.[2]

On one furniture trip they took extra saddle horses, for the Quinlan boys wanted to learn to ride. They took turns riding the horses with the boys so they would not be injured. Waters also taught them to swim.

One day as Quinlan was coming to his ranch in a buggy, he saw a man riding aimlessly about without a shirt and asked what was wrong. "I have only one shirt and I have worn it until I found gray backs in it. I took it off and laid it on an ant hill to let the ants pick them off, but I had to ride off in a hurry to turn back the cattle. When I returned, I couldn't find the shirt!" said the cowboy.

Quinlan drove on to his ranch house and procured another shirt for

297

him as the sun was shining mighty hot. He was afraid it would burn the fellow so he would not be able to work. The cowpuncher found red ants were not created in vain.

Rattlesnakes bit both horses and cattle. Since Quinlan had lost animals, he offered to pay twenty-five cents for each set of rattles that the boys would bring him. One cowhand, Bill Thompson, believed that rattlesnakes grew a complete set of rattles each year after they had lost the originals. He had a forked stick, three or four feet long, hanging to his saddle horn. When asked why he was carrying the stick, he told that when he saw a rattlesnake coiled, he set the prongs of the stick straddle of the snake's neck, pulled off the rattlers, and turned the snake loose. This made matters worse for the stock for they heard no warning sound before the snake struck. Quinlan soon heard about it; Thompson had a new name, "Rattlesnake Bill," but no job.

In the boom days of the 1880s Kansas cities and towns experienced the speculative effects more than the surrounding country. Wichita, Medicine Lodge, Winfield, and other western towns suffered more from the effects of inflationary prices than did towns and cities farther east. Groups of speculators organized associations of town builders and put advertisements in the paper of certain property to be sold. One of the members would buy the land by outbidding an outsider who was actually wanting to buy it for a home or a business building. Then he would divide the property and associate it with other property to advance the price rapidly. Occasionally he would sell to an honest buyer. Since the ring of speculators controlled the bulk of the property in a given town, they could make the business appear legitimate.[3]

They began to attract cattlemen with large cattle herds. Nick Sherlock had 1000 head of cattle which he sold and invested in Medicine Lodge property where he built a large stone and brick building. He expected greater returns from this business building than from his livestock. By the time he got ready, "there was no business." He began to brood over his losses, drank heavily, lost his mind, and died in an insane asylum. Thus was ended the life of a fine man of whom everybody thought well.[4]

"Barbecue" Campbell was another victim of the promoters. He was doing well in cattle business and was old enough to have better judgment than to bite at such propositions. But things looked so rosy and Wichita appeared to be a fine place to end his days so he built a $75,000 mansion there. When the boom collapsed, he was left with the property on which he couldn't pay the taxes because his income was so small.

Campbell turned over his business affairs to his ranch foreman, Charley Collins, in whom he had great confidence. When the U.S. soldiers ordered the cattlemen to vacate the Cherokee Strip, Campbell gave Collins power of attorney to buy a suitable range in the bluestem country of Kansas. Collins went west of Atchison, bought a range suitable for Campbell's herd, returned, and took him up to see it. He was well pleased and thought it was just what he wanted. When Collins quoted the price of $3000 to use the range, Campbell was surprised and wanted to know how that came about. Collins showed Campbell the contract and other papers which revealed the range had been sold to Collins. The old cattleman had to come to his terms.

This Collins deal and the collapse of real estate and cattle business left Campbell in mighty bad condition. He had two sons who eased him down so that his fall wasn't as bad as Nick Sherlock's. The collapse left empty business houses and dwellings in the Southwest for several years.

The Cherokee Strip Live Stock Association ranchers included Benjamin S. Miller, president; Milton H. Bennett, treasurer; Charles H. Eldred; James W. Hamilton; and S. T. Tuttle.[5] Eldred was an eastern man who came out for his health and belonged to a syndicate which held a large interest in the range. I was at his camp a time or two. He put in nearly all of his time reading magazines. He was friendly and did not try to high-hat a common cowpuncher. Tuttle had a ranch along Turkey Creek and remained until the opening of the Strip to settlement.

Hamilton, a former treasurer of Kansas, had a herd of big longhorn steers which were near starvation during the hard winter of 1885. His ranch was east of Billy Malaley's Pole Cat ranch where I had my cattle. I saw some of his cattle drifting over the snow, looking for something to eat. I could hear their teeth grinding and gritting.

Hamilton went to Caldwell and hired "Boff" Baughman as his foreman. "Boff" was not anxious to assume any duties, and he was afraid he might miss a meal at the Leland Hotel. They went out to look over the ranch. Cowpunchers were no longer carrying six-shooters; but Hamilton had sent down a bunch of fellows who had six-shooters, wide-rimmed hats with high crowns, heavy new cowhide leggings, and spurs with bells. Tim Birmingham called them "The Six-Shooter Mob."

299

Baughman seemed satisfied with the cattle, looked over the saddle horses, gave his opinion, then called for Hamilton's men who came out in all their regalia. "Boff" said, "Jim, in case of a stampede, what shall I do with your barnyard savages?"

I met Miller at his camp north of the Salt Fork River. Charley Curry and I stayed at his ranch headquarters in March 1880 when he was there. Curry was a great talker and originated in the same state as did Miller. They soon raked up old acquaintances through important men they had known and had a great visit. Miller, a graduate of one of the old eastern colleges, expressed regret that he had not gone to Europe to finish his education to give him a better understanding of affairs in the United States. He was elected mayor of Caldwell, later took sick and died there.

The officers of the Cherokee Strip Live Stock Association after 1883 sent huge sums of currency by Bennett to the Cherokee Nation's tribal treasurer. He told me of one of his trips from Texas in the early days with a herd of Texas cattle. He had quite a land holding south of the Salt Fork adjoining the Timberlake ranch on the east. His brother, "Cub," was with him during the 1880's. When the Cheyenne-Arapaho country was opened, "Cub" was in charge of one of the Hockaday hardware stores and died while in their employment.

I first met "Tony" Day from Fort Worth in Dodge City in 1878, then later in Caldwell. He took charge of a range in the western Strip in the summer of 1880 with 4000 head of cattle on 200,000 acres.[6]

When Cal Watkins moved his herd from the Osage country in 1879, he settled along the upper reaches of the North Canadian in the Cherokee Strip, just south of the Kansas line near the present site of Supply, Oklahoma. He occupied part of the Day Brothers' holdings. During the 1880 roundup both claimed cattle in the first roundup. Cal got to his feet and made a wonderful, eloquent speech for his right of domain. He had his hat in hand, using it to punctuate points. All listeners were highly entertained.

When Cal got his side demonstrated to a fine point, "Tony" said, "Well gentlemen, I'm no public speaker. I never made a speech in my life, but all you men who think I'm in the right, just follow me." He gave his horse a cut with his quirt and rode away in a gallop. All the men except Watkins went with him.

I last saw Day in 1886 in Yorke, Parker, and Draper's store in Caldwell. He was on his way back home. He had sold all of his cattle holdings. He was talking to B. W. Key, whose relatives lived in Texas. Day asked him when he was going to take his vacation, pulled out his notebook, and wrote out his house number in Fort Worth. He told him when he arrived in Fort Worth his carriage would meet Key at the railway station and take him sightseeing. After Day had gone, I said, "That'll be quite a treat for you."

Key replied, "Do you suppose I'd have the nerve to do that? He's worth a quarter of a million dollars."

I told him that "Tony" was just as common as the rest of us and would be certainly glad to see him. Key declared he would not have the nerve to do it solely because he had more money than the rest of us.

Since E. M. "Ed" Hewins was a pioneer of Chautauqua County, I knew him well. I met him in Caldwell, Hewins, and other points. He was the father of Hewins, Kansas. A great shipper of livestock, he dealt in both longhorn and domesticated cattle. He was the first shipper who threw fine pieces of coal into shipping cars for hogs. They ate the hunks of coal which tended to clog their intestinal tracts and they did not shrink much in going to market.

Major Drumm was a native of Ohio. When gold fever got hold of him in 1849, he went by way of the Isthmus of Panama by steamer up the Pacific coast to San Francisco, then to Eldorado County, California, where he mined for twenty years and gradually went into the cattle business in a small way. This gave him the idea he was cut out to be a cattle breeder and dealer.

He then went to Texas and drove large herds across Indian Territory in 1870, slowly grazing them on the rich growth of grass. By the time he reached Newport, now Kansas City, his cattle were fat enough to ship to market. When he was gathering his herds in Texas, the Wilson brothers—Abner, Tom, and Bill, hired out to Major Drumm and came up the trail with him. They stayed with him until the United States Government opened the Cherokee Strip for settlement. Jack Crewdson was his trail foreman. In passing through the Strip, Drumm became impressed with the idea of establishing a ranch there.

He was the first cattleman who turned his cattle loose on the Cherokee Strip in 1874 between the Medicine and Salt Fork Rivers. His ground was located on both sides of Salt Fork near the mouth of Medicine River with a range of 150,000 acres in 1879 near present Cherokee. I often stopped at his U ranch headquarters. This was

Maj. Andrew Drumm (1828–1919) from Ohio was the first man to run cattle in the Cherokee Outlet. He was elected chairman of several cattle pools as well as the Cherokee Strip Live Stock Association. Editor Thomas McNeal called him the "Nestor" of the range. Courtesy of Western History Collections, University of Oklahoma Library.

where the first old Texas Trail entered Kansas slightly west of Kiowa. He also located and built the first store in Kiowa. Crewdson was the first postmaster and storekeeper.

After the spring of 1879 the Texas Trail no longer crossed Drumm's "U ranch" but followed the Eagle Chief. It skirted the blackjacks on the north and followed the Eagle Chief northwest to the western trail. This was the trail which Jesse Evans and his outfit brought 20,000 cattle from New Mexico to Dodge City in 1878.

Young and George Short were holding cattle between the ⇞ and Major Drumm's ranches in the winter of 1881. They were trying to keep the herds apart, but the latter became too heavy and broke into the ⇞ range; I was sent to help.

While I was at Short's camp, a fellow rode in and told me that a letter addressed to me was at Major Drumm's headquarters. He was following the trail south and would not pass through the ranch. If he had known I was there, he would have brought it as it appeared to be rather urgent by the manner in which it was addressed. From my brother, Charles, it was addressed to Kiowa, Drumm's ranch, or any other way to get to L. S. Records.

That year Charlie King of Kiowa established a mail route from there to various cow camps in the Strip. I do not know how many subscribers he had, but he charged each man twenty-five cents a month. He drove Buck, a large buckskin-colored horse, hitched to a two-wheel cart. During the following winter, King got stuck in a snow drift and almost froze to death. Being a cripple, he decided that he was not suited to be a mail carrier.[7]

Bill McMillan, Major Drumm's foreman, sent over a number of men who drove back a large number of Drumm's cattle. This made work so light along the line between the two ranges that the Short brothers could handle the cattle easily, themselves. Instead of returning to the ⇞ ranch, I mounted and rode out with George as he rode his line. We saw about a dozen antelope, standing and looking at us.

George said, "Let's get our ropes ready, mebbe we can catch one of 'em." I told him they knew better than to let us get near and gave the suggestion no more thought. We rode but a short distance when Short said, "Here they come!"

It was too late to get our ropes ready when we noticed the antelope were determined to cross directly in front of us. We spurred our horses into a run and split the band into two sections. Some were

303

obliged to wheel about to keep from hitting our horses. I reflected how foolish it was that we hadn't prepared our ropes, for it would have been so easy to have caught one of them. Short rode to his line and I went on to Drumm's ranch and stayed all night. The ranch house was made from logs and was 1½ stories high.

Tom Wilson, a good violinist, was there and we stayed up until about 10 P.M. One of the cowhands stepped outdoors and came back a moment later and said, "There's an awful black cloud in the north and great big drops of rain are falling."

The Major jumped to his feet and said, "I zounds, I'll have to go and see about that." That was his favorite expression when something unusual happened.

The boys all began to laugh and asked him if he was going out to stop the storm. He was in such a hurry that he went without his hat.

A little later he came back into the house and said, "You fellers better put up that old fiddle, go to bed, and get a little sleep." He turned to McMillan and said, "Bill, get the cook up at 3 A.M. so he will get a good hot breakfast for the boys. Have them out, fed, their horses saddled, so they can get started by 4 A.M. Deploy your men up Salt Fork to catch the drift of the cattle and keep them from crossing Salt Fork."

All the boys got up and I asked some of them where they were going. They didn't know but would soon be on the way. After they had eaten and gone, I got up, went down to breakfast, then saddled and fed my horse. It was dark yet and snowing heavily.

Major Drumm came to breakfast, sat down, and said, "Young man, what do you suppose your cattle are doing down there on our range?"

I replied, "Everyone of them is curled up in a nice, warm grassy bed and they wouldn't get up on a bet."

He asked, "Do you think so?"

"I don't think so, I know so," I replied.

He said, "I'll bet you they're stringing out through those breaks, headed for the blackjacks."

When I left Drumm's ranch that morning, I came to the Salt Fork and found the current was still open but ice had frozen from the banks to the swiftly running water. A horse could break the ice easily and I rode across without any trouble. It was snowing so heavily that one could not see more than twenty-five yards ahead.

As I rode through the tall grass, a cow arose out of a buffalo wallow

304

which contained a stand of tall, heavy grass. I changed my course and rode around her; she immediately lay down again. I wished I had Major Drumm here to see how cattle would do under such circumstances. It might have been a favorable thing for his cowhands.

The major was a bachelor at that time and consequently he remained almost constantly at the ranch. Often I saw him engaged in doing something. While at his log house headquarters he read magazines, newspapers, and kept up with all the livestock reports. I also saw him writing out projects pertaining to his numerous business transactions. I met him on his fine saddle horse, seated in a fashionably quilted saddle, as far as ten miles from headquarters.

On the general roundup of 1881 when I was busy working a herd, cutting out the strays on Major Drumm's ranch south of the Salt Fork River, I heard Wheeler Timberlake calling for me. I noticed a two-or three-seated canopy-top surrey drawn by a span of fine horses with a driver and two women in the carriage. They stopped at a distance from the herd, and Timberlake motioned for me to come over. As I rode up, he said, "Well, this is him."

One of the women answered, "My name is Brown. I'm a cousin of yours. I asked Mr. Timberlake to call you over here as I wanted to see you."

I told her I did not know much about my relatives, as my father had pulled away from them when I was quite young. I told her it was my busy day; I could not neglect the cattle and I would have to be moving. I did not see her again. Major Drumm did not marry until he was sixty-four years old, and since he married a woman named Brown, I suspected this woman might have been the one.[8]

One day the Major came to the door of the room at headquarters where a bunch of us were seated. He had a Fort Worth paper, "Listen to this!" He read an account of John Terry's death. Terry was a cowman in the Strip who took sick, entered a Fort Worth sanitarium as a pauper, and died with $8000 hidden in his overall-pocket. The hospital staff found it. "I zounds!" said the Major, "A man that would represent himself as a pauper ought to die as one! If Terry had gone to a hospital and secured an additional nurse, he could have come out a well man. It probably would have cost him $100. Such foolishness as that cost him his fortune and his life besides."

There was one time when the Major forgot to say "I zounds!" That was the stampede of the Major's beef herd one summer in the eighties.

305

After beeves began to show good flesh, Major Drumm told the boys to cut out a shipment to take to the railroad to be shipped to eastern markets. The boys began by rounding up a part of the herd by cutting out the best in that bunch. About noon they took the cut near the camp ranch house. As the cattle seemed to be quiet, the men left a Kansas boy, John Greene, to watch the longhorns while they ate dinner. This was his first job and he was riding a company horse on his little pumpkin seed saddle. He had a long rope coiled and hanging on the horn of his human saddle. The longhorn steers grazed quietly and the thought of becoming a cowboy interested him.

Since no one was in sight to make fun of his awkward roping, he decided to rope, throw, and hogtie one of the old steers. This was one of the most ridiculous things which ever entered a fool boy's head. He tied one end of the long rope to the horn of the saddle, made a slip noose in the other end, then rode quietly beside a large beef steer and threw the rope at the steer's head. The rope went true to his aim and when the steer felt the rope hit, he started to run, then felt the rope tighten, let out a loud bellow which frightened the whole herd. Since the horse had his side toward the steer and was taken so by surprise, it threw the horse on its side. The power of the steer tore the saddle from the horse; the beeves stampeded at the first bellow and started off at a good rate of speed. When the steers saw the steer with the saddle coming after them, they were frightened worse than ever. The saddle sailed high in the air at one moment, hit the ground with a clattering sound, then soared into the air again. The herd scattered to the far corners of the range. The men heard the thunder of the stampeded beeves, mounted their horses, rode as fast as possible to the place where they had left the beeves so quietly. All they found was a badly scared boy and a crippled horse. Thus was brought to a sudden end the hopes of a would-be cowpuncher. The major's remarks were more forceful than his otherwise elegant "I zounds!"

After the Cherokee Strip run, Major Drumm went to Kansas City and affiliated with the livestock exchange and joined A. J. Snider and Flatol. He was active until two years before he "came to the end of the trail" at age ninety-one.

Tom Wilson traveled 1250 miles to attend Drumm's funeral. His estate was evaluated at $2,000,000 at his death. He showed interest in the welfare of generations to come by endowing a home and school which consisted of 370 acres, two miles southeast of Independence,

Missouri, for the education and training of young men. In 1932 many of the cowmen of the old Cherokee Strip dedicated a monument to Major Drumm on the site of the ranch house which he built on his famous U ranch, sixty-two years before.[9]

Experience taught me that a cowpuncher could stay all night quicker at Major Drumm's camp than at any other in the Southwest but I never worked for him. His men went to bed at 10 P.M. and got up at 4 A.M. to get ready to ride the lines. Abe Manee told me he carried an extra blanket while he rode his lines in the summertime. He spread it on the ground and dozed until the sun shone. As days were so long and the nights so short, it made almost a steady grind to get up so early and go to bed so late. Major Drumm told me if he fed his men too well, they became independent and were less apt to perform their work in an acceptable manner. Because of these ideas and because he lived at the headquarters ranch house instead of using a foreman, I did not care to become his employee.

THIRTY-ONE

A Shot Heard
around the Prairie

On 1 April 1892 back in Peru, brother Charlie suggested we take part
in the opening of the Cheyenne-Arapaho country on 19 April 1892. I
agreed, although I did not think much of an opening that was conducted in the outlandish manner of a horse race. We took a team and
an ordinary wagon with bows and a sheet. From father's home we
passed through Arkansas City southward to Indian Territory and traveled southwest to the old cattle trail at the present site of Waukomis,
Oklahoma.

When we were camped one night in the Cherokee Strip, a big, loud-
mouthed fellow came to our wagon and began to tell us how things
were done in the southwestern country; innocent men had been killed
and the killers set free. "John Potts was murdered in cold blood, lies
buried here in the lone prairie, and his murderer was not brought to
justice!"

"Are you related to Potts?" I asked.

"No," he replied. "I didn't know either of them."

"Well, I happen to know both parties," I remarked. "I wasn't there
the morning Potts was killed, but the next night I talked with Ben
Franklin! He informed me that he killed Potts in self-defense. Franklin had a great many friends. He was always straight and honorable in
all of his dealings. Potts was using an assumed name because he had
murdered a person in Texas and a reward had been posted for his
arrest!"

This seemed to cool off the gentleman mighty quick and he was able
to go back to his camp in peace. I made up my mind he was a "would-
be" who took me for a tenderfoot who could be impressed with his hot
air.

We followed the old cattle trail to Dover but found such a vast
crowd that we drove back up the Cimarron through Old Oklahoma
until we came to Mr. Cottam's farm. He was called "the last man in the
Horn." As Oklahoma was then constituted, the settlement of 1889

followed the Cimarron River from a point three miles west of King-fisher City thus making a natural boundary between the settled Old Oklahoma and the unsettled Cheyenne and Arapaho country. The northwesterly direction of the Cimarron caused the northwestern corner of Old Oklahoma to terminate in a point; hence, this long narrow strip was called "the Horn."

We camped east of the river which is very wide at that point along with Charley Norton and learned Cottam also had come from Indiana. He had good water and we bought hay and corn from him. The settlers had raised a remarkable corn crop in 1891 and shelled corn could be bought for thirty cents a bushel. We met a number of people before the day of the run, including Hanks, a middle-aged blacksmith, who lived in the sand hills nearby, and his son-in-law, King. Both had worked for a cowman whose camp lay along Spring Creek, a tributary of Salt Creek which empties into the Cimarron River southeast of the present site of Okeene. Both men had used their land rights, but they intended to participate in this opening for speculative purposes. They planned to run from the trail, crossing three-fourth's of a mile north of the Hennessey highway crossing and get the same distance advantage in the race. It was formerly a buffalo crossing, later used by cattle, and now settlers began using it.

Some men in our little group had time pieces and when it was approaching high noon, we saw the U.S. cavalryman ride out in front of the large crowd below us. We began to edge closer to the river. It was a misty, damp, and disagreeable April day, and the wind was out of the north. Three days before the land opening someone had set fire to the grass between Salt Creek and the Cimarron. The wind blew a fairly good gale from the south and the prairie fire roared like thunder. We felt the earth tremble from its force. The fire proved to be a good thing as we could easily find all of the cornerstones which bore the numbers corresponding to the range, township, section, and quarter-section.

Brother Charlie and I sat on our horses, straining to see the officer as he stuck his carbine above his head. In our group were Hanks astride his black mare; W. W. Haworth, a Civil War veteran from Indiana, with his sons, Louis and James, and son-in-law, Thomas Oliver;[1] King; a man named Carnes with his son; and thirty Negroes afoot. Most of the others were mounted. When we saw smoke fly from the gun, our horses were already on the run. Old man Hanks and I

309

were in the lead. I knew this river like a book from my line-riding days for the ⅀ ranch but Hanks did not. We were riding through shallow water neck and neck when I hollered, "Hold up, Mr. Hanks, there's a deep hole!" I checked my horse, but he slid down into the deep water which closed over him and his horse. Then up they came. Hanks thought I was trying to kid him, he later told me. I saw they were getting out all right as I passed. He led his mare out on a sand bar; he was so cold and stiff, he was afraid he could not mount for he had no saddle. He took hold of the mare's mane by one hand, put all the power he had left in him, and lit straddle of her at the first effort. He soon overtook me in some breaks west of the river.

When we got on top of the high ground a mile west of the crossing, we could see the whole country to the south. None of the swarming humanity we had seen was in sight. I let the horse go at a good gait until I was satisfied I was on the first full quarter from the river. "I think you are now on a full quarter. It will be safe to set your stake," Hanks said, "And here I am leaving you!"

He turned southwest to a ford on the little stream that crossed the southwest corner of my claim. I did not slacken speed but jumped to the ground, rolled on my back as I held to the long hitch-rein. The horse circled around me three times before I could get him stopped. He pulled me to my feet again. I stuck my four-foot cedar stake into the soft earth. It bore a penciled inscription, "This claim is taken by L. S. Records."

Brother Charlie ran on to the next quarter-section south of mine but when he arrived, there were already three claimants so he turned and rode back.

The first fellows I saw crossing my place on horseback were Bill Scarth, Jacob Chilcote, and Bill Sturgeon. Scarth was riding a sorrel, bald-faced horse at top speed and he staked the claim that cornered mine on the southwest. Sturgeon had a quarter-section in Old Oklahoma a few miles east of the Cimarron. He located Chilcote's claim prior to the opening, accompanied him, and told him where to set his stake just west of my claim. A few moments later I saw another fellow dismount near the east line of my claim; I had staked near the north line. I was glad to see him, for I believed then there wouldn't be more than one person to contest. I looked towards the southwest corner of my claim and saw two Sooners come out of the small creek on foot. They had stayed there all night. We had made the run so quickly, they

310

were not aware anyone was near until the country was "taken by storm." Because of inclement weather, they had taken refuge behind the creek banks. Those who saw the two men yelled, "Sooners!" This got a rise out of them; they took their packs and started back across the river, seeing they had made a mess of their claim taking since the country was already "settled up."

A few minutes later the thirty Negroes crossed my claim on foot towards the southwest and the Watonga Community. Each one carried a canteen and a pack on his back. Some carried axes or hoes, others had spades or shovels. They believed that area would be a good cotton country because it had blackjacks and sandy land. One of them walked near me and said, "Dat's right boss, stay with it. You wuz heah fust."

I rode over, met my young contestant, and asked if he did not see me before he stopped. He replied that he saw me riding in after he had staked the land. I did not challenge his word but told him he was too young to prove up the claim. The young fellow, Kern, asserted he would not take less that $250 for it.

"I'll tell you what I'll do. You've done me quite a favor by stopping there in plain sight, for someone or two might have staked the place and caused me some trouble. So I'll just give you $5 for your day's work!" I said.

"Well, all right, I'll take it," he replied.

I thought, then, that my brother's chance was all over, that everything was settled. But that was far from the truth. We started toward the river to recross to Mr. Cottam's farm where we had left our wagon and bedding. We noticed no one had staked the quarter-section which adjoined mine on the north. Charlie stopped and staked the land, believing there were no other contestants. He remained afoot as I took the two horses. Mr. Cottam permitted me to load his plow in our wagon, and he gave me two dozen small peach trees which I set out on the first plowed ground. One of the trees is still alive. In my absence Charlie met Chilcote, the man who staked the claim west of mine, also from Chautauqua County.

Chilcote slept on his claim that night, rolled his bed the next morning, and laid it on a knoll where everyone could see it. He walked over and told me he was going across the Cimarron to get a plow to break the sod. If I saw anyone hunting claims, he asked me to tell them what he was doing.

When he left, I started plowing a small plot to set out the peach

311

trees. Soon a man and his son drove by with two wagons and teams, headed for Kingfisher. "That is the way to do it. No man can shake you loose from that claim," he said. "Has anyone taken that claim?" He pointed to Chilcote's claim.

"Yes," I replied. I showed him the bed roll and told him the man's name was Chilcote and he had gone for a plow.

The two drove away and nearly caused Chilcote to lose his claim when they got to Kingfisher.

The next day Charlie, Chilcote, and I rode to Kingfisher to file our declarations of settlement with J. C. Robberts, receiver at the land office.[2] We got there early and had to wait until a quota of six was ready to enter. I had position No. 1. I handed Robberts my number; he looked in the books, came back, and told me that he would have to refuse my application. I asked, "Why?" He told me that Charles Sturgeon had made an application to amend his previous filing on a sand hill claim in Old Oklahoma to the claim which I had staked: SW quarter of section 17, township 19 north, range 9 west of Indian Meridian.

"You're going to hand them papers right back to me on that account without any acknowledgment from me that I ever offered to place my filing on the land?" I asked.

Then Robberts wrote out a statement that I had presented my application to file, stated the reason for refusing me the right, and entered the date I had appeared.

"You seem to have a perfect right to turn this application down," I said. "Haven't you equal authority to give your opinion about this?" I asked.

"I have no instructions about that," Robberts replied. "I'll give you my opinion. If you want that for your home and will settle there, you'll get the place." He added, "You'll have to see a lawyer and have him draw up your remonstrances, so it will cover all of the points at issue."

"I'm a stranger in this town and don't know any lawyer. Whom would you suggest?" I asked.

"Cummings and Whirlow,"[3] he replied.

I saw Judge Cummings alone in his office; he asked me what Robberts had said. I told him the whole story.

"Robberts is right!" he exclaimed. "If you want it for a homestead, all you'll have to do is live there. I haven't any blanks. If you'll go back to the land office and get the blanks, I'll fix them up for you." Cummings added.

I asked him to tell me the name of the man who would furnish me the blanks and what they would cost. He directed me to look for Jim McConnell, a red-headed man. There were only two fellows in the land office. I went up to the red-head. "I'm looking for Jim McConnell."

"That's my name," the younger man replied.

I told McConnell that Judge Cummings had advised me to see him and ask for a blank which could be used as a protest against an application to amend a filing for one quarter to another.

"Tell Judge Cummings I don't give anything out of this office," McConnell remarked. "But there are papers lying on that table over there. Look through them and see if you can find anything that will fit the case," he suggested.

I looked through the pile, picked out three, and carried them over to McConnell, "Will these papers fit the case?"

"You tell Cummings I never gave them to you, you just took them!" he remarked after looking at the forms.

"Oh, I see!" I said.

"That's the way you do it, eh?" laughed another fellow in the room who was listening to our conversation.

"Yes," McConnell answered.

When I returned to Cummings's office, Whirlow was there.

"Whirlow, that's Mr. Records there," Cummings said.

"Are you any kin to Moses T. Records who graduated at Baker University at Baldwin, Kansas?"

"Yes, I am his younger brother. He was in the same classes with you, John Holzapfel, and William A. Quayle at Baker,"[4] I answered. I named one other member.

Whirlow expressed pleasure at meeting me. This was the beginning of a friendship that lasted many years. I told Cummings what McConnell had said. He laughed, "Jim's a good boy."

Cummings and Whirlow filled out my protest form and sent it to the United States land office at Washington, D.C. They told me I could leave Oklahoma or do anything I wanted to do, for no one could file on the claim or contest it until an order came from Washington, removing my protest. Cummings set a day for me to appear with two witnesses to prove I staked my claim on 19 April. I took Kern, the boy who staked

313

my claim, and brother Charlie to Kingfisher before Cummings and Whirlow and they signed my affidavit.

When Jacob Chilcote's number was called, he stepped up to file. He found that Mrs. Benedict, mother of Omer Benedict,[5] a future Republican candidate for governor of Oklahoma in 1926, had filed a homestead entry on his claim. Chilcote filed notice of a contest on grounds he had made a prior settlement. He returned to his claim, plowed three acres of sod, dug a foundation for a house, dug a shallow well, and told me he would return to Kansas.

When Charlie stepped up to file, he found there were two other claimants and he filed notice of a contest. He was unsuccessful and consequently got no land. We soon learned that Hanks and his son-in-law had staked a claim which they had picked out before the run, about a mile west of my claim. They had built a dugout which King moved into and broken eight acres of sod. Charlie and I talked with them and they agreed to take $75 for their claim. Brother Frank wanted a claim. We told King and Hanks not to sell to anyone else until we could hear from Frank, then we drew a map to show Frank.

It was difficult to get money to pay for necessities to improve our claims. I wrote to my wife at Peru to send me a bank draft, then drove to Hennessey to buy a sod plow and barbed wire. The hardware man, L. A. King, had only two plows left which he would sell at reduced prices if I took them both. I agreed. I knew Chilcote would need one. I presented the bank draft to King who could not accept it unless I was identified. Just then J. D. P. Maroquind, the man who named Homestead, Oklahoma, in the Cheyenne-Arapaho country, came into the store. I had known him in Kansas. He and King were members of the Masonic lodge and had sat together in lodge the previous night. He told King that I was all right; he had known me a long time.

"But I don't know you," King said to Maroquind.

"Mr. King, this becomes a personal matter to me," Maroquind said as he stepped behind me toward the hardware man.

King seemed to be satisfied and let me have the hardware. When I returned to my claim, Chilcote purchased one of the plows and broke out a few acres of sod. I built a dugout, fenced twenty acres of pasture, broke ten acres of sod, and planted corn and maize.

My claim was in the range which Bill Quinlan had fenced for a horse pasture. The prairie fire had not burned the posts but the barbed wire had been removed. Many settlers of Old Oklahoma were so poor they

314

removed and sold it at Hennessey, while the settlers near the Strip took wire and posts from the great fenced ranges to improve their claims. The Cherokee Indians were supposed to get all of the Strip cattlemen's houses, sheds, pens, corrals, and fences but as usual, they got nothing. The removal of fences from the ranges created much trouble for farmers and range riders with cattle eating crops.

Chilcote told me he was ready to return to Hewins, Kansas. I told him if he would go to the Pawnee Agency, I would go with him to ask Frank about the Hanks and King claim. He agreed. I planned to ride on to Peru to visit my wife and son.

Chilcote had a wagon with a span of mules. When we arrived at the Cimarron's main crossing where that horse race started, the river was bank full. Two teams were waiting to cross. On the east bank was a four-horse team with one man in the wagon and another walking beside the team. The water came to his waist. The man on the west bank was Sim Dunmire, an old cowpuncher friend.[6] He appeared greatly pleased to see me once more. His fee was $2 to pull wagons across but he would not charge us.

Chilcote became nervous and suggested we go back. "I will tell you how we will fix it," Chilcote said when I argued that Dunmire should charge us. "This is my team and wagon and I don't want to risk it in the deep water!"

"Well that being the case, Chilcote wins!" I said to Sim. "So here goes for Guthrie."

We ate dinner next day at Guthrie and had fair traveling until we got to Pawnee. I showed Frank the map and described the country. He wrote out his resignation, presented it to Major Woods, the Pawnee agent, and it was accepted.

I advised Frank to go the way we came but since he had no time to lose, he used the main crossing. Frank liked the claim. King was living in a good dugout and had planted eight acres of corn and a good garden. They agreed to go with Frank to Kingfisher and serve as witnesses if he would give them $100 instead of $75. They made out an affidavit that they were the original claimants, there were no others, and they were relinquishing in favor of Frank.[7] He erected a four-room house and brought his family from Pawnee. Brother Charlie helped brother Frank and his family move. Then Charlie drove our wagon back to Peru.

John Kelso, Frank's brother-in-law, was at Pawnee when we arrived.

He had just traded for a good-looking horse and saddle and wanted to go to Hewins, seventy-five miles away. So we mounted his two horses, got an early start, and rode through the large pastures in the Strip, making the trip in one day. Presently we saw ripe, wild strawberries, dismounted, and soon had all we cared for.

A little farther ahead we saw a large roundup of longhorn steers. Several men were working the herd. A rider dashed out after a steer. I looked with disbelief, "If Sylvester Flitch is in this country, I would say that is he," I pointed him out.

Next we rode up to the ranch headquarters and found it was Ed Hewins' outfit. I remembered Flitch had been his foreman. Tom Waters told me he had worked on the Hewins ranch and Flitch had a full-grown bear there. We stopped for dinner and I asked, "Is Sylvester Flitch with the herd?"

"He is," was the reply, but I didn't get to see him.

I told them what I had said to Kelso, then told them I stood night-guard with him when we caught the cub bears in the Glass Mountains.

When we got to Big Caney, we found a man who had just crossed the temporary bridge, stuck in the mud with a big load of shelled corn. We tied our ropes to the wagon tongue, fastened them to the saddle horns, and pulled the load out of the way to cross. The river had receded from flood stage.

We rode to the Santa Fe station at Caney and found Ed Stevens in charge. It was getting late and we had ten miles to go. We reached Father's and turned the horses into the 200 acre pasture. When we went after them next morning, the horse I had ridden could not be found. We took his trail and noted he had gone around the pasture three times, then staggered into the brush and died.

I went to Sedan to see Tom King, United States Commissioner, but he was out of town. I went into the bank and found M. B. Light, a retired lawyer, transacting business.[8] He had not seen me for at least a year and inquired where I had been. I told him about my claim filing failure. He was influential in local politics and a great friend of Senator Plumb's. Nearly five years before this, he had introduced Father to the Senator.

"Now, while I've got hold of your hand, I want to tell you something," Father had said. "I voted for Tippecanoe twice. The first time he was defeated, but the second time we elected him. I intend to live to vote for his grandson, Ben Harrison!"

"I hadn't thought about that," Plumb had said, "but since you mention it, I'm going back to work for Harrison's nomination." He did. Harrison won both the nomination and the election and Father lived to vote for him.

When I finished my story, Light said, "Come over to my house where I keep my file and paper."

We crossed the street to his house. He sat down at his large roll-top desk and directed a letter to Senator Plumb of Washington, D.C.[9] He called his attention to the recent opening of the Cheyenne-Arapaho country. Laban S. Records entered the race according to schedule, secured a claim, presented his application to file with J. C. Robberts, receiver of the land office at Kingfisher, but was refused because Charles Sturgeon, who occupied a farm in Oklahoma, made an application to amend.

"Now, Senator," Light wrote, "this must be attended to at once so L. S. Records can build a house and make other improvements before winter sets in. You will remember the time I introduced the Rev. Samuel Records to you, who prophesied so accurately the nomination and election of Ben Harrison. Laban is his youngest son. As Oklahoma is to be admitted as a state soon, we are all anxious to have it come in as a Republican state and this is one way of doing it. See George Chandler and others to have word set to the receiver at Kingfisher to expunge the application to amend, then send to Records to appear and file on the aforementioned claim."

In August my wife's brother, Arthur Barker, and I took a small load of personal effects, eight or nine horses and mules, and drove to my claim. Some of them belonged to brother Frank. We cut the corn and maize, stacked it near the creek, broke another ten acres, and prepared the ground for wheat. Soon it rained and we broke out five more acres; later we sowed fifteen acres of wheat. We made a bank stable for my five horses and raised enough corn to fatten a couple of hogs. We fed maize to the horses. My brother-in-law got a job near Homestead and went to work.

That August I slept on a pallet in the grass and kept my team tied to the wagon box. About 2 A.M. one morning one of my horses became frightened, jerked back on his rope, and swung the wagon box toward me. I raised up and could see as plain as day. I picked up a corn cob, hit the horse with it, and he pulled the box to its former position. As I lay down again, I heard a heavy rolling thunder in the west but it was a

317

clear night. I called to Bill Scarth who was sleeping in a wagon box under bows and sheet across the creek from me. It was still so light that I saw Scarth as he climbed out.

"What caused the heavy thunder?" he asked. "Why it's getting darker!" he exclaimed.

Neither of us knew what had happened. The next day we talked to passersby, and one or two reported they had seen a large ball of fire, a meteorite, traveling from the southeast toward the northwest. All of them had heard the thunder but we never knew where the meteorite fell.

Since I wanted to drill a well shortly after we arrived from Kansas, Frank said I could use his drill-bit if I would take it to Kingfisher to get it sharpened. The bit and stem weighed 450 pounds so I put it in a spring wagon.

In Kingfisher I met Tom B. Ferguson who was later appointed governor of Oklahoma Territory.[10] I told him where Frank, Chilcote, and I were located. All three of us had known him in Kansas. Then I told him about Chilcote's contest.

"Where is Chilcote now?" he asked.

"He has gone to Kansas," I replied.

"On what grounds is he contesting the filing?" he asked.

"On prior settlement," I told Ferguson.

"Chilcote hasn't got a ghost of a chance to win. When he left, he took his rights with him. Tell him if he wants to keep the place not to let it come to trial but get some kind of a compromise," Ferguson advised.

I saw Judge Cummings, who was handling Mrs. Benedict's litigation, at his office in Kingfisher and told him what the circumstances were in respect to Chilcote's contest. He told me Mrs. Benedict had witnesses who would swear no one had staked the claim. I told him I knew who gave her the numbers on the land. He should not allow the old man who had been paid $5 to get up and swear that Chilcote had not staked the claim. There were too many of us who knew all the circumstances and were ready to swear that Chilcote was the first one to stake the claim. The best way out of the difficulty was to put a reasonable price of $100 as a compromise. Cummings said he would act on the suggestion; he believed it would be a basis for negotiation.

I told Chilcote what Cummings had said. He did not have $100 but borrowed it from Henry Thiele who received a five-year lease on forty acres of the claim after the contest had been settled. Mrs. Benedict then relinquished her claim and allowed Chilcote to file his homestead right. Soon afterward Chilcote brought his bride to the claim.

While I was in Cummings and Whirlow's office seeking legal assistance one morning, a colored man came into the office and asked for Cummings. He and other colored persons had staked claims along Cooper Creek in Kingfisher County, but a white man, "Ranicky Bill," had shot the stakes off their claims and chased them into the blackjacks where they had stayed until darkness. This Negro had walked all night to see Cummings who was the U.S. Commissioner. Cummings asked him if "Ranicky Bill" had killed anyone and did he know where he was at that moment?

The Negro answered, "No." He stated that bullets whistled over their heads and limbs fell as they ran into the timber.

"Do you fear for your life?" Cummings asked.

"Lawd man, I's afraid!" the Negro replied.

"Would you sign a warrant for the arrest of 'Ranicky Bill'?"

"Yas suh!" the Negro quickly told Cummings.

Cummings then told him to see a certain deputy sheriff and tell him to come to his office. The commissioner cautioned the Negro not to tell anyone else, for he wanted "Ranicky" brought to Kingfisher. The deputy came soon and wanted to know the true name of "Ranicky Bill." I told him it was William McKinney.[11] Cummings made out the warrant. The deputy soon returned and walked into Cummings' office with "Ranicky Bill" and a younger fellow named Johnson.

"Have you committed any violent acts?" Cummings asked.

"Ranicky" replied, "No, I was just having a little fun with the boys!"

Cummings place him under peace bond of $500 and gave him his freedom.

"Ranicky Bill" had staked the best claim in Turkey Creek valley in 1889 but later sold it to Bill Demmick for $1800. "Ranicky" invested this money in a bunch of poor horses, some "on the lift." I saw him ride up to one that was unable to get up unaided. He got off his horse and ran to it. When the horse saw "Ranicky" coming on his sleek, fat horse, it became scared and tried to get up. "Ranicky" grabbed it by the tail, gave it a lift, and set the horse on its feet.

Before the deputy sheriff left, I heard a considerable noise in the street. I looked out the window and saw a team and wagon with several men. Among them was Deck Spurlock whom I had known all his life.

He had served a short term in the Kansas State Penitentiary and had left Chautauqua County to avoid arrest for disturbing the peace. I first saw him when his father rushed into Father's house, carrying the little fellow in his arms and crying that his little son was dead. The boy was hurt when his father got out of the wagon to open a gate. Mother examined him and found a little scratch on the side of his head. She put some camphor and sugar on it and the boy soon recovered.

I told the deputy to step to the window and take a good look at the young fellow; he would likely meet him in an official capacity. Just then Deck looked toward the window, recognized me, and dodged around behind the wagon. He must have told the other fellows for they looked toward me. They all got into the wagon and drove south as if they were leaving town. Deck was soon caught stealing horses along the Arkansas River and was sent back to the penitentiary. He died there of tuberculosis.

The settlers had a hard time getting their mail. My wife sent me another bank draft to Kingfisher. There was a line of men strung across the front and through the door of the post office. I did not stop to investigate but walked to the window and asked for my mail. A deputy marshal took me by the arm, "Do you want your mail?"

"Yes," I replied.

He displayed his star, "Go take your place at the other end of the line."

I went to the door, turned north to the corner of the building, then east to the end of the line of men and more joining all the while. The men at the north end of the long brick building stood with their backs against the wall. As one person was waited on and left, everyone took one step ahead. It was afternoon; I might not get my mail by sunset and still had thirty-two miles to ride. I returned to the post office, thinking I might beat the game. I walked to a nice-looking lady standing north of the main delivery window, who did not appear to have much to do.

"Are there any advertised letters for Records?"[12]

"No, there aren't," she replied.

Of course I knew this was what she would say. I told her I was positive the letter was there. She asked what day it was advertised. I told her I lived thirty-two miles out in the country and did not know one day from another. When I asked her what day of the week it was, she good-naturedly told me.

320

"Do you suppose it is possible it could get back in the general delivery?" I asked.

"Just wait a minute until that man gets away from the box and I will see," she replied.

As the man turned away, she picked up a handful of letters, very deftly ran through them, and handed my letter to me. She saw the dates on the envelope and seemed greatly amused. I thanked her and said I was sorry to put her to so much trouble but it was very urgent. She replied it was very tiresome for her to stand there for so many hours without anything to do and was pleased to offer her help when it was needed.

This letter contained the draft I was expecting, but the bank cashier could not cash it unless I was identified. I told him I doubted if I could find anyone to identify me as there were "10,000 all around me and myself, alone." I asked what I should do. He suggested that I telegraph the Sedan, Kansas bank to assume responsibility for the draft.

When I left the bank, I noticed a familiar-looking man a few feet ahead of me. I began to force my way through the crowd to Bill Dunlap. Was I tickled! We were both pleased to see one another again after a few years. I asked him to identify me, he readily agreed. Smiling, I walked back to the cashier.

"Do you know Dunlap?" the cashier asked.

"Sure, I sometimes swear by him!" I replied.

The cashier and Bill laughed.

"I sometimes swear by him, too," Bill added.

The cashier knew the draft would be all right with Dunlap's name on it. He had taken a claim two miles north of Kingfisher. I told him where I lived, and several times thereafter either he or his ranch hands stopped, as my farm was about half way from his ranch on Barney Creek to Kingfisher.

The day I finished sowing wheat, 2 October 1892, a letter came, telling me to go to Kingfisher and file on my claim. The application to amend was removed. The land office was merely awaiting orders from the United States Land Commissioner. I was convinced that political influence had hastened things along for no one else had filed in the Cheyenne-Arapaho country until the next March, putting me ahead by five months.

So instead of going to Kansas then, as I had planned, I went to Kingfisher, returned to my claim, then drove to Peru, and found my second boy, Earl, was born the day I filed, 6 October 1892.

Since we would have to wait awhile before I could take the family to Oklahoma, I decided to stay until after the election. The forenoon of election day, I loaded our household goods in the wagon. After dinner I secured a ticket at the precinct polling place and presented it in the usual manner but was challenged by W. A. Tanksley, a candidate for probate judge. He had been selected as a challenger for the People's party, known as "calamity howlers."[13] We got into quite an argument. Soon Frank Floyd and Lyman Brooks came to my assistance but could do nothing about it. I told Tanksley that I would vote. He called for my filing papers, looked them over, then withdrew his challenge. He was defeated by a small majority.

I was detained so long that it was after dark before we arrived at Sedan where we stayed all night with Thomas W. King. His wife, Mary Etta, was my wife's oldest sister. When I told him about my voting trouble, he laughed heartily and said both sides had their challengers.

The next morning we drove to Cedar Vale, Arkansas City, then crossed the Kansas line into the Cherokee Outlet. We found a man and a boy about twelve years old, waiting for someone to come their way. They were afraid to cross the Outlet by themselves, for they had heard so many blood-and-thunder stories about the Strip. They hailed and asked to join us. The man was driving a span of horses hitched to a wagon; the boy was riding a horse and driving seven head of cattle. I drove our three cows while my wife's younger sister, Lillie, drove the team. The man told us they were going to Kiel, Oklahoma, now Loyal. He did not talk much but the boy talked freely. He soon found out I had spent several years in the Strip and thought nothing about lying down in the grass when night overtook me. The boy remarked he felt silly about their unfounded fears.

The boy's name was Bert Welty. Little did I think, then, this boy would fall under the tutelage of the notorious Ben Cravens who led him into trouble, killed a man, stole $1200, then shot Welty, and ran off with the money.[14]

We continued southwest until we struck the old Texas cow trail north of the present site of Enid. When we arrived at the present site of Waukomis, we cut out our three cows for the man and boy were not afraid to continue alone. They were near the settlements of Old Oklahoma. Before we left the trail, we camped at noon and let the cows and horses graze. While I was looking around, I found some ashes, charcoal, turtle shells, and small bones. I recalled the story of John Payne and John Langford who were working on a ranch west of Caldwell on the Kansas state line during the summer of 1880. Some of their cattle started south along the Texas Trail. They took food in their saddle pockets, enough to last them about a day. The cattle kept right on the trail until they got to where Kingfisher now stands, then began to scatter. They continued following the cattle for two or three days before they could locate them. There were no camps nearby and they became hungry. So they took the Indians' plan and began collecting land terrapins to roast. I tried to talk with them about it later but they wouldn't tell me a thing.

I called to my wife to come and asked as I pointed to the spot, "Look at the ashes. Do you know what that represents?"

"Oh, yes. You were telling me about the Indians roasting turtles and eating them, but I never expected to see where it was actually done," she replied.

We were at the same spot where many years before I had often observed young Indians wading in the pools of water and hunting for turtles to roast. When an Indian felt one, he reached down, picked it up and dropped it in the folds of his blanket. The squaws were usually on sand bars and banks, gathering driftwood to build fires to roast the turtles. When the wood burned to live coals, the young Indians shook the turtles out of the blankets upon the hot coals. They carried forked sticks; when a turtle crawled out of the fire, it was thrown back again. This was repeated until the turtle was too badly burned to move. When the shells began to pull apart, the Indians raked the turtles from the fire. Then the feast began. Indians ate them like a hungry cowpuncher tasting sourdough biscuits.

When I settled on my Cheyenne-Arapaho country claim, the land was covered with bluestem and bunch grass. There were a few buffalo wallows on it, but there were no buffalo bones or horns. There were signs of numerous prairie dog burrows which had been occupied years before. Prairie dog owls were occupying the old deserted dens. There were a few deer in the country when we settled. Coyotes were numerous and destructive of turkeys, chickens, and other domestic fowls.

There were large coveys of quail in every protected place throughout the country. Great flocks of sand-hill cranes and pelicans were numerous in fall and spring. Prairie chickens were plentiful. Wild turkey were found in the blackjack timber east of the Cimarron. There were many eagles—a few bald, but more numerous were the larger golden eagles. Wild ducks and geese were numerous.

When I rode the great cattle ranges in the seventies and eighties, I saw vast numbers of curlews feeding on bugs, beetles, and numerous insects that harbored under buffalo and cow chips. They had loud, piercing screams that carried far. If a weary cowpuncher could not make camp at night but slept on the open prairie near a large flock of curlews, he got a bad scare when they cut loose with those piercing cries just before daybreak. One can imagine his joy when he opened his eyes and saw those lovely birds moving all around him. The curlew was so equipped that it could live on the range better than any other native bird. For many years I watched them going north in the springtime, but I do not recall seeing them returning when fall came. Today the curlew has vanished—but so has the great open range that I knew so well, worked on so hard, and loved so much. These signs have long since vanished, as have the signs of the old cow trail.

324

Epilogue

Laban and Dora brought their young sons, Ralph Hayden and Earl Lester, with them to their Oklahoma homestead. They built a dugout on the banks of the Cimarron River, where two more children were born, Victor Laban and Edith Lucinda.

They built their farmhouse, where their last child, Dora Geneva was born. They lived there until their deaths; Geneva lived and farmed there with her husband, Oliver Campbell, until 1949. The house is now surrounded by wooded undergrowth, which makes it nearly impossible to reach.

Ralph attended Central State Normal in Edmond, Northwestern State Normal in Alva, the University of Oklahoma, and the University of Chicago. He was a public schoolteacher, superintendent, and history professor at the University of Oklahoma. Earl was manager of Goforth Motor Company in Okeene and was the first president of the International Association of Rattlesnake Hunters. Victor served in World War I and worked for the Southard Gypsum Company. Edith graduated from Hillcrest Medical Center, was a postgraduate nurse at Sea View Hospital in New York City, and was a navy nurse in World War I.

After forty-eight years on his Oklahoma homestead, Laban Records headed for his last roundup on 17 August 1940. His wife followed soon after, on 6 February 1943.

Laban Samuel Records's last photograph, taken in Enid, Oklahoma, in 1937, probably at a meeting of the Cherokee Strip Cowpunchers Association. Courtesy of Western History Collections, University of Oklahoma Library.

Abbreviations

BCM	Barber County Mail
BCSGA	Barber County Stock Growers Association
BON	Bill O'Neal
CC	*Caldwell Commercial*
CJ	*Caldwell Journal*
CFC	Charles Francis Colcord
CFCA	*Autobiography of Charles Francis Colcord 1859–1934*
CP	*Caldwell Post*
CS	Oliver Nelson, *The cowman's Southwest; being the reminiscences of Oliver Nelson; freighter, camp cook, cowboy, frontiersman in Kansas, Indian Territory, Texas, and Oklahoma, 1878–1893*
CSBB	Cherokee Strip Live Stock Association, *Cherokee Strip Brand Book*, 1881
CSBB 1883	Cherokee Strip Live Stock Association, *Cherokee Strip Brand Book*, 1883
CSLSA	Cherokee Strip Live Stock Association
CT	Cheyenne Transporter
HSK	A. T. Andreas, *History of the State of Kansas*
IT	Indian Territory
LSR	Laban Samuel Records
M&N	G[eorge] D[oud] Freeman, *Midnight and Noonday*
M&S	Nyle H. Miller and Joseph W. Snell
MLC	*Medicine Lodge Cresset*
MR&K	Medicine River and Kiowa
"OCO"	Joe B. Milam, "The Opening of the Cherokee Outlet," *Chronicles of Oklahoma*
OKH	T[homas] J[efferson] Dyer, *Old Kiowa in History and Romance*
RHR	Ralph Hayden Records
SF&EC	Salt Fork and Eagle Chief
ST-S	*Sedan Times-Star*
T&W, *OK*	Joseph Bradfield Thoburn and Muriel Wright, *Oklahoma: A History of the State and Its People*
WHC	Western History Collections, Norman
YPD	York, Parker, and Draper

Notes

Chapter 1: *Westward to Kansas*

1. Obituary of Lucinda Records, *Sedan Times-Journal*, 19 Apr. 1889; obituary of Samuel Records, *ST-S*, 24 Feb. 1904.

2. Chautauqua, *History*, 66–68. David Clark also had a general merchandise store. See also *HSK* 2:1219.

3. *HSK* 2:1216–17, 1219, 1222; Chautauqua, *History*, 40, 67, 187, 191. Samuel Records was called "Father Records."

4. *M&N*, 130–31. The drought in June was followed by the grasshopper invasion in August.

Chapter 2: *Bullwhackers, Mule Skinners, and Cattle Buyers*

1. *HSK* 2:1454–55 gives a detailed account of how the Benders were caught in IT, shot, and killed by the marshals. Dary, "Benders," 131–38 has photos of the mass graves and the Bender store [hotel]. See also Wilder, *Kansas*, 609–10; Rich, *Heritage*, 307. See the chapter on freighting in Ridings, *Trail*, 393–404.

2. Mathews, *Osages*, 241–42. No Pah Wallo's camp was in the northeastern part of the Osage reservation near the Caney River.

3. Congressman Sam R. Peters got the bill passed for Marshall, Milt Clements, and Harry van Trees, who had been caught on the south fork of the Nenesquaw River in Pratt County in winter 1874–75. *MLC*, 13 Mar. 1883.

Chapter 3: *Life in the Osage Nation*

1. This trail, sometimes called the "Eastern Trail" (RHR "Recollections of the Osages") or the "East Shawnee Trail" (Gibson, *Oklahoma*, 279–80), went from Colbert's Ferry via Boggy Depot to Baxter Springs, Kans.

2. *CFCA*, 100–101. Watkins was a big, rough-looking redhead. He settled early on the site of Oswego, Labette County, was their legislator, then moved to Chautauqua County. He preferred the "free dashing life of a cow man to that of a politician or a granger and was not a man to be trifled with" (*MLC*, 16 Dec. 1880). He and Stith had a camp on Elm Springs near Turkey Creek. Ibid., 24 Feb., 17 Mar. 1881.

3. Finney, "Osages," 424. Hard Rope is pictured with other Indian delegates at the 1874 conference in Lawrence, Kans. See also Berger, *Between the Rivers*, 12–14.

4. Burns, *Osage*, 413. Gibson was the first Quaker agent. Parsons, "Removal," 93–94. He served 1869–76 and is pictured with four of the eight Iowan agents. See also RHR, "Recollections of the Osages."

5. Douglas, *Cattle Kings*, 352. Burnett's profit was $10,000 from wintering his herd at the Osage reservation in fall 1874. Day, "Letters," 316n. Burnett was the "dean of the Texas cattlemen." See the short biographies in Brown and Schmitt, *Trail*, 35; *Prose*, 218–22.

6. Dickerson, *Osage Nation*, 82. Soderstrom drowned in 1902. Mathews, *Wah'Kon'Tah*, 40. His house is on the map facing this page.

7. Commissioner, *Annual Report*, 216–17. Gibson's report of 1873 lamented the Osages' unhealthy condition caused by wearing threadbare moccasins on damp earth.

8. RHR interviewed David Parsons about Conner, who was reduced to the ranks from second chief. Henderson, "Reminiscences," 279–81; Finney, "Osages," 423; Berger, *Between the Rivers*, 12–14. He was an interpreter for Hard Rope in negotiations with "Chief" Norton.

9. RHR concluded through his research that Ogese must have been Augustus Captain, one of the fourteen committeemen who assisted Agent Gibson in selecting their new home in IT.

10. Burns, *Osage*, 512–13. In Aug. 1888, Congress passed a law which prohibited a white man from allotment to the Osage rolls. If a person could prove he was on the rolls on 31 Dec. 1881, he could remain.

11. West Point, *1964*, 279. A George Washington Gatchell was in the West Point class of 1887.

Chapter 4: *Cowpunching in Dodge City*

1. Gibson, *Oklahoma*, 281; Rainey, *Strip*, 54, 580–85. The Texas or Chisholm Trail was established by trader Jesse Chisholm in 1865. It went from the mouth of the Arkansas at Wichita south into the Leased District via Caldwell to the Red River Station. Present U.S. Highway 81 follows parts of this trail closely. Skaggs, *Ranch*, 32–33, and Ridings, *Trail*, 27–41, contain maps. The Dodge City Trail branched off at Red Fork ranch and followed Turkey and Eagle Chief creeks on the Cimarron at the mouth of Buffalo Creek. J. W. Chastain, appointed by the CSLSA, lay a new trail for the Panhandle and northwest Texas ranchers, closed the Dodge Trail north of the Cimarron, left the Eastern Trail south of the South Canadian, and crossed the North Canadian west of Cantonment to intercept the old Dodge Trail on Buffalo Creek. *CP*, 1 May 1881. Another trail opened by J. W. Carter left the Western Trail near the Washita River crossing, went northeast until 5 mi. above Cantonment, crossed the North Canadian just east of Dickey Bros. range, went north to the Cimarron above Bill Quinlan's home ranch, crossed Walnut Creek to the Caldwell-Cantonment road, and followed it to the Pond Creek ranch to meet the Chisholm Trail. Ibid., 25 May 1882. See also Tennant, "Trails."

2. Johnson got his name by pursuing "a band of wild horses and never let up until he had walked them down and captured them" (Callison, *Bill Jones*, 194).

3. Hamner, *Longhorns*, 132. Supposedly, Johnson was a Scot. McNeal, *Kansas*, 178. He was not a good loser at poker against Maj. Andrew Drumm. He was the manager of four cattle companies, including the KC Cattle Co., IT (the 5̄). *MLC*, 30 Mar. 1882.

4. "OCO," 268; Morris, Goins, and McReynolds, *Atlas*, 47. Dickey Bros. had a range on the southern line of the Cherokee Outlet near Cantonment between the two Canadian rivers. W. W. Dickey was a stockholder in Caldwell Stock Exchange Bank. *CP*, 25 May, 10 Aug. 1882. See also Clay, *My Life*, 183; *CS*, 160.

5. T&W, *OK* 2:493. As late as autumn 1886, the freighters received $17 per ton at Wichita. See also M. Wright, *Story*, 153–54.

6. *OKH*, 12, 17–20. Oliver P. T. and Dr. A. D. F. Ewell and M. Socrates "Crate" Justis left their Virginia home in 1872 and went to Kansas; each took a quarter of land in Sumner County. They sold out in 1875, wintered in San Antonio, bought one thousand head of Texas cattle, and established a ranch on Little Mule Creek in Barber County. RHR, "Cowhand," 31n. It had 66,400 acres. Ewell was president of the SF&EC Pool. *MLC*, 4 Nov. 1881; *CP*, 23 Nov. 1882. See also Brown, Jean, *History of Kiowa*, 57–58. The Cherokee Outlet has been commonly known as the Strip. It was a 226 × 58 mi. strip of buffalo-hunting grounds for the Cherokee tribe in northwestern Oklahoma. Rainey, *Strip*, 1.

Chapter 5: *The Dull Knife Raid*

1. Sandoz, *Cheyenne Autumn*, is the story in detail, gathered from Indian interviews, conducted by the author and her father, and from voluminous printed resources and records. Dull Knife was interviewed by J. W. Alder. He had left Ft. Reno because the Indians were dying too fast. He had nothing to do with the unwise choices and tried to prevent bloodshed. *MLC*, 22 May 1879. See also H. Collins, *Warpath*, with picture facing 176; Grinnell, *Fighting Cheyennes;* D. Collins, *Dull Knife;* Canadian, *History*, 13; Covington, "Causes," 16–19; P. Wright, "Pursuit"; CFC "Reminiscences," 11–17. The fort was built to protect the Darlington Agency after a Cheyenne uprising in 1874. Morrison, *Military Posts*, 146. See also Bronson, *Cowboy Life*, 139–46.

2. Yost, *Medicine Lodge*, 56. The Comanche County Pool, with 6,000 sq. mi. and fifteen cowmen, was the largest in the United States, with headquarters at Evansville, named for Jesse Evans, on the Salt Fork. See also Barber County, *Chosen Land*, 8; *Caldwell Index*, 6 Jan. 1881; *CP*, Aug. 1882. *MLC* lists sixteen brands. *CFCA*, 64. The north-south line was from Big Mule Creek to the Cimarron; the east-west line was from the mouth of Buffalo Creek to Drumm's ranch. See also Hunter, *Trail Drivers* 1:289. RHR, "Cow-

hand," 31n. The Sheete Cow outfit was in Comanche County, as was Soldier Creek.

3. *MLC*, 24 Oct., 21 Nov. 1878 has articles and a poem about Murray's death and about Lindsay, boss herder for Quinlan.

4. *HSK* 2:1523. Wylie Payne (b. Missouri, 1847) was in Nebraska two years, in the Missouri legislature in 1876, and went to Kansas in 1877. He was a director of the CC Pool and the CSLSA, was elected president of the BCSGA in March, and was called impulsive. *CP*, 15 Mar. 1883. See also *MLC*, 2 Feb. 1882; BON, *Brown*, 125.

5. McNeal, *Kansas*, 142–44. Ben Lampton and his brother, Pete, were part of the nomads of the cattle ranges. Ben had a smile "fresh as dew of early morn" (*MLC*, 20 Mar. 1879).

6. Hunter, *Drivers* 1:717. Sullivan was a cowhand for William G. Butler on a cattle drive to Abilene from Karnes County, Tex., March 1868.

Chapter 6: *The Comanche County Pool*

1. Nelson was popular with the boys. *MLC*, 16 June 1881. He sold out to E. W. Payne and moved to Texas. Ibid., 12 July 1883. The well-known Evans was one of the first to herd cattle in Comanche County. Ibid., 9 June 1881. He bought black Galloway cattle. Ibid., 16 June 1881. His company—Evans, Hunter & Evans—was in District #6 on the Salt Fork. Ibid., 2 Feb. 1882. He was commission merchant of Platt & Evans, Kansas City, Mo. Ibid., 6 Sept. 1883. See also *CSBB*, 5; *CP*, 10 Aug. 1882.

2. From Wichita, Feb. 14 1882:

> The typical cowboy wears a white hat, with a gilt cord and tassel, high-top boots, leather pants, a woolen shirt, a coat, and no vest. On his heels he wears a pair of jingling Mexican spurs, as large around as a tea-cup. When he feels well (and he always does when full of what he calls "Kansas sheep-dip"), the average cowboy is a bad man to handle. Armed to the teeth, well mounted, and full of their favorite beverage, the cowboys will dash through the principal streets of a town, yelling like Comanches. This they call "cleaning out a town." (Wilder, *Kansas*, 964)

YPD were agents for L. C. Gallup of California and Colorado. *CP*, 10 Aug. 1882; *CT*, 25 Nov. 1881. Baughman, *Scout*, 161. The store was located on Main Street opposite the Leland Hotel.

3. *OKH*, 12. Iliff settled in Barber County before its organization. Yost, *Medicine Lodge*, 54. He and his brother-in-law, J. W. McNeal, bought the *Barber County Mail* on 20 Mar. 1879 and renamed it the *Medicine Lodge Cresset*. *Dictionary*. A hogleg was a large single action revolver.

4. *OKH*, 12. Bill and Ed Withers were undesirable citizens in Kiowa. William was with "wanted" horse thieves. *MLC*, 29 May 1879.

5. LSR often and CFC always wrote his name Mayer, indicating how it was pronounced. Streeter, *Prairie*, 149. He was Wichita's city marshal from 1871 to 1875. His twin brother, John, assisted him in 1871. M&S, *Great*, 80–84, 99–103, 162–63, 343–69. Mike was a Civil War veteran, a stage driver, and later a carpenter. He was with the Patrol Guard, organized after the Dull Knife Raid. *MLC*, 1 May 1879. Drago, *Wild*, 253, 256. He moved to Caldwell in 1880, opened a saloon, and was elected mayor in 1881. See also BON, Encyclopedia, 225–27; Wilder, *Kansas*, 964; *CP*, 22 Dec. 1881.

6. Yost, *Medicine Lodge*, 66. Rumsey was a founder of Kiowa. *OKH*, 5–10, 15, 21. He was postmaster from 1877 to 1884. His mercantile store was directly south across Main Street from the hotel. He owned a cattle ranch adjacent to town. See also *MLC*, 16 Dec. 1880, 3 Feb. 1881.

7. L. C. Bidwell was an honorary member of the first CSLSA meeting in 1883. *CP*, 15 Mar. 1883. "OCO," 268. His camp was just north of the Outlet above the Miller-Pryor lease. See also *CP*, Aug. 1882.

8. Someone jumped Bunker's claim. *MLC*, 16 Apr. 1880. His ranch was near Cedar Creek, brand **FB**. Ibid., 12 Nov. 1880. His bull in the well gave him nationwide fame. Ibid., 20 Jan., 2 Feb., 10 Mar. 1881. He left for Durango, Colo., to relocate his cattle business. Ibid., 11 Jan. 1883. Goddard changed his brand. Ibid., 14 Sept. 1882. For Springer, see ibid., 26 Nov., 9 Dec. 1880, 21 Apr. 1881.

9. Foreman, History 87:278–80, 11:504. In the early 1880s one of the IT gangs included Bill and Jim Barker and Hank Triplett. They operated around Vinita. Howard, "Cowtowns," 64. Jim was shot in 1879 and taken to Coffeyville, where he died.

10. *MLC*, 17 July 1879 ran the letter to Mrs. Stockstill about her husband's death. See also ibid., 25 July, 8 Aug., 29 Aug. F. H. Candee attended the Caldwell cattle meeting. *CC*, 10 June 1880.

11. "OCO," 268. Campbell's range was at the head of Turkey Creek, southeast of the ⑦ ranch, directly south of the Cragin Cattle Co. *CS*, 128. He was in Distrist #4, 1881 roundup. *CT*, 11 Apr. Brands are in *CSBB* 1883, 13; *CSBB*, 23. Dale, "Ranching," 44; Bethrong, *Ordeal*, 93. Denied a Cheyenne-Arapaho lease, he became "a troublesome occupant," grazing over three thousand head without consent of the tribal council. Douglas, *Kings*, 325. He became ranch manager for the XIT in the Texas Panhandle, 1885.

Chapter 7: *Roundup Time in the Spring*

1. "Burnt cattle" were cattle on which rustlers had altered the original brand to one of their own choosing.

2. *CSBB*, 5, 17. W. T. & T. Snow of Alton, Kans., had brands of **WS** or **WS**. Tom was appointed captain of the District #3, 1884 roundup. *MLC*, 29 Mar. *M&N*, 275, map, 195. He owned the Two Orphans Livery Stable in Caldwell in 1886.

3. Manee, who died of consumption, was described as "kind, generous, truly noble." *CP*, 18 Jan., 28 Mar., 3 May 1883.

4. The *MLC* ran many articles about D. A. Greever and his wife, from travels to illness. "OCO," 268. Greever & Houghton owned the 21 ranch, across the Cimarron southwest of the 5. D. A. attended the first CSLSA meeting. *CP*, 15 Mar. 1883. See also *CFCA*, 92; *CS*, 129.

5. Howard, "Cowtowns," 88 with maps. Texas fever infected the Kansas cattle. A "dead [quarantine] line" was established to keep Texas cattle out; it kept moving west with new settlements. See also Gard, *Trail*, 29–33, 35–37, 50–56; RHR, "Cowhand," 31n.

6. Dykstra, *Towns*, 181; *BCM*, 17 Oct. 1878, appealed for a new law. See also *MLC*, 17 Apr. 1879, 30 Jan. 1880, for both sides of the herd law issue.

7. *CSBB* 1883, 4. "Fine" Y. Ewing's brands were **UIN** and **UN**, both sides of the cow. Wilder *Kansas*, 833. Perry won by a ten-vote plurality. He had a big celebration party. *BCM*, 14 Nov. He sold his cattle interest to "Fine." *MLC*, 9 June 1881.

Chapter 8: *Line Riding on the 5 Ranch*

1. *CS*, 133. The gypsum crystals in the Glass Mountains cause them to glisten in the sunlight. Pelzer, *Frontier*, 126; *CS*, 100. Johnson came up the Texas Trail in 1874–75 for wages; he invested mostly in men, and they drove all they could across the Red River in 1876. He started the 5 with nine thousand head and sold 49 percent to a Scottish company. He "made periodic inspection trips to the 5 in his two-horse surrey" (RHR, "Cowhand," 26). He was an active buyer in the Dodge City markets. "OCO," 268. The 5 was southwest of Drumm's ranch, north of the Cimarron on the Eagle Chief. *CS*, 103–4. It was 30 × 25 mi. in area. The Cheyenne-Arapaho reservation lay to the south. Johnson shipped seventeen cars of cattle from Caldwell in 1880. *CC*, 2 Sept. See also *MLC*, 3 Sept. 1880, 30 Mar. 1882.

2. *CSBB* 1883, 14. Dunlap was foreman for the Quinlan range in 1883. Kingfisher, *Pioneers*, 74–75. He later moved to California. Isaac King Berry (b. 1850, Kentucky) was later "boss-herder" for Mayhew & Ellsworth. *MLC*, 16 Feb. 1882 (*Portrait*, 1252–53 with picture). Farris later worked for the Quinlan-Crawford outfit. *MLC*, 16 Nov. 1882. *OKH*, 12. He was Ewing's head foreman.

3. *CSBB*, 39. Maj. Barrett F. Buzard, St. Joe, Mo., was on the organizing committee of the CSLSA. The Buzard-Nicholson outfit had ⌒ and ⌒ brands.

4. *CS*, 101–2. The cabin was 30' × 16' with a door also on the north with a sash window east of each door by 1883. The camp was on the south bank of the Eagle Chief, 2 mi. west, 1 mi. south of present Carmen, Okla.

5. Ibid., 131. Elm Motte was 1 mi. above the cabin. Big Timber was 6 mi. southeast of camp in a heavy grove. Both were turkey roosts.

6. Drago, *Great*, 150–51. Print and Marion Olive took three thousand stock to Nebraska. Sandoz, *Cattlemen*, 68–76; Worcester, *Trail*, 162. They

334

burned and brutally eliminated little ranchers in Texas and Nebraska in their zeal to be rich cattlemen. Also see Jenkins, *Olive*.

7. John D. Miles was a former Kickapoo agent. *El Reno Tribune*, 6 June 1975. *M&N*, 148n. The agency was 110 mi. south of Caldwell. Canadian, *History*, 12. He replaced Darlington at the agency on 1 June 1872 and was "efficient" but was there at a volatile time. See also Hunter, *Drivers* 1:501–2; Covington, "Causes," pictured with Gibson and Darlington.

8. Berger, *Between the Rivers*, 36; *MLC*, 15 May. Scott was employed by Gov. John P. St. John on 14 Apr. 1879 as a government scout with Capt. Hibbset's cavalry to guard the Kansas border. See also ibid., 2 Sept. 1880; *CT*, 10 May, 25 June 1881; 10 Oct. 1884.

9. By then the thirty-eight-year-old Johnson was manager of thirteen different ranches owned by the Texas Land & Cattle Co. The lightning bolt struck him on top of his head, made a small hole in his hat, and also killed his horse. *MLC*, 6 July. Two men riding beside him were unharmed, reported Charley Collins in *CP*. His body was taken first to Dodge, then to Kansas City and Muscatine, Iowa, for burial. *Kansas City Star*, 4 July; *CC*, 6 July. A memorial was given at the CSLSA. *CP*, 8 Mar. 1883.

Chapter 9: *Wildlife on the Eagle Chief Range*

1. A prairie fire on Sparks's claim 7 mi. south of Medicine Lodge resulted in an appeal for help, since he was "past his prime." He captured two bear cubs while hunting in the Cimarron and planned to train one to interview people who set out fires. *MLC*, 20 Mar., 22 May 1879.

2. The somewhat slovenly Hildreth was later head cook for the 5 in 1882. He was ca. 6' tall with a "bacon rind complexion, long underjaw, keen gray eyes, and a long nose with a big hump in the middle" (*CS*, 101).

3. Articles about McAlister's many journeys to Texas to buy horses are in *MLC*, 10 Oct. 1878–18 Jan. 1883. See also *CT*, 31 Mar. 1881.

Chapter 10: *The Winter Trapping Expedition of 1879*

1. This was not the same Dull Knife as the one on the raid, as he stayed in Montana.

2. Cherokee, *Pioneer*, 139; *OKH*, 10. Cowan (1847–1924) was ranch foreman for the SF&EC Pool in 1883.

3. Estergreen, *Carson*, 15, 268, 278. Born Christopher Carson (1809–68), Kit was last in the area in October 1865, before the cattle traveled the western trail. No doubt this was another scout.

4. RHR "Ranching in Southern Kansas," 44–46. Curry came up the Texas Trail, settled in Barber County, and later went to No Man's Land, Oklahoma Panhandle. His range was on Elm Creek east of Medicine Lodge. In the 1881 roundup he traded hats for morrals and ran foot races. *MLC*, 7 Apr., 2 June.

Chapter 11: *Working for the ⭲ Ranch*

1. RHR, "Cowhand," 31n. The ⭲ ranch was 72,648 acres. *CS*, 176. It was established in 1877 by Bates and his uncle, J. D. Payne, both of Elmira, N.Y. The headquarters were 10 mi. northeast, of the ⛢ camp. Frank was a former proprietor of the Leland Hotel in Caldwell. *MLC*, 18 Oct. 1883. Sumner County Deeds, 15 July 1872–10 Oct. 1874. The two owned extensive property at Wellington. See also "OCO," 268; *CP*, 12 May 1881; *CSBB*, 25.

2. Caswell Tipton McCracken was later Campbell's "boss-herder." *CT*, 28 May 1883; *MLC*, 23 Mar. 1882. He m. Annie Smith of Little Mule Creek, where he settled on 30 Aug. 1883. *OKH*, 12.

3. "OCO," 268. Fling & Bates also owned land just north of the Outlet, east of Bidwell's camp.

4. BON, Encyclopedia, 25–26. Anderson was blinded from a bullet in the head in a fight at Beard's saloon in Wichita, Kans., on 27 Oct. 1873. He and Tom Hubbert, "famed horse thieves," made their headquarters at Kiowa in 1874. *MLC*, 6 Feb. 1880. See also M&S, *Great*, 158–67.

5. McCoy, *Sketches*, 289–91 with picture. A William H. Kingsbery was prominent in the cattle busines. See also Hunter, *Drivers* 2:1026.

6. West was in the Medicine Lodge bank robbery. The newspaper accounts called him John Wesley and admitted he had several aliases.

7. Foreman, *History* 9:382, 11:479. "Red Neck" Brown was foreman of the F S ranch in the Creek Nation. Morris, *Oklahoma*, 379. Charles is pictured with Osage council men.

8. RHR, "Cowhand," 31n. Brothers Young, George, and Luke Short came up the Texas Trail to work in cow country. *CSBB* 1883, 30. Young's brand was ⛢, address was Kiowa. See also Carriker, *Fort*, 194–96.

9. McMillen brought a Texas herd up to Wellington for the Dye brothers and attended the stock meeting. *MLC*, 23, 30 Mar. 1882. Drumm (1828–1919), called the "Nestor" of the cattle business, settled in Kansas in 1870. *CJ*, 17 May 1880. Jent recalled both Drumm and his brother, Milon. *Cedar Vale Messenger*, 14 Dec. 1961. When his brother sold out, he joined with A. J. Snider until 1891 when cattle were ordered off the range by Pres. Grover Cleveland. He was chairman of the first stockmen's meeting. *CC*, 10 June 1880. He was temporary chairman of the organizational meeting of the Medicine River & Sand Creek Winter Pool. *MLC*, 1 Sept. 1881. Rainey, *Strip*, 165. He was president of the third annual CSLSA meeting in 1883. *CSBB*, 3, 5, 13. His partner was A. Snider; their brand was U; their address was Kiowa in District #5. "OCO," 268. The Salt Fork ran through their ranch. McNeal, *Kansas*, 177–80, 186–88. He was considered an expert poker player but played only for excitement and adventure. Once someone was short of cash, he suggested that a steer be the ante. See also *Tulsa Daily World*, 1 May 1932, 5:5.

Chapter 12: *Medicine Lodge and Ranching in Barber County*

1. McNeal, *Kansas,* contains stories of the people in the Outlet. Crissman, *History,* 154; Baldwin, *Kansas,* 777; Yost, *Medicine Lodge,* 41–43. He was elected to the Kansas legislature in 1885–87, mayor in 1890, and was editor for many years of Topeka's *Nail and Breeze.* See also Connelley, *History,* 56–57 with picture, 144.

2. McCanless would have a corner on the well-cleaning business. *MLC,* 24 Mar. 1881; Ibid., "The Perils of Journalism," 31 Mar. In the first advertisement of the McCanless Restaurant on 26 Sept. 1879, meals cost 25 cents; they cost 35 cents in Aug. 1880. McCanless opened the Central Hotel in September with the same advertisement.

3. Chester L. Mann addressed a meeting at the courthouse with a debate on monopolies. *MLC,* 16 Mar. 1882.

4. Adrian Reynolds of the *ST-J,* 1888, considered Arthur Capper destined to make an honorable record in the newspaper business. See also Mechem, *Kansas* 1:58; Connelley, *Newspapers,* 44. McNeal travel articles appeared in the *Topeka Daily Capitol,* 9 Dec. 1920–28 Apr. 1929.

5. BON, *Brown,* "The Lincoln County War," 23–36.

6. See *Oklahoma Federal Tract* 40:55 for Aemillius J. Johns.

7. McNeal, *Kansas,* 111–13. Parsons was from New York. His widowed mother sent him West to keep him from the "primrose-lined" paths of sin. See also Yost, *Medicine Lodge,* 81. Short biographics of Hocraft and Russell are given in Edwards, *Historical Atlas,* 7.

8. They also had A. W. Little's cattle; his brand was **LON**. *HSK* 2:1522–23. He was from Kentucky, studied law, and moved to Mississippi, then Kansas, in 1879. *MLC,* 17 Mar.–26 Aug. 1881 reported his family trip back to Kentucky. *HSK* 2:1521. Patrick Henry Chapin came to Barber County in 1879. He had two hundred head of cattle 8 mi. northeast of Medicine Lodge, where he was elected mayor. *MLC,* 15 May 1879, 26 Nov. 1880, 2 Feb. 1882. See also Barber County, *Chosen Land,* 128–29 with picture of his home. Frank reported that the ranges in Barber County were better and less crowded than in IT. Ibid., 12, 26 Nov. 1882.

9. Frank's ranch was 6 mi. east of Kiowa. *MLC,* 16 Dec. 1880. His **AF** brand first appeared on 7 Apr. 1881.

10. Chapin returned home earlier. On his return Lard thought these cattle were the finest herd they had purchased there. They purchased cattle often in Arkansas. Lard's ranch was on Walnut Creek, 2½ mi. south of Medicine Lodge. Ibid., 11 June 1880; 15 Dec. 1881; 2 Feb., 16 Mar., 11 May, 8 June 1882; 25 Jan. 1883.

11. Frank's thank-you article to the Chapins mentioned "Dr. Bratain." Another article stated he was a shadow of his former self. Ibid., 31 Mar., 1880.

12. Frank Chapin was assistant cashier. Ibid., 8 May 1884. *M&N,* 219. A

teller had just gone to the post office. McCollom, *Meandering*, 66. Frank was later president of a bank in Medicine Lodge.

13. Hoig, *Land Rush*, 211. John Chapin came to Oklahoma in 1882 as an Indian trader. The Red Fork Ranch Trading Post was later sold to him. *Kingfisher Free Press*, 17 Apr. 1939. See also H. Collins, *Warpath*, 88–101; Barnard, *Rider*, 64–66; *CS*, 49.

14. Dr. W. A. Noble's advertisement. *CP*, 2 Jan. 1879.

Chapter 13: *The Roundup of 1881*

1. This first general roundup of some 300,000 cattle in the Outlet range east to the Arkansas River and west to the Eagle Chief country began on 22 Apr. Over two hundred men participated and ca. 60,000 cattle were shipped from Caldwell and Hunnewell. *MLC*, 30 June. On roundups, see Ridings, *Trail*, 326–44. Dale, "Cherokee Strip," 63, 76–78. The CSLSA was organized in Caldwell in 1880 to plan the spring roundup and matters of grazing in the Outlet with especial protection of their herds in a region without law; it authorized the printing of a brand book, became the largest stock organization in the world, and influenced the history of both Kansas and the United States. At the 16 Mar. 1881 meeting, six districts with captains were created. *CT*, 25 Mar. Savage, *Cherokee Strip*, 7–10. It was incorporated in 1883. See also T&W, *OK* 2:503–4. Wilson, a member of the MR&K Pool, was named roundup captain at the BCSGA. *MLC*, 16 June 1881, 20 July 1882.

2. Meigs had a narrow escape during a range fire, riding his line for the MR&K Pool. He sold his ranch southeast of town to return to Chautauqua County. *MLC*, 19 Jan. 1882, 2 Feb. 1883. Wilson, a member of the same pool, was on the roundup committee and was elected chairman of the BCSGA. Ibid., 6 Apr., 20 July, 14 Dec. 1882; 10 May 1883. Berkemeier, *Drumm*, 24, is a picture of Abner Wilson. For his brother, Tom, see ibid., 66–67. Springer was in several roundups—captain of Distrist #1, 1882, and in BCSGA District #2, 1883. Ibid., 14 Apr. 1881, 6 Apr. 1882, 10 May 1883.

3. Morrison, *Military Posts*, 142. The cantonment was built by Col. Richard Dodge on a site suggested by Gen. Philip Sheridan almost 60 mi. due northwest of Ft. Reno. Cassal, "Tour," 404n. It was garrisoned until June 1882.

4. The Melrose ranch was on Elm Creek, 4½ mi. north of town. *MLC*, 22 Feb. 1883.

5. Ridings, *Trail*, 179–81. Left Hand, an Arapaho principal chief, was beaten over the head by Jones, the Dickey Bros. foreman, who thought he had struck his horse. *MLC*, 12 May 1881. See also *CFCA*, 104–6.

6. Foreman, *History* 109:215–16. The battle of Buffalo Wallow was on 18 Sept. 1874. Ibid. 3:549–50, 78:281–83. Chapman (d. 8 July 1925) was daring in his dealings with cattlemen. See also Rill, "Chapman"; Carriker, *Fort*, 100, 116, 161; idem, "Mercenary"; *Daily Oklahoman*, 14 Apr. 1929 with picture.

7. Flitch (1847–1900), from Switzerland, was in the Civil War with the Ohio cavalry at the Florence and Andersonville prisons, where he studied English. He was a U.S. deputy marshal in Oklahoma Territory. Flitch file, WHC, with his gun and picture. *CSBB*, 23. He was an officer in the CSLSA. His brands were __K, on the left side, T + T; his address was Hunnewell.

8. Rain delayed roundups in IT. Cowboys reported the head of Driftwood was the worst dose yet. *MLC*, 26 May, 23 June 1881.

9. Pat had m. Julia Faulkner before his accident, which also was printed. B. W. Phillips used the **LU** brand. Ibid., 22 Oct., 2 Dec. 1880; 30 June 1881, 8 June 1882; 26 July 1883. *CFCA*, 93. Pat was one of the "Irish Brigade." Einsel, *Kansas*, 96. He had a ranch on Mule Creek.

10. The cattlemen of Distrist #6 were so pleased they voted Wilson the $100 saddle. *MLC*, 23 June, 7 July 1881. See also 6 Dec. 1883. Douglas, *Kings*, 243–57. Isaac Thomas Pryor (1852–1937), an orphan from the South who served as a mascot in the Civil War, drove fifteen herds of three thousand head each over the Chisholm Trail to Nebraska in 1881, with profits of $3–5 a head. Hunter, *Drivers* 1:93–94. He was an organizer of the Old Time Trail Drivers Association and was described as "good and stout." See also ibid. 1:178, 410–12, 2:706–7, 862, 872. *Prose*, 103–7; *MLC*, 10 Sept. 1880; *Kansas City Times*, 30 Sept. 1937 with pictures.

Chapter 14: *Ranching in Pratt County*

1. Several bad storms were reported that year. "The heaviest storm ever" was reported on 5 May, rain with hail. A severe storm on 11 May tore trees up by roots and a gable off the roof at Lance Creek ranch. Evansville reported a heavy storm on June 23. *MLC*, 26 May, 7 July.

2. Miller, Langsdorf, and Richmond, *Kansas*, 156 (picture of woman with wheelbarrow of cowchips).

3. Comanche, *Comanche*, 48. Col. Charles Colcord was one of the original members of the CC Pool. *CFCA*, 55–56. CFC, "Reminiscences," 8. He was head of the Jug Co., with the ⌇ brand. *CP*, 10 Aug. 1882. Other members were R. C. and Bob Campbell, Billy Carter, and Frank Thornton.

4. "Big George" Kalbflesh purchased four lots on the corner of 6th and Chisholm streets for $300 for his new stable and also owned one on 4th Street. *CC*, 26 Aug. 1880, 22 Dec. 1881. See also *CFCA*, 90.

5. His name was pronounced Boffman. H. Collins, *Warpath*, 108–9. He was tall, heavily built, and big-boned, with bushy red hair and eye brows. A drooping mustache partially covered large, thick lips on a red, coarse face with a constant sneer. His obscene wit with a jackass bray monopolized all conversation. He was never known to bathe; tobacco juice dripped from his mouth, staining his chin and shirt. He ate with a knife and his fingers and wiped his fingers on his trousers.

Chapter 15: *Back to the* ✢ *Ranch*

1. *CSBB*, 15. The Timberlake range was in District #5, 1881 roundup. H. W. was on the committee to set up the 1882 roundups; their brand was ᴸ, and their address was Kiowa. *CT*, 11 Apr. 1881, from p. 511 10 Mar. 1882.

2. Charles I. Cragin of Philadelphia was the president of the Cragin Cattle Co., which bought out M. H. Bennett and Timberlake & Hall for $155,000 for five thousand cattle and thirty-five horses. The brand was Ȓ; the address was Pond Creek; R. D. Cragin was manager. Ibid., 22 Mar. 1883. Their clubhouse had a ninety-two-piece china service with their brand, silver trays, spittoons, etc. *MLC*, 30 Oct. 1884.

Chapter 16: *The Talbot Raid*

1. M&S, *Great*, 362–69, is the most unbiased account of this raid. It printed the letter that the Talbot gang wrote to the *Kansas City Times*. *CFCA*, 111–14. After the raid they all came to CFC's camp, staying several days. *M&N*, 250–67; Talbot house on map, 195. Others involved were Dick Eddleman, Tom Love, Tom Delaney, and Comanche Bill Mankin. It was rumored that Talbot avenged the killing of his cousin, Slyvester Powell, and half-brother, George Flat. See also McNeal, *Kansas*, 189–93; BON, Encyclopedia, 226–27; *CS*, 31–34; Drago, *Great*, 184–86; idem, *Wild*, 251–61; Siringo, *Riata*, 191; Ridings, *Trail*, 470–87.

2. *M&N*, 186n with biography. Wilson was killed in Wellington on 6 Dec. 1884 after an argument following a card game.

3. Baughman, *Scout*, 161. Key (b. Alabama) was general manager of YPD during the 1870s. Thoburn, *History* 5:2177–78. He was with the company for over thirty years and became a full partner with F. B. York after the others died. When the Outlet opened, he moved to Woodward to open up the first mercantile house there.

4. *M&N*, 251n. Spear was one of the locals involved.

5. W. E. Campbell won sweepstakes at the Sedgwick County Fair on Herefords. He had shorthorns too. *CT*, 10 Oct. 1881; *Kiowa News*, 19 Nov. 1959. He wore a sling for several weeks after the raid. *MLC*, 23 Mar. 1882. Some writers confused him with "Barbeque" Campbell, i.e. Ridings, *Trail*, 480; RHR, "Ranching in Southern Kansas," 46n. He was president of the MR&SC Winter Pool. *MLC*, 1 Sept. 1881. His ranch was 48,000 acres with six thousand cattle. Ibid., 6 Aug. 1884. *OKH*, 22–23. He sold land in the western end of his range to the New Kiowa Town Co. He had a grand ball to dedicate a new barn in 1888. *CP*, 19 Nov. 1959. See also *CSBB*, 27; Brown, Jean, *History of Kiowa*, 50–57 with his picture.

6. Siringo, *Texas Cowboy* (his biography). BON, *Brown*, 117; Ridings, *Trail*, 275 (his picture). *M&N*, 482–83. After the trial Talbot returned to California and was mysteriously killed in 1896. Speculation was that the killer was John Meagher.

Chapter 17: *Neighborhood and General Roundups of 1882*

1. Bates's ᴓ brand turned to the left. *CP*, 27 Apr. 1882; *CSBB* 1883, 9; *OKH*, 22. Payne's ranch had the same brand.

2. *OKH*, 14. Leonard lay in the hotel several weeks. His was one of the first burials in the Old Kiowa Cemetery. Ibid., 7; *M&N*, 140–46 (Leonard family story).

3. The BCSGA was organized on 1 Apr. 1880. *MLC*, 26 Mar. Drumm, Campbell, and Streeter were members. *OKH*, 16; *CSBB*, 5, 7. D. R. Streeter's ranch was west of Drumm's, in District #5 with the **Z** brand. He was a member of the SF&EC Pool. Brown, Jean, *History of Kiowa*, 437,18. Streeter escaped from Andersonville Prison and had a stationary business in Ohio before coming to Kansas.

4. T&W, *OK* 4:777 with picture. CFC was a range rider from 1872 to 1889. See also *CFCA*; CFC, "Reminiscences." Rainey, *Strip*, 66–67 with picture.

5. The new shooting gallery was built that spring. *MLC*, 27 Apr. 1882.

6. McNeal, *Kansas*, 179. Priest was an inveterate gambler, an easy mark at the poker table. He had the reputation of being willing to take advantage of a crooked deal. See also *MLC*, 19 Nov. 1880, 14 Apr. 1881.

Chapter 18: *Cowboy Pranks in Caldwell*

1. The rate at the new brick Clifton Hotel on the east side of Main Street was $1.50 a day; Louie Segerman was the proprietor. *CP*, 5 Oct. 1883.

2. M&S, *Why*, 625–29. Wheeler (1854–84) was in the Medicine Lodge bank robbery and was described as "perhaps the most cold blooded murderer in the gang" (*MLC*, 1 May 1884). He was known as Robertson in his native Rockdale, Tex., with a wife and four children; his other alias was Burton. He m. Alice Wheeler in Indianola, Nebr., in 1881. Ibid., 14 May.

3. *M&N*, 286. John A. Blair was first a clerk for Cox & Epperson. He was one of the Caldwell "71'ers" and one of the most popular men; he was postmaster from 1874 to 1881, then owned the Grocery & Hardware House, north of the City Hotel, and finally went into partnership with C. P. Hood, the major's brother. In the cattle business he became the first secretary of the CSLSA. *CP*, 9 Jan., 20 Mar., 8 Apr., 22 May 1879; 15 Mar. 1883. B. Miller, *Ranching*, 157. The Leland Hotel was the first brick hotel in Caldwell. It was opposite the New Union Depot with rates of $2 a day. *CC*, 26 Aug. 1880. It had fifty bedrooms, a commodious dining room, and second-floor parlors with a broad view of the IT skyline. *CJ*, 3 Apr. 1884. See also *MLC*, 9 Dec. 1880.

4. The J. H. Wendels owned the hotel and the city livery stable. *CP*, 8 Jan. 1880.

5. Horan, *Authentic*, 181. Siringo quit the range and opened his "ice cream and lemonade" (later oyster) parlor in 1883. Advertisement, *CJ*, 18 Sept.

6. "The whole Johnson herd passed over me, but luckily only one

broke through" (Siringo, *Texas Cowboy*, 83–87). The horse's name was spelled "Whisky-peat." Berry bet on Gray-dog, one of the ranch horses.

7. Carnegie's range was at Coldwater, IT. He went to Colson's cattle camp in IT, had a sudden chill, was taken to Caldwell by M. H. Bennett, and died four days later at the Leland Hotel. *CP*, 8, 15 Mar. 1883.

8. Sumner County Marriage Record. Tim Birmingham, age twenty-five, and Lizzie Manley, twenty, were m. 29 Sept. 1883. The minister was S. R. Anderson. BON, *Brown*, 88. The Phillips was one of twelve saloons in the town.

9. *HSK* 2:1216. Ed M. Hewins was instrumental in the organization of Sedan, Kans. Mechem, *Kansas* 1:52. He was Chautauqua County commissioner and a state senator. He was also a director of the CSLSA. *CP*, 15 Mar. 1883. *CSBB* 1883, 16. The brand of the Hewins-Eli Titus partnership was +=;. "OCO," 268. Their range was on the southern border of the Outlet just east of the Texas Trail and present Waukomis. Jent described him as "open-hearted, his own worst enemy" (Leonard, *Hewins*, 33); he made it possible for stockmen to have an open market. He moved to Higgins, Tex., after he lost his herd and then to Wyoming, where he died.

Chapter 19: *Stagecoach Travel on the Frontier*

1. The route mileage from Caldwell to Pole Cat was 12 mi.; Pond Creek, 14; Skeleton, 21; Buffalo Springs, 16; Haines Ranch, 8; Little Turkey, 4; Red Fork, 4; Kingfisher, 10; Cheyenne Agency, 21; Ft. Reno, 2. *CC*, 27 May 1880.

2. Mrs. George Haines (Hanes) was "a heroine of the plains" (*Oklahoman*, 19 Apr. 1925, 9). See also Ridings, *Trail*, 418.

Chapter 20: *Working on the Skeleton Ranch*

1. Advertisements for cresylic ointment are in *MLC*, 8 Sept. 1881.

Chapter 21: *The Last Big Cherokee Strip Roundup*

1. Bradley was with the Layfette Cattle Co. Ibid., 18 Oct. 1883.

2. Gordon was attended by Drs. La Garde and Hodge. *CT*, 10, 28 May 1883.

3. Cherokee, *Pioneer*, 521–22 with picture. A. E. (Gene) Pardee was foreman of the Ewing ranch in the 1880s. See also *OKH*, 22.

4. Johnson had power of attorney from the CSLSA. *MLC*, 15 June 1881. He was renowned as a Kansas City inspector. *CP*, 31 Aug., 28 Dec. 1882, 5 Apr. 1883.

5. Ridings, *Trail*, 179–80. E. M. Horton, en route from Texas to Medicine Lodge with a herd of three hundred mares and colts, found the river crossing impassable. He proceeded to the Cantonment Trail, where he was met by Running Buffalo. *CT*, 10 May 1883.

6. Madsen (1851–1944) was Danish, a "fearless, crackshot, early day

outlaw-hunting deputy marshal" (BON, Encyclopedia, 211–13). He fought the Germans, was in the French Foreign Legion, helped bury the dead at Little Big Horn, and was with Buffalo Bill. *Oklahoman*, 16 Nov. 1935. See also ibid., 23 Nov. 1935–8 Mar. 1936; Barker, *Madsen;* Croy, *Marshal.*

7. RHR, "Round-up," 130n. E. M. Ford & Co. owned the ꟼꝹ outfit, with John Miller in charge. Their range was on Red Rock, Black Bear Creek. *CP*, 15 Mar. 1883.

8. Harrell, *Oklahoma*, 18. This cattle trail, named for the mountains, extended from near Willis on the Red River northwest to the Washita River, ca. 5 mi. southeast of Gene Autry to Pauls Valley and Purcell to cross the South Canadian at the Old Fairgrounds, Oklahoma City.

9. Bryce, "Historical," 282. White Bead was the Caddo Chief for whom the town was named.

10. Canadian, *History*, 13. The Darlington mission was established in 1880 at the north edge of the Cheyenne Agency. Mothershead, "Journal," 463 with sketch. Fire broke out on 29 Jan. 1882; the mission was then rebuilt as a three-story building, which the Mennonites took over from the Quakers. See also *El Reno American* 17 Feb. 1949 with picture. Barker, *Darlington*; Reynolds, "Darlington"; Kroeker, "Mennonites," 19; Ridings, *Trail*, 150–52 with picture.

Chapter 22: *Neighborhood and Kansas Roundups*

1. The Cimarron & Crooked Creek Pool was organized on 6 Sept. 1881. *MLC*, 15 Sept. It was in District #1, 1882 roundup. *CT*, 10 Mar.

2. *OKH*, 16. Mrs. Chatham bought the Kiowa House from Mrs. Davis in 1880 and moved it to New Kiowa. *MLC*, 2 Nov. 1882, 5 July 1883. *CS*, 179. She sold it to Tip McCracken for $1,200.

3. C. Henry Wisner (1824–1913) and his wife, Sarah, were physicians. They donated a water fountain and paid the remaining debt of the Lincoln Library at Medicine Lodge. *Barber County Index*, September 1985. They owned Spring Brooks ranch. His brand, H ◇ , first appeared on 27 Mar. 1884; his address was Chicago. *MLC*, 16 Nov. See also *CP*, Aug. 1882.

4. *OKH*, 7, 11, 13. The Blantons came to Kiowa in 1878. Fanny m. Streeter on 20 Dec. 1885. For their courtship, see *MLC*, 24 Feb., 25 Aug., 1 Sept., 15 Dec. 1881.

5. *OKH*, 11, 16. Flynn m. Mrs. Ada M. Chatham, one of the Blanton girls, on 19 Feb. 1887. He opened the first law office in Kiowa, was postmaster, and was co-editor and publisher of the *Kiowa Herald*. McNeal, *Kansas*, 227–31. He was b. in Pennsylvania in 1861, of Irish heritage, and had been an office boy in Grover Cleveland's law office. He opened the first post office in Guthrie as an Oklahoma "89er." *Oklahoman*, 19 Apr. 1925, 68. See also Thoburn, *History* 2:694 with picture; Rainey, *Strip*, 334–41 with picture; Brown, Jean, *History of Kiowa*, 19; idem., *More About Kiowa*, 277–86 with pictures of both Dennis and Adeline (Ada).

343

6. Charles, a member of the MR&K Pool, held the cattle between Pole Cat and Pond creeks. *MLC*, 20 Apr. 1882, 14 Feb. 1884. The Caldwell merchants had induced the cattlemen to reserve the Lane so that they could hold the cattle trade. LSR, manuscript, 1028.

Chapter 23: *Driving the ⇑ Cattle to Caldwell*

1. *CS*, 97. The pleasant, rather small Hamlet was in charge of the ⅀, in 1883.

2. *HSK* 2:1505. Witzleben (b. Germany, 1849), a college graduate, was reared in the banking business. A cashier at Bank of North America in St. Louis, he went first to Dodge, where he was bookkeeper for YPD until 1879, when he became copartner with York in Caldwell.

3. *M&N*, 24n, 282 with picture. Wilder B. "Buffalo" King settled 6 mi. west of Caldwell on Buffalo Creek bottoms in 1871. A superior buffalo hunter, then farmer, he migrated to Washington Territory in 1886. He weighed ca. three hundred lbs. "His yell would nearly knock your hat off" (*CS*, 34).

4. Garland's range was on Pond Creek. *CP*, 15 Mar. 1883.

Chapter 24: *Crime Comes to Cow Country*

1. Larkin was elected captain of Crooked & Pond Creek Winter Pool. *CP*, 15 Sept. 1881. He was appointed inspector by the CSLSA at St. Joe, Mo. 10 Aug., 26 Oct. 1882.

2. Hanlon was exonerated for killing Dodd. *MLC*, 22 Mar. 1883.

3. Brown, Jean, *More About Kiowa*, 241–44, gives the most completely researched story about Potts, alias Willis Scruggs, age twenty-five. He fired two shots at Franklin, grazing his eyebrow. Franklin returned fire and broke the pistol arm of Potts, who wrapped it with a handkerchief and fired again. Franklin shot him in the bowels, *MLC*, 13 Mar. 1884. See also ibid., 3 July, and *CT*, 28 Mar. Alfalfa, *Alfalfa*, 85. His grave was moved from the ⅀ to the Municipal Cemetery, Cherokee, Okla. Another version, sympathetic to Potts, said he seemed to be well educated and was popular with the ⅀ boys. Conversely, Franklin was pictured as dangerous and quarrelsome. *Oklahoman*, 14 Mar. 1915, B:1. See also *CS*, 193–200. Franklin was called "Adams."

4. (W. H. "Deacon") Bates & (David T.) Beals of Boston belonged to the great LX Texas Panhandle ranch syndicate. Their outfit was on Pond Creek. *CP*, 15 Mar. 1883.

5. *M&N*, 212n. B. B. Wood was deputy to Bat Carr in 1882. Ridings, *Trail*, 42. He was first a cowboy on the Snow & Rannels ranch on Red Rock, later a Wichita policeman, and finally a private detective in Kansas City, Mo. M&S, *Why*, 516–19. Thomas worked for the Washita Cattle Co. An inquisition justified his killing. Other citizens rose up in his defense.

6. *M&N*, 189n. Cassius M. "Clay" Hollister (1845–84) was elected mayor of Caldwell in 1879. He was in trouble with law officials for various

misdemeanors, then became deputy U.S. marshal and made several noteworthy arrests before he was killed on 18 Oct. near Hunnewell. Mrs. Cross helped her husband escape by standing between him and the posse; he wore "a night shirt and a Winchester rifle" (*MLC*, 23 Oct.). BON, Encyclopedia, 146–48, gives a different version. See also M&S, *Great*, 141–51; idem, *Why*, 221–31.

7. Drumm had recommended Brown (1857–84), who knew "Billy the Kid" intimately, as Caldwell marshal because of his nerve and fearlessness. Brown, twenty-six years old, had blue eyes, a light complexion, and a mustache; he was a native of Rolla, Mo. In a letter to his new wife, Alice Maude, on 30 Apr., he wrote, "I did not shoot anyone, and did not want the others to kill anyone" (*MLC*, 14 May). See also *CFCA*, 112–16; BON, *Brown;* M&S, *Why*, 67–84. The business houses were all draped in mourning for Geppert (b. Pennsylvania, 1842), who was one of the most enterprising citizens. *MLC*, 1 May, 8 May. *HSK* 2:1523. He moved to Kansas in 1879 and entered the hardware and lumber business. Joe McNeal, brother of Thomas, sold his newspaper interest (*MLC*, 13 Apr. 1882) and became county attorney in 1884. Foreman, *History* 76:152–54. Later as an early Guthrie settler, he became a banker. *M&N*, 219n. Payne lived to name his assailants. *MLC*, 8 May. Caldwell sent its condolences. Ibid., 14 May. Bradley was formerly of the Layfette Cattle Co., 18 Oct. 1883. *CS*, 117–22, 170–71, 189, 205–8; *M&N*, 217n. Smith, the foreman of the T5 ranch, had expert knowledge of horses. He was under medium size, with a dark complexion and a "hardened expression." He directed the crowd to sell his horse and saddle and send the money with his belongings to his mother in Vernon, Tex. *MLC*, 1 May. West had several aliases. Most sources called him "Wesley." Undersized, he had an "evil reckless expression" (ibid.). He shakenly told the crowd that he was from Paris, Tex. When the crowd opened the cell door, there was a sudden rush as Smith managed to get out of the handcuffs because of his large wrists and small hands, and West had gotten his shackled boot off. Ibid., 14 May. Before they died, they issued statements implicating "I Bar" Johnson, who immediately made a sworn statement. Ibid., 8 May. See also BON, Encyclopedia, 125–36; *M&N*, 212–28; McNeal, *Kansas*, 153–59; Drago, *Wild*, 266–68; M&S, *Great*, 47–64, 56–64, 88–90; Ridings, *Trail*, 488–500; McCollom, *Meandering*, 62–66; *Barber County Index*, September 1985.

Chapter 25: *Billy Malaley's Pole Cat Ranch*

1. Ridings, *Trail*, 100–15. Malaley (1850–1919), of Irish heritage from Alabama, was of medium size, was unassuming, intelligent, shrewd, cautious, and implicitly honest, and was known as the best rider in cow country. Dale, "Ranching," 43, 45. Miles's protégé as a former Cheyenne-Arapaho agency employee, he leased land from the agency and lost a fortune when the cattle were ordered off. After he m. Katie Lamb, he established residence in Caldwell. *CC*, 15 July 1880. *Portrait*, 249–50 with picture. He helped secure range

leases in the Outlet and had a ranch near Wheeler, Tex., in 1879, for 8 yr. He moved to Hennessey in 1893 and had a half interest in a livery barn. See also Carriker, *Fort*, 112; *CP*, 22 Feb. 1883; *CSBB*, 3, 5, 7, 17; *M&N*, 152–54; Ridings, *Trail*, 432–44. Hennessey was killed by Indians on 4 July 1874. *Oklahoman*, 28 Oct. 1955.

2. *HSK* 1:855; Connelley, *Plumb*, 221–23. Calvin Hood, from Sturgis, Mich., formed a partnership with Preston Plumb in Emporia, Kans., in spring 1872. *HSK* 1859. Plumb (1837–91), from Ohio, went to Kansas in 1856 and attended Cleveland Law School in 1858–59. A founder of Emporia, he established the *Emporia News;* he was a member of the Leavenworth Constitutional Convention in 1858, state legislator in 1862, speaker in 1867 and then a banker in 1873. See also Wilder, *Kansas*, 760. *HSK* 1:847–48. Thoburn, *History* 2:604. He took the side for settlement of the Outlet.

3. John H. Seger visited Malaley's camp and reported this story. *CT*, 26 Apr. 1883; *CP*, 8 May.

4. Sheridan, a member of the SF&EC Pool, was called the "most expert" cowman on the range. *MLC*, 29 Mar., 3 May 1883. *OKH*, 18–19. High Springs, Okla., was named for him. See also Brown, Jean, *More About Kiowa*, 200–16 with his picture.

5. *OKH*, 5–6, 13. August Hegwer established a store in Kiowa in 1874 and had 160 acres east of Kiowa, extending to the river bottom. He was hunting with his stepson, Dave Freemyer, age fourteen, when he was caught in the storm unaware, in his shirtsleeves, and died on Mule Creek southwest of Kiowa. See also Barber County, *Chosen Land*, 223–24.

6. McNeal, *Kansas*, 159–63. Tom Potter had 80 steers left of the 3,300 he drove up the trail. Chautauqua, *History*, 37. Hewins and Titus lost all but 62 head in their herd of 15,000.

7. T&W, *OK* 2:513–19. Prospective settlers to Oklahoma Territory were called "Boomers" as early as 1879. Savage, "Rock Falls." They were "booming" for the opening of the territory for settlement in their town at Rock Falls. See also Rister, *Land;* Dale and Wardell, *History*, 225–45; *CT*, 26 Nov., 24 Dec. 1880; 10 May 1881; *MLC*, 9 Dec. 1880, 12 May 1881.

Chapter 27: *Cattle Shipping Business in Kansas*

1. In a few hours $1,000 was subscribed to help those who had suffered from the storm. *MLC*, 23 Apr. 1885. Sharlotty Shepler's body was found near the old Blackstone crossing. Ibid., 30 Apr. Yost, *Medicine Lodge*, 106–16. The Shepler child, the eighteenth and last victim, was finally found. See also Barber County, *Chosen Land*, 414; *Barber County Index*, September 1985; McCollom, *Meandering*, 69–70.

2. Three other Male sons were caught in the flood. Two climbed trees; the other went into a stable. *MLC*, 7 May.

3. The complete story is in LSR, manuscript, 651. Yost, *Medicine*

Lodge, 38. Derrick Updegraff left eastern Kansas in Dec. 1872 for Medicine Lodge, where he set up a sawmill and a one-room house-hotel. See also *HSK* 2:1521–22. Cherokee, *Pioneer*, 266. Alpha m. Effie Moore in July 1893, was in the Strip run, homesteaded on Horse Creek near Carman, and was foreman for Drumm in 1886. Thoburn, *History* 2:920, 931, 934. He was representative and senator from Woods County. See also *CFCA*, 89; Richards, *Red Book*, 706 with picture; Seekers, *Alva*, 266.

4. McNeal, *Kansas*, 119–24. Orange Scott Cummings (1846–1928), from Ohio, was justice of the peace for a brief time. McNeal dubbed him the "Pilgrim Bard" and printed his poetry. *MLC*, 9 June 1881–27 Mar. 1884. Other books included *Owaaneo* (*Pale Flower*) and *Twilight Reveries*. Seekers, *Alva*, 153–55 with picture; T&W, *OK* 2:493; Cherokee, *Pioneer*, 154. He made the Strip run and homesteaded on the banks of the Salt Fork 3 mi. south and 7½ west of Hardtner, Kans.

5. Chautauqua, *History*, 67. The church was dedicated on 13 Jan. 1889.

6. Chautauqua County Marriage Record.

Chapter 28: *Frank Records Among the Pawnee Indians*

1. His inventory book and leather pouch are in Box 5, Folder 52, RHR Inventory, WHC.

2. Indian Agent D.J.M. Woods wrote that Frank began service on 7 Oct. 1889, had a full knowledge of farming five years before his service, had his family at the agency, was strictly temperate, had good moral character, and treated the Indians fairly. Indian Agent, Report, Indian Archives. Oklahoma City.

3. See Brown, "Ghost," for an account of Ghost Dance disturbances.

4. Shirley, *"Pawnee Bill,"* 105. Lillie met Dunlap on a cattle-buying trip in the Choctaw Nation. See also Rainey, *Trail*, 196 with a picture of Lillie.

Chapter 29: *Cowhands and Trail Drivers*

1. Douglas, *Kings*, 81. Richard King (1825–85), from Orange County, N.Y., and Mifflin Kenedy (1818–95), of Quaker heritage from Pennslyvania, had been cabin boys. See also *Prose*, 80–86 with picture of King; Hunter, *Drivers* 1:529–30, 2:954–56.

2. There were many legends about the colorful 6' 4", 220-lb. Abel Head Pierce from Rhode Island. He was "portly, tall, long-legged, with a thin high-pitched voice" (McCoy, *Sketches*, 142). He introduced the walking stick to Kansas. "He was 'King of the Sea Lions' [Matagora steers with his B U brand], uncouth as the cattle he drove, but at heart, one of the best men in this or any other land" (Douglas, *Kings*, 39). See also Hunter, *Drivers* 1:318, 2:923–24; Clay, *My Life*, 107; Brown and Schmitt, *Trail*, 70.

3. B. Miller, *Ranching*, 146. He called Birchfield "Old Uncle Steve." He was chairman of the 1881 stock meeting. *CSBB*, 3, 5. He was in District #4.

On a trip West, he found cattle prices higher in New Mexico. *CT*, 10 Jan., 25 Feb. 1882.

Chapter 30: *Cherokee Strip Ranchers*

1. *OKH*, 8, 11. A. J. Crewdsen, an early Kiowa landowner, was justice of the peace. See also *MLC*, 3 Feb. 1881.

2. Waters, Quinlan's foreman, later worked on the 101 ranch. Waters, Recollections. *CFCA*, 100. Quinlan was from Texas and weighed ca. 125 lb. He worked hard and attended strictly to business. He and Crawford began with five hundred cows and branded over two thousand in four years. They shipped twenty-five cars of cattle from Caldwell. *CP*, 26 Oct. 1882. They branded five thousand cattle. *MLC*, 1 Feb. 1883. *CSBB*, 4, 31. They were in District #1; their brands were **2S**, **OO**, **7-L**, **7-5**; their address was Kansas City, Mo.; their home camp was Indian Creek near the Cheyenne line. See also *CS*, 139; "OCO," 268; *CJ*, 16 Aug. 1883. A Quinlan sister-in-law appears as Nannie. U.S. Census, State of Missouri.

3. Zornow, *Kansas*, 165. Speculators bought land in 1881–87; the values rose 400 percent.

4. Sherlock was general superintendent of the roundup in Barber County. *MLC*, 23 Apr. 1880. He was captain of SF&EC Pool. Ibid., 3 Nov. 1881.

5. Thoburn, *History* 4:1539. Eldred (1836–1919), from Illinois, was a cattle shipper before the Civil War. He moved to Barber County in 1879 and joined Gregory to form a company with nearly 12,000 acres on its southwest border, extending east from the Salt Fork almost to Hardtner. Their brands were in *CSBB* 1883, 2. Eldred was "entertaining, well-posted on all general topics" (*MLC*, 24 Feb. 1881). He was "very social" and understood "business thoroughly" (ibid., 10 Mar. 1881). See also Crissman, *Woods*, 117 with picture; Eldred, Papers, WHC *HSK* 2:1504–5. Tuttle (b. N.Y., 1849) migrated to Illinois in 1861, then to Texas, driving cattle seven years to Kansas, where he m., 1883. He first owned a Texas Panhandle ranch, then a 15 sq. mi. ranch in IT. See also "OCO," 268; *CSBB* 1883, 5; *CP*, 25 May 1882, 19 Apr. 1883; *MLC*, 20 Mar. 1884. *HSK* 2:1499 with picture. Hamilton (b. Ohio, 1842) went to Wellington in 1879, where he was mayor in 1883. He bought 3,800 acres in Kingman, Pratt, and Barber counties. He was general manager of the Southern Kansas Border Land Co., which kept his ∧ brand. *CSBB*, 3, 5, 45. He was in District #4, 1881 roundup. *CT*, 11 Apr. As CSLSA director, he paid the second tax to Cherokees. *MLC*, 3 Apr. 1884. Mechem, *Kansas* 1:11, 63, 407. He was state treasurer (LSR wrote that he was governor) in 1887–90. See also *MLC*, 26 Oct. 1882. *HSK* 2:1504. Miller (b. New York, 1851) received a B.L.B. degree from Iowa University, went to Barber County in 1878, established a ranch in IT in 1879, and later was director of the Caldwell Stock Exchange Bank. "OCO," 268. His range was just east of the Great Salt Plain, and he was a member of the MR&K Pool. *MLC*, 1 Sept. 1881. *CSBB*, 3, 5, 37. He was in District #5, 1881 roundup. *CT*, 11 Apr.; *MLC*, 14 Apr.

1881. The author of *Ranching in Southwest Kansas* (see Bibliography), he was president of the *CJ. CP*, 3 May 1883. He built a house on lower Main Street (ibid., 10 Aug. 1882) and branched out with a half interest in a hog ranch in IT on 25 Feb. 1882. See also T&W, *OK* 3:504; Thoburn, *History* 2:536; Baughman, *Scout*, 208. *M&N*, 285. Bennett, from Zanesville, Ohio, worked for Drumm for three years after he came to Caldwell in 1871. T&W, *OK* 3:504. He attended the first stock meeting. *CC*, 10 June, 1 July 1880. *CSBB*, 11. He was captain of District #4, 1881 roundup (*CT*, 11 Apr.) and was authorized to publish the *CSBB* in 1883. His brand was —. See also *MLC*, 14 Apr. 1881.

      6. Goodnight described Day as "brave, honest, a good cowman who never whined or boasted" (Hamner, *Longhorns*, 72). Pelzer, *Frontier*, 197. He managed the Creswell "Turkey Track" Cattle Co. on Jones Creek west of Hetlinger. "OCO," 268. A. J. & C. P. Day had two ranges, one in the far northwestern Outlet below the Cimarron and the other southeast of there on both sides of the North Canadian, just west of Dickey Bros. RHR, "Cowhand," 31n. At one time he had over 12,000 cattle. He reported 500,000 strays on the second range (*CP*, 15 Mar., 5 Apr. 1883) and was captain of District #1, 1881 roundup. *CT*, 11 Apr. See also Clay, *My Life*, 183; Drago, *Great*, 175; CFCA, 99.

      7. *OKH*, 19–20. King also owned and operated a livery stable in Kiowa.

      8. Drumm's widow was named Cordelia, *Tulsa Daily World*, 1 May 1932, 5:5.

      9. Ibid. See also McClure, "Drumm." The Andrew Drumm Institute for Boys was his former home on a 360-acre farm with $1,800,000 endowment. Berkemeier, *Drumm*, 72.

Chapter 31: *A Shot Heard around the Prairie*

      1. *Oklahoma Federal Tract*, 5:39 (Haworth Claim). Ibid. 5:47. (Oliver Claim). See also RHR, "Recollections of April"; Barker, *Newspaper;* Tate, "Forgotten 'Run,'" 30–31.

      2. A street in Kingfisher is named for Robberts. Thoburn, *History* 2:913; Hoig, *Land Rush*, 106. A native of David City, Nebr., he was attorney general of Oklahoma Territory, 1902–4. Rockwell, *Garfield*, 766. He was district judge in Garfield County, 1915–24. See also Eighty-Niners, *Oklahoma*, 193–96. *Oklahoma Federal Tract* 5:42. (LSR and Chilcote Claims). Ibid. 5:43. (Scarth Claim).

      3. *Kingfisher Panorama*, 11.

      4. Eighty-Niners, *Oklahoma*, 334. Holzapfel was a charter member of the First Methodist Church in Oklahoma City, 23 June 1889. Quayle became president of Baker, then a Methodist bishop. Rice, *Quayle.*

      5. *Oklahoma Federal Tract* 5:42. T&W, *OK* 3:6 with picture. Omer's parents, Elias M. and Malinda Pemberton Benedict, were of Quaker heritage.

      6. Dunmire was in Mexico two years and found four-year-old steers at $9 a head just south of New Mexico. *MLC*, 2 July 1882.

7. *Oklahoma Federal Tract* 5:42.

8. *HSK* 2:1216, 1218. King was first district clerk of Chautauqua County. *ST-S*, 6 May 1926. *HSK* 2:1216. Light was deputy county clerk and attorney in 1882. ST-S, 26 Aug. 1873.

9. Connelley, *Plumb*, 431, 449. Plumb d. on 20 Dec. 1891. The letter must have been written to his successor, Bishop W. Perkins.

10. Fischer, *Governors*, 109–27. Ferguson (b. Iowa, 1857) was a school-teacher in Chautauqua County. He studied religion, then served as supply minister at Peru and Sedan. An Oklahoma "89er," he established the *Watonga Republican*. President Roosevelt asked Flynn if there was an honest man in Oklahoma to appoint as territorial governor. Flynn said, "Yes, Tom Ferguson." Roosevelt replied, "Send for him" (Eighty-Niners, *Oklahoma*, 66).

11. Rainey, *Strip*, 177–79. McKinney was first known as "Wild Cat Bill" because of a vest made from a wildcat he had killed. He had a heavy leather belt with cartridges for his two Colt six-shooters and wore large jagged spurs on his boots. He seldom wore a coat. He also wore a broad-brim high-crown hat with a rattlesnake-skin band, adorned with a red rooster feather. He had a slight drooping mustache. He was arrested for intimidating a German homesteader and was sent to the federal jail in Wichita, where the other prisoners tore off most of his clothing. He was also accused of horse stealing. He had frightened the officers away with his Winchester when they went to his claim to arrest him. *Kingfisher Free Press*, 17 Apr. 1939. See also Ridings, *Trail*, 348–51.

12. Unclaimed letters were advertised in the local papers.

13. Clanton, *Populism*, 29, 32. The bulk of the Populist movement was in the middle Kansas counties, where the boom was the most reckless in 1881–87. It rose on the wave of agrarian dissent. Populists demanded freeing farmers from crushing debts and making money more available to them. Mary Lease, the Populist orator for the Farmers' Alliance, reportedly cried, "What you farmers need to do is raise less corn and more Hell" (Bowman, *Almanac*, 238). See also Debo, *Prairie City*, 14–15.

14. BON, Encyclopedia, 76–77. Cravens (1868–1950) was a horse thief, whiskey smuggler, train robber, convict, and farmhand. Croy, *Marshal*, 222. He was the last of the notorious outlaws. Leonard, *Hewins*, 123–25. He and Welty robbed the combination store and post office at Red Rock, where Alva Bateman was killed on 19 Mar. 1901. Canton, *Autobiography*, picture opp. 226. Welty lived to identify Cravens.

Bibliography

Frequent use of one journal and one publisher have been identified by the following abbreviations:

CO *Chronicles of Oklahoma*
UOP University of Oklahoma Press, Norman

Books

Aldridge, Reginald. *Ranch Notes in Kansas, Colorado, Indian Territory, and Northern Texas.* London: Spottiswood & Co., 1884.

Alfalfa County Historical Society. *Our Alfalfa County Heritage, 1893–1976.* Cherokee, Okla.: Alfalfa County Historical Society, 1976.

Andreas, A. T. *History of the State of Kansas.* 2 vols. Chicago: A. T. Andreas, 1883. Reprint. Atchison: Atchison County Historical Society, 1976.

Atherton, Lewis. *The Cattle Kings.* Bloomington: Indiana University Press, 1961.

Baldwin, Sara Mullin, and Robert Morton, ed. *Illustriana Kansas.* Hebron, Nebr.: Illustriana, 1933.

Barber County Historical Committee. *Chosen Land: A History of Barber County, Kansas.* Dallas: Taylor Publishing Co., 1980.

Barker, Carolyn. *Chris Madsen.* Carolyn Barker Series, no. 60. El Reno, Okla.: N.p., 1989.

———. *Darlington: Indian Agency, Narcotic Farm, Oklahoma Wildlife Department Game Farm.* Carolyn Barker Series, no. 80. El Reno, Okla.: N.p., 1991.

———. *Newspaper Articles of the 1892 Land Run.* Carolyn Barker Series, no. 71. El Reno: N.p. 1990.

Barnard, Evan G. *A Rider in the Cherokee Strip.* Edited by Edward Everett Dale. Boston: Houghton Mifflin Co., 1936.

Barrett, Charles F. *Oklahoma after Fifty Years.* Oklahoma City: N.p., 1941.

Baughman, Theodore. *The Oklahoma Scout.* Chicago: Homewood, [1885].

Berger, Ruth. *Between the Rivers: Pioneer Tales of Arkansas City, Kansas.* Nichon-cka Series, vol. 1. North Newton, Kans.: Mennonite Press, 1969.

Berkemeier, George. *Major Andrew Drumm 1828–1919: An Adventurer Who Left A Living Memorial.* Topeka, Kans.: H. M. Ives & Sons, 1976.

Berthrong, Donald. *The Cheyenne and Arapaho Ordeal: Reservations and*

351

BIBLIOGRAPHY

Agency Life in the Indian Territory, 1875–1907. The Civilization of the American Indian Series. UOP, 1976.

Bowman, John S., ed. *The World Almanac of the American West.* New York: Random House, 1986.

Bronson, E. Beecher. *Cowboy Life on the Western Plains: The Reminiscences of a Ranchman.* New York: N.p., 1910. Reprint. Lincoln: University of Nebraska Press, 1962.

Brown, Dee, and Martin F. Schmitt. *Trail Driving Days.* New York: Charles Scribner's Sons, 1952.

Brown, Jean M. *A History of Kiowa, Old and New, on the Cowboy Frontier.* Lawrence, Kans.: House of Uske, 1979.

_____. *More About Kiowa and Other Stories.* Newton, Kans.: Mennonite Press, 1993.

Burns, Louis F. *A History of the Osage People.* Fallbrook, Calif.: Ciga Press, 1989.

Callison, John J. *Bill Jones of Paradise Valley, Oklahoma, and the Great Southwest.* Kingfisher, Okla.: John J. Callison, 1914.

Canadian County History Book Association. *History of Canadian County, Oklahoma.* El Reno, Okla.: Privately published, 1991.

Canton, Frank M. *"Frontier Trails": The Autobiography of Frank M. Canton.* Cambridge: Riverside Press of Houghton Mifflin Co., 1930.

Carriker, Robert C. *Fort Supply Indian Territory: Frontier Outpost on the Plains.* UOP, 1970.

Chautauqua County Heritage Association. *History of Chautauqua County.* N.p.: Curtis Media, 1987.

Cherokee Strip Live Stock Association. *Cherokee Strip Brand Book.* Kansas City, Mo.: Sam L. C. Rhodes, 1881.

_____. *Cherokee Strip Brand Book.* N.p., 1883. George Rainey Memorial Edition. Enid, Okla.: N.p., 1949.

Cherokee Strip Volunteer League. *Pioneer Footprints across Woods County.* Alva, Okla.: Privately published, 1976.

Clanton, O. Gene. *Kansas Populism: Ideas and Men.* Lawrence: University of Kansas Press, 1969.

Clay, John. *My Life on the Range.* New ed. UOP, 1962.

Colcord, Charles Francis, Jr. *Autobiography of Charles Francis Colcord.* New ed. Tulsa: N.p., n.d.

_____. *Autobiography of Charles Francis Colcord, 1859–1934.* Edited by C. C. Helmerich. Tulsa: N.p., 1970.

Collins, Dennis. *The Indians' Last Fight; or, The Dull Knife Raid.* Girard, Kans.: Press of the Appeal to Reason, 1913.

Collins, Hubert E. *Warpath and Cattle Trail.* New York: William Morrow & Co., 1928.

Comanche County Historical Society. *Comanche County History.* Coldwater, Kans.: Comanche County Historical Society, 1981.

352

Connelley, William Elsey. *History of Kansas Newspapers.* Topeka: Kansas Historical Society, 1916.

————. *The Life of Preston B. Plumb, 1837–1891.* Chicago: Browne Howell, 1913.

Crissman, George. *A History of Woods County, Oklahoma.* N.p., n.d.

Croy, Homer. *Trigger Marshal: The Story of Chris Madsen.* New York: Van Rees Press, 1958.

Cummins, Orange Scott. *Musings of the Pilgrim Bard.* Winchester, Okla.: Eagle Press, 1903.

————. *Reminiscenses of Early Days.* Medicine Lodge, Kans.: Canema, 1886.

Dale, Edward Everett. *Cow Country.* New ed. UOP, 1965.

————. *The Range Cattle Industry.* UOP, 1930.

Dale, Edward Everett, and Jesse L. Rader. *Readings in Oklahoma History.* Evanston, Ill.: Row Peterson & Co., 1930.

Dale, Edward Everett, and Morris L. Wardell. *History of Oklahoma.* Englewood Cliffs, N.J.: Prentice Hall, 1948.

Dary, David. "The Bloody Benders." In *True Tales of the Old-Time Plains.* New York: Crown Publishers, 1979. Rev. ed. *True Tales of Old-Time Kansas.* Lawrence: University of Kansas Press, 1984.

Debo, Angie. *Prairie City.* New York: Alfred A. Knopf, 1944.

Dickerson, Philip. *History of the Osage Nation.* Pawhuska: Privately published, ca. 1906.

Dictionary of the American West. Springfield, Mass.: G. & C. Merriana Co., 1981.

Douglas, C. L. *Cattle Kings of Texas.* Dallas: Cecil Baugh, 1939.

Drago, Harry Sinclair. *Great American Cattle Trails: The Story of the Old Cow Paths of the East and Longhorn Highways of the Plains.* New York: Dodd, Mead, & Co., 1965.

————. *Wild, Wooly, and Wicked: The History of the Kansas Cow Towns and the Texas Cattle Trade.* New York: Clarkson N. Potter Publishers, 1960.

Dyer, T[homas] J[efferson]. *Old Kiowa in History and Romance.* N.p., 1934.

Dykstra, Robert R. *The Cattle Towns.* New York: Alfred A. Knopf, 1968.

Edwards, John P. *Historical Atlas of Sumner County, Kansas.* Philadelphia: F. Bourquin, 1883.

Eighty-Niners, The. *Oklahoma: The Beautiful Land.* Oklahoma City: Times-Journal Publishing Co., 1943.

Einsel, Mary. *Kansas, the Priceless Prairie.* Coldwater, Kans.: N.p., 1976.

Estergreen, M. Morgan. *Kit Carson: A Portrait in Courage.* UOP, 1962.

Fischer, Leroy H., ed. *Territorial Governors of Oklahoma.* The Oklahoma Series, no. 1. Oklahoma City: Oklahoma Historical Society, 1975.

Fletcher, Baylis John. *Up the Trail in Seventy Nine.* UOP, 1968.

BIBLIOGRAPHY

Freeman, G[eorge] D[oud]. *An Incidental History of Southern Kansas and the Indian Territory, 1871–1890.* Caldwell: Freeman, 1890. Reprint. *Midnight and Noonday.* Edited by Richard Lane. UOP, 1984.

Gard, Wayne. *The Chisholm Trail.* UOP, 1954.

Gibson, Arrell. *Oklahoma: A History of Five Centuries.* Norman: Harlow Publishing, 1965.

Gittinger, Roy. *Formation of the State of Oklahoma.* Berkeley: University of California Press, 1917.

Grinnell, George Bird. *The Fighting Cheyennes.* New York: Charles Scribner's Sons, 1915. Reprint. The Civilization of the American Indian Series, no. 44. UOP, 1956. 6th ed., 1977.

Hamner, Laura Vernon. *Short Grass and Longhorns.* UOP, 1943.

Harlow, Victor. *Oklahoma: Its Origins and Development.* Oklahoma City: Harlow Publishing Co., 1935.

Harrell, Mrs. J. B. *Oklahoma and Oklahomans.* N.p.: Privately published, 1922.

Historical and Biographical Record of the Cattle Industry of Texas and Adjacent Territory. 2 vols. N.p., 1895. Reprint. New York: Antiquarian Press, 1959.

History of Canadian County Oklahoma. El Reno, Okla.: Canadian County Historical Book Association, 1991.

History of Chautauqua County. N.p.: Curtis Media, 1987.

Hoig, Stan. *The Oklahoma Land Rush of 1889.* Oklahoma City: Oklahoma Historical Society, 1984.

Horan, James D. *The Authentic Wild West: The Lawmen.* New York: Crown Publishers, 1980.

Hunter, J. M., comp. and ed. *The Trail Drivers of Texas.* 2 vols. 2d ed., rev. Nashville: Cokesbury, 1925. Reprint. New York: Argosy-Antiquarian, 1963.

Jenkins, A. O. *Olive's Last Round-up.* Loup City, Nebr.: N.p., 1930.

Kingfisher Historical Society. *Pioneers of Kingfisher County, 1889–1976.* N.p.: Kingfisher Historical Society, 1976.

Kingfisher Panorama. Oklahoma Semi-Centennial Year of Statehood. Kingfisher, Okla.: Kingfisher Free Press, 1957.

Lea, Tom. *The King Ranch.* 2 vols. Boston: Little, Brown, & Co., 1957.

Leonard, Esther. *From Whence They Came: A Little History of Hewins, Kansas.* San Antonio: Arrow Press, 1983.

McCollom, Beverly. *Meandering Medicine Lodge: The 1880's.* Privately published, n.p., 1991.

McCoy, Joseph Geiting. *Historic Sketches of the Cattle Trade of the West and Southwest.* Kansas City, Mo.: Ramsey, Millet & Hudson, 1874.

McNeal, Thomas A. *When Kansas Was Young.* New York: Macmillan Co., 1922.

Mathews, John Joseph. *Wah'Kon-Tah: The Osage and the White Man's Road.* Civilization of American Indian Series. UOP, 1932.

Mechem, Kirke, ed. *Annals of Kansas, 1886–1925*. 2 vols. Topeka: Kansas Historical Society, 1925.

Miller, Benjamin S. *Ranching in Southwest Kansas and Indian Territory*. New York: Fless & Ridge Co., 1896.

Miller, Nyle H., Edgar Langsdorf, and Robert W. Richmond. *Kansas, A Pictoral History*. Topeka: Kansas Historical Society, 1961.

Miller, Nyle H., and Joseph W. Snell. *Great Gunfighters of the Kansas Cowtowns, 1867–1886*. A Bison Book. Lincoln: University of Nebraska Press, 1963.

————. *Why the West Was Wild*. Topeka: Kansas Historical Society, 1963.

Miner, H. Craig. *Wichita: The Early Years, 1865–80*. Lincoln: University of Nebraska Press, 1982.

Morris, John W., Charles R. Goins, and Edwin McReynolds. *Historical Atlas of Oklahoma*. 3d ed., rev. and enl., 1986.

Morris, Lerona Rosamond, ed. *Oklahoma, Yesterday, Today, Tomorrow*. Guthrie, Okla.: Co-operative Publishing Co., 1930.

Morrison, William Brown. *Military Posts and Camps in Oklahoma*. Oklahoma City: Harlow Corp., 1936.

Nelson, Oliver. *The Cowman's Southwest, being the reminiscences of Oliver Nelson; freighter, camp cook, cowboy, frontiersman in Kansas, Indian Territory, Texas, and Oklahoma, 1878–1893*. Edited by Angie Debo. Western Frontiersmen Series, no. 4. Glendale, Calif.: Arthur H. Clark Co., 1953.

Okeene Historical Committee. *Blue Skies and Prairie: Okeene Family Histories*. N.p., 1977.

Oklahoma Federal Tract Book. 53 vols. Lawton, Okla.: Southwestern Genealogical Society, 1984. Washington, D.C.: U.S. Department of Interior Bureau of Land Management, 1956. Microfilm. 22 rolls.

O'Neal, Bill. *Encyclopedia of Western Gunfighters*. UOP, 1979.

————. *Henry Brown, the Outlaw-Marshal*. Early West Series. College Station, Tex.: Creative Publishing Co., 1980.

Pelzer, Louis. *The Cattlemen's Frontier*. Glendale, Calf.: Arthur H. Clark Co., 1936.

Portrait and Biographical Record of Oklahoma. Chicago: Chapman Publishing Co., 1901.

Prose and Poetry of the Live Stock Industry of the United States with Outlines of the Origin and Ancient History of Our Live Stock Animals. New York: Antiquarian Press, 1959.

Rainey, George. *The Cherokee Strip*. Guthrie, Okla.: Co-operative Publishing Co., 1933.

Rice, Merton Stacher. *William Alfred Quayle: The Skylark of Methodism*. New York: Abingdon Press, 1928.

Rich, Everett, ed. *The Heritage of Kansas*. Lawrence: University of Kansas Press, 1960.

355

BIBLIOGRAPHY

Richards, William B. *Oklahoma Red Book*. 2 vols. Oklahoma City: N.p., 1912.

Ridings, Sam P. *The Chisholm Trail*. Guthrie, Okla.: Co-operative Publishing Co., 1936.

Rister, Carl Coke. *Land Hunger: David L. Payne and the Oklahoma Boomers*. UOP, 1942.

Rockwell, Stella Campbell, ed. *Garfield County, Oklahoma, 1893–1982*. 2 vols. Enid, Okla.: Garfield County Historical Society, 1982.

Sandoz, Mari. *The Cattlemen: From the Rio Grande across the Far Marias*. New York: Hastings House Publishers, 1958.

_____. *Cheyenne Autumn*. 4th ed. New York: Hastings House Publishers, 1953.

Savage, William W., Jr. *Cherokee Strip Live Stock Association*. Columbia: University of Missouri Press, 1973.

_____, ed. *Cowboy Life: Reconstructing An American Myth*. UOP, 1975.

Seekers of Oklahoma Heritage Association. *The First One Hundred Years of Alva, Oklahoma, 1886–1986*. N.p.: Curtis Media, 1987.

Seymour, Flora Warren. *Indian Agents of the Old Frontier*. New York: D. Appleton-Century Co., 1941.

Shirley, Glenn. *"Pawnee Bill": A Biography of Major Gordon W. Lillie, White Chief of the Pawnees, Wild West Showman, Last of the Land Boomers*. Albuquerque: University of New Mexico Press, 1958.

Siringo, Charles A. *Introduction to a Texas Cowboy; or Fifteen Years on the Hurricane Deck of a Spanish Pony*. Chicago: M. Umbdenstock & Co., 1885. Reprint. New York: Wm. Sloan, 1950.

_____. *Riata and Spurs: The Story of a Lifetime Spent in the Saddle as Cowboy and Rancher*. Boston: Houghton Mifflin Co., 1931.

Skaggs, Jimmy M., ed. *Ranch and Range in Oklahoma*. The Oklahoma Series, no. 8. Oklahoma City: Oklahoma Historical Society, 1978.

Streeter, Floyde Benjamin. *Prairie Trails and Cow Towns*. Boston: Chapman & Grimes, 1936.

Thoburn, Joseph Bradfield. *A Standard History of Oklahoma*. 5 vols. Chicago: American Historical Society, 1916.

Thoburn, Joseph Bradfield, and Muriel Wright. *Oklahoma: A History of the State and Its People*. 4 vols. New York: Lewis Historical Co., 1929.

Webb, Walter Prescott. "The Cattle Kingdom." In *The Great Plains*. Boston: Ginn & Co., 1931.

West Point Alumni Foundation. *The 1964 Register of Graduates and Former Cadets of the United States Military Academy*. West Point, N.Y.: West Point Alumni Foundation, 1964.

Wilder, D. W. *Annals of Kansas, 1541–1885*. New ed. Topeka: T. Dwight Thacher, Kansas Publishing House, 1886.

Woods, H. Merle. *Fort Reno, Okla.: The Protector*. El Reno, Okla.: El Reno American, 1975.

356

Worcester, Don. *The Chisholm Trail: High Road of the Cattle Kingdom.* Lincoln: University of Nebraska Press, 1980.

Wright, Muriel H. *A Guide to the Indian Tribes of Oklahoma.* UOP, 1951.

————. *The Story of Oklahoma.* Guthrie, Okla.: Co-operative Publishing Co., 1929. 4th ed., 1949.

Wright, Robert M. *Dodge City: The Cowboy Capitol.* Wichita, Kans.: Wichita Eagle Press, 1913.

Yost, Nellie Snyder. *Medicine Lodge: The Story of a Kansas Frontier Town.* Sage Books. Chicago: Swallow Press, 1970.

Zornow, William Frank. *Kansas: A History of the Jayhawk State.* UOP, 1957.

Articles

Beck, T. E. "When the Territory Was Young." *CO* 14 (September 1936): 360–64.

Brown, Donald N. "The Ghost Dance Religion among the Oklahoma Cheyenne." *CO* 30 (Winter 1952–53): 408–16.

Bryce, J. Y. "Temporary Markers of Historical Points." *CO* 8 (September 1930): 282–90.

Carriker, Robert C. "Mercenary Heroes: The Scouting Detachment of the Indian Territory Expedition, 1874–75." *CO* 51 (Fall 1973): 303–24.

Cassal, Hilary. "Missionary Tour in the Chickasaw Nation." *CO* 34 (Winter 1956–57): 397–416.

Colcord, Charles. "Reminiscences of Cow Country." *CO* 12 (March 1934): 5–18.

Covington, James W. "Causes of the Dull Knife Raid—1878." *CO* 26 (Spring 1948): 13–22.

Crockett, Bernice Norman. "Health Conditions in the Indian Territory from Civil War to 1890." *CO* 36 (Spring 1958): 21–39.

Dale, Edward Everett. "The Cherokee Strip Live Stock Association." *CO* 5 (March 1927): 58–78.

————. "Ranching on the Cheyenne-Arapaho Reservation, 1880–1885." *CO* 6 (March 1928): 35–59.

Day, James M. "Two Quanah Parker Letters." *CO* 44 (Autumn 1966): 313–18.

Finney, Frank F. "The Osages and Their Agency during the Term of Isaac T. Gibson." *CO* 36 (Winter 1958–59): 416–28.

Henderson, James C. "Reminiscences of a Range Rider." *CO* 3 (September 1925): 253–88.

Kaufman, Edmund G. "Mennonite Missions among the Oklahoma Indians." *CO* 40 (Spring 1962): 41–54.

Le Van, Sandra. "Quaker Agents at Darlington." *CO* 51 (Spring 1973): 92–99.

Martin, George W., ed. "Dull Knife Raid." *Kansas Historical Collection* 9 (1906): 388–89n.

357

BIBLIOGRAPHY

Milam, Joe B. "The Opening of the Cherokee Outlet." *CO* 9 (September 1931): 268–86.

Mothershead, Harmon. "Journal of Ado Hunnius, Indian Territory, 1876." *CO* 51 (Winter 1973–74): 451–72.

Records, Ralph Hayden. "At the End of the Trail; Range Riding and Ranching, 1878." *West Texas Historical Association Yearbook* 19 (October 1943): 109–20.

————. "A Cowhand's Recollections of Southwestern Cowmen of the 1870s and 1880s." *Cattleman* 30 (June 1943): 26–31.

————. "Range Riding and Ranching in Southern Kansas, 1879–1881." Parts 1, 2. *Cattleman* 30, 31 (March, October 1944): 40, 42–46; 68–69, 74–84.

————. "Range Riding in Oklahoma." *CO* 20 (June 1942): 159–71.

————. "Recollections of April 19, 1892." *CO* 21 (March 1943): 16–27.

————. "Recollections of the Osages in the 70s." *CO* 22 (Spring 1944): 70–82.

————. "The Round-up of 1883: A Recollection." *CO* 23 (Summer 1945): 119–38.

————. "Wildlife on the T-5 and Spade Ranches." *CO* 21 (September 1943): 280–99.

————. "Wildlife Plentiful in Early Oklahoma." *Oklahoma Cowman* 10 (November 1970): 14–17, 28.

Savage, William W., Jr. "The Rock Falls Raid: An Analysis of the Documentary Evidence." *CO* 49 (Spring 1971): 75–82.

Tennant, H. S. "The Two Cattle Trails." *CO* 14 (March 1936): 86–108.

Wright, Peter M. "The Pursuit of Dull Knife from Fort Reno in 1878–1879." *CO* 46 (Summer 1968): 141–54.

Newspapers

Baker University News-Bulletin 18 (April 1925). Quayle Memorial Edition.

Barber County Index. Special Peace Treaty Edition. September 1985.

Barber County Mail. 23 May 1878–20 March 1879.

Caldwell Commercial. 10 June 1880–6 July 1882.

Caldwell Index. 6 January 1881.

Caldwell Journal. 2 January 1879–3 April 1884.

Caldwell Post. 2 January 1879–5 October 1883.

Cedar Vale Messenger. 14 December 1961.

Cheyenne Transporter. 26 November 1880–10 October 1884.

Daily Oklahoman.

    1. "First Mail Coach 'Sneaked' into City," "'Flynn's Livery Stable' at Guthrie." Eighty-Niner Homecoming Edition. 19 April 1925, 9, 68.

    2. "Four Score Years a Fighter." 18-part serial on the life of Chris Madsen. 16 November 1935–8 March 1936.

3. "Madsen, Man of War on Outlaws." 16 November 1935, 1.

4. "With Empty Gun He Goes into Fight and Is Killed." 14 March 1915, sec. B:1.

El Reno American. "Darlington, Mennonite Mission as It Appeared in 1886." 17 February 1949.

El Reno Globe. "Ghost Dance a Myth—Cheyenne and Arapaho." 25 May 1894.

El Reno Tribune. 6 June 1975.

Kansas City Star. "A Cattle King Killed." 4 July 1882, 1.

Kansas City Times. "A Saga of the Cattle Country in the Life of Col. Ike Pryor." 30 September 1937.

Kingfisher Free Press. "Red Fork Ranch at Present Site of Dover Was Trading Post," "G. H. Riese Tells Difference Between Cowboy and Cowpuncher." Golden Anniversary Edition, 17 April 1939.

Kiowa News. 19 November 1959.

Medicine Lodge Cresset. 20 March 1879–30 October 1884.

Oklahoma Orbit. Thetford, Francis, "This Is Oklahoma: Canadian County." 10 July 1960.

Sedan Times-Journal. 19 April 1889.

Sedan Times-Star. 26 August 1873, 24 February 1904, 6 May 1926.

Topeka Daily Capitol. 9 December 1920–28 April 1929.

Tulsa Daily World. "Monument Will Mark Site of Old U Ranch." 1 May 1932, 5:5.

Theses, Dissertations, and Other Unpublished Works

Hayes, Jennie L. "Kansas Cow Town, 1865–1885." Master's thesis, University of Oklahoma, 1938.

Howard, Dwight Martin. "Southeastern Kansas Cowtowns." Master's thesis, University of Kansas, 1946.

Kroeker, Marvin. "Mennonites of Oklahoma to 1907." Master's thesis, University of Oklahoma, 1954.

McClure, Meade L. "Major Andrew Drumm: 1828–1919." Paper presented at Missouri Valley Historical Society, Kansas City, Mo., 1919.

Parsons, David. "The Removal of the Osages from Kansas." Ph.D. diss., University of Oklahoma, 1940.

Reynolds, George C. "Darlington: The Man and the Place." Research Paper. Southwest State College, Weatherford, Okla., 1965.

Tate, Leo G. "The Forgotten 'Run': The Cheyenne-Arapaho Run, April 19, 1892." Research Paper. University of Central Oklahoma, Edmond, n.d.

Waters, Tom. Personal Recollections. Recorded by Dr. J. V. Frederick. In possession of Esther Schilberg, 319 W. Scenic Dr., Monrovia, CA 91016.

BIBLIOGRAPHY

Reports

Commissioner of Indian Affairs. *Annual Report to the Secretary of the Interior for 1873.* Washington, D.C.: Government Printing Office.

Indian Agent D.J.M. Woods, Report to T. J. Morgan, Commissioner of Indian Affairs, 17 January 1890, Microfilm. Indian Archives. Oklahoma Historical Society. Oklahoma City.

Mooney, James. "Ghost Dance Religion and the Sioux Outbreaks of 1890–91." Part 2:771–72. *Fourteenth Annual Report of the Board of American Ethnology.* Washington, D.C.: N.p., 1891.

Manuscript Collections

Baker University Student Records, Baldwin, Kans.

Eldred, Charles. Papers. Western History Collection. Norman, Okla..

Flitch, Sylvester. File. Western History Collection. Norman, Okla.

Foreman, Grant. Indian-Pioneer History Collection. Project S-149. 114 vols. Works Progress Administration, 1937–38. Indian Archives. Oklahoma Historical Society. Oklahoma City.

Records, Laban Samuel. "Recollections." 1937. Manuscript. 1131 pp. Copy in Western History Collection. Norman, Okla.

Records, Ralph Hayden. File. Western History Collection. Norman, Okla.

Rill, Arthur. "Amos Chapman: Plainsman, Scout, Squaw Man." Cleo, Okla. 21 September 1905. Cheyenne-Arapaho Files, Section X, Indian Scouts. Indian Archives. Oklahoma Historical Society, Oklahoma City.

Waters, Tom. File. Cowboy Hall of Fame. Oklahoma City.

Public Documents

Chautauqua County [Kans.] Marriage Record. 28 December 1888, C:355.

Sumner County [Kans.] Deeds. Book 2. 15 July 1872–10 October 1874.

Sumner County [Kans.] Marriage Record. 29 September 1883, 261.

United States Census. State of Missouri, Jackson County, Kaw Township. Vol. 44:74. Sheet 11, Line 54. William C. Quinlan.

Index

INDEX

369